Environmental Gerontology

Graham D. Rowles, PhD, is Professor of Gerontology, founding Director of the Graduate Center for Gerontology, and Chairman of the Department of Gerontology in the College of Public Health at the University of Kentucky. He holds joint appointments in Nursing, Behavioral Science, Geography, and Health Behavior. He has a BA and MSc from Bristol University, Bristol, UK, and a PhD from Clark University, Worcester, MA. His research focuses on the lived experience of aging. A central theme of this work is the exploration, employing qualitative methodologies, of the changing relationship between older adults and their environments with advancing age and the implications of this relationship for health and well-being. He has conducted in-depth ethnographic research with elderly populations in urban (inner city), rural (Appalachian), and nursing facility environments. Recent research includes leadership of the Kentucky Elder Readiness Initiative (KERI), a statewide project to explore the implications for communities of the aging of the Baby Boom cohort. His publications include *Prisoners of Space?* and five co-edited volumes, in addition to more than 60 book chapters and articles. He is a Fellow of the Gerontological Society of America and the Association for Gerontology in Higher Education and serves on the editorial boards of the *Journal of Applied Gerontology* and *Journal of Housing for the Elderly*. Dr. Rowles is Past National President of Sigma Phi Omega, Past President of the Southern Gerontological Society, Past President of the Association for Gerontology in Higher Education, and Chair of the Commonwealth of Kentucky Institute on Aging.

Miriam Bernard, PhD, is Professor of Social Gerontology, Director of the Centre for Social Gerontology at Keele University, Staffordshire, UK, and President of the British Society of Gerontology (2010–2012). Since completing a Combined Honors degree in English Literature and Geography and a PhD in Social/Human Geography (both at Keele), her research career has been distinguished by a commitment to inter- and multidisciplinary perspectives. Building on a background of innovative participatory action-research with older people in the voluntary sector (as Research Officer with the Beth Johnson Foundation), Dr. Bernard joined Keele University's internationally recognized Centre for Social Gerontology in 1988, to help set up the first postgraduate diploma/master's courses in Gerontology outside London. She is now a leading figure in social gerontology nationally and internationally, and an experienced and successful supervisor of PhD students. Dr. Bernard has extensive experience in policy and practice-relevant research with older people in urban environments and in purpose-built retirement communities, and long-standing research interests in women's lives as they age and in intergenerational relationships. She currently leads the interdisciplinary "Ages & Stages" project (www.keele.ac.uk/agesandstages). Dr. Bernard is the author/editor of 17 books and monographs, over 70 book chapters and journal articles, and many research reports. She serves on the editorial boards of the *Journal of Intergenerational Relationships: Programs, Policy and Research* and the Policy Press's book series *Ageing and the Lifecourse*.

Environmental Gerontology

Making Meaningful Places in Old Age

Graham D. Rowles, PhD
Miriam Bernard, PhD
Editors

SPRINGER PUBLISHING COMPANY
NEW YORK

Springer Publishing Company, LLC
11 West 42nd Street
New York, NY 10036
www.springerpub.com

Acquisitions Editor: Sheri W. Sussman
Production Editor: Michael O'Connor
Composition: diacriTech

ISBN: 978-0-8261-0813-5
e-book ISBN: 978-0-8261-0814-2

14 15 16 17 / 6 5 4 3 2

The author and the publisher of this Work have made every effort to use sources believed to be reliable to provide information that is accurate and compatible with the standards generally accepted at the time of publication. The author and publisher shall not be liable for any special, consequential, or exemplary damages resulting, in whole or in part, from the readers' use of, or reliance on, the information contained in this book. The publisher has no responsibility for the persistence or accuracy of URLs for external or third-party Internet websites referred to in this publication and does not guarantee that any content on such websites is, or will remain, accurate or appropriate.

Library of Congress Cataloging-in-Publication Data
Environmental gerontology : making meaningful places in old age / Graham D. Rowles, Ph.D., Miriam Bernard, Ph.D., editors.
  pages cm
  Includes bibliographical references.
  ISBN 978-0-8261-0813-5 — ISBN 978-0-8261-0814-2 (e-book)
  1. Older people—Housing—Planning. 2. Public spaces—Social aspects. 3. Home—Social aspects. 4. Aging—Social aspects. I. Rowles, Graham D. II. Bernard, Miriam.
  HD7287.9.E577 2013
  363.5′946—dc23   2012039805

Printed in the United States of America by McNaughton & Gunn.

We dedicate this book to our mothers, Eileen Mary Rowles and Margaret Emily Bernard, who taught us the meaning of home by making warm, nurturing places to which we can always return.

Contents

Contributors   *ix*
Preface   *xi*

PART I THE MEANING OF PLACE IN RESIDENTIAL AND PUBLIC SPACES

1. The Meaning and Significance of Place in Old Age   *3*
   Graham D. Rowles and Miriam Bernard

2. Social Interactions in Public Spaces and Places:
   A Conceptual Overview   *25*
   Sheila Peace

PART II PRIVATE RESIDENCES

3. Creating and Sustaining Homelike Places in Residential
   Environments   *53*
   Frank Oswald and Hans-Werner Wahl

4. A Place of One's Own: Reinterpreting the Meaning of
   Home Among Childless Older Women   *79*
   Kate de Medeiros, Robert L. Rubinstein, and Patrick J. Doyle

PART III LONG-TERM CARE ENVIRONMENTS

5. The Complex Process of Becoming At-Home in Assisted
   Living   *105*
   Malcolm P. Cutchin

6. Transforming Long-Stay Care in Ireland   *125*
   Eamon O'Shea and Kieran Walsh

7. Developing a Physical Environmental Evaluation
   Component of the Dementia Care Mapping
   (DCM) Tool   *153*
   Habib Chaudhury, Heather Cooke, and Krista Frazee

PART IV PUBLIC SPACES

8. Mobility in Outdoor Environments in Old Age   **175**
Susanne Iwarsson, Agneta Ståhl, and Charlotte Löfqvist

9. Older People's Use of Unfamiliar Space   **199**
Judith Phillips

10. Intergenerational Pathways for Building Relational
Spaces and Places   **225**
Leng Leng Thang and Matthew S. Kaplan

11. Creating Homelike Places in a Purpose-Built Retirement
Village in the United Kingdom   **253**
*Bernadette Bartlam, Miriam Bernard, Jennifer Liddle,
Thomas Scharf, and Julius Sim*

PART V CHALLENGES OF APPLICATION

12. Past, Present, and Future in Designing Private and Public
Environments for Creating and Sustaining Place   **283**
Miriam Bernard and Graham D. Rowles

Index   **305**

Contributors

Bernadette Bartlam, PhD, is Lecturer in Mixed Methods in the Research Institute for Primary Care and Health Sciences, and a member of the Centre for Social Gerontology, Keele University, England

Miriam Bernard, PhD, is Professor of Social Gerontology, Director of the Centre for Social Gerontology at Keele University, England, and President of the British Society of Gerontology (2010–2012)

Habib Chaudhury, PhD, is Associate Professor of Gerontology at Simon Fraser University, Vancouver, Canada

Heather Cooke, MA, is a PhD candidate in the Centre on Aging at the University of Victoria, Canada

Malcolm P. Cutchin, PhD, is Professor of Occupational Science and Occupational Therapy, Adjunct Professor of Geography, and Senior Scientist of the Institute on Aging at the University of North Carolina at Chapel Hill, North Carolina

Patrick J. Doyle, PhD, is Assistant Professor of Gerontology in the Department of Human Services at Bowling Green State University, Bowling Green, Ohio

Krista Frazee, MA, is affiliated with the Department of Gerontology, Simon Fraser University, Vancouver, Canada

Susanne Iwarsson, PhD, is Professor of Gerontology, Registered Occupational Therapist in the Department of Health Sciences, and Director of the Centre for Ageing and Supportive Environments, Lund University, Lund, Sweden

Matthew S. Kaplan, PhD, is Professor of Intergenerational Programs and Aging in the Department of Agricultural Economics, Sociology, and Education at The Pennsylvania State University, University Park, Pennsylvania

Jennifer Liddle, MA, is Research Associate on the Longitudinal Study of Ageing in a Retirement Community (LARC) in the Centre for Social Gerontology, Keele University, England

Charlotte Löfqvist, PhD, is Senior Lecturer in the Department of Health Sciences, Registered Occupational Therapist, and Study Director in the Centre for Ageing and Supportive Environments, Lund University, Lund, Sweden

Kate de Medeiros, PhD, is Assistant Professor of Gerontology and a Scripps Fellow in the Department of Sociology and Gerontology at Miami University, Oxford, Ohio

Eamon O'Shea, PhD, is Professor in Economics at the National University of Ireland, Galway, Ireland

Frank Oswald, PhD, is Professor of Interdisciplinary Ageing Research, Faculty of Educational Sciences, Goethe University, Frankfurt, Germany

Sheila Peace, PhD, is Professor of Social Gerontology in the Faculty of Health and Social Care, The Open University, England

Judith Phillips, PhD, is Professor of Gerontology, Director of the Research Institute for Applied Social Sciences, and Deputy Pro-Vice Chancellor at Swansea University, Swansea, Wales, United Kingdom

Graham D. Rowles, PhD, is Professor of Gerontology, Director of the Graduate Center for Gerontology, and Chairman of the Department of Gerontology in the College of Public Health at the University of Kentucky, Lexington, Kentucky

Robert L. Rubinstein, PhD, is Professor of Anthropology and Director of the Center for Aging Studies in the Department of Sociology and Anthropology at the University of Maryland, Baltimore County, Baltimore, Maryland

Thomas Scharf, PhD, is Professor of Social Gerontology and Director of the Irish Centre for Social Gerontology at the National University of Ireland, Galway, Ireland

Julius Sim, PhD, is Professor of Health Care Research in the School of Health and Rehabilitation, and a member of the Centre for Social Gerontology, Keele University, England

Agneta Ståhl, PhD, is Professor of Transport Planning, Department of Technology and Society, and Assistant Director of the Centre for Ageing and Supportive Environments, Lund University, Lund, Sweden

Leng Leng Thang, PhD, is Associate Professor in the Department of Japanese Studies, National University of Singapore

Hans-Werner Wahl, PhD, is Professor and Chair of the Department of Psychological Aging Research, Institute of Psychology, University of Heidelberg, Heidelberg, Germany

Kieran Walsh, PhD, is Research Fellow and Deputy Director of the Irish Centre for Social Gerontology at the National University of Ireland, Galway, Ireland

Preface

Increasing sophistication in understanding older adults' experience of their environment and the way this evolves with advancing years has not been paralleled by translation of this insight into practice and design. Growing knowledge of the effects of physical barriers on mobility, the way in which older adults perceive space, deeper understanding of the meaning of home to longtime residents, and more sophisticated and differentiated insight into the consequences of relocation have been well documented. Yet, we are only in the early stages of grappling with the implications for environmental design, social care, and public policy. This book is an attempt to begin to address this situation.

An exchange of correspondence in 2008, in anticipation of the 2009 19th World Congress of Gerontology and Geriatrics in Paris, resulted in our contacting a number of colleagues with a view to contributing a session on environmental gerontology to the conference. While this initiative did not pan out, it began a dialogue that resulted in this volume. We contacted an array of scholars, primarily from North America and Western Europe, who we knew were conducting innovative research on the relationship between older people and their environment. Our request was that they contribute an original chapter on their work, placing special emphasis on the applied implications of what they were discovering.

As the project evolved it became clear that it was important to make a distinction between residential spaces and public spaces. With respect to residential spaces, we found that the theme of home and the transformation of spaces into places of personal identification and attachment was a recurrent topic. Beyond the threshold of home, there were also a variety of themes emerging in contemporary work, including the need for shared intergenerational spaces and inclusiveness in the design of public spaces to facilitate their becoming places embracing diverse populations. Our intent in this volume is to provide a coherent perspective not only on the distinctive characteristics of private and public spaces and the ways in which they become transformed into private and public places, but also to consider the way in which these places fit together within the framework of people's lives.

It is important at the outset to understand the difference between spaces (locations within a Cartesian world that, in and of themselves, have no meaning) and places (those same locations transformed through processes of habitation and life experience into sites of great meaning that reinforce individual and group identity). Each person's life is a blending, to greater or lesser extent, of involvement in both private and public spaces and places. This blending varies from day to day, from year to year, and over the life course as we spend varying amounts of time in each type of space and develop ways of transitioning backward and forward from the private to the public domain. The key, of course, is the manner in which our private and public lives and personas are manifest and reinforced by the places we create for ourselves and the spaces that others create for us. These spaces either support or constrain the creation of place. As many of our contributors note, identification with the spaces of our life is closely linked to the control we have over the way in which they are transformed and maintained, either positively or negatively, as places linked to our identity and ongoing sense of being in or being alienated from the world.

In old age, indeed throughout the life course, processes of making and remaking place by both individuals and social groups are facilitated or hampered by environmental design, by models of social care and human service practices and, on a larger scale, by public policy. Consequently, a major focus of the chapters that follow is an attempt to begin to translate an understanding of environmental experience into a set of recommendations in each of these domains.

This volume is strongly interdisciplinary, with contributions from individuals with backgrounds and expertise in anthropology, architecture, economics, education, geography, gerontology, planning, psychology, sociology, architecture, occupational therapy, rehabilitation sciences, and other health sciences. There is also something of an international flavor. While the contributions do not embrace the diversity of more than a limited number of cultures and the coverage is by no means comprehensive, we do include perspectives from scholars in England, Ireland, Sweden, Germany, Canada, and Singapore as well as the United States.

The book consists of five sections. In Part I we set the context and provide a conceptual overview. In Chapter 1 we explore the meaning and significance of place in old age, focusing primarily on the manner in which individuals experience and create meaning in the private space of the residence and how this may change with advancing years and as a result of relocation. Chapter 2 provides a conceptual complement to this introduction by exploring the ways in which public spaces become places through social interactions and the creation of communal identity. Building on this background, Part II takes a deeper look at private residences, in chapters exploring how homelike places are created and sustained (Chapter 3) and the distinctive meanings of home for childless older women (Chapter 4), one of a number of groups that are marginalized and underrepresented within mainstream research in environmental gerontology. In Part III we turn our attention to long-term care environments. The focus is on understanding the processes whereby people make meaning and attempt to become at home following a move to assisted living (Chapter 5) or are provided with a context and support to create homelike places when they find themselves in long-stay facilities (including nursing homes), which for many provide a final residence (Chapter 6). Introducing the theme of measurement, Chapter 7 provides important insight on ways in which we can come to understand how persons with dementia use and experience institutional space.

Moving outside the residence and focusing on public spaces, Part IV considers the meaning of mobility in outdoor environments (Chapter 8) and considers processes through which people come to know and transform unfamiliar public spaces into places with which they can engage and identify (Chapter 9). Chapter 10 adds an intergenerational perspective, presenting exemplars from different parts of the world of ways in which inclusive public spaces can be created to foster interactions and communication among different age cohorts. A final contribution to this section (Chapter 11) emphasizes the importance of ensuring that those who design and manage retirement villages are attuned to the manner in which these spaces are used and are imbued with meaning. In a synthesizing conclusion to the book, Part V, we bring together the diverse themes introduced throughout the volume within the framework of a set of guidelines and recommendations for moving forward. Our aspiration is for Chapter 12 to serve not only as an integrative summary, but also as a launching pad for others to pursue the many lines of research and intervention advocated by our contributors.

We view this book as a step in the continuing journey of transforming knowledge into action to enhance the quality of people's lives. As the reader, we hope you will use the ideas expressed in the following pages as a starting point for pondering the best ways to harness expanding knowledge about, and sensitivity to, the subtleties of environmental experience for this purpose. We challenge you to consider ways in which you might contribute to this goal—in creating and understanding your own personal places, in the support of others as they create theirs, and in contributing to the development of environmental design, social interventions, and public policy that has nurturing, positively meaningful places as a core underlying theme. In order to facilitate this process, we have included a brief Editors' Introduction at the beginning of each of the contributed chapters. We hope that these comments will provide additional stimulus to your thinking and some ideas for discussion with colleagues.

In compiling the volume, we discovered that there is great variation in terminology, not only on different sides of the Atlantic but also throughout the world. For example, emergence over the past three decades of "assisted living" has given rise to an array of differing interpretations of what this actually means. Within the United States, there is a wide range of definition and interpretation of the term among individual states. Even within this volume, there are variations in definitions and nuances of terminology. We have encouraged each author to make explicit their own particular definitions of terms and phrases that appear ambiguous or subject to alternative interpretations.

One of the pleasures of compiling this book has been working with people of vision and commitment who from the outset understood—sometimes better than we did—the potential significance of the venture. Thanks are due to our editor at Springer Publishing Company, Sheri W. Sussman, for guiding us in initially shaping the volume. She encouraged us to make sure that we did not prepare merely the amalgam of disparate chapters that typifies some edited books, but rather a coherent work within which each contributor provided a key component in developing an overall argument. We will also be forever grateful to Sheri for her personal support and guidance over several years as each of us dealt with unforeseen challenges of illness and death in our families that delayed completion of the book. Sheri is an editor who realizes that while deadlines are necessary, families are even more important.

The degree to which we have succeeded in achieving our aspirations for this book is due to the diligence of our contributors in trying to make their chapters conform to what has emerged as a shared vision.

We thank them for their willingness to adjust their contributions to address our many comments and suggestions on initial drafts, and for responding so rapidly and thoughtfully to specific requests for refinement and clarification.

Compiling an edited volume is not only a work of intellect; it is a challenge of organizational and administrative skill and commitment. We were blessed to have an editorial and project associate at the University of Kentucky, Julie A. Brown, who handled the process of corresponding with our authors, and the numerous administrative chores that accompany the development of an edited volume, with skill, efficiency, good humor, and grace.

During the development of this book we both encountered a number of unexpected personal challenges that sometimes made it necessary to delay or to modify our plans. That we were able to complete the work despite these circumstances is testament to the forbearance of our respective spouses, Ruth and Steve, who ungrudgingly gave up what should have been family time, enabling us to work long hours, engage in lengthy trans-Atlantic telephone conversations, and meet in Boston following the 2011 Gerontological Society of America annual conference to work on the project. We thank you.

—*Graham D. Rowles*
Georgetown, Kentucky

—*Miriam Bernard*
Keele, Staffordshire

PART I

The Meaning of Place in Residential and Public Spaces

CHAPTER 1

The Meaning and Significance of Place in Old Age

Graham D. Rowles and Miriam Bernard

> How hard it is to escape from places. However carefully one goes they hold you—you leave little bits of yourself fluttering on the fences—like rags and shreds of your very life.
> —Katherine Mansfield

> The ache for home lives in all of us, the safe place where we can go as we are and not be questioned.
> —Maya Angelou

We are shaped by the physical and social environments of our life—where we were born, where we grew up, where we live today, and where we grow old. In turn, through processes of habitation and habituation we transform the spaces of our life into places of meaning and significance within what Husserl defined as our *Lebenswelt* or life-world (Husserl, 1970/1936; Schutz & Luckmann, 1973). For each person, the outcome of this complex trans-action is a unique experience of "being-in-the-world" that evolves with each passing year (Dreyfus, 1991; Heidegger, 1962). In recent decades, the significance of the human/environment relationship, its influence on the nature of our being in the world, and its association with well-being in old age has been increasingly acknowledged as a primary component of the emergence of environmental gerontology (Kendig, 2003; Phillipson, 2004; Scheidt & Windley, 2006; Schwarz & Scheidt, 2012; Wahl & Weisman, 2003).

In this chapter, and throughout most of this book, we focus on one sub-domain of environmental gerontology. Since the 1970s, the strongly applied and theoretical focus of the field has been accompanied by a less prominent school of thought that has grappled with trying to understand the environmental experience of growing old. Adopting an emic perspective, researchers such as Chaudhury, Howell, Peace, Rowles, Rubinstein, Smith, and Watkins have focused heavily on experiential aspects of the older adult's relationship with the environment. Specifically, these researchers have been trying to understand the meaning of place and home to older adults and the manner in which, as a result of advancing age and environmental change (both *in situ* and as a result of relocation), such meaning evolves over time. Early work by Howell (1983), O'Bryant (1982), Willcocks, Peace, and Kellaher (1987), Rowles (1978), Rubinstein (1989, 1990), and Scheidt and Norris-Baker (1999) has been complemented in recent years by contributions from Chaudhury (2008), Cutchin (2003, 2004), Evans (2009), Sixsmith (2002), and others, who have been concerned with phenomenological aspects of environmental meaning, attachments to place, and the notion of "home" (Rowles & Chaudhury, 2005). We have learned far more about the importance of "being in place" and the way in which this changes over the life course (Rowles, 1991, 2000) as well as the negative consequences and emotional issues resulting from severance (especially involuntary severance) from familiar places and objects (Castle, 2001; Danermark & Ekstrom, 1990). We have learned about the role of the surveillance zone as a significant zone of space, especially for those who are homebound (Rowles, 1981). We have been introduced to the notion of "place therapy" (Scheidt & Norris Baker, 1999). And we are beginning to understand the critical importance of the process of *casser maison* (breaking the house) as people are forced to give up the possessions of a lifetime when they relocate to a smaller dwelling (Ekerdt, Sergeant, Dingel, & Bowen, 2004; Morris, 1992). Increasingly too, research is focusing on themes of environment and personal identity in old age (Peace, Holland, & Kellaher, 2006; Rubinstein & de Medeiros, 2005).

Of course, life is also lived in the public realm. Public and shared spaces are critical environments shaping the conduct of everyday life. Our use of and identification with public spaces is an essential component of an overall sense of being in place. There are public places in which we feel safe, welcomed, and within which we can experience a sense of belonging and identification. Other public spaces are dangerous, hostile, and alienating. The design and ambiance of these spaces is a critical element in determining our ability or willingness to venture forth from the relative security of our residence. An older person may feel safe and may identify with the space of the dwelling but be fearful of engaging in a hostile changing environment outside (Balint, 1955). The interwoven relationship between perceptions of private and public spaces molds daily behavior and individual lifestyles.

As knowledge of the subjective world of the older person has evolved, we have now reached a level of sophistication that merits a focused attempt to translate deepening insight into practical suggestions and outcomes for the design of both interior (private) and exterior (public) environments. Beyond simply acknowledging and becoming more sensitive to the meaning of place to older adults, how can we constructively use a growing knowledge base to effect change that will improve the quality of life in old age? How can we translate what we are learning about the meaning and significance of place to older people and their well-being into concrete recommendations for practice, policy, and design?

In this chapter we set the stage for a set of contributors to this volume who are beginning to address these questions. We and our contributors also address a series of interrelated questions: What is the current state of knowledge about the manner in which individuals' mold and experience private spaces? How do spaces become transformed into places? How does the individual's experience of place change in old age? To what extent does environmental change (either *in situ* change resulting from the transformation of a neighborhood or a relocation necessitated by reduced personal competence) threaten our sense of being in the world and, more specifically, "being in place" or "at home"? Is such disruption inevitable, irrevocable, and irreconcilable with maintaining a sense of self and well-being in old age? How does the physical form of our environment, the objects it contains, and the social context it provides, reinforce or threaten identity and a sense of being in place?

Acknowledging that private and public spaces are integrally intertwined in the fabric of individual lives, we focus in this chapter on private spaces (primarily the place of residence) over which, in most cases, the individual generally has some level of control. In Chapter 2, Sheila Peace provides the necessary complement to our treatment as she sets a context for considering public space. We begin, though, with a brief overview of developments in the field from both sides of the Atlantic.

DEVELOPMENTS IN ENVIRONMENTAL GERONTOLOGY

The roots of environmental gerontology are both theoretical and empirical. Theoretically, environmental gerontology builds on the seminal "field theory" ideas of Kurt Lewin (1951) and has been historically oriented around a simple conceptual equation: $B = f(P.E)$, where B represents Behavior, P represents Person, and E represents Environment. Early development of the field was strongly intertwined with the foundation and growth of environmental psychology in the late 1960s and 1970s (Canter & Craik, 1981; Craik, 1973; Proshansky, Ittelson, & Rivlin, 1976). During this

FIGURE 1.1   The Ecological Model

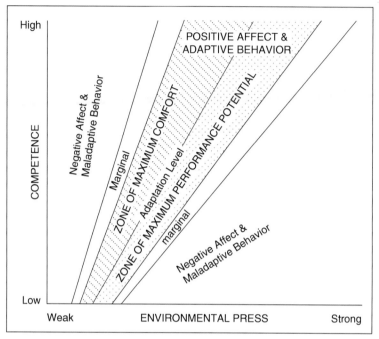

Source: Redrafted from Lawton and Nahemow (1973, p. 661).

period, a series of theoretical conceptualizations including Pastalan's "age-loss continuum" (1970) and Kahana's "environmental congruence" theory (1982), and Rowles' "hypothesis of changing emphasis" (1978) began to develop a domain in gerontology that was premised upon investigating the "fit" between older people and their environmental context. The most influential of these conceptualizations was M. Powell Lawton and Lucille Nahemow's (1973) ecological theory, which was an elaboration of the "environmental docility hypothesis" (Lawton & Simon, 1968, p. 108) that:

> The more competent the organism—in terms of health, intelligence, ego strength, social role performance, or cultural evolution—the less will be the proportion of variance in behavior attributable to physical objects or conditions around him . . . With high degrees of competence he will, in common parlance, rise above his environment. However, reduction of competence, or deprived status, heightens his behavioral dependence on external conditions.

A frequently reproduced diagram of the ecological theory provided visual representation of environmental adaptation as the outcome of a dynamic relationship between changing individual competence (needs) and the changing constraints of the environmental context (press) (Figure 1.1).

Development of these perspectives was reinforced by growing societal concern during the 1960s and 1970s with developing special living environments for older adults. The creation and proliferation of age-segregated retirement communities, societal acceptance of sheltered housing schemes in the United Kingdom, the emergence of high-rise publicly subsidized elderly housing in the United States, and the development of a plethora of innovative alternative residential models for older adults in both North America and Western Europe, spawned the need for novel designs and assessment of the effectiveness of these approaches for accommodating a rapidly growing elderly population (Carp, 1966; Jephcott, 1971; Lawton & Hoover, 1981; Regnier & Pynoos, 1987). Many critical evaluations of the new forms of housing arrangement were undertaken by the same people who were concurrently developing the theoretical basis of environmental gerontology—Frances Carp, Tom Byerts, Leon Pastalan, M. Powell Lawton, Eva Kahana, Sandra Howell, Victor Regnier, Robert Rubinstein, and Anthony Warnes; indeed, there was a happy interweaving and concordance of theory and practice.

During the 1980s, 1990s, and the first decade of the twenty-first century, a new generation of environmental gerontologists, including Miriam Bernard, Habib Chaudhury, Malcolm Cutchin, Simon Evans, Caroline Holland, Susanne Iwarsson, Leonie Kellaher, Frank Oswald, Sheila Peace, Judith Phillips, Chris Phillipson, Thomas Scharf, Rick Scheidt, Hans-Werner Wahl, and Gerald Weisman, have come to the fore. Building on the theoretical and applied work of the pioneers, this strongly inter- and multidisciplinary cadre of researchers has provided a growing level of sophistication in reinterpreting and refining and elaborating the $B = f(P.E)$ equation. Wahl and Lang (2004) argued for elaboration of the equation through greater integration of the social component of environment. Working from the perspective of occupational therapy, Iwarsson developed the person-environment-activity model (P-E-A), which she operationalized through the housing enabler concept (Iwarsson, 2004). Cutchin, harnessing the ideas of John Dewey, developed a strongly transactional perspective focused on research showing how over time people develop "place integration" within the environments of their life (Cutchin, 2003, 2004). Peace and her colleagues provided new perspectives on inclusivity in housing and the role of environment in shaping identity in later life (Peace & Holland, 2001; Peace, Holland, & Kellaher, 2005). And Evans (2009) provided fresh insight into social well-being and the experience of community among frail people living in "housing with care." In addition, interdisciplinary collaboration from within the social and behavioral sciences has been increasingly complemented by contributions from engineers, computer scientists, ergonomists, designers, and other technological fields.

As was the case during the early years of environmental gerontology, theoretical work has been interwoven with innovation in housing options and with increasingly sophisticated evaluations of their effectiveness (Ball et al., 2005; Peace & Holland, 2001). In particular, the emergence of universal design (Story, 1998), lifetime homes (Kelly, 2006), smart homes (Fisk, 2001), and a variety of assisted living alternatives (Golant & Hyde, 2008; Wilson, 2007; Zimmerman, Sloane, & Eckert, 2001), in association with the expansion of options such as co-housing (Brenton, 2001), has given rise to increasing interest in trying to reduce the tendency toward residential segregation that had characterized the previous generation of housing alternatives. In parallel with these developments, the mantra of aging-in-place has emerged to become a pervasive element of public policy, in association with an increasing emphasis, verging on an obsession, of enabling older adults to maintain independent living circumstances (Bookman, 2008; Rowles, 1993; Tilson, 1990). The outcome has been diversification of environmental gerontology as a heavily applied sub-field. While the late 1980s and 1990s were a period of theoretical quiescence (Schwarz, 2012), the first decade of the twenty-first century has seen the emergence of increasingly sophisticated person/environment transactional theory. It is against the backdrop of these broad trends that we now turn our attention to providing a contemporary perspective on individual experience of residential environments.

HUMAN EXPERIENCE OF THE ENVIRONMENT

Making Spaces Into Places

Life involves an ongoing process of making spaces into places with more or less success over the life course. Transforming spaces into places is a complex process that occurs on many levels. It may involve unpacking our overnight suitcase as we settle in to our hotel room and try to make ourselves comfortable for a one-night stay; we place items in accustomed locations, our socks in the top drawer and the picture we carry of our spouse on the nightstand on the left side of the bed—the side where we sleep at home. In the United States, it may involve claiming the space of our college dormitory room by placing identity-defining posters on the walls. Or it may involve a process, often extending over decades, of creating a permanent home as we decorate and redecorate our residence, design and maintain a garden, and gradually accumulate furniture and artifacts that define the space as ours.

On every level, the process involves transforming what is at the outset a sterile and meaningless piece of geographic space, for example an empty apartment, into a place that has personal meaning in the context of our ongoing life. In the process, we are engaged in converting something that is neutral and often alien into something that is a meaningful expression of our identity. This is not a trivial pursuit, because it is a process that provides a sense of familiarity, centering, security, ownership, control, territoriality, comfort, display, and identity.

On the most basic level, the creation of place involves the *use* of an environment, our pattern of behavior within a setting. For example, for those who work away from home, over time we develop a familiar pattern in our use of the space of our residence—a daily routine that provides a rhythm to life. We rise at about the same time each morning, and stumble, semi-awake, to the kitchen to plug in the coffee maker, before moving to the bathroom to perform our morning ablutions. On the way back to the kitchen, the daily ritual may include pausing at our front door to pick up the mail. Returning to the kitchen, we turn on the radio or our digital reader to catch up on the news before moving to the bedroom to dress for the day. We leave for work at about the same time each day, traveling the same route and often passing and interacting with the same people. And on most working days, the pattern of the rest of the day follows a similar preordained ritual in our use of the environment. A comparable pattern of ritualized behavior in the use of interior space may be traced if we work from home and spend most of the day in this setting. Regardless of our particular lifestyle, over time we develop a level of familiarity and comfort with our daily routine such that it becomes subconscious and habitual—taken for granted.

The habituation of daily activity patterns is reinforced by cognitive *awareness* of the configuration of the inside of our residence and the regular pathways we traverse as we move through the day. Indeed, our learned comfort and familiarity with our environment may only be fully brought into consciousness when the "automatic pilot," what David Seamon (1979) terms our pre-conscious "body subject," breaks down when we bump into a piece of furniture our spouse has moved from its appointed place, or we realize with a start that we have traveled almost the whole distance to work without consciously thinking about our driving. Over time, the reassurance of routines of using space and the "mental maps" that guide our behavior provide a level of comfort in traversing space. This may be adaptive as routine takes over from declining cognitive and sensory capability (Kastenbaum, 1980/1981; Norris-Baker & Scheidt, 1989).

Use and awareness of space are complemented as components of the way in which we transform spaces into places by the development of *emotional attachment* and a sense of ownership of known and familiar places—the corner of the locker room at the gym where we routinely change becomes "our place" (we feel a sense of intrusion when we arrive to find that someone has taken our customary locker). Attachments may become far more intense with respect to locations where significant life events transpired. The room in our residence where a relative died, the site of an accident on the way to work, the coffee shop where we first met our spouse, all, over time, become part of the rich landscape of place that forms the backdrop to the tapestry of our life and a constant source of reinforcement of identity. Each location becomes a potential cue to resurrecting in consciousness the events that transpired within it. The spaces of our life gradually become the places of our life as they become suffused with layer upon layer of meaning, sometimes recalled and sometimes merely latent, but always available as a potential source of self-affirming recollection.

Habitation of an environment over an extended period gener-ates temporal depth in the experience of place through repetition of patterns of use, increasingly differentiated awareness, and the accu-mulation of layers of emotional attachments. This facilitates *vicarious engagement* (Rowles, 1978). In our mind's eye, it is possible to travel back in time or across space to places where we have lived (including our current residence as it was in the past) and memorable locations we have visited and to reconstruct the events that transpired in these locations. We can also traverse contemporary space and visit places far away as we use the vast reservoir of our history of involvement with place to conjure up images of what is currently transpiring in these locations. Who among us has not taken such a journey as our thoughts stray while attending a particularly boring presentation? Of course these places are not real in the sense that they constitute an accurate representation. Rather they are constructions, often honed over many years as we selectively reconstruct the places of our life in ways that reinforce identity. Over time, place gradually comes to embody the self as it provides a reservoir of experiences grounded in our life experience that we can resurrect and vicariously relive and reconfigure as we develop, refine, and reinforce our identity. As layer upon layer of meaning in place is accumulated, the outcome is a sense of being in place.

House and Home and Being at Home

For many people, the most intense expression of being in place is provided by the concept of "home" and the experience of being at home. A large and growing literature on the idea of home has included a significant amount of work on the meaning of home in old age (Rowles & Chaudhury, 2005). At the outset it is important to make two distinctions. First, we differentiate between house and home because too often the former term is confounded with the latter. As Amos Rapoport notes so cogently, there is a critical difference between a house, apartment, assisted living residence, or nursing facility, indeed any type of living space, and a "home" (Rapoport, 2005; Rowles, 2006). In and of themselves, houses and apartments have no meaning. They are merely locations—empty spaces. They can only be brought to life and assume meaning as "home" through a process of habitation or "dwelling" in which space is claimed as a part of individual or group identity. Second, our concern is with home as an expression of our relationship with a concrete entity, a physical location, a place that becomes imbued with meaning through our habitation or dwelling within its confines. While there is certainly significant conceptual overlap, we are not directly concerned with more ethereal notions of home such as are evoked at the end of life when some people refer to "going home to God."

As we have noted, bringing spaces to life and developing a sense of being at home in these spaces is a complex process involving use, awareness, and the development of emotional attachments, all filtered through ongoing processes of vicarious immersion. It involves an intimate interweaving of person and location over time that results in a sense of familiarity, comfort, and at-oneness with places that finds expression in many dimensions of a person's being in the world and is closely related to well-being. It is only with the deepening awareness and understanding of these dimensions that we are able to contemplate providing effective interventions to truly enhance quality of life by creating spaces that are supportive of human need for being in place and being at home. So what are the dimensions of being at home?

For most people, "home" provides a place of centering. It is a location, characteristically our residence, from which we depart and to which we return each day, a reference point from which we build our spatial world. As such it provides an anchoring point for the flow of daily life (Bollnow, 1961). Our residence as home imbues life with a sense of permanence that contrasts with the alienation of being homeless and without an inner space (Watkins & Hosier, 2005). Home is associated with a sense of ownership. In an ethological sense it is our territory—our lair, burrow, or nest (Porteous, 1976); it provides a place of refuge from a threatening world outside and a place of privacy where we are safe and able to let down our guard, to relax, and where we are released from the constraints of the face that our culture obliges us to present to the world.

Having a home and being at home in most western societies is not without culturally imposed responsibility. We are expected to maintain our property and, if we have a garden, to exercise control over this space by ensuring that our lawn is mowed, our hedges are trimmed, and the gate is not hanging off its hinges.

The rewards of having a home, whether it be a high-rise apartment, a terraced house or a suburban residence, and being able to generate and maintain a place where we feel at home, are great. In addition to feelings of safety and comfort, home provides a place where we are in control and where we have the freedom of self-expression. Within interior space, we are free to decorate the rooms according to our whim, assemble furniture that reflects our aesthetic preference, and fill the space with artifacts and treasured possessions accumulated over our lifetime that reinforce our identity and personal history (Marcus, 1995; Rowles, Oswald, & Hunter, 2004). Outside, we can express ourselves in ways that range from an expansive lawn upon which our children play, through a productive garden where we grow herbs and vegetables, to elaborate flower beds providing a profusion of color through the changing seasons.

Ultimately, home is a place of belonging. It is a sacred place where we can simply be—where we can find ourselves through retreat from a profane world (Eliade, 1959). Nowhere is this essential function of the house as home more eloquently expressed than in the writing of Otto Bollnow (1961, p. 33), who more than 50 years ago wrote:

> Outer space is the space of openness, of danger, and abandonment. If that were the only space, then the existentialists would be correct and man would really be the eternally hunted fugitive. He needs the space of the house as an area protected and hidden, an area in which he can be relieved of continual anxious alertness, into which he can withdraw in order to return to himself. To give man this space is the highest function of the house.

Conversely, as we shall argue, to take it away is an often unknowing but generally pernicious cruelty.

Considered in concert, the dimensions of being in place and being at home reflect the essence of the way in which human beings relate to their environmental context. While home is the most intense expression of relationship with place, the same dimensions apply to greater or lesser degree to all of the spaces of life as they are used and as relationships develop within them. Consequently, we can feel quite "at home" at our favorite table at a local restaurant, or quite alienated when patronizing a cafe that is clearly designed for an entirely different clientele, especially when we experience the embarrassment of inappropriate dress for the setting. We can mark our ownership of our house (now our home) by building a fence, or reserve our place in an airport waiting room by arranging our luggage in a defensive pose and daring anyone to invade what has become our temporary albeit ephemeral home space.

ENVIRONMENTAL EXPERIENCE IN OLD AGE

Patterns of Adjustment Within Private Space

It is now well known and documented that older adults spend an increasing proportion of their time at home, in many cases more than 80% (Baltes, Maas, Wilms, & Borschelt, 1999; Kuster, 1998). Within the home, and especially as people move into their ninth decade, increasing frailty, difficulty in moving around and climbing or descending stairs, as well as fear of falling may lead to closing off rooms and to a process of environmental centralization (Clemson, Cusick, & Fozzard, 1999; Rowles, Oswald, & Hunter, 2003; Rubinstein, 1989). Older people may spend an increasing amount of their time in a single room or on a single floor of a multilevel residence, as they accommodate to changing capability. Indeed, they may "set up," sometimes with assistance from family members, to maintain the highest possible level of independence for as long as possible by placing their favorite chair with a clear view to the outside and may surround themselves with items they need, the television remote control, their sewing project, their telephone, and food for snacks, making sure that these items are within easy reach to minimize the need for movement during the day (Rowles, 1981).

These processes are often facilitated by external support from family members, neighbors, or social services. Typical is the experience of Peggy, an older women in one of the first author's studies who was "set up" in this manner every morning by her son, who would visit before going to work and make sure that his mother was provided with a flask of coffee and a lunch prepared by his wife, and that she was comfortably ensconced in her favorite chair by the window (Rowles, 1981, 1983). Each evening he would return to conduct comparable activities to make sure that she was set up for the night. Similarly, as people grow older in the community, they increasingly come to rely on support from neighbors and friends. In the same study, Audrey had, over the years, cultivated a relationship of "obligation" with her immediate neighbors, who would bring in her mail from the roadside mailbox, observe her window to make sure that the curtains were opened each morning, and visit frequently to provide assistance with daily chores. In some cases, neighbors may also act as a liaison with children who live far away. In less stable and less socially integrated neighborhoods, similar support may be provided by paid caregivers or by a growing array of community-based home care services.

Patterns of Relocation: Remaking Home

Eventually, for some older adults there comes a point when they can no longer sustain themselves or be sustained in their home by family, neighbors, or social services. Characteristically, this results in the need to relocate to a new setting that provides an increasing array of supports to sustain activities of daily living (Oswald & Rowles, 2007). In the past, the options were limited. Generally, they entailed relocation from a community residence to a nursing facility. But in recent decades, a plethora of intervening opportunities have emerged, ranging from supportive housing through assisted living to an array of personal care options designed to sustain individuals in a less medically oriented and restrictive environment than the nursing facility. Consequently, the process of relocation may involve a series of moves to successively more supportive environments.

The key point here is that making such moves involves the disruption of the person's being in place or being at home and necessitates transferring or remaking a new mode of being in place. This process is complex and involves adjustment with respect to all of the dimensions of being in place that we have discussed. The process is repeated with every move (Figure 1.2).

Abandonment of a familiar home and remaking a sense of being in place and at home in a new setting is not only stressful, but also is a skill. For example, early work on retirement communities showed that some people are particularly adept at this process, having developed the capacity over their life course to easily transition from place to place (Jacobs, 1974; Osgood, 1982). Others are not. For these people, relocation is often associated with significant stress. The stresses are magnified for older adults, who tend to have a lower level of physiological reserve

FIGURE 1.2   The Experience of Relocation: Remaking Home

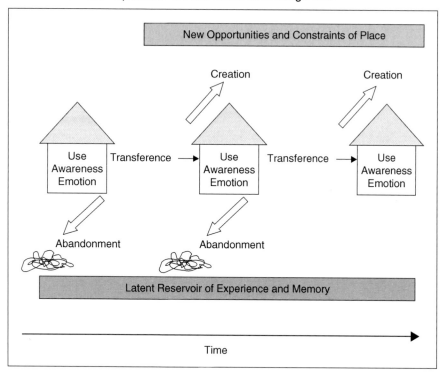

capacity and ability to adapt to environmental change. Experience is also a key factor here. Census data for 2005–2006 indicate that U.S. residents relocate, on average, 10.1 times during their life, a far cry from the relative residential inertia of previous generations. Of course, many people relocate many more times and many on fewer occasions. For a person with lifelong residence in a single dwelling or who relocates only once or twice over the course of their life, each move has the potential to be traumatic. It may involve tearing up deeply burrowed roots and abandoning a sense of being in place that is a key element of the persona. In contrast, those who relocate frequently generally, although not invariably, have less-intense associations with the abandoned locations and are more likely to have refined their place-making skills in a manner that minimizes the disruption of each move.

A key element of the process will be one of *transference*, as older people move not only themselves but also many aspects of their being in place, including the possessions they load into the moving van and the many aspects of their lifestyle and daily routine of behavior that they try to accommodate to the new setting. For example, there is evidence that when people move to a new residence, they have a tendency to place furniture in a spatial configuration replicating the arrangement of these items in the residence from which they have departed (Toyama, 1988). Each new setting will offer many new opportunities: the opportunity to engage in new activities, to make new friends, and perhaps to devote more time and energy to preferred occupations rather than having to continue routine chores of home and self-maintenance that have become increasingly taxing and problematic. But there will also be constraints; for example, in the case of movement to assisted living or other types of supportive care environment, there will generally be the need for downsizing (giving up furniture and artifacts that cannot be accommodated in a reduced space), a need to change aspects of daily routine in order to conform with dining times at a new facility, a potential loss of privacy, and the need to develop familiarity with new routes and pathways in negotiating new residential space and becoming familiar with the surrounding neighborhood.

Reconciling the opportunities and the constraints will involve the active *creation* of a new mode of being in place and at home. Also involved is a process of *abandonment*, as much that has been central to life may have to be given up: the ease of a long-established daily routine, the taken-for-granted familiarity with often-frequented spaces, the garden nurtured over two decades that became a sanctuary and so much a part of life and identity as new plants and trees were added over the years, a network of close personal friends, strong relationships with neighbors, and, because each new space is characteristically smaller than the one given up, many of the cherished possessions accumulated over a lifetime. There is also the fear of loss of memories as the physical cues in the environment that evoked and preserved images of a daughter playing on the swing in the backyard, a spouse working at the bench in the garage, and countless other key events that took place in what was "home" are given up, become part of the detritus of life, and gradually fade from immediate consciousness to become part of a latent reservoir of experience and memories. Reconciling processes of transference, creation, and abandonment during the experience of relocating is repeated with every move.

Placing this model in the broader context of the experience of relocation and its relationship to our being in place or at home throughout the life course, there is an ongoing relationship between *proactivity*, defined as anticipating, preparing for, and making a home or planning a relocation over which one has control, and *reactivity*, defined as an experiential response to unanticipated or unwelcome relocation, generally in situations where one has reduced or limited control (Lawton, 1990). The balance between the two processes is different at different points in the life course and over each person's lifetime relocation trajectory. For example, as a child our autonomy and involvement in planning and anticipating relocations is limited even though place attachment may be an important element of our identity and well-being (Jack, 2010). We simply react and accommodate to decisions to move made by our parents as we transfer, create, and abandon aspects of our being in place or at home during relocations over which we have little control. But as we grow older and perhaps establish our own family, assuming we have the resources to do so, we tend to become increasingly proactive in making the places of our life, in creating the kind of private and residential space in which we feel most comfortable and at home. We envisage a dream home, establish a comfortable lifestyle or mode of being in place, and gradually accumulate artifacts that reinforce our identity and our preferred mode of being in the world. Toward the end of a working life, as we envisage retirement, we may become even more proactive as we anticipate and prepare for this event, and perhaps eventually engage in retirement relocation to a residence and setting supporting our preferred mode of being in place. Striving to live a life imagined, we make our ideal home.

Our sense is that this is a common process for many people who have the necessary resources. Unfortunately, many people do not. Too many powerless older adults still live in poverty and isolation in environmentally and socially hostile neighborhoods (Minkler, 1985; Scharf et al., 2006; Scharf, Phillipson, & Smith, 2005, 2007); in Maslow's (1943) terms their lives are framed at the base of the needs hierarchy with a focus on survival rather than the element of self-actualization that results from being at home.

Even if we could envisage the opportunity for all people to create a place where they can be at home as a central motif of their life, there should be no illusion that such a state is likely to be perpetual. As we age and potentially become more environmentally vulnerable, we are likely to find ourselves in a much more reactive mode as we are obliged to accept increasing levels of care in order to remain at home or as we consider relocation to a more supportive environment. In such a setting, although we may receive all the care we need, we will invariably be forced to react to circumstances in which we have significantly reduced control and independence with a far less rich mode of being in place, and in an environment where our level of autonomy and ability to remake place is likely to be significantly diminished.

Consequences of Relocation

As we have noted, there is abundant evidence that relocation, particularly when such relocation is involuntary and—in the terms employed in this chapter—reactive, has negative consequences. Beyond the effects on mortality and morbidity so widely documented and discussed in the literature (Danermark & Ekstrom, 1990; Smith & Crome, 2000), we suggest that the fundamental issue is one not only of physical separation, but also of psychological and, specifically, experiential separation from place. To be "out of place" and "homeless," essentially the fate of many older people when they become vulnerable, is no way to spend the final months or years of life.

WHY PLACE IS IMPORTANT

We are now approaching a point where being out of place and homeless may no longer be an inevitable companion of old age. As we accumulate knowledge of the manner in which people experience space and make place, we are increasingly able to identify options for intervention that on the one hand enable people to sustain accustomed modes of being in place and at home and, on the other, ease the process of transition and remaking place when environmental change or a relocation becomes necessary. Diverse options are now available for supporting aging in place. There is growing emphasis on creating livable cities and elder-friendly neighborhoods that nurture a sense of being in place (Abbott, Carman, Carman, & Scarfo, 2009; Clark & Glicksman, 2012; Lui, Everingham, Warburton, Cuthill, & Bartlett, 2009). Design innovations, including universal design, smart home technologies, benign surveillance equipment and emerging ambient intelligence technologies, are making it easier for older adults to remain at home (Fisk, 2001; Hwang, Cummings, Sixsmith, & Sixsmith, 2011; Melenhorst, Rogers, & Fisk, 2007; Sixsmith, 2000; Story, 1998).

When relocation is necessary, we are discovering that not only actual preliminary visits to the new setting but also simulated ones can ease the process of transference (Hertz, Rossetti, Koren, & Robertson, 2005; Hunt & Roll, 1987). The value of assisting individuals faced with downsizing in the process of sorting through their possessions, with a view to identifying and saving those that provide the strongest cues to ongoing identity and potential to minimize the stress of severance from familiar place, is increasingly recognized (Luborsky, Lysack, & Van Nuil, 2011). So, too, is the integral role of the family in the process and its relationship to the creation of legacy through the handing down of possessions during the process of household disbandment (Ekerdt & Sergeant, 2006; Hunter & Rowles, 2005).

Providing support in the remaking of home is possible through the design of long-term care facilities that provide adequate space in rooms and residents' private spaces for the retention, storage, and display of familiar and treasured artifacts. Supporting residents in the remaking of home is also facilitated by staff education to increased sensitivity to the significance of being in place and the meaning of home to older residents.

Easing the negative impacts of giving up a home and sustaining a sense of continuity, can be accomplished by return visits to the abandoned residence or neighborhood or by strategies to reinforce the retention of previous social relationships—for example, maintaining membership in, and continuing to participate in and retain social ties with, one's former church. The increasingly widely utilized option of reminiscence groups in long-term care facilities also provides an important medium for vicariously reconnecting people to their past and to places that have been physically abandoned (Gibson, 2004; Haight & Webster, 1995). One particularly interesting and potentially adaptable option is provided in the work of Habib Chaudhury (2008), who demonstrates how both generic photographs of residences as well as actual photographs of former homes (obtained from family members) can provide critical environmental cuing to enable persons with Alzheimer's disease to recapture places of their past and hence retain and reinforce identity. Within this process of "photo-linking," the picture becomes a medium for re-entering and remaking place. Finally, the emergence of the Internet and the growth of social media including Facebook, MySpace, Skype, Tumblr, Reddit, and Twitter is transforming the nature of people's social relationships and modifying the ways in which lives are confined by space. Embracing aspects of contemporary social media that are becoming increasingly prominent in the lives of future older adults, offers the potential for sustaining and reinforcing existing modes of being in place and perhaps creating new modes of being in the world and at home that we have yet to imagine (Bradley & Poppen, 2003; Carter, 2005; Sum, Matthews, Pourghasem, & Hughes, 2009).

We are on the threshold of a new era in our knowledge and understanding of older people's relationship to place, an era in which environmental gerontology has the potential to use deepening understanding of the manner in which older adults relate to place as a basis for sensitive and empathic interventions to improve the quality of life in old age. This book is a response to this opportunity. Our authors are not only contributing to the development of a more sophisticated and finely nuanced environmental gerontology, but also are helping us make progress along a path toward greater environmental sensitivity and awareness of the lived experience of older adults, which has the potential to improve quality of life for us all.

As you read the following chapters, we hope that you will ponder the many ways in which our contributors are grappling with the challenge of translating knowledge of the meaning and significance of place in old age into practical suggestions for environmental design, human service intervention, community development, and public policy. We sense that many of these suggestions are merely scratching the surface of the possible. Our hope is that you, the reader, will use this information and the insights of our contributors as a stimulus for your own thinking.

Of one thing we are sure: space matters, but place matters even more, because it captures the essence of meaning in life. To be placeless is to be alienated from the world and is a threat to identity. It is a fate that in our contemporary society confronts many people as their residential circumstances change toward the end of life. Our contributors demonstrate why this need not be so.

REFERENCES

Abbott, P. S., Carman, N., Carman, J., & Scarfo, B. (2009). *Recreating neighborhoods for successful aging.* Baltimore, MD: Health Professions Press.

Balint, M. (1955). Friendly expanses–horrid empty spaces. *International Journal of Psychoanalysis, 36,* 225–241.

Ball, M. M., Perkins, M. M., Whittington, F. J., Hollingsworth, C., King, S. V., & Combs, B. S. (2005). *Communities of care: Assisted living for African American elders.* Baltimore, MD: The Johns Hopkins University Press.

Baltes, M. M., Maas, I., Wilms, H.-U., & Borchelt, M. (1999). Everyday competence in old and very old age: Theoretical considerations and empirical findings. In P. B. Baltes & K. U. Mayer (Eds.), *The Berlin aging study* (pp. 384–402). Cambridge, UK: Cambridge University Press.

Bollnow, O. F. (1961). Lived space. *Philosophy Today, 5*(1), 31–39.

Bookman, A. (2008). Innovative models of aging in place: Transforming our communities for an aging population. *Community, Work & Family, 11*(4), 419–438.

Bradley, N., & Poppen, W. (2003). Assistive technology, computers and internet may decrease sense of isolation for homebound elderly and disabled persons. *Technology and Disability, 15,* 19–25.

Brenton, M. (2001). Older people's cohousing communities. In S. M. Peace & C. Holland (Eds.), *Inclusive housing in an ageing society* (pp. 169–188). Bristol, UK: Policy Press.

Canter, D. V., & Craik, K. H. (1981). Environmental psychology. *Journal of Environmental Psychology, 1*(1), 1–11.

Carp, F. M. (1966). *A future for the aged.* Austin, TX: University of Texas Press.

Carter, D. (2005). Living in virtual communities: An ethnography of human relationships in cyberspace. *Information, Communication and Society, 8*(2), 148–167.

Castle, N. G. (2001). Relocation of the elderly. *Medical Care Research and Review, 58*(3), 291–333.

Chaudhury, H. (2008). *Remembering home.* Baltimore, MD: The Johns Hopkins University Press.

Clark, K., & Glicksman, A. (2012). Age-friendly Philadelphia: Bringing diverse networks together around aging issues. *Journal of Housing for the Elderly, 26,* 121–136.

Clemson, L., Cusick, A., & Fozzard, C. (1999). Managing risk and exerting control: Determining follow through with falls prevention. *Disability and Rehabilitation, 21*(12), 531–541.

Craik, K. H. (1973). Environmental psychology. *Annual Review of Psychology, 24,* 403–422.

Cutchin, M. P. (2003). The process of mediated aging in place: A theoretically and empirically based model. *Social Science and Medicine, 57*(6), 1077–1090.

Cutchin, M. P. (2004). Using Deweyan philosophy to rename and reframe adaptation to environment. *American Journal of Occupational Therapy, 58*(3), 303–312.

Danermark, B., & Ekstrom, M. (1990). Relocation and health effects on the elderly: A commented research review. *Journal of Sociology and Social Welfare, 25,* 25–49.

Dreyfus, H. L. (1991). *Being-in-the-world: A commentary on Heidegger's being and time, Division I.* Cambridge, MA: MIT Press.

Ekerdt, D. J., & Sergeant, J. F. (2006). Family things: Attending the household disbandment of elders. *Journal of Aging Studies, 20,* 193–205.

Ekerdt, D. J., Sergeant, J. F., Dingle, M., & Bowen, M. E. (2004). Household disbandment in later life. *Journals of Gerontology, Social Sciences, 59*(5), S265–S273.

Eliade, M. (1959). *The sacred and the profane: The nature of religion.* New York, NY: Harcourt, Brace & World.

Evans, S. (2009). *Community and ageing: Maintaining quality of life in housing with care settings.* Bristol, UK: Policy Press.

Fisk, M. J. (2001). The implications of smart home technologies. In S. M. Peace & C. Holland (Eds.), *Inclusive housing in an ageing society* (pp. 101–124). Bristol, UK: Policy Press.

Gibson, F. (2004). *The past in the present: Using reminiscence in health and social care.* Baltimore, MD: Health Professions Press.

Golant, S. M., & Hyde, J. (Eds.). (2008). *The assisted living residence: A vision for the future.* Baltimore, MD: The Johns Hopkins University Press.

Haight, B. K., & Webster, J. D. (Eds.). (1995). *The art and science of reminiscing: Theory, methods and applications.* Washington, DC: Taylor & Francis.

Heidegger, M. (1962). *Being and time* (J. Macquarrie & E. Robinson, Trans.). New York, NY: Harper & Row.

Hertz, J. E., Rossetti, J., Koren, M. E., & Robertson, J. F. (2005). *Management of relocation in cognitively intact older adults.* Iowa City, IA: University of Iowa, Gerontological Nursing Interventions Research Center, Research Dissemination Core.

Howell, S. C. (1983). The meaning of place in old age. In G. D. Rowles & R. J. Ohta (Eds.), *Aging and milieu: Environmental perspectives on growing old* (pp. 97–107). New York, NY: Academic Press.

Hunt, M. E., & Roll, M. K. (1987). Simulation in familiarizing older people with an unknown building. *The Gerontologist, 27*(2), 169–175.

Hunter, E. G., & Rowles, G. D. (2005). Leaving a legacy: Toward a typology. *Journal of Aging Studies, 19,* 327–347.

Husserl, E. (1970). *The crisis of European sciences and transcendental phenomenology.* Evanston, Ill.: Northwestern University Press. (Original work published in 1936).

Hwang, E., Cummings, L., Sixsmith, A. J., & Sixsmith, J. (2011). Impacts of home modification on aging-in-place. *Journal of Housing for the Elderly, 25*(3), 246–257.

Iwarsson, S. (2004). Assessing the fit between older people and their physical home environments: An Occupational therapy research perspective. *In Annual Review of Gerontology and Geriatrics* Vol. 23 (pp.85-109). New York, NY: Springer Publishing Company.

Jack, G. (2010). Place matters: The significance of place attachments for children's well-being. *British Journal of Social Work, 40,* 755–771.

Jacobs, J. (1974). *Fun city: An ethnographic study of a retirement community.* Austin, TX: Holt, Rinehart and Winston Inc.

Jephcott, P. (1971). *Homes in high flats,* Edinburgh, UK: Oliver & Boyd.

Kahana, E. (1982). A congruence model of person-environment interaction. In M. P. Lawton, P. G. Windley, & T. O. Byerts (Eds.). *Aging and the environment: Theoretical approaches* (pp. 97–121). New York, NY: Springer Publishing Company.

Kastenbaum, R. J. (1980–81). Habituation as a model of human aging. *International Journal of Aging and Human Development, 12*(3), 159–169.

Kelly, M. (2006). Lifetime homes. In S. M. Peace & C. Holland (Eds.), *Inclusive housing in an ageing society* (pp. 55–75). Bristol, UK: Policy Press.

Kendig, H. (2003). Directions in environmental gerontology: A multidisciplinary field. *The Gerontologist, 43*(5), 611–615.

Kuster, C. (1998). Zeitverwendung und Wohnen im Alter [Use of time and housing in old age.] In Deutsches Zentrum fur Altersfragen (Ed.), Wohnbedurfnisse, Zeitverwendung, und soziale Netzwerke alterer Menschen. *Expertisenband I zum Zweiten Altenbericht der Bundesregierung.* [Housing needs, use of time, and social networks of older adults.] Frankfurt am Main: Campus.

Lawton, M. P. (1990). Residential environment and self-directedness among older people. *American Psychologist, 45,* 638–640.

Lawton, M. P., & Hoover, S. (1981). *Community housing and choices for older Americans.* New York, NY: Springer Publishing Company.

Lawton, M. P., & Nahemow, L. (1973). Ecology and the aging process. In C. Eisdorfer & M. P. Lawton (Eds.), *The psychology of adult development and aging* (pp. 619–674). Washington, DC: American Psychological Association.

Lawton, M. P., & Simon, B. B. (1968). The ecology of social relationships in housing for the elderly. *The Gerontologist, 8,* 108–115.

Lewin, K. (1951). *Field theory in social science: Selected theoretical papers* (Dorwin Cartwright, ed.). Oxford, UK: Harpers.

Luborsky, M. R., Lysack, C. L., & Van Nuil, J. (2011). Refashioning one's place in time: Stories of household downsizing, *Journal of Aging Studies, 25,* 243–252.

Lui, C. W., Everingham, J. A., Warburton, J., Cuthill, M., & Bartlett, H. (2009). What makes a community age-friendly? A review of international literature. *Australian Journal on Aging, 28*(3), 116–121.

Maslow, A.H. (1943). A theory of human motivation. *Psychological Review* 50(4) 370–396.

Marcus, C. C. (1995). *House as a mirror of self: Exploring the deeper meaning of home.* Berwick, ME: Nicholas Hays.

Melenhorst, A.-S., Rogers, W. A., & Fisk, A. D. (2007). When will technology in the home improve the quality of life for older adults? In H.-W. Wahl, C. Tesch-Romer, & A. Hoff (Eds.), *New dynamics in old age: Individual, environmental and societal perspectives* (pp. 253–269). Amityville, NY: Baywood Publishing Company.

Minkler, M. (1985). Building supportive ties and sense of community among the inner-city elderly: The Tenderloin Senior Outreach Project. *Health Education and Behavior, 12*(3), 303–14.

Morris, B. R. (1992). Reducing inventory: Divestiture of personal possessions. *Journal of Women and Aging, 4*(2), 79–92.

Norris-Baker, C., & Scheidt, R. J. (1989). Habituation theory and environment aging research: Ennui to joie de vivre? *International Journal of Aging and Human Development, 29*(4), 241–257.

O'Bryant, S. L. (1982). The value of home to older persons: Relationship to housing satisfaction. *Research on Aging, 4*(3), 349–363.

Osgood, N. J. (1982). *Senior settlers: Social integration in retirement communities.* Westport, CT: Greenwood Press.

Oswald, F., & Rowles, G. D. (2007). Beyond the relocation trauma in old age: New trends in elders' residential decisions. In H.-W. Wahl, C. Tesch-Romer, & A. Hoff (Eds.), *New dynamics in old age: Individual, environmental and societal perspectives* (pp. 127–152). Amityville, NY: Baywood Publishing Company.

Pastalan, L. A. (1970). Privacy as an expression of human territoriality. In L. A. Pastalan & D. H. Carson (Eds.), *Spatial behavior of older people* (pp. 88–101). Ann Arbor, MI: University of Michigan-Wayne State University Institute of Gerontology.

Peace, S. M., & Holland, C. (Eds.). (2001). *Inclusive housing in an ageing society: Innovative approaches.* Bristol, UK: Policy Press.

Peace, S., Holland, C., & Kellaher, L. (2006). *Environment and identity in later life.* Maidenhead, UK: Open University Press.

Peace, S.M., Holland, C., & Kellaher, L. (2005). The influence of neighborhood and community on well-being and identity in later life: An English perspective. In G.D. Rowles & H. Chaudhury (eds.). *Home and identity in Late Life: International Perspectives.* (pp. 297–315). New York, NY: Springer Publishing Company.

Phillipson, C. (2004). Urbanization and ageing: Towards a new environmental gerontology. *Ageing and Society, 24*(6), 963–971.

Porteous, J. D. (1976). Home: The territorial core. *Geographical Review, 66*(4), 383–390.

Proshansky, H. M., Ittelson, W. H., & Rivlin, L.G. (Eds.). (1976). *Environmental psychology: People and their physical settings* (2nd ed.). Oxford, England: Holt.

Rapoport, A. (2005). On using home and place. In G. D. Rowles & H. Chaudhury (Eds.), *Home and identity in late life* (pp. 343–360). New York, NY: Springer Publishing Company.

Regnier, V., & Pynoos, J. (1987). *Housing the aged: Design directives and policy considerations.* Amsterdam, The Netherlands: Elsevier.

Rowles, G. D. (1978). *Prisoners of space? Exploring the geographical experience of older people.* Boulder, CO: Westview Press.

Rowles, G. D. (1981). The surveillance zone as meaningful space for the aged. *The Gerontologist, 21*(3), 304–311.

Rowles, G.D. (1983). Geographical dimensions of social support in rural Appalachia. In G.D. Rowles & J.R. Ohta (eds.). *Aging and Milieu: Environmental Perspectives on Growing Old.* (pp. 111–130). New York: Academic Press.

Rowles, G. D. (1991). Beyond performance: Being in place as a component of occupational therapy. *American Journal of Occupational Therapy, 45*(3), 265–271.

Rowles, G. D. (1993). Evolving images of place in aging and aging in place. *Generations, 17*(2), 65–70.

Rowles, G. D. (2000). Habituation and being in place, *Occupational Therapy Journal of Research, 20* (Special Supplement), S52–S67.

Rowles, G. D. (2006). A house is not a home: But can it become one? In H.-W. Wahl, H. Brenner, H. Mollenkopf, D. Rothenbacher, & C. Rott (Eds.), *The many faces of health, competence and well-being in old age: Integrating epidemiological, psychological and social perspectives* (pp. 25–32). Dordrecht, The Netherlands: Springer.

Rowles, G.D. & Chaudhury, H. (2005). *Home and Identity in Later Life: International Perspectives.* New York, NY: Springer Publishing Company.

Rowles, G. D., Oswald, F., & Hunter, E. G. (2004). Interior living environments in old age. In H.-W. Wahl, R. J. Scheidt, & P. G. Windley (Eds.), *Aging in context: Socio-physical environments. Annual review of gerontology and geriatrics* (Vol. 23, pp. 167–194). New York, NY: Springer Publishing Company.

Rubinstein, R. L. (1989). The home environments of older people: A description of the psychosocial processes lining person to place. *Journal of Gerontology, 44*(2), S45–S53.

Rubinstein, R. L. (1990). Personal identity and environmental meaning in later life. *Journal of Aging Studies, 4*(2), 131–147.

Rubinstein, R.L., & de Medeiros, K. (2005). Home, self and identity. In G.D. Rowles & H. Chaudhury (eds.). *Home and Identity in Late Life: International Perspectives* (pp. 47–62). New York, NY: Springer Publishing Company.

Scharf, T., Bartlam, B., Hislop, J., Bernard, M., Dunning, A., & Sim, J. (2006). *Necessities of life: Older people's experiences of poverty.* London, UK: Help the Aged.

Scharf, T., Phillipson, C., & Smith, A. E. (2005). *Multiple exclusion and quality of life amongst excluded older people in disadvantaged neighborhoods*. London, UK: Social Exclusion Unit, Office of the Deputy Prime Minister.

Scharf, T., Phillipson, C., & Smith, A. E. (2007). Aging in a difficult place: Assessing the impact of urban deprivation on older people, In H.-W. Wahl, C. Tesch-Römer, & A. Hoff (Eds.), *New dynamics in old age: Individual, environmental and societal perspectives.* Amityville, NY: Baywood.

Scheidt, R. J., & Norris-Baker, C. (1999). Place therapies for older adults. *International Journal of Aging and Human Development, 48*(1), 1–15.

Scheidt, R. J., & Windley, P. G. (2006). Environmental gerontology: Progress in the post-Lawton era. In J. E. Birren & K. W. Schaie (Eds.), *Handbook of the psychology of aging* (6th ed). Amsterdam, The Netherlands: Elsevier.

Schutz, A., & Luckmann, T. (1973). *The structures of the lifeworld (Strukturen der Lebenswelt)* (R. M. Zaner & H. T. Engelhardt, Trans.). Evanston, IL: Northwestern University Press.

Schwarz, B. (2012). Environmental gerontology: What now? *Journal of Housing for the Elderly, 26,* 4–19.

Schwarz, B., & Scheidt, R. J. (Ed.). (2012). Environmental gerontology [Special Issue]. *Journal of Housing for the Elderly, 26,* 1–3.

Seamon, D. (1979). *A Geography of the Lifeworld: Movement, Rest and Encounter.* New York, NY: St. Martin's Press.

Sixsmith, A. J. (2000). An evaluation of an intelligent home monitoring system. *Journal of Telemedicine and Telecare, 6,* 63–72.

Sixsmith, A. J. (2002). *Home and later life: An experiential study.* London, UK: University of London.

Smith, A. E., & Crome, P. (2000). Relocation mosaic: A review of 40 years of resettlement literature. *Reviews in Clinical Gerontology, 10*(1), 81–95.

Story, M. F. (1998). Maximizing usability: The principles of universal design. *Assistive Technology, 10*(1), 4–12.

Sum, S., Matthews, R. M., Pourghasem, M., & Hughes, I. (2009). Internet use as a predictor of sense of community in older people. *Cyber Psychology and Behavior, 12*(2), 235–239.

Tilson, D. (1990). *Aging in place: Supporting the frail elderly in residential environments.* Glenview, IL: Scott, Foresman & Company.

Toyama, T. (1988). *Identity and milieu: A study of relocation focusing on reciprocal change in elderly people and their environment.* Stockholm, Sweden: Department for Building Function Analysis, The Royal Institute of Technology.

Tuan, Y. F. (1977). *Space and place: The perspective of experience.* Minneapolis, MN: University of Minnesota Press.

Wahl, H-W., & Lang, F.R. (2004). Aging in context across the adult life course: Integrating physical and social environmental research perspectives. In H-W. Wahl, R.J. Scheidt & P.G. Windley (eds). *Annual Review of Gerontology and Geriatrics* Vol. 23. (pp. 1–33). New York, NY: Springer Publishing Company.

Wahl, H.-W., & Weisman, G. D. (2003). Environmental gerontology at the beginning of the new millennium: Reflections on its historical, empirical and theoretical development. *The Gerontologist, 4*(5), 616–627.

Watkins, J. F., & Hosier, A. F. (2005). Conceptualizing home and homelessness: A life course perspective. In G. D. Rowles & H. Chaudhury (Eds.), *Home and identity in late life* (pp. 197–216). New York, NY: Springer Publishing Company.

Willcocks, D. M., Peace, S. M., & Kellaher, L. A. (1987). *Private lives in public spaces: A research-based critique of residential life in local authority old people's homes.* London, UK: Tavistock Publications.

Wilson, K. B. (2007). Historical evolution of assisted living in the United States, 1979 to the present. *The Gerontologist, 47*(Special Issue), 8–22.

Zimmerman, S., Sloane, P. D., & Eckert, J. K. (2001). *Assisted living: Needs, practices, and policies in residential care for the elderly.* Baltimore, MD: The Johns Hopkins University Press.

CHAPTER 2

Social Interactions in Public Spaces and Places: A Conceptual Overview

Sheila Peace

EDITORS' INTRODUCTION

This chapter complements the focus on private space and the intimate space of home of Chapter 1 by providing an overview perspective on public places and spaces, the world beyond the threshold. The chapter provides a transition from individual to social constructions of space and place. In her discussion, Peace emphasizes the importance of considering the interaction of micro and macro spaces, the private and the public. In particular, she frames our growing knowledge of the meaning and significance of place within the larger context of intergenerational social interactions in public spaces and ongoing actions and debates in the movement toward creating age-friendly communities. She makes a convincing case for recognizing environmental complexity and the need to improve efforts to bring together physical/material, social, and psychological dimensions in understanding the way in which older people relate to environment. Such a melding necessitates a perspective that recognizes the diversity of human experience and the diversity of older people. It is important to acknowledge varied needs over a period of later life that may span more than 40 years. In order to develop this level of understanding, Peace emphasizes the value of longitudinal community ethnography and the need to understand the intergenerational characteristics of public spaces. This particular focus is elaborated in the contribution by Thang and Kaplan (see Chapter 10).

Public spaces allow people to meet on ostensibly neutral ground in planned and unplanned ways, to interact with others within the context of the whole community.

—Holland, Clark, Katz, and Peace (2007, p. ix)

This quotation comes from a study of social interaction in an urban public place carried out in the British town of Aylesbury. I shall return to the findings of this study later in the chapter; here, it is used to introduce a series of underpinning concepts and themes—space; public; neutral ground; planning; context; community—that underpin the discussion. To these I add the associated issues of "place" and "interaction" between people and their environment, particularly in later life, as it is the understanding of these concepts that grounds the arguments presented by authors in all sections of this book, but particularly in Part IV. How people interact with each other and how environment encapsulates personal behavior is an ecological position that, when focused on development in later life, recognizes how issues of personal identity, embodiment, and sociability can make the environment more or less enabling (Rubinstein & de Medeiros, 2004).

The chapter is divided into two main sections. In the first, the aim is to consider the spatiality of aging on both conceptual and experiential levels. What are the issues that influence the experience of the public in terms of space and place in later life, and how may these issues be addressed? With this understanding, the second section views empirical research on two levels: intergenerational interactions within one town, and the global move toward age-friendly communities. Conclusions will be drawn over future directions and the challenges to be faced in developing meaningful public spaces and places.

DEFINING PUBLIC SPACES AND PLACES

Recent views on space and place are used to position the discussion. This is a multidisciplinary area of study, but fundamental is the work of social geographers such as Linda McDowell (1999), Tim Cresswell (2004) and Doreen Massey (2005), who have all debated the concept of place and made the case for a rethinking of spatial imagination. It can be argued that space is an intangible concept that enables location. Space may be traversed or navigated and situated in historical time, economic time, and personal time. In this way, space and time, interpreted through human interaction, create diverse understandings of spatiality. While the world is becoming ever more interconnected through the migration of labor, capital, technological development, and lifestyle, which at one level seem to reduce distance, such globalization does not have to lead to a uniformity of experience where place loses the importance of personal meaning, attachment, and spatial uniqueness that can be both familiar and unfamiliar.

The use of space is the essence of place, a social construction that McDowell (1999, p. 4) defines this way:

> It is socio-spatial practices that define places with multiple and changing boundaries, constituted and maintained by social relations of power and exclusion (Massey, 1991; Smith, 1993). Places are made through power relations which construct the rules which define boundaries. These boundaries are both social and spatial—they define who belongs to a place and who may be excluded, as well as the location or site of the experience.

Such power relations underlie the "ostensibly" that defines the "neutral ground" identified by Holland et al. (2007) in the quotation that begins this chapter. Here we can see that for different individuals or groups, boundaries in place can be overlapping or distinct, and can influence different levels of spatial mastery or, as discussed here, levels of connectivity.

Levels of Connectivity in Later Life

McDowell talks of the "social relations of power and exclusion," and certain authors have been prominent in examining how spaces and places are experienced and understood in different ways by women and men, and the impact of gender and gender relations (see Bondi, 1998; McDowell & Massey, 1984). In these analyses, age and gender have not been considered together. There is a need to explore the impact on spatiality of the multiple jeopardy experienced through the interface among age, gender, sexuality, ethnicity, and socioeconomic status.

In contrast, other academic activists have been concerned with campaigning over rights for change and the reduction of social exclusion. In the field of disability, ongoing discussion of the social model of disability recognizes the social consequences of living with impairment (Shakespeare & Watson, 2001; Swain, French, Barnes, & Thomas, 2004). These social consequences can be seen as attitudinal, structural, and environmental barriers that prevent people from participating in aspects of everyday life. Environmental barriers may relate to the design and layout of buildings, neighborhoods, and communities and have led to national legislation and ongoing discussion concerning universal design, accessibility, and visitability within public spaces (Ackroyd, 2005; Habinteg, 2011; Imrie, 2004; Milner & Madigan, 2001; Schneidert, Hirst, Miller, & Ustrun, 2003). Such barriers are often an expression of a society's underlying attitudes toward disabled people, which are played out in structures that exclude people (Kitchin, 1998; Manzo, 2003).

Obviously there are parallels between the experiences of people of all ages living with ongoing physical/cognitive impairments and older people who experience chronic or acute health conditions later in life. However, the discussion of barriers to everyday living has resonance for people as they age who may not see themselves as disabled or experiencing ongoing physical or mental impairment. For, as noted above, barriers are not only environmental, but also attitudinal and structural. Here it is useful to consider a comment by Massey (2005, pp. 5–6), which raises issues of power and place attachment:

> For some it is the sphere of the everyday, of real and valued practices, the geographical source of meaning, vital to hold on to as "the global" spins its ever more powerful and alienating webs. For others, a "retreat to place" represents a protective pulling up of drawbridges and a building of walls against the new invasions. Place, on this reading, is the locus of denial, of attempted withdrawal from invasion/difference.

Inclusion in the everyday, and the dichotomy outlined here, leads me to reflect on how over time many multidisciplinary environmental gerontologists have been most concerned with aspects of the micro environment, defined here in relation to the situation of "aging within setting" at the private level of the individuals and their residence (see Chapter 1). This has been at the expense of considering the wider issues encompassed by the "spatiality of aging" within the public spaces of cities, towns, and neighborhoods and beyond the bounds of employment to wider confines of active citizenship. Only in recent decades has there been a call for age-friendly cities that take onboard both micro and macro aspects of environment. The "retreat to place" can also be seen in the way in which many people in later life "stay put" in their own homes, often having been long-term members of a particular community (Peace, Holland, & Kellaher, 2006). Within the United Kingdom (UK), the policy rhetoric of "independence" and "independent living" is seen in parallel with moves toward "Lifetime Homes, Lifetime Neighbourhoods" (Department for Communities and Local Government [DCLG] 2008; Home and Communities Agency [HCA], 2009).

Of course, outstanding social geographers/gerontologists such as Glenda Laws (1994, 1997) have been exceptions in seminal early conceptual work, showing how space and place are central to the development of social identity in later life and championing the relationship among age, space, and place. She argued that in relation to age there are

> several dimensions of spatiality—accessibility, mobility, motility, spatial scale, and spatial segregation—which are involved in the mutual constitution of places and identities. (Laws, 1997, p. 93)

These are issues that can be used to examine both the environmental and structural barriers that may prevent the older person from being integrated into and connected with the wider community. In developing her argument, Laws considered different forms of residential experience to focus on identity construction associated with age-integrated and age-segregated communities. Her discussion of the development of homes for the aged, retirement communities, and the more recent pre-eminence of home ownership in later life, complements Massey's dichotomy between the "retreat to place" and integrated everyday living. Laws (1997, p. 98) commented:

> The experience of being old, for example, varies according to one's environment. Situation can thus actively affect ageing. That age relations are constrained in, mediated by and constrained by space begs a refocusing of attention in social gerontology.

In this chapter we must be aware that dimensions of spatiality occur in places that may crudely be considered age-integrated (town centers) or age-segregated (retirement villages), with various circumstances leading to different experiences of inclusion and exclusion and intergenerational relations. Here I concentrate on public places and spaces predominantly in the wider age-integrated community. To conclude this section, the work of Scharf and colleagues needs to be recognized as providing an important context for focusing on the structural causes of inequality in later life, against which to situate applied empirical research concerning person-environment interaction (Scharf, Phillipson, & Smith, 2005; Smith, 2009). Phillipson (2004) has also drawn our attention to the need for environmental gerontology to reconsider the increasing global urbanism of the growing UK older population, where 90% are classed as "urban residents" (Phillipson, 2011). His comments concerning social exclusion through urban living, versus "elective belonging" in place (Phillipson, 2007), add weight to the arguments raised above. In contrast, the research of Scharf and Bartlam (2006a, 2006b; 2008) raises the issue of social exclusion for older people living in rural communities, where concerns regarding restricted mobility and lack of access to transportation are particularly pertinent and integral to a discussion of public places. I come back to the impact of this diversity of location when discussing empirical work.

Description of the conceptual grounding underpinning the spatiality of aging provides a context for discussion of everyday experience. But first there is a need to consider how levels of connectivity relate to the very public nature of space.

The "Public" Nature of Public Space

How do we define the "public" nature of public space[1] and what issues does this raise? Once again our understanding is truly multidisciplinary and concerned with how behavior may reflect cultural, generational, and environmental differences. In defining the public, it is common to invoke the dichotomy of public and private. In terms of space, "public" may be explained in the language of communal, civic, free, open, and unrestricted, but it can also be owned independently and can be a consumerized space such as in markets, shopping malls, parks with some restricted activity space, sports stadia, the transportation hub or bus stop; spaces that have become both regulated and open to surveillance and in this sense political (Madanipour, 1999, 2003). Public space may be known or unknown territory; somewhere that people find easy to travel through following familiar routes and shortcuts; or unfamiliar—which may be disorienting, leading to a sense of insecurity or stimulating and leading to new experiences (see Chapter 9). In contrast "private" may be recognized in the language of individualized, familial, domestic, concealed, privileged, restricted, elite, or intimate and may also be known or unknown; defined widely or only open to a limited group, such as a family home or the consulting rooms of the doctor's surgery, in contrast with the waiting rooms. Historically, this duality of public/private has been linked to social constructions of gender, so that there are stereotypical associations of public with masculine and work, and private with feminine and home (Arendt, 1958; McDowell, 1999). In more recent decades, changing lifestyles, particularly in relation to employment and care, have come to challenge these assumptions (Bondi, 1998).

To continue, consider two sets of issues, the first relating to personal behavior in space and the second, to the impact of wider social factors. Worpole and Knox (2007, p. 4), reporting on a program of research concerned with a diversity of public spaces funded by the Joseph Rowntree Foundation (JRF) during the first decade of this century, stress the importance of association and exchange in person-environment interaction:

> There has been a tendency to confine notions of public space to traditional outdoor spaces that are in public ownership, but opportunities for association and exchange are not so limited. Gatherings at the school gate, activities in community facilities, shopping malls, cafés, and car boot sales are all arenas where people meet and create places of exchange. To members of the public, it is not the ownership of

places or their appearance that makes them 'public,' but their shared use for a diverse range of activities by a range of different people. If considered in this way, almost any place regardless of its ownership or appearance offers potential as public space.

Earlier discussion of social exclusion indicates that a diversity of social capital will influence levels of engagement, but public spaces are supposedly spaces for all. Indeed, all age groups need representation in the life of any community. So, does the social construction of space differ for people of different ages or generations and affect the nature of the "public?" To a degree, this can relate to the type of interaction experienced and the behavior that ensues. A focus on activity and human relations brings to the fore the symbolic interactionist Erving Goffman's (1959) consideration of the presentation of self which continues to have relevance for behavior in particular places. Utilizing the dramatic analogy of performance in front and back regions, with or without a public audience, Peace et al. (2006, p. 87) report and note re Goffman's work:

> He makes this comment in relation to the "front regions": "The performance of an individual in the front regions may be seen as an effort to give the appearance that his activity in the region maintains and embodies certain standards" (1959, p. 110). Such standards relate to rules and codes by which people behave, to the respect that is shown for a "region," and the order that is maintained. Failure to maintain such standards or appearances may lead others to question the person's independence or for them to feel increasingly insecure. In contrast "back regions" allow the person to "relax": ". . . he can drop his front, forgo speaking his lines, and step out of character." (Goffman, 1959, p. 115)

While it may be assumed that public spaces have greater association with "front regions" in terms of interactions, some of the locations outlined above have the potential to incorporate both regions within public places with specific meaning. For example, areas of a park, a river side, and the graveside or cemetery garden are all places with potential through the natural environment, situation, and use to enable privacy, formality, and informality. We can also appreciate how people at different points in their lives, occupying a variety of roles, may feel more or less comfortable and may express greater confidence in different places.

The "maintenance of standards or appearances" within public places may reflect particular generational behavior, and differing value bases may also influence attitudes that reinforce generational stereo-types. This quote from a study of environment and identity in later life shows how an incident situated—through time, locality, and iso-lation—can undermine an older woman's self-confidence and control over space, thus influencing her attachment to place:

> I suppose it was in April just before I was ill and I had to come home by bus. . . . and [as] I walked up. . . . I was very conscious of some-body following me. And I wouldn't look around, but I got quite het up within and I crossed over. . . . and I felt the footsteps coming nearer and nearer. And I couldn't resist it, I turned around, I had to you know, and it was a fellow. So I went on walking and suddenly he brushed past me, just touched my arm and said "you needn't be so scared, I am only going home" and it was a young man. He didn't do anything, he just brushed past. . . . Whether he intended doing anything or not and decided not to. . . . I don't know. But you see until then I never thought about it, but ever since then it has just left me with that uneasy feel-ing. . . . And you see there was not a soul around, it was just before midnight, there wasn't a soul around, only a fence down the bottom, there was no house there when I crossed over, there was nobody who would have come anywhere near to help me, if he'd decided to mug me. I had a handbag of course. . . I didn't know the man. But it was a very uneasy feeling. And it has left me, this is the trouble, it has left me, I suppose I was lucky and got away with it, but another time it could happen. So [today] I thought "I must get these two letters in the post" and so I went in the car, which is ridiculous because it is only around the corner, and the walk would have done me good, but I thought "no, I am not walking round there." It is a shame because we never used to feel like that, did we? (Helen, aged 81 years, London Borough of Haringey, from Peace et al., 2006, pp. 67–68)

Such examples are not uncommon; they show how incidents can influence behavior. This quote also points to a wider understanding of the politics of "public" space and issues of ownership, security, regu-lation, and rights, which all shape social interaction. In any locality, public spaces can include a wide variety of places—shopping centers, markets, libraries, civic centers, transportation depots, parks, allot-ments, religious buildings, graveyards, cemeteries, canal and river banks, seaside promenades, beaches and piers, as well as all manner of streets and walkways; some dominated by cars and other forms of pub-lic transport; some well-lit, some without lighting; some known to all and others known only to those "in the know." Such locations are gov-erned by planning regulations and, while we are not concerned with this level of detail (RTPI, 2004), the implications of public/private partnership over ownership and management of space and public "rights of way" and regulations over usage can influence the way people act. For example, the list of places above involve different levels of ownership/ management but may share a common goal with respect to the potential for open accessibility. Ownership and management also influences issues of security and safety and the potential for creating meaningful places for all.

In the United Kingdom, there is variation in levels of community policing. On the ground, the public presence of the statutory policeman or policewoman is subject to great debate (Police Recruitment, 2011) and not the focus of this chapter. However, the literature does indicate the concerns of older people over feeling safe in their own communities (Pain, 1997), and there is evidence that they are more likely to communicate with the police than other age groups: "Last year, 49% of people who spoke to us at one of our engagement events were 60 and over" (Merseyside Policy Authority, 2011).

Comments from the reports of the "Older People's Advocate" in Northern Ireland (Northern Ireland Office, 2007), and the vision statement for working with older people from the Scottish Police Service (Association of Chief Police Officers in Scotland [ACPOS], 2011), indicate not only the beginnings of a greater understanding of people's needs as they age, but also the diverse concerns for safety and security within particular locations—both rural and urban: "Older people need constant re-assurance that those responsible for community safety are visible and accessible and that their interests are being protected" (Older People's Advocate, 2011).

Of course, security guards, particularly in shopping malls, also have a community policing function, although with a different focus. For those responsible for these public spaces, help and advice to the public, crowd management, Closed-Circuit Television (CCTV) monitoring, dealing with unruly behavior, fire safety, and evacuation may be seen as part of their role, alongside liaison with the police (Elite Safeguarding Security Services, 2012).

This difference between public and private security also raises the issue of the use of cameras for surveillance in public space. In 2004, it was reported that over 4 million cameras were in use in Britain (Gras, 2004), but little is known concerning the impact of such surveillance on personal behavior in later life and on the use of public space. Do such cameras offer more individual security or is this just part of the more recent need to address corporate and national security?

It is interesting to note that the Royal Town Planning Institute set up a working group early in this century to consider the planning implications of an aging population (RTPI, 2004). Their report considered the need for planners at national, regional, and local levels to be aware of demographic change and the diversity of cohort needs in later life. They focused on issues relating to housing, leisure, recreation, and tourism, as well as the retail sector and shopping and town centers. While raising the need for partnership with health, social care, and housing services, they do not mention the police and community safety. This work preceded the publication of the British social policy *"Lifetime Homes, Lifetime Neighbourhoods"* (DCLG, 2008) which began to capture the infrastructure needed to enable people in later life to remain a part of their community. Since this report, political change has brought to the fore the need for greater localism in the development of community strategies (Kneale & Sinclair, 2011).

Consideration of issues that influence how people define public space, the impact of social construction on behavior, and the spatiality of aging provides essential background for looking at examples from empirical research. I begin by considering intergenerational interactions within the public spaces of one English town and then move to the wider picture of how localities at all levels—neighborhood, town, and city—may be made more age-friendly with regard to the inclusion of older people.

THE SPATIALITY OF AGING

Watching Aylesbury

A study of the town of Aylesbury in the southeast of England was part of the JRF program of research reported earlier and undertaken between 2003 and 2006 (Holland et al., 2007). Aylesbury is a commuter settlement for metropolitan London, 33 miles north of the city, with a population of approximately 69,000 people within a defined urban area. The town center is compact, and the aim of this research was ambitious: to consider intergenerational interaction; shared and contested use of space; safety and security in public areas; and the management and maintenance of public space. To achieve a comprehensive assessment, the researchers[2] decided that data needed to be recorded daily over a 12-month period to include potential seasonal and diurnal diversity. In doing this they developed a unique form of participatory research where 46 lay co-researchers, who were members of the community and were aged between 16 years and 73 years, were trained to undertake observations and record interactions at a range of public spaces. Nine micro observation sites covering public spaces were identified within the following locations: two central market squares, two shopping malls, the high street, a path alongside the canal, a central park, plus two postwar and more recent housing estates within 2 to 3 miles of the center.

Observations were carried out by the co-researchers, working in pairs, using a semi-structured observation method. Research funding enabled them to be paid by the hour. For each micro-site an observation sheet was devised that included an outline map of the key features of the site, and a matrix on which observers could record the demographic characteristics of people using the site and any interactions among them. This was a combination of recorded observation and "ethnographic diary." During the course of 12 months from October 2004 to September 2005, the lay observers worked across all days of the week and in all weathers, making observations from approximately 8:00 a.m. through to 9:00 p.m.

The lay observers were invited to participate in the research for as long as they wished, and a small core group stayed with the observation for most of the study period. Their research experience is reported in Clark, Holland, Katz, and Peace (2009). The academic research team maintained constant communication with the lay co-researchers through mobile telephone, and undertook observations early in the mornings and late into the evenings and night. The academic team also undertook further research, which included street surveys and interviews with key stakeholders, so that findings could influence local initiatives to develop the use of public places by diverse users. Here, consideration is given to those aspects of the research that contribute to an understanding of the spatiality of aging and influence how we can maintain and develop an age-friendly community.

Intergenerational Interaction

The findings highlight age-related modes of socialization and ways of being "out and about" in town. Older people were usually seen to be alone or in twos (less often in threes or fours), and there were few observations of intergenerational interactions between what were defined through observation as non-family/kin groups. Young children were very seldom unsupervised in town center areas, whereas secondary (high) school children and young adults/teens might be in ones and twos but were often in larger, more mobile groups. This had an effect on some adults and authorities, who reported being uncomfortable with such congregations, regardless of their degree of passivity.

The most dominant group at all sites and times consisted of "young adults" in the 20- to 50-year-old age group. Such groups dominated the whole area, especially in the evenings and at night. Indeed, the whole town space could be seen to be designed primarily for this group as key consumers, sometimes to the detriment of the very young and old. Farther away from the town center, observations showed a greater intermingling of age groups at the less affluent suburban small shopping and service center (including health care services) within the mixed tenure housing estate, where people of different ages sometimes knew each other and would exchange greetings. There was a level of invisibility for older people, the more public or commercial the setting and the less communal the rationale for behavior.

Shared and Contested Use of Space

We noted particular patterns of shared and contested use of space. Time impacts on spatial behavior and seasonal observations provided essential evidence. In central locations, the activities of older people and younger children were strongly affected by the economic and educational rhythms of the town, noted in transportation patterns. Hence, the working day, school day, market day, school term times, and vacations affected who would be around at particular times, periods, and seasons, in the context of the distance of residential areas from leisure and retail facilities. In the town center, it was apparent that the activity patterns of many older people were governed by bus timetables and rules concerning financial costs through bus passes and "special offers." Observation showed that older people came into the town early but avoided large crowds of school children or commuting workers. In this way, age groups had different behavioral flows; it was noted that, for older people, issues of mobility and motility were crucial to accessibility in the town center. These "behavioral flows" reflect the "place ballet" identified by Seamon and Nordin (1980) and demonstrate the importance of identifying variation in the use of space and the need to make place enabling. The historical development of the town, where one market square had cobbled paving stones, meant that some people could have been excluded from entering certain streets and wheelchair access had to be negotiated. The observations only focused on those who entered the frame, and so there is no record of older people with mobility problems who may not have ventured to the town center. However, street furniture was welcomed and comments from the street surveys, made by middle-aged and older people, identified concerns with benches where there was a need for back and arm support.

The research showed that certain places/times/patterns of occupancy were seen as "legitimate," such as "shoppers" of all ages in the malls, and the "locals" in neighborhood centers. This dominance of certain people in places at certain times gave a sense of acceptability. It was noted that, in the center of the town, both adults and young children avoided deserted spaces or spaces occupied by particular groupings. Most of the time people seemed to avoid conflict by taking account of others' use of shared spaces and accommodating them to some extent. This was particularly noticeable in the park, where groups of young people made space for each other. At a micro level, this shared usage could also be seen in the way that people of all ages sat together on busy benches and seats at particular points of the day. This shared use of space was not contested. However, it was observed that those feeling marginalized in some situations could express their feelings publicly—such as through graffiti adorning a neighborhood bandstand, or by locating themselves in marginal public places. For example, street drinkers had moved from one of the town squares to the main park when the square was being redeveloped (Aylesbury Vale District Council [AVDC], 2004) and then again within the park when it became busy with families. These observations reflect aspects of non-normative behavior demonstrating the legitimation of certain types of behavior in certain places, as discussed in the seminal work on "behavior settings" of environmental psychologists Roger G. Barker and colleagues (see Barker, 1968; Barker & Barker, 1961; Barker & Schoggen, 1973).

Safety and Security in Public Areas

The ownership and regulation of public spaces was considered earlier in this chapter, and the Aylesbury study provides for a closer examination of this theme. Some places in the town were heavily regulated, with uniformed guards, CCTV, and rules about smoking, congregating, and antisocial behaviors. This was especially true of the shopping malls, where proprietorial ownership of the retail sector leads to a high level of security enforcement. This kind of regulation was reassuring for some, especially older people questioned in the study; but others needed to resist it—for example, young people wanting to gather in groups to chat and browse rather than spend money they might not have. Of course, there would have been people of all ages with limited financial resources for whom "town center" shopping would prove unusual.

The park was an example of space where sometimes "forbidden" activities were almost the only things happening, linking with earlier comments on the interchange of public and private space, where behavior seen as "formal" or "informal," "communal" or "personal," "appropriate" or "inappropriate," can all take place. But then, as indicated by a sign at the entrance to the park, the researchers saw that the following behaviors were also regulated, affecting all age groups:

- No skate-boarding or rollerblading through the park
- Dogs to be kept on leads
- No cycling through the park
- No ballgames except in designated areas
- In the interest of safety, please do not bring glass, alcohol or barbecues into the area.
  —Aylesbury Vale District Council, 2005.

In this case, it could be argued that the behavior that has been regulated is "informal," both "communal" and "personal," and seen by many as highly "appropriate" in a park. Indeed, there seemed to be little that you could do in this park.

Formal regulation cannot manage all places at all times, and there was a noticeable amount of self-regulation by people to make public spaces viable. People observed in the study knew their own capabilities and level of risk-taking and could choose whether or not to be in certain places at certain times and decide what they could do in them. For example, older people could leave town early; younger people could choose to be in semi-secluded places, but close enough to help should it be needed. It was felt that public places are not viable without a significant sense of security deriving from public behavior and self-regulation, and that this needs to be fostered by inclusion of all age groups. We have already noted that town center facilities were directed toward the needs of the young to middle-aged groups, yet there is something about the very nature of intergenerational living that needs to be acknowledged here. Everyday behavior may range across a continuum from solidarity to tolerance to hostility among generations. For older people, the importance of "being there" challenges all ages through visibility, seniority, and experience, which in turn demands a recognition of the spatiality of aging.

The Management and Maintenance of Public Space

Places are interconnected. Management in one location may have an effect on other locations; consequently, any locality needs to be seen as part of a planned system. Through the central urban regeneration policy, introduced by the New Labour government from 1997 onwards, the aim was to develop greater social inclusion within the community. Part of this policy enabled local government to bid for funding through the Single Regeneration Budget (Furbey, 1999) to target certain areas for redevelopment. Toward the end of the research fieldwork in Aylesbury, planned regeneration of one of the two market squares was completed, and the research team was able to survey members of the public to gain early views on this development. In the main, people were pleased with the changes made, although the demolition of old public toilets raised comment. It was not the case that the old facilities should have been retained and maintained. Rather, the local government's suggestion that people should adopt a "café culture" and ask local retailers if they could use their toilet was not a popular suggestion with any age group; walking to facilities within the shopping malls was the preferred alternative, but was not necessarily convenient for people with poor mobility. The new open sitting space with a central water feature could be seen as innovative and unusual, but comment was also made about both the lack of greenery and the inadequacy of bench-type seating for people needing body support. While the research advisory group for this study, involving local government staff, had access to the research data, the timing was too late to influence this development immediately, but it did show the value of community consultation. Indeed, all sectors of the population need to feel that they have an investment in the public spaces of the town center—not just the commercially active adults.

This research identified some of the patterns of intergenerational interaction for one English town, highlighting issues where greater accessibility and more sympathetic design could have facilitated participation by different age groups. Self-regulation prevented different groups from conflicting with each other, but it was a situation where certain age groups were still seen to dominate. The value of longitudinal community ethnography needs to be recognized as such observations consider the behavior of a wide range of people over time, even though by treating people *en masse* we are unaware of individual community history and of who is missing from the community picture.

Age-Friendly Communities

How then may the experience of observing intergenerational interactions within public spaces in one town help to identify how the spatiality of aging can be made more inclusive? Consider the literature on the development of "age-friendly communities"—both urban and rural. An international review by Lui, Everingham, Warburton, Cuthill, and Bartlett (2009) from Australia identifies the relationship between policy that encourages aging in place and the growing need for an age-friendly community where change is seen across physical/material, social, and psychological aspects of environment, resulting not only in increased mobility but enhanced independence, interdependence, and quality of life. The concept is relevant to both rural and urban populations and is defined in terms of both communities and cities. Early developments concerning age-friendly cities evolved through the World Health Organization's *Healthy Cities Project* in the 1980s, leading to the *Global Age-Friendly Cities Project*, launched in 33 cities worldwide in 2005 (WHO, 2007). Underpinning the work has been the premise that an age-friendly city should promote active aging—seen as "optimizing opportunities for health, participation, and security in order to enhance quality of life as people age" (WHO, 2002, p. 12). Across the 33 cities—from Mexico to Istanbul, from New Delhi to New York—focus groups were set up to hear the views of people aged 60 years and older from across the income range. One hundred and fifty-eight groups, with 1,485 older participants, were involved, as well as 250 caregivers and 515 service providers (WHO, 2007).

London, England, was one of the world cities that took part in this project and Help the Aged (HTA), the Institute of Gerontology at Kings College, London, and Ipsos MORI's Social Research Institute (a leader in public sector research in the United Kingdom), undertook detailed research (Help the Aged, 2007). The following comments contextualize the situation of the age-friendly cities:

> Here, many of the factors which influence the character of a world city—fast-moving international populations, differences in wealth and in embeddedness in local neighbourhoods—are balanced by progressive policies toward social inclusion of older people and people with disabilities, which have radically influenced the all-important detail of everyday urban life. (Help the Aged, 2007, p. 6)

The research was carried out in Waltham Forest and Newham, both London boroughs to the North East of the city; Newham has one of the highest ethnic minority populations. Group-work centered on outdoor spaces and buildings; transportation; housing; respect and social inclusion; social participation; communication and information; civic participation and employment; and community support and health services (Help the Aged, 2007, p. 13). It is interesting to compare the findings from this study with the Aylesbury data.

In Waltham Forest and Newham, participants saw the nature of living in an "age-friendly" place as related to certain local resources. Older people commented on the importance of engagement with others—not necessarily family, but others met particularly at community centers; facilities that people treasured and wished to be maintained and advertised. Alongside these facilities, good public transportation was essential, as well as accessible transportation that was sometimes door-to-door. In London, the Freedom Pass currently gives free travel if you were 60 or older before April 6, 2010; the age of issue is currently rising. Given times of financial recession, such affordable travel needs to be maintained (Transport for London, 2011). The wider infrastructure of the physical/material environment—clean streets, adequate lighting, street furniture, wheelchair accessibility through ramps and parking facilities—was considered by these participants to be age-friendly. Also, in these locations, supportive social housing was seen as an asset. In making wider recommendations, the researchers extended a call for good housing within an age-friendly community.

These positive views were qualified by some barriers. It was apparent that, despite adequate material infrastructure, people reported that their own well-being could be affected by the social environment. The participants commented on the behavior of the general public and on the importance of personal attitudes toward older people, showing how rowdy behavior and lack of consideration by others could influence how they lived their lives. The comment was made: "There is a general view that ageism is endemic and institutionalized" (Help the Aged, 2007, pp. 15–16).

Alongside this view, a fear of crime was discussed; feelings of vulnerability led people not to go out at night-time and to go out less during the winter months, leading some to feel housebound. More visible community policing was recommended, which links not only to earlier discussion concerning safety and security, but also to issues of overregulated space where little happens.

In Waltham Forest and Newham, participants reported that an age-friendly community needed to be one where adequate support, ranging from help with home adaptation to assistance with a wide range of household tasks, enabled people to continue living at home, if that was their wish. Also, it was clear that if people were active in the community, they might gain the information they needed to stay engaged within their community; but some people were isolated and their information needs needed to be targeted. Finally, in terms of barriers to creating an age-friendly city, the participants returned to the material environment and, despite commenting that the infrastructure was adequate, they repeated a need for clean public toilets as they were in short supply.

Given these findings, it is not surprising that the London research team made the following recommendations to the WHO project (summarized from Help the Aged, 2007, p. 19):

1. Think beyond families; people need support and social contact with people of a similar age.
2. The accessible local environment should be perceived as "short distances strung together with staging posts"—benches, sitting places at bus stops, public toilets, well-maintained pavements, good road crossings.
3. Develop interest between the generations—intergenerational interaction is essential.
4. Older people aging in place become "a point of stability and continuity" for the community.
5. "Neighborhood" is the goal to be achieved, rather than the starting point.

To implement these recommendations, the involvement of older people in both central and local decision-making was seen as essential.

Returning to Lui et al. (2009), it is interesting to note that in reviewing the literature since 2005 on "what makes a community age-friendly?," they were able to distinguish not only definitions of "age-friendly communities," "age-friendly cities" and "lifetime neighborhoods," but also to chart how concerns ranged from those focused predominantly on the physical/material environment to those focused predominantly on the social environment, alongside a further continuum that adopted a more or less participatory approach to engaging older people in the process of understanding connectivity. Three important areas were identified as absent or undeveloped within the literature: a lack of attention to rural areas; the need to encompass diversity and complexity when considering the development of intergenerational solidarity; and the need to evaluate the impact of consciously developing "age-friendly communities" through aspects of the physical/material and social environment (Lui et al., 2009, p. 119).

Attention has already been drawn to variation in urban and rural living (Phillipson & Scharf, 2005). In addition, Eales, Keefe, and Keating (2008), working in Canada, extend our understanding of age-friendly environments by focusing on the resource base of rural communities and commenting on how natural, human-built, and social environments may simultaneously offer a different "best-fit" for people who have diverse lifestyles driven by variation in personality, identity, or culture. Humphrey et al., in a British study for the Department of Work and Pensions (DWP, 2011, p. 85) concerning aspirations for later life, show that adults across the lifespan are more likely to feel that their neighborhood is a good one to grow old in if it is safe, in a quiet area with lots of amenities such as good public transport, shops, and general practitioners.[3] This is also a place that is well maintained and tidy; where people have friends and the opportunity to meet other older people as well as getting involved in groups and decision-making concerning their area. Given the different ways in which empirical and conceptual research contributes to the understanding of what is meant by age-friendly in relation to place, some conclusions can now be drawn as to future development.

UNDERSTANDING TO IMPLEMENT CHANGE

The focus in this chapter has been on public spaces and places within age-integrated communities; how age affects the social construction of space and how age-friendly design can enhance participation in old age. Through policy initiatives, ongoing research, new design guidance, and the personal participation of older people in decision making, changes to the physical/material environment—from navigable pathways for pedestrians to more plentiful public toilets—may occur (see Bichard, 2011; Burton & Mitchell, 2006; Commission for Architecture and the Built Environment [CABE], 2004, 2007, 2009; DCLG, 2008; Help the Aged, 2008; Inclusive Design for Getting Outdoors [I'DGO], 2011; Mitchell, Burton, & Raman, 2004) and, through work beginning with the physical/built environment, personal well-being can also be enhanced. For example, the I'DGO research project, concerned with older people's use of outdoor space, has demonstrated the cumulative effect of change through providing facilities, and how addressing this one aspect of personal need affects behavior:

> We found that good facilities, including the existence of toilets, predicted the amount of time participants spent outdoors either walking (to go to places or for recreation) or pursuing other activities, such as gardening. In other words, toilet facilities, perhaps in combination

with other facilities, made it more likely that respondents would spend longer out of doors. (I'DGO, 2011)

Of course, such facilities also have wider benefit to the whole community.

In spite of changing financial circumstances, local government is already being seen to acknowledge the needs of their aging population through direct planning (Planning Advisory Service/IDeA, 2009) and local planning strategies are beginning to recognize those dimensions of spatiality identified earlier by Laws (1997): accessibility, mobility, motility, spatial scale, and spatial segregation. In 2009, six local authorities in the British county of Berkshire (Berkshire Authorities, 2009, pp. 26, 27) identified these issues in their discussion of accessibility summarized as:

> Access to services and facilities were explored through the consultation workshops in order to define good accessibility. The issues below were raised as important when considering accessibility:
> - Access to public transport
> - Access to friends and family
> - Access to local shops
> - Access to health care
> - Access to community facilities
> - Access to information

These issues are similar to those mentioned by earlier participants in the London boroughs of Waltham Forest and Newham (Help the Aged, 2007). The Berkshire report (Berkshire Authorities, 2009, p. 32) goes on to say this about public space:

> Understanding how people use places and giving priority to pedestrians should also be extended to an evaluation of public spaces and the important role these can play in the life of a local community. Experience shows that too often the provision and planning of public spaces is designed around what land is left once roads and buildings have been planned. Putting open space at the heart of local communities can have social and community benefits which provide an opportunity for older people as a meeting place and as a local amenity enhancing the individual's experience of their local environment.

Beyond such environmental determinism, and even with potential for personal empowerment, our understanding of the interface between the physical/material and the social environment continues to develop. At the beginning of this chapter, I showed how social relations of power and exclusion could determine the social construction of space, with age being a determining characteristic. The research undertaken in Aylesbury indicated that both children and young people, and older people, lacked dominance when it came to interactions within a British town center. But in the main, younger people were more easily able to congregate and "do their own thing!" Intergenerational interaction is also about experience and attitudes and recognition of ageism.

FROM KNOWLEDGE TO OWNERSHIP TO PRACTICE

The environmental complexity outlined above—the physical/material, the social, the psychological—is perhaps best understood by everyone if they take a life-course perspective and ask, "What does the age-friendly community mean for me?" and "How does my contribution address the needs of all ages?" Practically, if involved as a professional stakeholder—a planner, a community leader, a designer, a spiritual leader, a community police person, an engineer—it will be important to recognize the need to discuss ideas with people of all ages and facilitate their participation; to communicate good ideas to the public as well as to peers; and, when trying out new thinking, to go back and evaluate what worked and what did not. It will be important to capture these ideas and innovations in design guidance, standards, and regulations, so that they become part of the everyday, accepted and expected in a lifetime neighborhood. Communication is essential and becomes more diverse as technology advances and people develop these skills into old age. For stakeholders who see themselves as members of the public, consideration of intergenerational community life needs to take on board the roles of grandparents, grandchildren, neighbors, organizers, volunteers, without which the social environment would be incomplete.

We could argue that a focus on the views of older people, while necessary and long in coming, needs wider acceptance to be developed into practical initiatives and maintained (see Riseborough & Jenkins, 2004). Change needs to be recognized as necessary and needs to be owned collectively and intergenerationally. The age-friendly community would then be based on an all-embracing definition of age that was based on greater solidarity, for without this there will continue to be greater segregation between ages and the potential for greater social exclusion. Here, the conceptualization of public space and place in relation to intergenerational interaction has acted as a crucial example. As Worpole and Knox (2007, p. 1) comment:

> The success of a particular public space is not solely in the hands of
> the architect, urban designer, or town planner; it relies also on people

adopting, using, and managing the space—people make places, more than places make people.

NOTES

1. Throughout this chapter the term "space" is used to refer to public locations, whereas the term "place" is used in relation to social constructions or representations of such spaces.
2. The research team were Caroline Holland, Jeanne Katz and Andrew Clark, with Sheila Peace as the Principal Investigator.
3. General Practitioners are local health professionals in the UK.

REFERENCES

Ackroyd, J. (2005). *Where do you think you're going? Report of the John Grooms inquiry into needs of young disabled people*. London, UK: John Grooms.

Arendt, H. (1958). *The Human Condition*. Chicago, IL: University of Chicago.

Association of Chief Police Officers in Scotland. (ACPOS). Policing for older people. Older people issues: A strategy. Retrieved from http://www.northern.police.uk/Older-People-Strategy/older%20people%20strategy%20document.pdf

AVDC (Aylesbury Vale District Council). (2004). Aims, objectives and activities of town centre partnership. Retrieved from http://www.aylesburyvaledc.gov

Barker, R. G. (1968). *Ecological psychology: Concepts and methods for studying the environment of human behavior*. Stanford, CA: Stanford University Press.

Barker, R. G., & Barker, L. S. (1961). The psychological ecology of old people in Midwest, Kansas, and Yoredale, Yorkshire. *Journal of Gerontology, 16*(2), 144–149.

Barker, R. G., & Schoggen, P. (1973). *Qualities of community life: Methods of measuring environment and behavior applied to an American and an English town*. San Francisco, CA: Jossey-Bass.

Berkshire Authorities. (2009). *Positive Planning for an Aging Society: The Berkshire authorities' response to lifetime homes, lifetime neighbourhoods*. Wokingham Borough Council, Bracknell Forest Council, Royal Borough of Windsor and Maidenhead, Slough Borough Council, West Berkshire Council, Reading Borough Council, November 2009, WYG Planning and Design (see www.wyg.com), London.

Bichard, J. A. (2011). Research into public toilet: the inclusive design of away from home (public) toilets in city centres. Retrieved from http://www.enfieldover50sforum.org.uk/Research%20Public%20Public20Toilets.htm

Bondi, L. (1998). Gender, class and urban space: Public and private space in contemporary urban landscapes. *Urban Geography, 19*, 160–185.

Burton, E., & Mitchell, L. (2006). *Inclusive urban design: Streets for life*. London, UK: Architectural Press.

CABE (Commission for Architecture and the Built Environment). (2004). *Manifesto for better public spaces*. London, UK: CABE Space.

CABE (Commission for Architecture and the Built Environment). (2007). *Building for life: Delivering great places to live*. London, UK: CABE Space.

CABE (Commission for Architecture and the Built Environment). (2009). *Future health: Sustainable places for health and well-being*. London, UK: CABE Space. Retrieved from www.cabespace.org.uk

Clark, A., Holland, C., Katz, J., & Peace, S. (2009). Learning to see: Lessons from a participatory observation research project in public space. *International Journal of Research Methodology, 12*(4), 345–360.

Cresswell, T. (2004). *Place: A short introduction*. London, UK: Blackwell Publishing.

Department for Communities and Local Government (DCLG). (2008). *Lifetime homes, lifetime neighbourhoods: A national strategy for housing an aging society*. London, UK: Department for Communities and Local Government.

Eales, J., Keefe, J., & Keating, N. (2008). Age-friendly rural communities. In N. Keating (Ed.), *Rural aging: A good place to grow old?* (pp. 109–120). Bristol, UK: The Policy Press.

Elite Safeguarding Security Services. (2012). Retrieved from http://www.eliteguarding.co.uk/shopping centres.html

Furbey, R. (1999). Urban 'regeneration': Reflection on a metaphor. *Critical Social Policy 61, 19*(4), 419–445.

Goffman, E. (1959). *Presentation of self in everyday life*. Harmondsworth, UK: Penguin Books.

Goodman, C., & Watson, L. (Habinteg Housing Association Ltd.). (2010). *Design guidance for people with dementia and for people with sight loss, research findings*, No.35. London, UK: Thomas Pocklington Trust.

Gras, M. L. (2004). The legal regulation of CCTV in Europe. *Surveillance and Society, 2*(2/3), 216–229.

Habinteg Housing Association. (2011). *Habinteg Lifetime Homes Design Guide*. Garston, Watford, UK: IHS BRE Press.

Help the Aged. (2007). *What makes a city age-friendly? London's contribution to the WHO's AFC project*. London, UK: Author.

Help the Aged. (2008). *Towards common ground: The help the aged manifesto for lifetime neighbourhoods*. London, UK: Author.

Holland, C., Clark, A., Katz, J., & Peace, S. (2007). *Social interaction in urban public places*. York, UK: Joseph Rowntree Foundation. Retrieved from http://www.jrf.org.uk/publications/social-interactions-urban-public-places

Home and Communities Agency (HCA). (2009). *Housing our ageing population: Panel for innovation*. London, UK: Homes and Communities Agency.

Humphrey, A., Lee, L., & Green, R. (2011). *Aspirations for later life, research report No.737*. London, UK: Department of Work and Pensions. Retrieved from http://research.dwp.gov.uk/asd/asd5/rports2011-2012/rrep737.pdf

Imrie, R. (2004). From universal to inclusive design in the built environment. In J. Swain, S. French, C. Barnes, & C. Thomas (Eds.), *Disabling barriers—enabling environments* (2nd ed., pp. 279–284). London, UK: Sage Publications.

I'DGO Inclusive Design for Getting Outdoors. Retrieved from www.idgo.ac.ujk/design_guidance/streets.htm and www.idgo.ac.uk/design_guidance/factsheets/public_toilets.htm

Kitchin, R. (1998). 'Out of place', 'knowing one's place': Space, power and the exclusion of disabled people. *Disability and Society, 13*(3), 343–356.

Kneale, D., & Sinclair, D. (2011). *Localism and neighbourhoods for all ages: Is localism sounding a death knell or a wakeup call for creating neighbourhood for all ages?* London, UK: International Longevity Centre (ILC)-UK.

Laws, G. (1994). Contested meanings, the built environment and aging in place. *Environment and Planning A, 26*, 1787–1802.

Laws, G. (1997). Spatiality and age relations. In A. Jamieson, S. Harper, & C. Victor (Eds.), *Critical approaches to ageing and later life* (pp. 90–100). Buckingham, UK: Open University Press.

Lui, C. W., Everingham, J. A., Warburton, J., Cuthill, M., & Bartlett, H. (2009). What makes a community age-friendly?: A review of international literature. *Australian Journal on Aging, 28*(3), 116–121.

Madanipour, A. (1999). Why are the design and development of public spaces significant for cities? *Environment and Planning B: Development and Design, 26*, 879–891.

Madanipour, A. (2003). *Public and private spaces of the city*. London, UK: Routledge.

Manzo, L. C. (2003). Beyond house and home: Toward a revisioning of emotional relationships with places. *Journal of Environmental Psychology, 23*, 47–61.

Massey, D. (1991). A global sense of place. *Marxism Today*, pp. 24–29. June (Reprinted in Massey, D. (1994). *Space, place, and gender* (pp. 146–156). Cambridge, UK: Polity Press).

Massey, D. (2005). *For space.* London, UK: Sage Publications.

McDowell, L. (1999). *Gender, identity and place: Understanding feminist geographies.* Cambridge, UK: Polity Press.

McDowell, L., & Massey, D. (1984). A woman's place? In D. Massey & J. Allen (Eds.), *Geography matters! A reader* (pp. 124–147). Cambridge, UK: Cambridge University Press in Association with the Open University.

Merseyside Policy Authority. (2011). Older People. Retrieved from http://www.mersey sidepolicesuthroity.gov.uk/older-people html

Milner, J., & Madigan, R. (2001). The politics of accessible housing in the UK. In S. Peace & C. Holland (Eds.), *Inclusive housing in an aging society* (pp. 77–100). Bristol, UK: Policy Press.

Mitchell, L., Burton, E., & Raman, S. (2004). *Neighbourhoods for life: A checklist of recommendations for designing dementia friendly outdoor environments.* London, UK: OCSD, Oxford and Housing Corporation. IGP Database Ref No G01-14255. Life-Checklist.pdf

Northern Ireland Office. (2007). Proposals for the safety of older people, consultation document. Retrieved from www.nio.gov.uk/proposals_for_the safety_of_older_people.pdf

Older People's Advocate. (2011). Responses to the Department of justice consultation on a new community safety strategy for Northern Ireland. Retrieved from http://www. dojni.gov.uk/index/public-consultations/archive-consultations/consultation_on_a_new_community_safety_strategy_for_ni/older_people__8217_s_advocate.pdf

Pain, R. H. (1997). Old age and ageism in urban research: The case of fear of crime. *International Journal of Urban and Regional Research, 21*(1), 117–128.

Peace, S., Holland, C., & Kellaher, L. (2006). *Environment and identity in later life.* Maidenhead, UK: Open University Press/McGraw-Hill Education.

Phillipson, C. (2004). Urbanization and aging: Towards a new environmental gerontology. *Ageing & Society, 24*(6), 963–972.

Phillipson, C. (2007). The 'elected' and the 'excluded': Sociological perspectives on the experience of place and community in old age. *Ageing & Society, 27*(3), 321–342.

Phillipson, C. (2011). *Growing older in urban environments: Perspectives from Japan and the UK.* A report on a symposium held in Church House Conference Centre, Westminster. London. March, 2011. Retrieved from www.ilcuk.org.uk

Phillipson, C., & Scharf, T. (2005). Rural and urban perspectives on growing old: Developing a new research agenda. *European Journal of Ageing, 2*(1), 67–75.

Planning Advisory Service/IDeA. (2009). *Knitting together: Planning and our ageing population.* London, UK: Improvement and Development Agency.

Police recruitment. Retrieved from http://www.police-recruitment.co.uk/community-policing.html

Riseborough, M., & Jenkins, C. (2004). *Now you see me. . .now you don't. How are older citizens being included in regeneration?* London, UK: Age Concern England.

Royal Town Planning Institute (RTPI). (2004). *Planning for an ageing population.* London, UK: RTPI.

Rubinstein, R. L., & de Medeiros, K. (2004). Ecology and the aging self. In H.-W. Wahl, R. J. Scheidt, & K. W. Schaie (Eds.). (2003). *Aging in context: Socio-physical environments, annual review of gerontology and geriatrics* (Vol. 23, pp. 59–84). New York, NY: Springer Publishing Company.

Scharf, T., & Bartlam, B. (2006a). *Rural disadvantage: Quality of life and disadvantage amongst older people: A pilot study.* Cheltenham, Gloucestershire: Commission for Rural Communities.

Scharf, T., & Bartlam, B. (2006b). *Quality of life and disadvantage among older people living in rural communities, Crc 19.* London, UK: Commission for Rural Communities. Retrieved from www.ruralcommunities.gov.uk/publications/crc19

Scharf, T., & Bartlam, B. (2008). Ageing and social exclusion in rural communities. In N. Keating (Ed.), *Rural ageing: A good place to grow old?* (pp. 97–108). Bristol, UK: The Policy Press.

Scharf, T., Phillipson, C., & Smith, A. (2005). Social exclusion of older people in deprived urban communities of England. *European Journal of Ageing, 2*(2), 76–87.

Schneidert, M., Hirst, R., Miller, J., & Ustrun, B. (2003). The role of environment in the International Classification of Functioning, disability and health (ICF). *Disability and Rehabilitation, 25*(11–12), 588–595.

Seamon, D., & Nordin, C. (1980). Marketplace as place ballet: A Swedish example. *Landscape, 24*(3), 35–41.

Shakespeare, T., & Watson, N. (2001). The social model of disability: An outdated ideology? *Research in Social Science & Disability, 2,* 9–28.

Smith, A. E. (2009). *Ageing in urban neighbourhoods: Place attachment and social exclusion.* Bristol, UK: Policy Press.

Smith N. (1993). Homeless/global: Scaling places. In J. Bird, B. Curtis, T. Putnam, G. Robertson, & L. Tickner (Eds.), *Mapping the futures: Local cultures, global change.* London, UK: Routledge.

Swain, J., French, S., Barnes, C., & Thomas, C. (Eds.). (2004). *Disabling barriers—enabling environments* (2nd ed.). London, UK: Sage Publications.

Transport for London. Retrieved from www.tfl.gov.uk/tickets/14305.aspx

WHO. (2002, April). *Active ageing: A policy framework.* The Second United Nations World Assembly on Ageing, Madrid, Spain.

WHO. (2007). *Global age-friendly cities: A guide.* Geneva, Switzerland: Author. Retrieved from www.who.int/aging/publications/Global_age_friendly

Worpole, K., & Knox, K. (2007). *The social value of public space.* York, UK: Joseph Rowntree Foundation. Retrieved from www.jrf.org.uk?publications/social-value-public-spaces

PART II

Private Residences

CHAPTER 3

Creating and Sustaining Homelike Places in Residential Environments

Frank Oswald and Hans-Werner Wahl

EDITORS' INTRODUCTION

*A*dopting a strongly psychological perspective, Oswald and Wahl focus
on the dual and reciprocal themes of belonging and agency. Using
data from the European Enabling Autonomy, Participation, and Well-
Being in Old Age: The Home Environment as a Determinant for Healthy
Ageing (ENABLE-AGE) project, they document how these themes are
related to older people's autonomy and well-being. The chapter introduces
a developmental perspective on environmental experience in later life by
suggesting that the evolution of the person-environment relationship is
related to the task of remaining independent for as long as possible as well
as maintaining one's integrity and identity. This task is manifest through
the individual's ability to control their environmental use (agency) and
their ability to make meaning (belonging) through the creation and
re-creation of homelike places. The data confirm that an understanding of
both belonging and agency is important in interpreting the effectiveness
of barrier-free building standards. But, beyond this, Oswald and Wahl's
work reveals the potential for reliably assessing both the individual's sense
of belonging and agency and the way these determinants of environmental
experience evolve over time. The perspective presented on the process of
person-environment adaptation provides for an expanded perspective on
developmental theories that have conspicuously lacked an environmental
component. In addition, the quest for understanding the way in which
belonging and agency are manifest every day in older people's lives, and
how they change as they move into advanced old age, has important implications for facilitating environmental design that embraces both subjective
and objective elements of experience.

Creating and sustaining homelike places is a developmental task for people across the lifespan. Better understanding of the person-environment (*P-E*) processes involved in this long-term developmental challenge has been, and continues to be, a major theme in aging research, particularly in social gerontology and the psychology of aging. That said, the aim of this chapter is to present our view of *P-E* interchange processes and their outcomes in the immediate home environment in later life. We first introduce a conceptual framework that refers to two key processes of *P-E* interchange in later life, which we have coined in our previous work as *belonging* and *agency* (Wahl & Oswald, 2010). Second, we draw on a selection of cross-sectional and longitudinal data from the European project ENABLE-AGE (in which both authors were participants) to support the notion that both processes capture significant portions of the psychological makeup of people's lived experience of housing in later life. Belonging and agency are also strongly related to key elements of the "good life" (Lawton, 1983) in old age, including autonomy and subjective well-being. The empirical findings presented in this chapter have been generated in collaboration with fellow researchers from the ENABLE-AGE consortium (see Chapter 8) (Iwarsson et al., 2007; Nygren et al., 2007; Oswald et al., 2007; Wahl, Oswald, Schilling, & Iwarsson, 2009).

TOWARD AN INTEGRATIVE THEORETICAL FRAMEWORK FOR HOUSING IN LATER LIFE

Human development is characterized by *P-E* exchange processes (Bronfenbrenner, 1999) involving subjective experiences as well as objective behavior. In order to address the complexity of aging in place, a conceptual framework is suggested that emphasizes two processes of *P-E* exchange in later life—*belonging* and *agency* (see Figure 3.1). In our view, the two constructs are particularly useful for integrating theoretical approaches offered in environmental gerontology in recent years (Oswald & Wahl, 2004; 2005; Scheidt & Windley, 2006; Wahl, 2001; Wahl, Iwarsson, & Oswald, 2012; Wahl & Lang, 2004, 2006; Wahl & Oswald, 2010; Wahl, Scheidt, & Windley, 2004).

In the framework outlined in Wahl and Oswald (2010), "processes of belonging" incorporate various facets of *P-E* experience, while "processes of agency" emphasize goal-directed *P-E* cognitions and behavior. As people have experienced life-long bonding to certain places, "processes of belonging" reflect environmental experience, subjective evaluation, interpretation of places, how meaning is made, as well as emotional bonding and place attachment. One key aspect of *P-E*

FIGURE 3.1 Conceptual Framework of Person-Environment Processes in Later Life

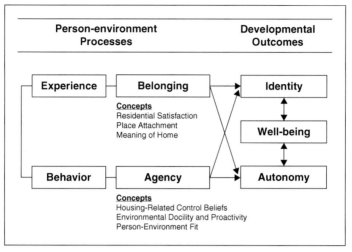

Note. Originally published in Wahl, H.-W., & Oswald, F. (2010). Environmental perspectives on ageing. In D. Dannefer & C. Phillipson (Eds.), *International handbook of social gerontology* (pp. 111–124). London: Sage.

belonging is the individual's cognitive orientation toward his or her own environmental past, present, and future, which may find expression as home-related reminiscence or in discussion of housing plans.

By contrast, "processes of agency" concern physical-environment-related cognitions including the perceived controllability of the physical environment in which one lives (Wahl & Oswald, 2010). At a behavioral level, agency is about reactive and proactive aspects of using, compensating, adapting, retrofitting, creating, and sustaining places. This is especially important in old age, because of limitations in functional capacity and behavioral flexibility. Both processes are particularly important for *P-E* exchange in the immediate residential environment, given that place of residence becomes more relevant to people as they age; that older people tend to spend more time in their home; and that many activities take place in this setting (Baltes, Maas, Wilms & Borchelt, 1999). In addition, the physical environment may or may not fit or be attuned to the older individual's functional impairments and needs.

Processes of belonging and agency are therefore two fundamental aspects of aging in place. Both processes are not independent of each other in everyday life for, as Figure 3.1 illustrates, processes of *P-E* exchange are related to major developmental outcomes as people age. These outcomes echo fundamental developmental tasks in later life—namely, to remain independent for as long as possible as well as to maintain one's integrity in terms of identity. As far as the aging self at home is concerned, a major goal in later life is to maintain identity and personality. As far as the aging body is concerned, the goal is to remain independent for as long as possible. Finally, we argue that both these outcomes are related to subjective well-being. The important feature of our framework is that autonomy, identity, and well-being are simultaneously considered as major endpoints of *P-E* interchange as people age, while the traditional view in environmental gerontology has concentrated separately on well-being (e.g., Lawton & Nahemow, 1973), on autonomy (e.g., Carp, 1987), or on identity (e.g., Neisser, 1988). In order to illustrate the integrative potential of the constructs of *P-E* belonging and *P-E* agency, we subsume and discuss the following classic approaches of environmental gerontology under these conceptual umbrellas.

Processes of Housing-Related Belonging

Processes of belonging are grounded in conceptualizations and theories of residential satisfaction addressing, for instance, variations in subjective global evaluations of the residence due to age of the inhabitant or geographic location, or the manifestation of place evaluation processes (Aragonés, Francescato & Gärling, 2002; Pinquart & Burmedi, 2004; Weideman & Anderson, 1985). Often, residential satisfaction is assessed by single item self-evaluations (Oswald, Wahl, Mollenkopf & Schilling, 2003). The criticism of this approach is reflected in the well-known residential satisfaction paradox, that is, evaluations are typically biased toward the positive and the correlation between subjective and objective ratings of the house, neighborhood, or city district tends to be low-to-medium at best, reflecting apparent satisfaction despite a poor objective environment (Fernandez-Ballesteros, 2001).

Theories of place attachment and identity (Altman & Low, 1992; Neisser, 1988; Proshansky, 1978; Proshanky, Fabian & Kaminoff, 1983; Stedman, 2002) emphasize domains of belonging in a more process-oriented and differentiated way. Place attachment is not only related to attitudes, but also to a gamut of processes operating when people form affective, cognitive, behavioral, and social bonds to the environment (Brown & Perkins, 1992), thereby transforming "space" into "place" (Altman, & Low, 1992; Rowles & Watkins, 2003). These aspects of bonding can be assessed by objective evaluations, for example, measures of indoor versus outdoor place attachment (Oswald, Hieber, Wahl & Mollenkopf, 2005), but there are also efforts to proceed using qualitative approaches, which empirically probe place attachment and identity (Peace, 2005).

Conceptualizations of the meaning of home are directly related to place attachment as they deal with the most frequent manifestation of attachment processes. Since older adults have often lived a long time in the same residence, cognitive and emotional aspects of the meaning of home are often strongly linked to biography. Such cognitive and emotional links may become manifest through processes of reflecting on the past, symbolically represented in certain places and cherished objects within the home. Thus, belonging covers non-goal-oriented cognitive and emotional aspects of bonding. It embraces behavioral and physical bonding as familiarity and routines develop over time. Meaning of home has been empirically explored mainly via qualitative methodologies (Rowles, 1983; Rubinstein, 1989; Sixsmith & Sixsmith, 1991), but there have also been efforts to quantify aspects of the meaning of home (Oswald & Kaspar, 2012; Oswald et al., 2006).

In terms of outcomes, one major conclusion drawn from the literature with regard to non-goal-directed processes of housing-related belonging in old age is that belonging contributes to housing-related identity (Born, 2002; Neisser, 1988). According to the landmark work of Graham Rowles (1983), processes of place attachment and allocation of meaning (of home) reflect different patterns of physical, autobiographical, and social "insideness" as a result of the long duration of living in the same place. Or as Rowles (1983, p. 114) has put it: "Place becomes a landscape of memories, providing a sense of identity" (see also Rowles & Watkins, 2003). Such a theoretical view of *P-E* interchange processes may explain why older adults often perceive the risk of losing their home (e.g., due to loss of competence) as closely related to losing crucial parts of self and, concomitantly, as a threat to their personal integrity. Substantial links between self or identity and well-being, as in our framework, have also been expressed in major psychological theories of lifespan development such as Erikson's (1950) psychosocial crisis approach and Levinson's (1986) conception of adult development, as well as in theories on successful aging (Ryff, 1989). Interestingly, none of these lifespan developmental scholars have put much emphasis on the home environment, a prominent portion of the everyday world of aging. Although the focus is on non-goal-oriented cognitive and emotional bonding, processes of belonging are nevertheless also instrumental in daily life as the home is cognitively represented "inside" the person. For instance, if my home means a lot to me because it is the place where I can do whatever I want to do, this may include everyday routines and activities and thus can be a resource for both autonomy and identity.

Processes of Housing-Related Agency

As people age, their residence may serve as an important compensation for age-related loss of competence, especially when significant loss in functional capacity occurs. But aging individuals are at the same time actively using, underusing, or misusing their home environments. For instance, if a person stays out of a room because he or she is not able to maintain it anymore, this could be labeled underuse. Misuse means that a person might, for example, stay in the kitchen all day long although there is a living room available which, paradoxically, cannot be used due to a number of barriers. In addition, people may just try to continue with their routines and daily behaviors without making environmental or person-related changes. By contrast, to maintain independence and avoid institutionalization, some people adapt (e.g., retrofit) their residential environment, while others choose instead to move to another, more barrier-free environment (Lawton, 1977; Oswald & Rowles, 2006; Scheidt & Windley, 1985; Wahl, 2001).

This brings us to processes of agency, which are embraced within established concepts and theories of environmental gerontology, including the environmental docility hypothesis (Lawton & Simon, 1968) and the ecological theory of aging (ETA) (Lawton, 1982; Lawton & Nahemow, 1973; Nahemow, 2000). The main proposition inherent in these models is that older people need to react to environmental press in order to remain independent (Lawton & Nahemow, 1973; Scheidt & Norris-Baker, 2004). The ETA describes behavior and affect as a function of the relationship between a level of personal competence and environmental press (Lawton, 1982, 1989, 1998; Nahemow, 2000). Behavioral adaptation in this sense is reduced to a docile or passive response to existing personal and environmental circumstances. In extending this model, the environmental proactivity hypothesis makes the case that older adults are not simply pawns in their environment, but can proactively change housing conditions according to their own wishes and needs in order to maintain independence. Such proactivity allows older adults to cope with environmental press and to profit from environmental richness (Lawton, 1985, 1989) by, for example, moving from residence to residence to better fulfill housing needs (Oswald & Rowles, 2006; Warnes & Williams, 2006). An important methodological implication of using environmental docility and environmental proactivity ideas is that both objective person-related information (e.g., on functional limitations), as well as physical-social-environment-related information (e.g., comprehensive assessment of barriers in a residence) is necessary. Although the ETA has achieved widespread prominence in research and application, assessment methods still seem far from achieving any gold standard, even though many unevaluated personal and environmental checklists have entered the field (Wahl & Iwarsson, 2007).

Other theoretical concepts address the level of *P-E* fit or lack of fit on several domains of *P-E* exchange as a prerequisite or manifestation of *P-E* agency—for example, in the congruence model of *P-E* fit suggested by Kahana (1982), and in the complementary/congruence model proposed by Carp and Carp (1984). A critical message inherent in *P-E* fit concepts is that the level of behavioral competence in a certain domain corresponds with the given level of environmental press (e.g., barriers at home), leading to adaptation (fit) versus maladaptation (lack of fit). This also means that establishing qualified *P-E* fit assessment opens a major research and practice perspective on *P-E* agency for those who are especially at risk in later life. At this point, assessment instruments have seldom surpassed the status of pure research devices and entered the field of practice and social service intervention. A rare exception is the concept of accessibility, and of measurement approach, suggested by Iwarsson and Slaug (2001, 2010; see also findings below).

Processes of *P-E* agency cover cognitions and evaluations and precede adaptive behavior aimed at regulating *P-E* dynamics as people age. A prominent construct in this vein is psychological control theory (Lachman, 1986; Lachman & Burack, 1993), which has been extended to the housing domain in our previous work (Oswald, Wahl, Schilling, & Iwarsson, 2007). Housing-related control beliefs explain home-related occurrences and experiences as people age, either as contingent upon one's own behavior (internal control), or upon luck, chance, fate, or powerful others (external control). The argument is that control beliefs related to the regulation of *P-E* exchange at home become increasingly important in old age. As was revealed in longitudinal studies, external control beliefs are especially sensitive to age-related changes, particularly due to health and functional ability losses, and thus are crucial in explaining autonomy and well-being (Baltes, Freund, & Horgas, 1999; Clark-Plaskie & Lachman, 1999).

Interplay of Housing-Related Belonging, Agency, and Outcomes of Aging Well

Within environmental gerontology theorizing, the families of concepts speaking to either *P-E* belonging or agency processes in later life are typically addressed separately. It makes sense to assume that both *P-E* interchange processes are closely intertwined as aging individuals "work" on the developmental task of creating and regulating homelike places. Consequently, *P-E* belonging and agency processes deserve consideration in tandem, not only at the conceptual level but also in empirical research. Depending on the research question, integrative empirical research examining both components that is able to address the synergies and possible constraints that one component may impose on the other, is a higher-order goal. For example, older people living at home and suffering from severe competence loss can adapt to environmental problems in terms of behavioral, cognitive, and emotional adaptation (Oswald & Wahl, 2005). They may objectively reduce their action range and subjectively re-evaluate their interior spaces as more valuable, in contrast to an out-of-home environment that has become less accessible. Thus, *P-E* adaptation in later life does not just refer to behavior, or experience; rather, it refers to both (Rowles, Oswald, & Hunter, 2004). The methodological consequence is that a balanced set of behavioral (objective) as well as experiential (subjective) data related to the physical-social environment needs to be assessed by empirical research.

As far as potential relationships between *P-E* processes of agency and belonging and general outcomes of autonomy, identity, and well-being are concerned, we would assume a greater age-related vulnerability for changes in the *P-E* agency component in relation to the outcome domain of autonomy. In other words, lowered *P-E* agency is expected to coincide with reduced functional competence (e.g., Wolinsky, Stump, Callahan, & Johnson, 1996). In contrast, processes of belonging are expected to remain stable, even after major loss of functional competence or health has occurred, for example, in very old age. Such *P-E* belonging stability may then play a role in the preservation of identity and well-being, which generally do not show much variability across the age continuum (e.g., Smith, Fleeson, Geiselmann, Settersten, & Kunzmann, 1999).

HOUSING AND HEALTHY AGING IN VERY OLD AGE

In the remaining part of this chapter we present data from the research project ENABLE-AGE. To our knowledge, this study represents the most comprehensive empirical attempt so far to assess *P-E* agency and belonging as well as the related outcomes of healthy aging, particularly autonomy in daily life, subjective well-being, and the absence of depression. The focus of ENABLE-AGE has been on single-living and community-dwelling very old men and women from different European urban settings. The study sites in Germany and Sweden continue to follow participants over time in order to explore the predictive quality of different aspects of housing for stability and change in autonomy and well-being as people developmentally move into very old age. In this chapter we refer only to the one-year follow-up assessment of ENABLE-AGE. First, we report findings on relationships among facets of agency and belonging. This is followed by discussion of findings on the relationships of *P-E* processes of belonging and agency on one side, and indicators of healthy aging on the other. Finally, emphasizing facets of agency, we present findings on the predictive quality of different indicators of agency on outcomes of autonomy and well-being over time.

Housing-Related Belonging and Agency

The first aim of the ENABLE-AGE project was to explore the relationship between housing-related belonging and agency. The findings presented here are based on data from a random sample of 1,918 people aged 75 to 89 years, living alone in their private urban residences in Sweden, Germany, Latvia, Hungary, and the United Kingdom. In the survey, a range of well-validated measures from various disciplines (e.g., psychology, occupational therapy) were administered within the home of the participants.

To address housing-related agency on the behavioral level, *P-E* fit in terms of housing accessibility was assessed with the Housing Enabler instrument (Iwarsson & Slaug, 2001, 2010). This instrument was administered in three steps. The first step consisted of assessment of functional limitations of the person. The second was identification of environmental barriers in the home and the immediate outdoor environment, as well as the subsequent computation of an individual accessibility score measuring the level of *P-E* fit, with higher scores indicating more accessibility problems. Third, on the level of cognition and evaluation, agency was assessed with the Housing-Related Control Beliefs Questionnaire: a questionnaire based on the dimensions of internal and external control, although only the external control subscale was included (Oswald, Wahl, Martin & Mollenkopf, 2003).

To address housing-related belonging, a set of quantitative measures was administered: the questionnaire on Usability in My Home (Fänge & Iwarsson, 2003); the questionnaire on Meaning of Home (Oswald, Mollenkopf & Wahl, 1999); and a global evaluation of housing satisfaction adapted from the Housing Options for Older People questionnaire (Heywood, Oldman, & Means, 2002). In assessing usability,

TABLE 3.1   Objective and Perceived Housing Indicators in the ENABLE-AGE Survey

(*N* = 1918)	Sweden (*n* = 397)	Germany (*n* = 450)	UK (*n* = 376)	Hungary (*n* = 392)	Latvia (*n* = 303)	Diff.
Objective housing variable set						
No. of environmental barriers[a]	64 (34–92)	66 (1–92)	37 (7–70)	39 (0–86)	55 (4–85)	***
Total accessibility score[a,b,c]	124 (0–670)	122 (0–596)	20 (0–371)	52 (0–531)	103 (0–563)	***
Perceived housing variable set						
Usability of the home, UIMH[d]						
- Activity aspects	19 (3–20)	19 (1–20)	19 (5–20)	20 (4–20)	15 (1–20)	***
- Physical environmental aspects	28 (8–30)	28 (10–30)	26 (12–30)	26 (6–30)	19 (5–30)	***
Meaning of home, MOH[e]						
- Physical aspects	8.9 (1.1)	8.9 (1.1)	8.2 (1.5)	7.3 (1.7)	6.6 (1.4)	***
- Behavioral aspects	8.5 (1.6)	8.9 (1.3)	7.6 (1.7)	8.2 (1.5)	7.1 (1.7)	***
- Cognitive/ emotional aspects	8.4 (1.0)	8.7 (0.9)	8.0 (0.9)	8.8 (1.0)	7.6 (1.2)	***
- Social aspects	8.6 (1.4)	7.8 (1.6)	8.3 (1.5)	7.8 (1.9)	6.8 (1.8)	***
Housing-related control, HCQ[f]						
- External control	2.8 (0.5)	2.8 (0.7)	2.6 (0.5)	2.3 (0.6)	3.1 (0.4)	***
Housing satisfaction[g]						
- Satisfaction with home conditions	4.8 (0.6)	4.6 (0.7)	4.5 (0.9)	4.2 (1.2)	3.6 (1.3)	***

Note. Originally published in Nygren et al. (2007). Accessibility was assessed by means of the Housing Enabler.
[a]Md (median) and range for each national sample.
[b]Higher scores indicate higher magnitude of accessibility problems.
[c]The total accessibility score is generated by the profile of functional limitations and dependence on mobility devices in the person (data not presented) and no. of environmental barriers.
[d]UIMH (1–5) Md (median) and range, higher scores indicate higher usability.
[e]MOH (0–10) M (mean) and SD, higher scores indicate more meaning.
[f]HCQ (1–5) M (mean) and SD, higher scores indicate higher control.
[g]Satisfaction with housing condition M (mean) and SD, higher scores indicate higher satisfaction. Statistical test for difference was performed with Kruskal-Wallis or with F-test with $p < .001$***.

we included two subscales on activity and the physical environment (Fänge & Iwarsson, 2003). To measure meaning, we investigated physical, behavioral, cognitive/emotional, and social aspects of the meaning of home (Oswald et al., 1999; for details see Iwarsson et al., 2007; Nygren et al., 2007; Oswald et al., 2007). Basic descriptive findings, and differences among settings, are depicted in Table 3.1.

In order to explore relationships among the sets of variables, that is housing-related indicators and healthy aging outcomes, we computed canonical correlations, as they parsimoniously describe the number and nature of mutually independent relationships among different sets of variables. In the first set of analyses, we juxtaposed objective environmental assessment of barriers and accessibility problems with data from several parts of the questionnaire covering issues of agency and belonging (see Table 3.2). The findings (reported in detail in Nygren et al., 2007) show that it is not the number of environmental barriers at home, but accessibility that interplays with different aspects of housing-related belonging and control beliefs. This indicates the cognitive facet of agency. Good accessibility was particularly associated with high scores in perceived usability, high amounts of behavioral meaning of home (e.g., "managing things without the help of others," "doing everyday tasks," "being able to change or rearrange things as I please") and low external control beliefs (e.g., "having a nice place is all luck," "where and how I live has happened more by chance than anything else").

Although there were different levels of accessibility in different European settings (see Table 3.1), the findings revealed comparability of the relationship between aspects of agency and belonging, simultaneously controlling for basic health and socioeconomic status. That is, there was a strong and consistent link between housing-related belonging and agency in very old age across the different settings. This was reflected in measures of accessibility, control beliefs, usability, and behavioral meaning.

Housing-Related Agency, Belonging, and Healthy Aging

The second aim of the ENABLE-AGE study was to explore relationships between housing (in terms of agency and belonging) and healthy aging. Indicators for healthy aging were autonomy, in terms of independence in daily activities, and subjective well-being. We assessed independence in activities of daily living (ADLs) (based on professional judgment) by using the ADL Staircase (Sonn & Hulter-Åsberg, 1991). Perceived independence in ADL was assessed using a single-item self-evaluation measure from the Neuropsychological Aging Inventory (Oswald, 2005). Subjective well-being included both cognitive (life satisfaction and environmental mastery) and emotional dimensions (affect and depression). We assessed life satisfaction through a single-item self-evaluation measure and assessed environmental mastery by the Environmental Mastery subscale of the Psychological Well-Being Questionnaire (Ryff, 1989). We assessed affect using the Positive and Negative Affect

TABLE 3.2 Correlations of Objective and Perceived Housing Variables (First Canonical Variates)

	Sweden	Germany	UK	Hungary	Latvia
Eigenvalues	0.5***	0.2***	0.4***	0.4***	0.5***
Canonical correlations (%)	.56 (83)	.42 (93)	.52 (88)	.51 (78)	.57 (81)
Objective housing variable set[a]					
Environmental barriers	**−.39 (.10)**	−.11 (.03)	.25 (−.04)	**−.74 (−.43)**	.18 (−.15)
Magnitude of accessibility problems	**−1.0 (−97)**	**−1.0 (−1.0)**	**1.0 (1.0)**	**−.92 (−.74)**	**.99 (1.0)**
Perceived housing variable set[b]					
Usability in the home					
Physical environmental aspects	**.78 (.38)**	**.69 (.29)**	**−.67 (−.24)**	.35 (−.11)	**−.61 (−.21)**
Activity aspects	**.82 (.56)**	**.63 (.37)**	**−.67 (−.21)**	**.75 (−.54)**	−.26 (−.02)
Meaning of home					
Behavioral aspects	**.60 (.31)**	**.70 (.45)**	**−.76 (−.50)**	**.71 (.20)**	**−.89 (−.70)**
Physical aspects	.19 (−06)	**.48 (.14)**	**−.63 (−19)**	**.79 (.23)**	**−.38 (.21)**
Cognitive/emotional aspects	.02 (−14)	.17 (−20)	−.14 (.33)	**.76 (.12)**	**−.46 (.18)**
Social aspects	.25 (.00)	.14 (.05)	−.27 (.07)	**.69 (.18)**	**−.61 (−.32)**
Housing-related ext. control beliefs	**−.50 (−18)**	**−.60 (−.37)**	**.61 (.32)**	**−.64 (−.19)**	**.63 (.28)**
Housing satisfaction	.12 (−.16)	.09 (−.12)	**−.40 (−.17)**	.18 (−.14)	.14 (.19)

Note. Originally published in Nygren et al. (2007).
[a]Correlations of objective housing variables with first canonical variate of objective housing variable set. Objective housing variables according to the Housing Enabler.
[b]Correlations of perceived housing variables with first canonical variate of perceived housing variable set. Perceived housing variables according to the Usability in My Home Questionnaire, UIMH, the Meaning of Home Questionnaire, MOH, the Housing-Related Control Beliefs Questionnaire, HCQ, and adapted satisfaction with condition of the home. Standardized canonical coefficients are shown in parentheses; correlations >.35 are boldfaced. ***$p < .001$.

Schedule (Watson, Clark, & Tellegen, 1988). This yielded a score for both negative (e.g., distressed, guilty, nervous, afraid, and ashamed) and positive affect (e.g., interested, excited, strong, active, inspired). Finally, we assessed depressive symptoms with the Geriatric Depression Scale (Yesavage et al., 1983).

The findings (reported in detail in Oswald et al., 2007) show that both processes of housing-related agency and belonging are related to autonomy and well-being (see Table 3.3).

TABLE 3.3 Correlations of Aspects on Housing and Healthy Aging (First Canonical Variates)

	Sweden ($n = 346$)	Germany ($n = 343$)	UK ($n = 350$)	Hungary ($n = 337$)	Latvia ($n = 267$)
Eigenvalues	1.2***	1.3***	1.6***	1.6***	1.8***
Canonical correlations (%)	.74 (73)	.75 (79)	.78 (74)	.78 (72)	.80 (68)
Housing variable set					
Environmental barriers	−.03 (.15)	−.08 (−.01)	−.09 (.07)	−.21 (.21)	.02 (.12)
Magnitude of accessibility problems	**−.73 (−.48)**	**−.61 (−.30)**	**−.67 (−.32)**	**−.69 (−.45)**	**−.69 (−.34)**
Usability in the home					
Physical environmental aspects	**.45 (.05)**	**.42 (.03)**	**.58 (.09)**	**.43 (.06)**	**.36 (.03)**
Activity aspects	**.64 (.24)**	**.71 (.35)**	**.55 (.08)**	.27 (.03)	**.72 (.28)**
Meaning of home					
Behavioral aspects	**.81 (.45)**	**.74 (.38)**	**.85 (.45)**	**.82 (.40)**	**.86 (.36)**
Physical aspects	.17 (−.08)	**.57 (.17)**	**.68 (.15)**	**.63 (.04)**	**.59 (.03)**
Cognitive/emotional aspects	.34 (.18)	.35 (.03)	**.45 (.10)**	**.61 (.19)**	**.58 (.11)**
Social aspects	.30 (−.03)	.13 (−.08)	.35 (−.09)	**.46 (−.03)**	**.52 (.01)**
Housing-related ext. control beliefs	**−.53 (−.21)**	**−.58 (−.20)**	**−.64 (−.33)**	**−.75 (.34)**	**−.66 (−.26)**
Housing satisfaction	.05 (.06)	.16 (−.03)	.15 (−.09)	.28 (.02)	.08 (.01)
Healthy aging variable set					
Independence in daily activities (ADL)	**.83 (.52)**	**.68 (.37)**	**.75 (.34)**	**.68 (.30)**	**.78 (.37)**
Perceived functional independence	**.80 (.41)**	**.76 (.38)**	**.82 (.37)**	**.80 (.23)**	**.87 (.46)**
Life satisfaction	**.36 (.04)**	**.50 (.13)**	**.47 (−.01)**	**.64 (.08)**	.29 (−.07)
Environmental mastery (Ryff)	**.59 (.23)**	**.76 (.45)**	**.66 (.20)**	**.84 (.41)**	**.58 (.18)**
Depression (GDS)	**−.55 (−.12)**	**−.53 (.01)**	**−.76 (−.42)**	**−.78 (−.24)**	**−.70 (−.32)**
Positive affect (PANAS)	.33 (.05)	**.43 (.10)**	**.39 (.02)**	**.46 (.09)**	**.49 (.04)**
Negative affect (PANAS)	−.22 (−.06)	−.32 (.01)	−.28 (.06)	**−.39 (.01)**	−.26 (.04)

Note. Originally published in Oswald et al. (2007).
ADL = Activity of Daily Living; GDS = Geriatric Depression Scale; PANAS = Positive and Negative Affect Schedule. Subsamples are reduced as a result of listwise deletion in canonical correlation procedures. Standardized canonical coefficients are shown in parentheses; correlations >.35 are boldfaced. ***$p < .001$.

Again, it was not the mere number of barriers in the home environment, but accessibility that proved important for autonomy in terms of independence in daily life and well-being. Additionally, behavioral aspects of the meaning of home, in particular, correlated with autonomy and well-being, indicating housing-related belonging. In other words, those participants with good accessibility (high *P-E* fit) at home, who perceived their home as useful and valuable for activities, and who thought that others or fate were marginally responsible for their housing situation (low external control beliefs), had better autonomy in daily life, a better sense of well-being (environmental mastery), and suffered less from depressive symptoms. Taken together, these cross-sectional findings suggest that when striving for barrier-free building standards it is also important to consider psychological issues of meaning and control beliefs and thus to encompass a holistic approach that takes both processes of *P-E* agency and *P-E* belonging into account.

Housing-Related Agency and Healthy Aging Over Time

The third aim of the ENABLE-AGE project was to explore home environments as a determinant of healthy aging in very old age. To do this, we explored empirical links between selected indicators of *P-E* exchange processes and indicators of healthy aging over time, as well as changes in these indicators. For this part of the study, we focused on aspects of agency in terms of accessibility and control beliefs, as well as on outcomes of autonomy and subjective well-being. Based on our understanding of agency, we reasoned that housing accessibility and housing-related control beliefs should be considered in concert, because they are complementary, both conceptually and empirically. Accessibility focuses on behavior; control-beliefs highlight evaluation and cognition. Outcomes were assessed using measures of ADL functioning, general well-being, positive and negative affect, and depression. Data were drawn from a sub-sample of 847 participants (at Time 1) in Sweden and Germany, 636 of whom were reassessed one year later (Time 2).

We expected that both indicators of agency would be important for both outcomes, but that accessibility would be more important for daily independence, whereas control beliefs would be more important for well-being-related outcomes. In addition, we assumed that behavioral and cognitive aspects of agency interact and that such interaction also relates to outcomes. That is, having accessibility problems and having at the same time strong external control beliefs would result in negative outcomes, because pronounced lack of fit between competence and environmental press would be intensified by the perception that attempts to modify or optimize one's home environment were subject to uncontrollable external forces. In contrast, if one lives in an accessible place, being high in external control may not be that important, because overall independence is still high. Thus, we assumed that a combination of low accessibility and high external control beliefs further increases the risk for negative outcomes, while external control should not play a role in the case of good accessibility.

As far as potential longitudinal changes in outcomes of autonomy and well-being in relation to agency at baseline were concerned, we expected that accessibility problems and control beliefs would reveal a substantial relationship with change in daily independence, but not so much with well-being. More specifically, we expected that having many accessibility problems and external control beliefs at baseline, would be associated with decreasing daily independence over one year.

The findings (reported in detail in Wahl et al., 2009) from cross-sectional regression analyses revealed that both aspects of agency, accessibility and control beliefs, were consistently associated with outcomes of autonomy and well-being, with accessibility being more strongly associated with daily independence and external control beliefs more strongly associated with well-being-related outcomes. All relationships were confirmed in the expected direction, that is, a low accessibility was linked with less daily independence, lower life satisfaction, lower positive affect, and higher levels of depressive symptoms. Similarly, higher external control beliefs were associated with less daily independence, lower life satisfaction, lower positive affect, higher negative affect, and higher levels of depressive symptoms (see Table 3.4).

Significant and marginally significant interaction terms underscored that being high in external control beliefs in a situation of low accessibility was linked with more negative outcomes, while external control did not play a role in the situation of high accessibility. In other words, particularly if a participant experienced low accessibility and felt that others were responsible for his or her own home environment, this came with an increase in depression and vice versa.

In the longitudinal regression analysis, accessibility at baseline was predictive for short-term changes (i.e., over one year) in daily independence and depression, while external control beliefs did not show a substantial relationship with any change in outcomes (see Table 3.5).

We found significant effects of the interaction between both aspects of agency in relation to changes in life satisfaction and depression. The predictive role of accessibility on changes in life satisfaction and

TABLE 3.4 Findings of Regression Analyses (Cross-sectional Analyses at T1, N = 847)

Predicting Variable	ADL Independence/ Dependence		Life Satisfaction		Positive Affect		Negative Affect		Depression	
	Stand. β	Semi-partial[c] R^2	Stand. β	Semi-partial R^2	Stand. β	Semi-partial R^2	Stand. β	Semi-partial R^2	Stand. β	Semi-partial R^2
Country (Germany = 0; Sweden = 1)	-.048	.002	-.102*	.008	-.24***	.049	.083*	.006	.085*	.006
Age	-.111**	.011	.044	.000	-.013	.000	-.023	.000	.003	.000
Sex (f = 0, m = 1)	.118***	.013	.054	.000	.133***	.018	.091*	.008	-.023	.001
Perceived health (1–5)	-.022	.000	-.282***	.070	-.263***	.049	.108*	.008	.315***	.071
Magnitude of accessibility problems (MAP) (0–596)[a]	-.342***	.088	-.077(*)	.007	-.076(*)	.004	.028	.000	.098*	.007
External housing related control beliefs (Ext. HCB) (1–5)[b]	-.156***	.021	-.088*	.025	-.145***	.025	.129**	.015	.167***	.025
Interaction MAP × ext. HCB	-.059(*)	.003	-.042	.011	-.024	.000	.015	.000	.107**	.011
Model R^2	.23		.11		.16		.05		.18	

Note. Originally published in Wahl et al. (2009). Data from the project ENABLE-AGE, T1, N = 847 (Sweden, Germany), with $p < .10(^*), p < .05^*, p < .01^{**}, p < .001^{***}$.

[a]Higher scores indicate larger magnitude of accessibility problems.

[b]Higher scores indicate higher external housing related control beliefs.

[c]Proportion of the dependent variable's total variance explained by regression on the predictor *uniquely*; not to sum up to the model's total R^2.

TABLE 3.5 Findings of Regression Analyses (Longitudinal Analyses Considering 1-year Change in Outcomes, $N = 636$)

Predicting Variable	ADL Independence/ Dependence		Life Satisfaction		Positive Affect (PANAS)		Negative Affect (PANAS)		Depression (GDS)	
	Stand. β	Semi-partial[c] R^2	Stand. β	Semi-partial R^2	Stand. β	Semi-partial R^2	Stand. β	Semi-partial R^2	Stand. β	Semi-partial R^2
Country (Germany = 0; Sweden = 1)	-.033	.000	.088(*)	.006	-.076	.005	.078	.005	.012	.000
Age	-.034	.001	.010	.000	-.077	.005	-.010	.002	.039	.001
Sex (f = 0, m = 1)	-.069	.005	-.056	.003	.018	.000	.053	.003	.046	.002
Perceived health (1–5)	-.050	.001	-.000	.000	.087(*)	.005	.049	.002	-.059	.003
Magnitude of accessibility problems (MAP) (0–596)[a]	-.252***	.048	-.051	.002	-.016	.000	-.010	.000	.134**	.014
External housing related control beliefs (ext. HCB) (1–5)[b]	.064	.004	.051	.002	-.007	.000	.005	.000	.017	.000
Interaction MAP × ext. HCB	.030	.000	.104*	.011	-.013	.000	-.005	.000	-.112*	.012
Model R^2	.08		.02		.02		.01		0.4	

Note. Originally published in Wahl et al. (2009). Data from the project ENABLE-AGE, T2, $N = 636$ (Sweden, Germany), with $p < .10(*), p < .05*, p < .01**, p < .001***$.

[a]Higher scores indicate larger magnitude of accessibility problems.

[b]Higher scores indicate higher external housing related control beliefs.

[c]Proportion of the dependent variable's total variance explained by regression on the predictor *uniquely*; not to sum up to the model's total R^2.

depression declines with increasing levels of external control beliefs, and amplifies with decreasing external control beliefs. In other words, if a participant lived in a situation with pronounced lack of accessibility, and at the same time felt that others were responsible for his or her home environment, this seemed to lead to an increase in depression and decrease in life satisfaction. In contrast, participants low in accessibility and, at the same time, feeling themselves responsible for their own home were not so much at risk for an increase in depressive symptoms and lowered life satisfaction.

In sum, these data document substantial relationships between types of agency and outcomes of autonomy and well-being. Such evidence is required to further improve housing-oriented prevention and intervention strategies in advanced old age. In terms of specific implications for planners and designers, we need to make sure that everyone who is involved in the process of providing and optimizing living circumstances for older adults is obliged to consider *P-E* relationships in his or her work. Based on our findings, it is not just the number of accessibility problems or the psychological attitude toward housing, but a combination of these factors which may heighten one's risk of losing independence over time among a group of particularly vulnerable older adults.

FROM KNOWLEDGE TO PRACTICE

It has long been argued that older adults are pawns of their environmental conditions, particularly of inadequate housing characteristics. But it is now clear that this relationship is complex and multifaceted. In a sense, adulthood and aging means the ongoing creation and re-creation of homelike places, although this does not imply observable "objective" *P-E* change in many instances but, rather, processes of psychological adaptation operating "under the surface." The aim of this chapter was to extend such understanding of *P-E* interchange in the immediate home environment into a consideration of later life. Based on a conceptual framework on processes of *P-E* interchange and related outcomes in later life, we presented data from the European project ENABLE-AGE to explore empirically three areas: the relationship between housing-related agency and belonging; the relationship between housing (in terms of agency and belonging) and healthy aging; and the home environment as a determinant of healthy aging in very old age. We believe strongly that our perspective has important implications for future research within environmental gerontology, but also far-reaching implications for interventions that will facilitate improved environmental adaptation.

In terms of future environmental gerontology research, our work supports the notion that it is possible to reliably and validly assess both processes of belonging and agency (Iwarsson & Slaug, 2010; Oswald & Kaspar, 2012; Oswald et al., 2006; Oswald & Wahl, 2004). We also argue that seeking a balanced assessment of both processes is important and is the only way to learn about the interplay of belonging and agency. It seems that most environmental gerontology research in the past has focused on *either* belonging *or* agency-related processes. The interplay between these constructs is still far from clear and our research only offers first steps in this direction (e.g., Wahl et al., 2009). It may be a good strategy to develop a minimum data set covering both belonging and agency-related processes and integrate such an assessment in large-scale cross-sectional and longitudinal studies. As we see it, this would provide better linkage between environmental gerontology oriented research and other areas of aging research and practice.

We also see more general conceptual (and empirical) implications. For example, the consideration of *P-E* belonging and agency processes may facilitate refinement of now classic views of developmental adaptation and "successful" aging such as Baltes and Baltes' (1990) model of selection, optimization, and compensation (SOC). SOC mechanisms can be expected to go hand-in-hand with *P-E* agency processes as addressed in our approach. For example, changing one's home (moving to another site or making housing modifications) in later life may reflect important selection and compensatory agency which has not been explicitly explored in the SOC model. On the other hand, processes of *P-E* belonging seem to be systematically underrated in many models of lifespan development and adaptation such as the SOC. That is, these models are all very much agency oriented (maintain or lose agency) and leave not much room for non-goal-directed processes of *P-E* belonging. It may be the case that processes of belonging may be more important for successful human development, and this may be particularly true for very old age (Wahl, Iwarsson, & Oswald, 2012; Wahl & Lang, 2006). If we consider aging in very late life as a mixture of active (even proactive) and reactive behavioral adaptation (of the environment) to compensate for age-related losses, as well as processes aiming to maintain stability of the given living situation as long as possible, then the interactive roles of agency and belonging in aging in place might be even more effective.

This perspective is underrepresented in projects on technological environments, such as in the field of ambient assisted living (e.g., Lindenberger, Lövdén, Schellenbach, Li, & Krüger, 2008), although it is true that belonging processes play a strong role in traditional lifespan developmental models such as Erikson's (1950) psychosocial crises approach. The classic Eriksonian switch from generativity to ego-integrity as central to later life and particularly very old age (see also Erikson, Erikson, & Kivnik, 1989) is not too far from a shift from agency to belonging. Similarly, Carstensen's (2006) extensive empirical work, driven by socio-emotional selectivity theory, has demonstrated a transition from information-seeking to intimacy-oriented social motivations as people age. In sum, focusing explicitly on processes of belonging without any a priori primacy of agency-related processes may be important in order to counterbalance the "modern" trend in developmental science and aging research to use predominantly "agency glasses" to better understand developmental dynamics. At the same time, our understanding of belonging processes has nothing to do with "classic" disengagement, but shows some overlap with concepts such as reminiscence, life review, and attachment processes in adult life (Lopez & Brennan, 2000).

In the light of our framework and findings, it is an important requirement that programs of housing adaptation and work to locate older people in optimal environmental settings are driven by agency and belonging considerations. For example, if we look for ways to adapt housing in very old age in order to improve or maintain daily independence, we should not ignore how psychological processes, like feeling oneself responsible for one's own home, can also have substantial consequences for autonomy and well-being, in combination with barrier-free amenities. Based on our extended set of empirical measures, we were able to show that older adults who have many accessibility problems are at high risk of decreasing daily independence over time. We were also able to show that accessibility problems and a feeling of limited control over the home environment can lead to depression and decrease in life satisfaction, whereas those who felt less externally controlled were at less risk for increased depressive symptoms. In practical terms this could mean, for instance, that counseling programs could be devised not only to address observed behaviors and objective barriers but also to include measures (e.g., questionnaires) to learn more about the inhabitant's attitudes toward his or her environment. One might even think of developing separate individual agency and belonging profiles which could help to tailor individual environmental adaptation/maintenance programs. We suggest that in terms of practical objectives, *P-E* fit (accessibility), usability, and housing-related control beliefs may provide important guidelines for such consultations. At the same time, it is important in terms of belonging to get a good understanding of residential satisfaction, of the meanings with which home is imbued, and of the strength and flexibility of given place attachment processes.

To our knowledge, very little research exists on the role of belonging and agency in demented and cognitively impaired older adults (as well as in those with other specific age-related diseases). It seems, in any case, to be a consistent clinical finding that the "cultivation" of belonging is important for older adults with dementia and may even compensate for deteriorated agency capabilities. In the final analysis, aging societies should be increasingly aware that planning for housing in old age is clearly about more than just considering barrier-free buildings. Indeed, adopting a more sophisticated view of the role of housing and well-being in old age may provide an important pathway to learning much more about personhood and psychological adaptation in later life.

ACKNOWLEDGMENT

The project "Enabling Autonomy, Participation, and Well-Being in Old Age: The Home Environment as a Determinant for Healthy Ageing" (ENABLE-AGE) was funded by the European Commission from 2002 to 2004 (QLRT-2001-00334). We thank all study participants, consortium and national team members, and sub-contractors for their contributions.

REFERENCES

Altman, I., & Low, S. M. (Eds.). (1992). *Human behavior and environment: Place attachment* (Vol. 12). New York, NY: Plenum.

Aragonés, J. I., Francescano, G., & Gärling, T. (2002). *Residential environments: Choice, satisfaction, and behavior.* Westport, CT: Bergin & Gervey.

Baltes, P. B., & Baltes, M. M. (Eds.). (1990). *Successful aging. Perspectives from the behavioral sciences.* Cambridge, UK: Cambridge University Press.

Baltes, M. M., Freund, A. M., & Horgas, A. L. (1999). Men and women in the Berlin aging study. In P. B. Baltes & K. U. Mayer (Eds.), *The Berlin aging study* (pp. 259–281). Cambridge, UK: Cambridge University Press.

Baltes, M. M., Maas, I., Wilms, H.-U., & Borchelt, M. (1999). Everyday competence in old and very old age: Theoretical considerations and empirical findings. In P. B. Baltes & K. U. Mayer (Eds.), *The Berlin aging study* (pp. 384–402). Cambridge, UK: Cambridge University Press.

Born, A. (2002). *Regulation persönlicher identität im Rahmen gesellschaftlicher Transformationsbewältigung* [Regulation of personal identity in the face of societal transformation]. Münster, Germany: Wasmann.

Bronfenbrenner, U. (1999). Environments in developmental perspective: Theoretical and operational models. In S. L. Friedman & T. D. Wachs (Eds.), *Measuring environment across the life span* (pp. 3–28). Washington, DC: American Psychological Association.

Brown, B., & Perkins, D. (1992). Disruptions in place attachment. In I. Altman & S. M. Low (Eds.), *Human behavior and environment: Place attachment* (Vol. 12, pp. 279–304). New York, NY: Plenum Press.

Carp, F. M. (1987). Environment and aging. In D. Stokols & I. Altman (Eds.), *Handbook of environmental psychology* (Vol. 1, pp. 330–360). New York, NY: Wiley.

Carp, F. M., & Carp, A. (1984). A complementary/congruence model of well-being or mental health for the community elderly. In I. Altman, M. P. Lawton, & J. F. Wohlwill (Eds.), *Human behavior and environment: Elderly people and the environment* (Vol. 7, pp. 279–336). New York, NY: Plenum Press.

Clark-Plaskie, M., & Lachman, M. E. (1999). The sense of control in midlife. In S. L. Willis & J. D. Reid (Eds.), *Life in the middle: Psychological and social development in middle age* (pp. 181–208). San Diego, CA: Academic Press.

Carstensen, L. L. (2006). The influence of a sense of time on human development. *Science, 312,* 1913–1915. doi:10.1126/science.1127488

Erikson, E. H. (1950). *Childhood and society.* New York, NY: Norton & Company.

Erikson, E. H., Erikson, J., & Kivnik, H. (1989). *Vital involvement in old age.* New York, NY: W. W. Norton & Co.

Fänge, A., & Iwarsson, S. (2003). Accessibility and usability in housing—construct validity and implications for research and practice. *Disability and Rehabilitation, 25*(23), 1316–1325.

Fernandez-Ballesteros, R. (2001). Environmental conditions, health and satisfaction among the elderly: Some empirical results. *Psicithema, 13*(1), 40–49.

Heywood, F., Oldman, C., & Means, R. (2002). *Housing and home in later life.* Buckingham, UK: Oxford University Press.

Iwarsson, S., & Slaug, B. (2001). *The housing enabler: An instrument for assessing and analyzing accessibility problems in housing.* Nävlinge och Staffanstorp: Vote & Skapen HB & Slaug Data Management.

Iwarsson, S., & Slaug, B. (2010). *The revised version of the housing enabler: An instrument for assessing and analyzing accessibility problems in housing.* Nävlinge och Staffanstorp: Veten & Skapen HB & Slaug Data Management.

Iwarsson, S., Wahl, H.-W., Nygren, C., Oswald, F., Sixsmith, A., Sixsmith, J., . . . Tomsone, S. (2007). Importance of the home environment for healthy aging: Conceptual and methodological background of the European ENABLE-AGE project. *The Gerontologist, 47*(1), 78–84.

Kahana, E. (1982). A congruence model of person-environment interaction. In M. P. Lawton, P. G. Windley, & T. O. Byerts (Eds.), *Aging and the environment. Theoretical approaches* (pp. 97–121). New York, NY: Springer Publishing Company.

Lachman, M. E. (1986). Locus of control in aging research: A case for multidimensional and domain-specific assessment. *Journal of Psychology and Aging, 1,* 34–40.

Lachman, M. E., & Burack, O. R. (Eds.). (1993). Planning and control processes across the life span: An overview. *International Journal of Behavioral Development, 16,* 131–143.

Lawton, M. P. (1977). The impact of the environment on aging and behavior. In J. E. Birren & K. W. Schaie (Eds.), *Handbook of the psychology of aging* (pp. 276–301). New York, NY: Van Nostrand Reinhold.

Lawton, M. P. (1982). Competence, environmental press, and the adaptation of older people. In M. P. Lawton, P. G. Wildly, & T. O. Byerts (Eds.), *Aging and the environment* (pp. 33–59). New York, NY: Springer Publishing Company.

Lawton, M. P. (1983). Environment and other determinants of well-being in older people. *The Gerontologist, 23*(4), 349–357.

Lawton, M. P. (1985). Housing and living environments of older people. In R. H. Binstock & E. Shanas, (Eds.), *Handbook of aging and the social sciences* (2nd ed., pp. 450–478). New York, NY: Van Nostrand Reinhold.

Lawton, M. P. (1989). Environmental proactivity in older people. In V. L. Bengtson & K. W. Schaie (Eds.), *The course of later life* (pp. 15–23). New York, NY: Springer Publishing Company.

Lawton, M. P. (1998). Environment and aging: Theory revisited. In R. J. Scheidt & P. G. Windley (Eds.), *Environment and aging theory. A focus on housing* (pp. 1–31). Westport, CT: Greenwood Press.

Lawton, M. P., & Nahemow, L. (1973). Ecology and the aging process. In C. Eisdorfer & M. P. Lawton (Eds.), *The psychology of adult development and aging* (pp. 619–674). Washington, DC: American Psychological Association.

Levinson, D. J. (1986). A conception of adult development. *American psychologist, 41,* 3–13.

Lindenberger, U., Lövdén, M., Schellenbach, M., Li, S.-C., & Krüger, A. (2008). Psychological principles of successful aging technologies: A mini-review. *Gerontology, 54,* 59–68.

Lopez, F. G., & Brennan, K. A. (2000). Dynamic processes underlying adult attachment organization: Toward an attachment theoretical perspective on the healthy and effective self. *Journal of Counseling Psychology, 47,* 283–300.

Nahemow, L. (2000). The ecological theory of aging: Powell Lawton's legacy. In R. Rubinstein, M. Moss, & M. Kleban (Eds.), *The many faces of aging* (pp. 22–40). New York, NY: Springer Publishing Company.

Neisser, U. (1988). Five kinds of self-knowledge. *Philosophical psychology, 1,* 35–59.

Nygren, C., Oswald, F., Iwarsson, S., Fänge, A., Sixsmith, J., Schilling, O., . . . Wahl, H.-W. (2007). Relationships between objective and perceived housing in very old age. *The Gerontologist, 47*(1), 85–95.

Oswald, F., Hieber, A., Wahl, H.-W., & Mollenkopf, H. (2005). Ageing and person-environment fit in different urban neighbourhoods. *European Journal of Ageing, 2*(2), 88–97. doi:10.1007/s10433-005-0026-5

Oswald, F., & Kaspar, R. (2012). On the quantitative assessment of perceived housing in later life. *Journal of Housing for the Elderly, 26,* 72–93. doi:0.1080/02763893.2012.673391

Oswald, F., Mollenkopf, H., & Wahl, H.-W. (1999). *Questionnaire on the meaning of home.* The German Centre for Research on Ageing. University of Heidelberg: Unpublished manuscript.

Oswald, F., & Rowles, G. D. (2006). Beyond the relocation trauma in old age: New trends in today's elders' residential decisions. In H.-W. Wahl, C. Tesch-Römer, & A. Hoff (Eds.), *New dynamics in old age: Environmental and societal perspectives* (pp. 127–152). Amityville, New York, NY: Baywood Publishing Company.

Oswald, F., Schilling, O., Wahl, H.-W., Fänge, A., Sixsmith, J., & Iwarsson, S. (2006). Homeward bound: Introducing a four domain model of perceived housing in very old age. *Journal of Environmental Psychology, 26*(3), 187–201.

Oswald, F., & Wahl, H.-W. (2004). Housing and health in later life. *Reviews of Environmental Health, 19*(3–4), 223–252.

Oswald, F., & Wahl, H.-W. (2005). Dimensions of the meaning of home in later life. In G. D. Rowles & H. Chaudhury (Eds.), *Home and identity in later life: International perspectives* (pp. 21–46). New York, NY: Springer Publishing Company.

Oswald, F., Wahl, H.-W., Martin, M., & Mollenkopf, H. (2003). Toward measuring proactivity in person-environment transactions in late adulthood: The housing-related control beliefs questionnaire. *Journal of Housing for the Elderly, 17*(1/2), 135–152.

Oswald, F., Wahl, H.-W., Mollenkopf, H., & Schilling, O. (2003). Housing and life-satisfaction of older adults in two rural regions in Germany. *Research on Aging, 25*(2), 122–143.

Oswald, F., Wahl, H.-W., Schilling, O., & Iwarsson, S. (2007). Housing-related control beliefs and independence in activities of daily living in very old age. *Scandinavian Journal of Occupational Therapy, 14,* 33–43.

Oswald, F., Wahl, H.-W., Schilling, O., Nygren, C., Fänge, A., Sixsmith, A., . . . Iwarsson, S. (2007). Relationships between housing and healthy aging in very old age. *The Gerontologist, 47*(1), 96–107.

Oswald, W. D. (2005). *Neuropsychological aging inventory (NAI).* Göttingen: Hogrefe.

Peace, S. M. (2005). *Environment and identity in later life.* Berkshire, UK: Open University Press.

Pinquart, M., & Burmedi, D. (2004). Correlates of residential satisfaction in adulthood and old age: A meta-analysis. In H.-W. Wahl, R. Scheidt, & P. G. Windley (Eds.), *Annual review of gerontology and geriatrics: Aging in context: Socio-physical environments* (pp. 195–222). New York, NY: Springer Publishing Company.

Proshansky, H. M. (1978). The city and self-identity. *Environment & behavior, 10*(2), 147–169.

Proshansky, H. M., Fabian, A. K., & Kaminoff, R. (1983). Place-identity. *Journal of Environmental Psychology, 3,* 57–83.

Rowles, G. D. (1983). Geographical dimensions of social support in rural Appalachia. In G. D. Rowles & R. J. Ohta (Eds.), *Aging and milieu: Environmental perspectives on growing old* (pp. 111–129). New York, NY: Academic Press.

Rowles, G. D., Oswald, F., & Hunter, E. G. (2004). Interior living environments in old age. In H.-W. Wahl, R. Scheidt, & P. G. Windley (Eds.), *Annual review of gerontology and geriatrics: Aging in context: Socio-physical environments* (pp. 167–193). New York, NY: Springer Publishing Company.

Rowles, G. D., & Watkins, J. F. (2003). History, habit, heart and hearth: On making spaces into places. In K. W. Schaie, H.-W. Wahl, H. Mollenkopf, & F. Oswald (Eds.), *Aging independently: Living arrangements and mobility* (pp. 77–96). New York, NY: Springer.

Rubinstein, R. L. (1989). The home environments of older people: A description of the psychological process linking person to place. *Journal of Gerontology, 44,* 45–53.

Ryff, C. D. (1989). Beyond Ponce de Leon and life satisfaction: New directions in quest of successful aging. *International Journal of Behavioral Development, 12,* 35–55.

Scheidt, R. J., & Norris-Baker, C. (2004). The general ecological model revisited: Evolution, current status, and continuing challenges. In H.-W. Wahl, R. Scheidt, & P. G. Windley (Eds.), *Annual review of gerontology and geriatrics: Aging in context: Socio-physical environments, 2003* (pp. 35–48). New York, NY: Springer Publishing Company.

Scheidt, R. J., & Windley, P. G. (1985). The ecology of aging. In J. E. Birren & K. W. Schaie (Eds.), *Handbook of the psychology of aging* (pp. 245–258). New York, NY: Van Nostrand Reinhold.

Scheidt, R. J., & Windley, P. G. (2006). Environmental gerontology: Progress in the post-Lawton era. In J. E. Birren & K. W. Schaie (Eds.), *Handbook of the psychology of aging* (6th ed., pp. 105–125). Amsterdam, The Netherlands: Elsevier.

Sixsmith, A. J., & Sixsmith, J. A. (1991). Transition in home experience in later life. *Journal of Architectural and Planning Research, 8*(3), 181–191.

Smith, J., Fleeson, W., Geiselmann, B., Settersten, R. A., & Kunzmann, U. (1999). Sources of well-being in very old age. In P. B. Baltes & K. U. Mayer (Eds.), *The Berlin aging study. Aging from 70 to 100* (pp. 450–471). Cambridge, UK: Cambridge University Press.

Sonn, U., & Hulter-Åsberg, K. (1991). Assessment of activities of daily living in the elderly. *Scandinavian Journal of Rehabilitation Medicine, 23,* 193–202.

Stedman, R. S. (2002). Toward a social psychology of place: Predicting behavior from place-based cognitions, attitude and identity. *Environment & Behavior, 34*(5), 561–581.

Wahl, H.-W. (2001). Environmental influences on aging and behavior. In J. E. Birren & K. W. Schaie (Eds.), *Handbook of the psychology of aging* (5th ed., pp. 215–237). San Diego, CA: Academic Press.

Wahl, H.-W., & Iwarsson, S. (2007). Person-environment relations in old age. In R. Fernandez-Ballesteros (Ed.), *Geropsychology: European perspectives for an ageing world* (pp. 49–66). Göttingen: Hogrefe.

Wahl, H.-W., Iwarsson, S., & Oswald, F. (2012). Aging well and the environment: Toward an integrative model and research agenda for the future. *The Gerontologist, 52,* 306–316. doi:10.1093/geront/gnr154

Wahl, H.-W., & Lang, F. R. (2004). Aging in context across the adult life: Integrating physical and social research perspectives. In H.-W. Wahl, R. Scheidt, & P. G. Windley (Eds.), *Annual review of gerontology and geriatrics: Aging in context: Socio-physical environments, 2003* (pp. 1–33). New York, NY: Springer Publishing Company.

Wahl, H.-W., & Lang, F. R. (2006). Psychological aging: A contextual view. In P. M. Conn (Ed.), *Handbook of models for human aging* (pp. 881–895). Amsterdam, The Netherlands: Elsevier.

Wahl, H.-W., & Oswald, F. (2010). Environmental perspectives on aging. In D. Dannefer & C. Phillipson (Eds.), *International handbook of social gerontology* (pp. 111–124). London, UK: Sage.

Wahl, H.-W., Oswald, F., Schilling, O., & Iwarsson, S. (2009). The home environment and quality of life related outcomes in advanced old age: Findings of the ENABLE-AGE project. *European Journal of Ageing, 6*(2), 101–111.

Wahl, H.-W., Scheidt, R., & Windley, P. (Eds.). (2004). *Annual review of gerontology and geriatrics, 23, issue on aging in context: Socio-physical environments.* New York, NY: Springer Publishing Company.

Warnes, A. M., & Williams, A. (2006). Older migrants in Europe: A new focus for migration studies. *Journal of Ethnic and Migration Studies, 32*(8), 1257–1281.

Watson, D., Clark, L. A., & Tellegen, A. (1988). Development and validation of brief measures of positive and negative affect: The PANAS scales. *Journal of Personality and Social Psychology, 54*, 1063–1070.

Weideman, S., & Anderson, J. R. (1985). A conceptual framework for residential satisfaction. In I. Altman & C. M. Werner (Eds.), *Human behavior and environment: Home environments* (Vol. 8, pp. 153–182). New York, NY: Plenum Press.

Wolinsky, F. D., Stump, T. E., Callahan, C. M., & Johnson, R. J. (1996). Consistency and change in functional status among older adults over time. *Journal of Aging and Health, 8*, 155–182.

Yesavage, J. A., Brink, T. L., Rose, T. L., Lum, O., Huang, V., Adey, M., & Leirer, V. O. (1983). Development and validation of a geriatric depression screening scale: A preliminary report. *Journal of Psychiatric Research, 17*, 314–317.

CHAPTER 4

A Place of One's Own: Reinterpreting the Meaning of Home Among Childless Older Women

Kate de Medeiros, Robert L. Rubinstein, and
Patrick J. Doyle

EDITORS' INTRODUCTION

*Focusing on older women who do not have children, this chapter adds a new dimension to the way in which we consider the private domain of the home by introducing the concept of **environmental positioning**; the idea that the meaning of place, in this case, home, is a fluid and dynamic mutual creation of the person living in the particular home environment and the observer/researcher who is attempting to understand the phenomenon. Each brings his or her own life experience and way of viewing life to an exchange in which the physical setting and the objects it contains serve as cues to framing and presenting a time-, place-, and situation-contingent view of home. By adding this level of interpretive sophistication, the authors facilitate the development of a more nuanced and deeper understanding of how the meaning of home differs for various populations. The perspective of environmental positioning is especially important in understanding the environmental experience of the increasing numbers of people whose lives and derivation of meaning in old age do not conform to the stereotypical models of the nuclear or the extended family. Of particular importance in this regard will be explorations of gay and lesbian older adults, older prisoners, older adults with lifelong physical or intellectual disabilities, older Native Americans, and older adults in other diverse cultures. Environmental positioning provides strong evidence of the need to reframe and expand the manner in which we interpret the meaning of home to older people and the ways in which we translate such interpretations into practice and policy.*

Childlessness has distinctive and complex meanings in all societies. In later life, childlessness may take on additional layers of meanings, some of which clearly relate to issues of *home*. We introduce "home" in relation to childlessness in old age for several reasons. In the West, home is a place often associated with raising families; it has long been considered the private domain of women and children, especially in times when few women worked outside the place of residence, in contrast to the public domains of men, which centered on their place of employment (McDowell, 1999). The strong conceptual link between home and family (children in particular) can also be found in many residential options for older adults (e.g., retirement communities, assisted living facilities and nursing homes). Many in the United States, for example, assume that children play a large role in their parents' decisions to move and therefore market themselves to the children of older adults (Carder & Hernandez, 2004). Thus, this personal transition of an older adult into a long-term care setting is expected to be a shared experience within a family system. The need for continued family engagement in personal and social care of the elder within long-term care settings has been widely touted within the academic and professional literature (Gaugler, 2005). Similarly, the renegotiation of the meaning of home when living in long-term care settings is often examined in the context of intergenerational/family interactions. Models of long-term care reform, such as the Eden Alternative, posit that family involvement within nursing homes is essential for the achievement of "homelike" settings and in turn, for improving quality of life for residents (Thomas, 1996). This focus on the familial context of long-term care and home overlooks the potentially unique experiences and meanings of childless older women. This chapter will address what meaning(s) can be found in home for people who do not have children.

In considering home, meaning, and culture in old age, we start from two contradictory ideas: (1) that objects such as houses and personal belongings can carry a heavy symbolic load and can symbolize various aspects of the self (Csíkszentmihályi & Rochberg-Halton, 1981; Rubinstein, 1987) and (2) that symbols associated with home and self run the risk of, or may be mistakenly seen as, appropriating order and patterns of meaning that may simply not exist for a given individual. In short, symbols associated with home can be simultaneously meaningful and meaningless, depending on the position the individual takes regarding them.

We then focus on a particular group of older adults—older women who do not have children—to help disentangle the confounding notions of family and home, and of home and house (or place) (Rapoport, 2005). We note that the purpose of the chapter is not to discuss the meaning of childlessness to older women, but to explore ways in which the meanings of home are negotiated and expressed when children are not involved, especially for a group (women) who have been conceptually tied with home. A focus on childless older women allows us a way of disentangling common assumptions about home by looking at a group for whom common assumptions may not apply.

Older women without children are important in considering the meaning of home for several reasons. Women comprised the majority of people age 65 and over in the world in 2000 (237 million women compared to 182 million men) (Richards, 2003). Also of concern is "motherhood," a socially constructed norm for women and a key concept in ideas of home and its association with family. The old sayings, "A woman's place is in the home" and "A man's home is his castle" underscore commonly held beliefs that women belonged within the private sphere of the house, separated from paid work, responsible for childrearing and meal preparation, and under the direction of the man of the house. The idea of home as a woman's place again is linked to family (fathers, husbands, and children). As such, family and home are expected to be key components of a woman's identity.

A dark side to family and home for women is often overlooked. Women who reached adulthood before the 1960s (or later) in the United States experienced systematic discrimination based on gender, race, and socioeconomic status, which created barriers to their participation in the job market and their ability to achieve financial independence. Home ownership in their own right was difficult if not impossible for most women. Home could also be the site for domestic violence and child abuse. In short, although home was a woman's place, she may have had little or no control within it. These historical events and perceptions, along with personal choices (e.g., to remain single or marry; to remain outside the formal workforce or seek paid employment), have inevitably influenced the experience of later life for many women.

To help understand the possible meanings of home for childless older women and to examine these meanings in light of common symbols associated with home, we introduce a new concept, *environmental positioning*. Environmental positioning is drawn from the larger "positioning theory" in psychology (Harré & Moghaddam, 2003; Harré & van Langenhove, 1999) and further understood through "narrative positioning" as it is applied in linguistics (Davies & Harré, 1990).

Key to "positioning" is the idea that one's place in a social framework such as a conversation or, in our construct, the home environment or society, may be intentional or unintentional and is not necessarily fixed. As Harré and Moghaddam (2003, p. 5) explain, the idea of "positioning" describes "a loose set of rights and duties that limit the possibilities of action." For example, someone positioned as "incompetent" by one person or group may have their right to be taken seriously limited by the others. This same person may also position the others as "uninformed," "irrelevant" or some other status that in turn may limit the possibilities of action by that group for the individual. Positioning can occur on the individual level, as in the example, or on the institutional level, where one's position may have actual consequences within the larger society (e.g., nursing home administrator, government official).

Like positioning theory, which developed as a dynamic response to the more static concept of roles, environmental positioning is developed in contradistinction to a position that sees the relationship and the meaning between a person and an environment as unchanging. Meanings within the environment, as in a conversation, are viewed as relational, fluid, and sometimes contradictory or contested. In the context of the home environment, this approach is especially useful in helping to better understand how older women negotiate multiple meanings of self and home, since it does not presuppose any meanings that are not made relevant by the women themselves.

We then go on to look at three case examples of older women without children and consider how they use environmental positioning to negotiate a combination of symbolic representation of meanings and identities crafted from their experiences and concerns. For each woman, home is inextricably linked to a struggle for success and to find a home of her own. Aspects of the physical and social details that the women reveal about their current homes tell complicated stories and offer complex representations of their lifetime experiences, personal and societal expectations and goals, and the historical context that framed each woman's life. We note that meanings of home for these women differ markedly from those one might expect to find in older women with children and grandchildren. In their difference from the "expected," these examples illustrate the nuanced quality of home. Finally, we consider how we can take the concept of "environmental positioning" and apply it in a practical sense, through policy, social planning, and design for living spaces for older women and men.

Shaping Norms and Symbolic Meanings

Before addressing the symbolic meaning of home for women, we first discuss "house," "place," and "home" and how we see them in the larger meaning system. As Rapoport (2005) points out, words like "house," "home," and "dwelling" are at times used interchangeably; at times with some distinctions. For example, "house" or "dwelling" may imply the structure alone whereas "home" implies an emotional attachment, a sense of belonging, to a structure. We see these overlaps not as a conflation of ideas or concepts, but rather as multidimensional aspects of possible meanings that we can attach to a place. The focus of our chapter is on the meaning of home. At times, "house" as a place and "home" as the meaning associated with that place are separate, at times conjoined. Therefore, clear separation of place and meaning are not always possible or warranted.

Much of the work about the meaning and symbolic value of home stresses two elements, family and self, whether implicitly or explicitly (Mallett, 2004; Rubinstein, 2005). The idea of home in relationship to family is a *de facto* norm, since the vast majority of people connect homes and families. Individuals grow up in a particular home or homes. Most eventually pass out of co-residence with their family of origin and go out on their own. Sixsmith (1986) described this aspect of home as the "social home." Whether or not a new home is connected with a new family is dependent on a number of factors, perhaps foremost of which is personal predilection. We consider the range of personal situations—without children or family—to which the symbol of home might be attached. Because symbols exist in arbitrary relationship to their referents, there is no necessary or absolute relationship. Indeed, home can stand for any number of things, depending on how an individual shapes and handles the meanings in the person's life. Thus, ultimately, the meaning of home relates significantly to the second common symbolic use of home—as a symbol of the self. Through the environmental positioning perspective, we are interested in learning how different aspects of the self are made known through environmental references in narratives and in physical space.

Women in Historical Context

To better understand the symbols used in the construction of meaning and home for childless older women, we consider how past life experiences shape the experience of old age. We focus primarily on events from the 1920s through the late 1960s in the United States, since this timeframe corresponds to childhood and early adulthood for people currently over age 65. Motherhood was (and still is) viewed as a primary role for women (Koropeckyj-Cox, Pienta, & Brown, 2007; Letherby, 2002) and women's identities have been historically constructed through their ability to bear children or not. While "fatherhood" is arguably also viewed as a primary role for men, women's fertility has been a barrier to their gaining access to jobs and financial independence, while having the opposite effect on men (Browne, 1998). These barriers in turn limit a woman's ability to directly "control" her home through her economic dependence on others, usually fathers or husbands (Calasanti & Slevin, 2001; Darke, 1994).

Most countries in the world, including the United States, manifest strong "pronatalist" views, with two overriding assumptions regarding children: (1) all married couples should have children, and (2) all married couples should want to have children (Koropeckyj-Cox & Call, 2007; Rempel, 1985). In many societies, the desire to want to have children is seen as "natural" and as a social imperative. In contrast, not wanting to have children is often viewed as a selfish, deviant, and/or an antisocial behavior, although this view is perhaps less dominant now than in earlier decades (Dykstra & Hagestad, 2007; Koropeckyj-Cox, 2002; Park, 2002), and there has been an active "childless by choice" movement for years. It is important that we are cognizant of the effect that historical societal expectations of familial trajectories for women may have had on the childless older women of today.

Despite pronatalism, rates of childlessness for women in the United States and in many countries around the world have varied but continue to increase. For example, 15% of women born in 1900 were childless compared with 25% of those born in 1910, who reached childbearing age during the Depression. Around 10% of women born in 1935 were childless while 22% of women born in 1962 were childless (Heaton, Jacobson, & Holland, 1999). Some have predicted that, given current trends, childlessness among Americans aged 70 to 85 may exceed 30% by 2030 (Dykstra & Hagestad, 2007).

Reasons for not having children include the obvious: not all women want to be mothers, regardless of cultural myths of motherhood as a natural instinct and despite marital status. For women who were over age 65 in 2010, access to employment was denied or limited based on their fertility (real or potential) through much of their adulthood. In the United States, most pregnant women were required to resign from jobs well into the late 1960s and fewer than 5% of employers offered any type of maternity leave for those few who were not fired (Kelly & Dobbin, 1999; Solinger, 2005). Formal legislation protecting pregnant workers was not permanently in place until 1978 (Kelly & Dobbin, 1999). Despite legislation, subtle forms of discrimination against women (either pregnant or of childbearing age) remain (Hebl, King, Glick, Singletary, & Kazama, 2007).

Choosing between independence in the workforce or dependence in a marriage has been attributed as the reason for intentional childlessness prior to the 1960s (Dykstra & Hagestad, 2007). Many employers refused to hire married women (because of the assumed likelihood of their having children) or women with children. Lack of reliable birth control methods to prevent pregnancy often resulted in children and financial dependence on a husband for married women, or social stigma for the unmarried. In either case, self-support was difficult. Women therefore were often forced to choose between a career without children or spouse and family life. More recently, childlessness has not been tied to marital status. There is an increase in married couples who choose to not have children (Dykstra & Hagestad, 2007; Koropeckyj-Cox, et al., 2007). Increased equity in job opportunities and earning potentials for men and women will likely contribute to the meaning of home in older age in the future.

Whatever the reason for childlessness, this reality has the potential to provide an individual with certain opportunities that may not be available to those whose energies are more fully tied up in child rearing. For women in our study, many of the energies that were not used for child rearing were in fact used for other goals, often toward career goals. Home, then, may not have been an embodiment of security and family, but more the embodiment of self-accomplishment. Owning one's own home can become a symbol of life accomplishment. The meaning of home reflected one's own work or other accomplishments, rather than functioning both practically and symbolically as a family home.

Home

"Home," like "motherhood," is a constructed source for social norms and the construction of ideals. Mallett (2004) distinguishes among several concepts of home: (1) home as a physical place or structure, where the assumption is that spatial organization restricts or encourages interaction of inhabitants; (2) as relational space, where home is constructed as part memory, part social relationship, and part idealization; (3) as a haven or private sphere; or (4) home as linked to family, which can include one's birth home or the place where one's extended family lives.

Mallett provides a very thorough discussion of "home" in the broad sense, but does not distinguish the possible differences in how "home" may be experienced differently by men and women.

In considering women and home, it is important to recognize that women historically had little autonomy within the home precisely because of its "private" nature (Holmes, 2009). They experienced control by their fathers until able to either work or marry and then control by their husbands (Browne, 1998; Darke, 1994). As married women, domestic violence often went unrecognized since marital disputes were considered within the "private" sphere of home (Gelles, 1985). Ironically, although women have been traditionally seen as the center of a "home," they often had little or no power within this place. Straight (2005, p.1), in writing about how women experience home, suggests that "the modernist idea of home as stable center and domestic virtue often assumes women as the very embodiment of that center while men offer the financial support to enable women to uphold home's ideal qualities." Straight (2005) is specifically interested in how women use stories to create and claim "home," even though the idealized notion of home may be unattainable. Although Straight describes "home" as an imagined state more than a lived reality, the act of telling or writing about home allows one to experience home simply through the telling. In other words, "I can experience a sense of home when I construct a story about home."

POSITIONING

Positioning Theory

As noted earlier, we draw our concept of environmental positioning from the larger psychological and cultural framework of positioning theory (Harré & Moghaddam, 2003; Harré & van Langenhove, 1999). In addition, we define the self as the "culturally constituted individual" (Rubinstein & de Medeiros, 2005, p. 61) who acts as the mediator and interpreter of experience (Herzog & Markus, 1999). Important components of the self are first, continuity and permanence, or the sense of having $\underline{a}$ self; second, discriminative relevance or the ability to distinguish one's self from other selves; and third, biographical meaningfulness in reference to the memories that one has of a past and the relevance that these past memories and experiences have to the present and the future (Rubinstein & de Medeiros, 2005, p. 61). Identity includes a portion of the larger notion of the self, but is less encompassing than the self-concept as a whole. Identity describes how a person views himself or herself and how others view that person (Cain, 1991). We note that identity is not a singular concept; one can have multiple simultaneous identities, some of which are chosen and managed by the person (e.g., choice of clothing, mannerisms, participation in selected groups) and some of which have been attached to a person through some aspect of the larger cultural context (e.g., race, ethnicity, age, gender, sexual orientation, socioeconomic status) and are externally defined (Browne, 1998; de Medeiros, 2005; Nelson, 2001; Tappan, 2000). Like the self, identity is culturally established (Bruner, 1990; Goffman, 1959; Nelson, 2001).

Positioning theory developed as a dynamic response to overreliance on the "static" concept of roles (Harré & Moghaddam, 2003; Harré & van Langenhove, 1999). Harré and others argued that the notion of roles was not able to explain how actors in a social situation were able to continuously alter their presentations based on their perceptions of how they were being positioned within the social situation. It seemed too simple a notion to assume that a social actor would remain within the confines of a role; instead, he or she would rather use aspects of a role, or abandon a role altogether if needed, depending on the situation. The social meaning of a given encounter will depend on where each participant "positions" himself or herself within the conversation. Position is not a "given." Rather, participants may find themselves negotiating for the position they desire and may not always be successful in doing so.

Narrative positioning was meant to explain something more complex and more reactive that was at work. Participants may continue to change their narrative positions based on how the conversation is unfolding. Davies and Harré (1990) present an example of two colleagues—a male and female—who are in a foreign city, looking for a pharmacy. The female colleague is ill. After they learn that there are no pharmacies nearby, the male colleague states: "I'm sorry to have dragged you all this way when you are not well," to which the female colleague responds, "You didn't drag me. I chose to come." An argument subsequently ensures. In the analysis, the male colleague's position can be interpreted as helpful, paternalistic, or other depending on the position of the conversational partner, while the female colleague's position could be interpreted as empowering, defensive, or representing a variety of other descriptors. This example illustrates that one's position can be intentional or unintentional; one's position may change; and positions may be interpreted differently by different participants. The strength in examining the interaction comes from considering how these different positions present themselves and what these positions say about the views of self and identity expressed by the participants.

Environmental Positioning

The concept of environmental positioning places positioning theory and narrative positioning in the context of the home environment and helps to describe the mutual creation of meaning between the actor living in a given home environment (e.g., a childless older woman) and the observer (the researcher). Environmental positioning suggests that selves and identities are expressed in various intentional and unintentional ways through the home environment that, analogous to a position in conversation, may be interpreted differently by different participants and by different parties at different times. In addition, the positions held by the person within the home (e.g., the homeowner) and the visitor (e.g., research interviewer) may change and may be interpreted differently by the other. The key in environmental positioning is that the environment itself—the objects, the structures, even the location—all contribute to the positioning of the actors and observers.

In the large body of work on the meaning of home in old age, emphasis is placed on the various symbols associated with home and their subsequent meanings. Several have suggested that personal objects become a form of the expressed self in older age (Rubinstein, 1987; Schwartz, Brent, & Barry, 1996). From an environmental positioning perspective, we are concerned with more than just the objects themselves, but instead are also interested in how the actor/subject positions him or herself in relation to these objects, physically, metaphorically, and narratively. Physical positioning implies the actual location of the objects in the environment in relation to the actor/subject. Metaphoric position refers to the symbolism that can be derived from the object and its placement. Narrative refers to the stories the informants tell about their homes and the objects within.

For example, from an environmental positioning perspective, family photographs placed on a prominent shelf may invoke different meanings, depending on the position of the actor. For the outside visitor, presence of family photos may be interpreted as a testament to the individual's commitment to family. Conversely, lack of such photos may be viewed as deviant or as suggesting that family is not important. For the individual, the display might be, on one level, a recognition of the cultural expectations that one must display such photos in particular places—on the fireplace mantel, on the wall, on the refrigerator—to be considered "normal," even though the pictures themselves may hold less personal meaning for that individual than other items— an old book that invokes a memory, other photos (informal snapshots) that are not as esthetically pleasing or culturally appropriate, a piece of clothing or jewelry that holds special meaning. In addition, in the presence of a researcher, family photographs may take a more significant position relative to the individual as they may help to explain some parts of his or her past more easily than a narrative would. Having an opportunity to show something like a photograph, tell a story about its meaning and importance, and let the researcher see where it is placed within the home environment adds more meaning than either seeing or telling alone.

In perhaps a less obvious example, orderliness (or lack therefore) may be a type of positioning as well. The person whose home is filled with stacks of books may be positioning him or herself as an engaged learner, but may be positioned by the observer as "unorganized" or lacking in other ways.

What we are suggesting is that relationships contain, in some way, the totality of possible future or previous relationships as options. The relationship between person and environment is not singular but multi-layered. The placement or display of photos (or stacks of books) is likely not a singular act that has only one meaning; instead, there are multiple layers of complexity.

As mentioned earlier with narrative positioning, one's position may be intentional or unintentional and is not necessarily fixed. The important aspect of environmental positioning is that meanings within the environment are relational, fluid, and often contradictory. There are the physical items (e.g., couch, kitchen table) which, as with language, people select and place using a known set of environmental codes associated with objects and uses of space. For example, environmental rules may include ideas such as: a couch belongs in a living room or den and is used for sitting and conversing and/or reclining; a living room is for entertaining others and is arranged to maximize socializing to include proximity of chairs, placement of end tables, and so on. How that person uses the cultural store of object and space rules—whether adhering to or deviating from convention—becomes a discursive process or form of expression through which the self can be made known.

In addition to the physical aspects of home (e.g., the actual structure, personal objects, and surrounding neighborhood) present in environmental positioning, there are relational aspects between biographical past, present, and anticipated future. For example, one's current view of home could be seen in contrast to or opposition to his or her childhood home (e.g., current advantages or disadvantages of then versus now), as a stepping stone from the past to the future, where the present is viewed as temporary, or as a linear progression from past, through the present, to the future, whatever that future might be.

Three Case Examples

We have selected three women to present as case examples in our wider discussion of the meaning of home for childless older women. These cases were selected from a larger study on childless older women and were chosen since they illustrate nuanced symbols of home and self. The focus of the four-year study was on the meaning of childlessness and generativity in later life for childless older women. We recruited and interviewed 180 women who described themselves as childless. About half of our sample were African American, half were White. In addition, approximately half were between age 65 and 79 years of age; half were aged 80 or older. Each woman participated in three face-to-face interviews, lasting about 90 minutes each, and was asked to discuss her life story, views on not having children, meaningful aspects of her current life, and other areas important to her. We selected three women from the larger sample to present as cases, based on methods described by Yin (2003). Yin argues that case examples are effective when the broad goals of the study have been defined but when an observed social phenomenon is not clearly understood. Cases therefore should bring some previously unknown or little understood perspective to the larger question at hand. In our study, the three case examples illustrate the concept of environmental positioning in three slightly different ways. We note that the women differ in age, race, retirement status (working, retired with pension, retired with no pension), type of residence (informant-owned house, military retirement community, housing-authority subsidized retirement community) and location (e.g., city versus suburb). We include our three informants' year of birth, since the historical context in which they were born and grew into adulthood is an important part of how their experiences are constructed.

The first woman, Ms. Day, was a widowed, 79-year-old African American woman (born in 1930) who owned a row home[1] in a large mid-Atlantic city in the United States. The second, Ms. George, was an 89-year-old European American (born in 1921) who never married, retired from the military, and lived in a housing community exclusively for retired military personnel. The third, Ms. Wallace, was a 77-year-old European American (born in 1934). She was a former office worker who never married and currently lived in a government-subsidized housing community for older adults in a suburban area. For each woman, we use environmental positioning to view how she creates meaning(s) for home through its physical space and temporal relationships.

Ms. Day

Ms. Day lived in a two-storey row home in a high-crime area of a large mid-Atlantic city. She had a small pension from factory work she did most of her life and currently held a part-time job as a secretary for a public agency: "the dream job" she said she was able to obtain only recently, when she was in her late 50s. Inside, floor and furniture spaces were covered in a seeming disarray of knickknacks, stuffed animals, dolls, photos to be hung, and clothing folded in stacks. The couch and sitting chairs in the main living room area were covered with protective plastic. This, combined with the items stacked upon them, suggested that this room was not used socially and instead functioned simply as an entryway to the kitchen and the upstairs. The kitchen, located in the back of the row home, was where Ms. Day spent most of her time. She had a small television on a shelf across from three seats at the kitchen table. The kitchen table had a telephone in the middle, knickknacks, picture frames, and a collection of salt and pepper shakers, letters, and other items. Ms. Day mentioned early in the interviews that she was proud that she had a friend, a woman, who lived in the upstairs bedroom. The friend, Ms. Williams, was a prominent political figure in the local community. Ms. Day explained that she let Ms. Williams live with her without paying rent. Having such a well-known local celebrity live with her was presented by the informant as a testament to Ms. Day's success and generosity.

Ms. Day described herself as someone able to beat the odds to get things done. She said, "I have been around people that always say, 'Well, you can't do this and you can't do that.' But I went on back to school and showed them that I could do, you know? I was able to get this house as a single person and I've been here since 1984 [after her husband's death]." The idea of buying the house as a single woman figured very prominently in the interviews. When the interviewer asked the question, "What in your life do you think will outlive you?" Ms. Day responded, "This house."

In telling her life story, Ms. Day said she had grown up on a "small street like I'm in now," with a mother, sister, and brother who were on welfare until her brother finished school and found a job. She described her childhood as having "a lot of love in our house." Ms. Day married her high school boyfriend to "get away from home." She was married for 19 years until her husband died. Although she said early in one interview that she had wanted children but was never able to get pregnant, she later confided that, actually, she had not wanted them. She said, "For one thing, I never liked housework and I knew if you had children, you had to be doing this and that." She also said that she never liked being married because her husband wanted her to stay home and keep house but she "insisted on working." Her husband ended up being responsible for the housework and, after he died, her mother and brother moved in with her and took over cleaning. Ms. Day even felt that being tied to the house through housework led to a shorter life expectancy. She said that the older people she knew as a child "had a much more inactive life, really, because a lot of them never worked. They were there to take care of the house and the husband worked and they raised the children. But the [way things are] today, the people live longer."

In looking back at her life, Ms. Day described feeling a great sense of accomplishment. She said:

> My mother, we didn't have much. She had one house dress. She would wash it at night and hang it over the line over the stove and get up in the morning, iron it, and put it on. And one pair of shoes. We used to go to school with paper in our shoes because they had no soles. But she always said, "Whatever you have, keep it clean. You never know when you might fall out in the street and have to go the hospital." But now, you know, I just sit back and I look and I think, "I got more shoes now than I'll ever wear, more clothes than I'll ever wear. . . . It just goes to how, how far you come."

Using an environmental positioning approach, we can see the multiple decorative items stacked throughout the house in contrast to her mother's lack of possessions. The items are in many ways symbols of success and accomplishment. For the observer to position Ms. Day as "messy" or "disorganized" would be to overlook a key part of how her environmental choices speak to her concept of self as someone with a "dream job" and "more clothes than she'll ever wear." Her excess is her success.

Ms. Day's sense of accomplishment (and her dislike of housework) is also clearly symbolized in her house/home. The permanence of the physical structure of the house, something that will outlive her, illustrates its strength. It is also the culmination of her working, earning money that she was able to save to eventually buy the house. Because she owned the house, she was able to offer her politician friend a place to stay in her *home*. House and home converge at this point to be both a physical place and an emotional idea. Having such an important guest further manifests her success. She also credits the house and her home—through her work—for her longevity.

She describes her childhood home as one filled with love despite the hardships and she has created, in her older age, a place where people, such as her own mother and brother and Ms. Williams, are welcome. She now extends that sense of welcome to her house guest, positioning her home and surroundings as a place that others may share.

Ms. George

Ms. George lived in a dorm-like room in a retirement community specifically for people with prior military service. The rooms were approximately 12 feet by 12 feet and contained a small single bed, a chair, and a small desk. The room also had an adjacent private bathroom. Unlike most retirement communities where women comprise over 75% of the residents, less than 10% of the 800 residents in this community were women, because of the military service requirements for all residents, even married couples. Where Ms. Day's home exemplified permanence-as-accomplishment, the entitlement to live in this community through a lifetime of service symbolized success to Ms. George.

Ms. George enlisted in the Navy in 1942 at age 21 after seeing a billboard advertisement that said "Uncle Sam Needs You." When she went home to tell her parents, she said, "Dad looked at me and I think if looks could have killed, I would have been dead on the spot. However, he said, 'You're 21, you can do what you want to do, but you're going to be sorry.' And I always say, 'I was so sorry I stayed for 23 years.'" She described the military as giving her more freedom than she had at home with an overprotective father. Her father would not let his older daughters attend high school since he said they only needed to know how to run a house and raise a family. Although her father finally relented and acquiesced to Ms. George's request to go to school, she said it was mostly because he did not think she was pretty enough for marriage. Later, when she got an office job, she said her father cried because he viewed this as an embarrassment to his family since it pointed to his inability as a father to keep his daughter home.

Ms. George never married and said that in later life, her biggest regret was in knowing that today it was no longer necessary for a woman to be married to have a baby. She talked about the stigma of unwed mothers she witnessed with friends who had become pregnant, and nieces who were kicked out of their homes. She became the "go to" person and offered support and housing to pregnant women in need.

Throughout her military and post-military career as an office administrator, Ms. George lived in several houses she purchased, usually because of family need. For example, she purchased a home and moved to the Midwest at one point to care for her adult disabled sister and even purchased a home for her parents so they could move closer to her siblings. She also moved into the military retirement community several years earlier as a way of convincing a friend, who was in the early stages of dementia, to move in as well and be cared for. Ms. George mentioned that this was the third time she had moved back into the retirement community, and that she liked it specifically because there was flexibility. She described it as a place where you only needed to shut the door behind you and not worry. It was also a place where she could connect with women who had similar life experiences.

Ms. George found meaning in her current house, also her home, through its military status as exemplified in her environmental positioning. She sat in an easy chair, across from a small desk. To her left, on the wall, was a photograph of herself in uniform early in her career. Next to the photograph was a shadow box, which is typically presented to military personnel when they retire. Shadow boxes are small glass-enclosed cases that usually contain a U.S. flag, a flag from their service branch (e.g., Navy), and the medals and awards that they earned throughout their military career. Ms. George's shadow box held what she said was the only military ribbon that women were able to earn at that time. The rest of her room was sparsely decorated.

By joining the military in her early 20s, Ms. George left a controlling father in a small Eastern United States town and traveled to big cities around the world. The military also trained her for a "respectable" career (female office workers at the time were considered to be "loose" women she said) and gave her a source of income in retirement, something that many working women her age did not have. The military retirement community where she lived had a sliding scale of payment: one-third of a resident's income, regardless of what that income was. With that one-third income payment, residents were offered a continuum of care from independent living to nursing home care. Ms. George therefore had no concerns about her financial future. When we asked her if she had enough money to make ends meet, she said, "I have more than I've ever had. Yeah, because, you know there was always a home to keep up and this to buy and that to buy and now I just spend money, uh, I say I don't even look at the price I just buy it, like I did the computer, I didn't even look at the price."

In thinking about her current house/home, she said what brought her the most satisfaction was that "I have nobody to boss me around; I can just come and go as I please and do what I want to." While personal autonomy is certainly a concept that has been addressed in the literature on retirement living, Ms. George's explanation seems to speak to some bigger notion of gendered autonomy regarding house/home. Within the confines of her room, she alone had choice in what to display and how to display it, just like in the military housing units she lived in while in the Navy. The fact that her current room was similar to rooms she would have had while on active duty, and that her prior service gave her the privilege of living here in later life, allowed her to position herself as in control of her past, present, and future.

It is interesting to note that the community does maintain rather strict rules. No one is allowed to cook in their rooms. All meals must be taken in the dining hall, which seats 800 people, and only during certain hours. In addition, all residents receive an automated "check in" call at 6:00 a.m., which they must answer or else staff will be sent to check on their well-being. The autonomy and freedom she feels in this particular living environment, and presumably her familiarity with military rules, make the structure advantageous rather than inconvenient. This structure is also one which she chose, unlike in her childhood home where the structure and limits imposed by her father were beyond her control.

Lack of personal decorations such as family photographs or non-military mementos also underscores the military life represented in her home. It is not that she does not have a family—siblings, nieces, and nephews—to whom she is close. They are simply not a core part of her home environment. Even the craftwork for which she is known throughout her retirement community and family—creating small statues out of old jewelry—is not displayed anywhere in her room, suggesting again that her control of space and her life are what represent who she is.

Ms. Wallace

Ms. Wallace said she reluctantly moved into a subsidized housing community after nearly becoming homeless eight years earlier. As an office worker throughout her life, she earned low wages and did not have a pension of any kind nor any money saved. The community where she lived, built within the last ten years, was located in a safe suburban neighborhood within walking distance of several stores and shops. Although part of federally subsidized Housing and Urban Development (HUD) housing and therefore officially non-denominational, the properties were managed by a large religious organization. Ms. Wallace did not like where she lived and found the residents and staff to be unfriendly. In the first few minutes of being interviewed, she said:

> My biggest problem with living here, I've lived here about 8 years now, is that I didn't really choose to live here. I really didn't have any

other place to go. I lived in the city. I thought it would be good to get out to here, the country life and all sorts of good things—the animals, the air. It was shocking to me that the manager here . . . I was very shocked to find out that he had been a priest. I'm not Catholic. I had never been around a priest in my life. I thought, "Oh, that's good, he's going to care about us and be very spiritual. But that's not the case at all. He can be hard and cynical . . ."

Ms. Wallace's mention of her shock at learning that the administrator was a former priest speaks to her views about what she saw as a callous and unfeeling place that was unresponsive to her needs as a person.

Many of Ms. Wallace's challenges with her apartment stemmed from the lack of space to accommodate her furniture and books. She said she had been repeatedly reprimanded by the manager at the annual housing inspections for having too many belongings according to staff. She described the inspections as:

Once a year they inspect your apartment to make sure you're really neat and clean and tidy. That you're not bringing in bugs, mice and roaches. They don't want you to have too much stuff in your apartment. It goes from one extreme to another. Some people hardly have anything here. Some people have too much. And I'm one of the too much. They try to give me a hard time about it, but I can't live with less. I didn't come here to just sit around on a couch and have a table and a chair and a bed. I brought a big desk, and I have a computer, and I have a lot of books. I have permission for them. My wall is lined with books. And they weren't wild about that, because they see things like that as fire hazards . . . We had a HUD inspector who came in and didn't find one thing wrong with my apartment.

She mentioned several times that the books and the desk were extremely important to her; she liked reading nonfiction and researching various topics on holistic health. Although neither the books nor her other belongings were tied to her past, per se, they were tied to her sense of identity and spoke to who she saw herself as a person. She said that by her own choice, she had nothing from her family or childhood in her apartment because of bad memories. Instead, the books and desk were linked to her present and imagined future self as a writer living in a log cabin in West Virginia. It is interesting to note in imagining her future, Ms. Wallace positions herself in a log cabin in the West Virginian mountains, despite having never visited West Virginia nor having either the health (she had difficulty walking and breathing) or the money (she was totally dependent on government subsidies) to make such a move possible. Her imagined future home would be her accomplishment, the culmination of her love of reading, learning, and writing. Rather than imagining a home from the past that offered security and affirmation, Ms. Wallace imagined a home of the future.

Ms. Wallace described her childhood as having grown up in a small rural town with an alcoholic father and stern disciplinary mother. After withdrawing from college because of poor grades, she moved eastward and never returned home. She said:

> I did go back home after college and I wanted to come out East. I felt I just, I have to get away from home, I don't want to be in this small [Midwestern] town. I was extremely frustrated. I thought, even if I don't get through college, I am not going to stay in my hometown. I want to get out into the world. I want to get to the East Coast and I'm still going to find a way to travel eventually although I never did that.

She never returned home, not even when her mother asked her to move home to provide care after a stroke, or when her mother eventually died. Ms. Wallace explained that she had no intention of putting her life on hold and returning home to provide care for her mother and, at that point, cut off all ties with her sisters and brother. She does not know if they are still living.

Ms. Wallace attributed other negative thoughts of her childhood home to the fact that her father would not let her date, and that she was embarrassed by where she lived. She said:

> But I was just so terribly caught, you know, caught that I wasn't allowed to date and we were not living in the greatest section of town. Actually it wasn't that bad, it was just, it was really middle class but a little lower middle class and it was across the tracks and the, the really better people lived on the other side of the tracks on better streets. And that really bothered me a lot and I felt they didn't want; they wouldn't want to date me because I don't live in the right end of town.

She was embarrassed by her family's lack of means then and expressed similar dissatisfaction with her current apartment which was government subsidized.

Ms. Wallace spent some time during the interviews talking about how her childhood and the events that she linked with home have affected where she is now. She said:

> So the reason I'm going back over all this is because I know it has so much to do with where I really am now and now that I'm not

doing very much of anything else except existing I can reflect upon all of this. And I realize a lot of it is, uh, responsible for where I am today. We think, once we get out of the house, get away from our parents, go to college or whatever it is we want to do, we're on our own now and we're going to be making all of our decisions and you don't, this, that's been the hardest thing for me my whole life. And we don't realize that, that all these things in our background are influencing us still today.

She then somewhat contradicts herself by saying:

So many times I tell myself, "you haven't gotten yourself any-where." It seems that successful people are pushed and driven at home. Although I hear of other people who were extremely success-ful and for who that was not the case. They just did it all on their own.

Ms. Wallace seems unsure whether she views herself as a survivor, as someone who, despite a poor childhood and lifetime of struggles to make ends meet, managed to live in a nice place surrounded by things she enjoyed; or a failure, someone who could have pushed herself fur-ther and be living in her dream home, a log cabin.

It is her imagined home in West Virginia on which she currently places her hope. When asked why she chose West Virginia, she said:

The best word I can come up with right now is all that holistic activity. I think it's wonderful and all that they do and how they physically workout and mentally workout and, you know, have their own gar-dens. I just think that is so wonderful, I would love to live that way . . . I realize I'm building it up because the truth of it is I don't know very much about West Virginia. I might get there and feel oh, this has just all been a dream, this is not the way it really is. But I would really like to try . . . It's supposed to be a lot less expensive and people are a lot more natural and real . . . Someone said, "What if you don't like it, what are you going to do?" I don't know, I guess I would just come back. No, I would just make the best of it.

It is the promise of something "real, natural" on which Ms. Wallace places her dreams of the future, in contrast to her present, even though it is unlikely that she will ever see her dream realized because of her financial and physical challenges.

DISCUSSION

In this chapter, we introduced the concept of environmental positioning as a means through which "home" and its potential meaning(s) could be better understood. By focusing on three older women who did not have children, we hoped to separate the strong connection between home and children that currently dominates most discussions of home in older age. The goal was to disentangle the meaning of home from reliance on symbolic interpretation of meaning alone. Also, our intention was to examine "home" as expressions of self. Environmental positioning allowed us to consider the physical aspects of home (items, the actual house or apartment), relational aspects of personal objects and of time (e.g., past, present, future); and focus on the narratives that provide insight into the physical and relational. Given this, it is clear that the meaning of home itself is fluid and conditional but at the same time can hold secure meaning, depending on the position of the social actors involved, which varies over time and condition. This reflects the ability of symbols to directly and strongly represent particular, secure meanings but at the same time to be nuanced, floating, and to have multiple meanings. Further, given pronatalist attitudes, it would be easy (and mistaken) to view these homes as somehow "less" since there is no presence of children and, in two of the three cases, little presence of family of any kind, through either pictures or objects that have been passed down. To assume that family is a key symbol found as a core part of the meaning of home would mean to privilege an assumption about symbols that may not apply to these women, and to disregard others, such as the link between the women's views of home and their tie to their perceptions of personal success.

It is also important to consider the events shaping the women's life courses and how they may affect the current meaning of home for them. The women in our chapter came into adulthood during a time in which few opportunities outside of the family existed for women. Jobs were often menial and low paying. Women whose lives differed from the societal ideal of being married with children were stigmatized. Given these challenges, home ownership by women was difficult. For each of the three women, their current residence—by choice or by circumstances—figured prominently in her self-concept. How she placed herself within this residence—as proud achiever in the cases of Ms. Day and Ms. Williams or as yet-to-succeed in the case of Ms. Wallace—greatly informed the meaning that home held for her. The temporal aspect of biographical past, present, and imagined future play an important role in the creation of meaning. Where past choices were important to all three women's current lives, dreams for the future, especially in Ms. Wallace's case, were what made the present meaningful.

Implications for Policy and Practice

Taking a more holistic view of the home environment and ways in which meanings are constructed is an important interpretive strategy for future work on this setting. Rather than relying on traditional explanations of symbols and their meanings, for example, defining home as a specific place for family and children, one should consider the possibility that the person's position within an environment, whether fixed or shifting, helps to illuminate how he/she finds meaning within home. For some women, the mere fact of having a home of their own that they bought and paid for is itself a singular accomplishment, regardless of the specific form of the home or what possessions are represented there. And even in such a stance, a person may take a number of fixed or varied positions about what other meanings of that home might be. In determining the range of such positions and their attendant meanings, one might find differences between older adults and others that may be critical in understanding the use of space, the nature of physical houses and the meanings of home.

Another implication relates to the varying definitions of house, home, and place. We strongly feel that it is unrealistic to separate the various meanings of the dwelling such as house, home, and place entirely, and that they are all linked. They essentially represent different positions that may be taken by the person at various times in relating to a home environment. To tease them apart is an academic exercise that moves away from the manner in which individuals actually relate to home environments at different times and under different conditions.

NOTES

1. A row home describes a type of housing that has its own outside entrance, is typically two to three stories, and shares a wall with one or more neighboring units. Row homes in Ms. Day's neighborhood were built in the early 1900s in a working class area.

ACKNOWLEDGMENTS

Data reported in this paper derive from a study titled, "Lifestyles and Generativity of Childless Older Women" (K. de Medeiros and R. Rubinstein, Co-PIs). This research is supported by the National Institute of Aging Grant Number AG03061-01A1. We are grateful to the NIA for its support of our research.

REFERENCES

Browne, C. (1998). *Women, feminism, and aging.* New York, NY: Springer Publishing Company.

Bruner, J. (1990). *Acts of meaning.* Harvard University Press: Cambridge.

Cain, C. (1991). Personal stories: Identity acquisition and self-understanding in Alcoholics Anonymous. *Ethos. 19*(2): 211–253.

Calasanti, T. M., & Slevin, K. F. (2001). *Gender, social inequalities, and aging.* Lanham, MD: Alta Mira Press.

Carder, P., & Hernandez, M. (2004). Consumer discourse in assisted living. *Journals of Gerontology Series B Psychological Sciences and Social Sciences, 59*(2), S58–S67.

Csíkszentmihályi, M., & Rochberg-Halton, E. (1981). *The meaning of things: Domestic symbols and the self.* Boston, MA: Cambridge University Press.

Darke, J. (1994). Women and the meaning of home. In R. Gilroy, & R. Woods (Eds.), *Housing women* (pp. 11–30). New York, NY: Routledge.

Davies, B., & Harré, R. (1990). Positioning: the discursive production of selves. *Journal for the Theory of Social Behavior, 20*(1), 43–63.

de Medeiros, K. (2005). The complementary self in old age. *Journal of Aging Studies: 19*(1): 1–13.

Dykstra, P., & Hagestad, G. (2007). Roads less taken—Developing a nuanced view of older adults without children. *Journal of Family Issues,* 1275–1310.

Gaugler, J. E. (2005). Family involvement in residential long-term care: A synthesis and critical review. *Aging & Mental Health, 9*(2), 105–118.

Gelles, R. J. (1985). Family violence. *Annual Review of Sociology, 11,* 347–367.

Goffman, E. (1959). *The presentation of self in everyday life.* Garden City, NY: Doubleday and Company.

Harré, R., & Moghaddam, F. (2003). *The self and others: Positioning individuals and groups in personal, political and cultural contexts.* Westport, CT: Praeger.

Harré, R., & van Langenhove, L. (1999). *Positioning theory: Moral contexts of intentional action.* Malden, MA: Blackwell Publishers.

Heaton, T. B., Jacobson, C. K., & Holland, K. (1999). Persistence and change in decisions to remain childless. *Journal of Marriage and Family, 61*(2), 531–539.

Hebl, M. R., King, E. B., Glick, P., Singletary, S. L., & Kazama, S. (2007). Hostile and benevolent reactions toward pregnant women: complementary interpersonal punishments and rewards that maintain traditional roles. *Journal of Applied Psychology, 92*(6), 1499–1511. doi:10.1037/0021-9010.92.6.1499

Herzog, A. R., & Markus, H. R. (1999). The self-concept in life span and aging research. In V. Bengston & K. W. Schaie (Eds.), *Handbook of theories on aging* (pp. 227–252). New York: Springer Publishing.

Holmes, M. (2009). *Gender and everyday life.* New York, NY: Routledge.

Kelly, E., & Dobbin, F. (1999). Civil rights law at work: sex discrimination and the rise of maternity leave policies. *American Journal of Sociology, 105*(2), 455–492.

Koropeckyj-Cox T. (2002). Beyond parental status: Psychological well-being in middle and old age. *Journal of Marriage and the Family, 64,* 957–971.

Koropeckyj-Cox, T., & Call, V. (2007). Characteristics of older childless persons and parents: cross-national comparisons. *Journal of Family Issues, 28*(10), 1362–1414.

Koropeckyj-Cox, T., Pienta, A., & Brown, T. (2007). Women of the 1950s and the "normative" life course: the implications of childlessness, fertility timing, and marital status for psychological well-being in late midlife. *International Journal of Aging & Human Development, 64,* 299–330.

Letherby, G. (2002). Childless and bereft? Stereotypes and realities in relation to 'voluntary' and 'involuntary' childlessness and womanhood. *Sociological Inquiry, 72*(1), 7–20.

Mallett, S. (2004). Understanding home: a critical review of the literature. *The Sociological Review, 52,* 62–89.

McDowell, L. (1999). *Gender, identity and place: Understanding feminist geographies.* Minneapolis, MN: University of Minnesota Press.

Nelson, H. L. (2001). *Damaged identities, narrative repair.* Ithaca, NY: Cornell University Press.

Park, K. (2002). Stigma management among the voluntarily childless. *Sociological Perspectives, 45*(1), 21–45.

Rapoport, A. (2005). On using "home" and "place". In G. D. Rowles, & H. Chaudhury (Eds.), *Home and identity in late life: International perspectives* (pp. 343–360). New York, NY: Springer Publishing Company.

Rempel, J. (1985). Childless elderly: what are they missing? *Journal of Marriage and Family, 47*(2), 343–348.

Richards, S. C. (2003). Infertility around the globe: new thinking on childlessness, gender and reproductive technologies. *Medical Anthropology, 17*(4), 515–517.

Rubinstein, N. J. (2005). Psychic homelands and the imagination of place: a literary perspective. In G. D. Rowles, & H. Chaudhury (Eds.), *Home and identity in later life: International perspectives* (pp. 111–142). New York, NY: Springer Publishing Company.

Rubinstein, R. L. (1987). The significance of personal objects to older people. *Journal of Aging Studies, 1*(3), 225–238.

Rubinstein, R. L., & de Medeiros, K. (2005). Home, self and identity. In G. D. Rowles, & H. Chaudhury (Eds.), *Home and identity in later life: International perspectives* (pp. 47–62). New York, NY: Springer Publishing Company.

Schwartz, B., Brent, R., & Barry, D. (1996, August). Priceless, meaningful, and idiosyncratic: Attachment to possessions. In J. L. Nasar, & B. B. Brown (Eds.), *Public and private places.* Proceedings of the Twenty-Seventh Annual Conference of the Environmental Design Research Association, Salt lake City, Utah, June 12–16.

Sixsmith, J. (1986). The meaning of home: an exploratory study of environmental experience. *Journal of Environmental Psychology, 6*(4), 281–298.

Solinger, R. (2005). Pregnancy and power: a short history of reproductive politics in America. New York, NY: New York University Press.

Straight, B. (2005). *Women on the verge of home.* New York, NY: State University of New York Press.

Tappan, M. B. (2000). Autobiography, mediated action and the development of moral identity. *Narrative Inquiry. 10*(1), 81–109.

Thomas, W. H. (1996). *Life worth living: How someone you love can still enjoy a nursing home: The Eden Alternative in action.* Acton, MA: VanderWyk & Burnham.

Yin, R. K. (2003). *Case study research: Design and methods* (3rd ed.). Thousand Oaks, CA: Sage.

PART III

Long-Term Care Environments

CHAPTER 5

The Complex Process of Becoming At-Home in Assisted Living

Malcolm P. Cutchin

EDITORS' INTRODUCTION

*The theme of the dynamism in the construction of home and place discussed by de Medeiros and her colleagues (Chapter 4) and the co-constitution of self and environment is reinforced by Cutchin in his consideration of **place integration**. Employing a Deweyan pragmatist perspective, Cutchin explores the diverse ways in which people become at-home following a move to assisted living. A key theme is the way in which place and home are defined in an ongoing manner by the actions and interactions of people with each other and with the environmental context. In exploring practical implications of this process, Cutchin emphasizes the role of transferred habits and the role of imagination and habits of thought in facilitating the process of accommodation through relocation and the ever ongoing process of place integration within a new setting. Providing illustrations through case studies, he illustrates how this is a process that some are more equipped to handle than others, but that nonetheless provides an important option for supportive intervention. Practical suggestions including an "integration handbook," peer mentoring, and professional intervention options are provided as opportunities for translating our emerging understanding of the process of place integration into an applied arena. In making these suggestions, Cutchin illustrates the critical role of education as a focal aspect of facilitating the transference of knowledge about the ways in which people experience place into practice and policy.*

THREE VIGNETTES

Ted was a month shy of his 90th birthday. A former editor for a university press, Ted was still doing some editorial work for pay and was working on an autobiography to leave to his family. He had lived in his assisted living residence for five years, since the building and organization were refurbished as a modern assisted living residence. Ted had moved over two dozen times in his life, but he had lived in his current community for several decades. He referred to moving as a "painful" experience and explained the process of downsizing in his recent past as especially so. Ted's primary motive for making the move to assisted living was to have "three meals a day prepared for me." He also wanted to feel more secure than he had felt alone in his six-room home. An unexpected benefit of moving to assisted living was being around others more often and developing new friendships, something Ted had not considered before moving. Those friendships were augmented with ongoing associations with friends and groups in the surrounding community. Even though his body was exhibiting the troubles of advanced age, Ted's active social life as well as his writing and editing provided him with meaning and purpose, and he was proud that he was still accomplishing such projects at his age. His success at making the most of his situation after the move to assisted living was notable.

Diana seemed an especially complex case, perhaps because of her distinct ability to reflect upon and articulate her experience before, during, and after her move to assisted living. An 81-year-old psychotherapist who was still practicing part-time, Diana had lived in her assisted living residence for two years. She moved there because of a health "scare" and general loneliness (she was divorced). Still very independent in behavior and thought, after two years in her residence Diana was not yet feeling settled. She had lived in several states and about ten residences during her life. One child lived in her city and the others were scattered about the world (New York, England, and Israel). Diana strongly identified with her Jewish heritage, and even though she was in that sense a minority in her residence—and at times felt other residents were slightly anti-Semitic—this was "not a problem" for her. Having grown up with prominent Jewish parents, a rabbi and school principal, Diana had always lived in integrated neighborhoods and did not want to live in a predominantly Jewish residence. The dynamics of her assisted living residence that bothered her and kept her thinking about another move were somewhat surprising. One was a conflict with the management over her right to practice therapy in the residence. Another was her dislike of residents' "resignation" with regard to their "assisted" status and dependence on staff. Yet another was her feeling of being patronized and other forms of ageism that she perceived in the residence. In spite of these issues, Diana believed her assisted living residence was a relatively good place to live. Nonetheless, she worried about becoming "resigned" herself, and felt "restlessness" about living in her congregate setting.

Rose did not seem an unhappy person by nature, but she seemed especially bitter about her situation in assisted living. She insisted that staff at her residence were very attentive, kind, and respectful and that she appreciated the health monitoring she received. But after living for two and a half years in her residence, Rose was still upset about her move. A widow whose only son had died several years earlier, Rose had lived her entire life in the Vermont community where her assisted living residence was located. She had moved very little in her lifetime. Not long after moving to a smaller home in her town, she had a heart attack and was hospitalized. Rose believed she was all but forced to move to assisted living and that the relocation had not been necessary. She was particularly "sick" about leaving her own house and "losing" all of her precious furniture, belongings, and the dog that was not allowed in her assisted living residence. Rose proudly shared photographs of her former house and furniture with visitors. Although she still maintained a driver's license and owned a car, she did not drive from the assisted living campus on a regular basis. She was still involved in her church, but had cut back on many of her responsibilities there. Some of her old friends from church now lived in the assisted living residence with her, but Rose was not well integrated into life in the residence. To her it was "very routine living." Much of her time was spent in her room with her cat.

These brief vignettes, developed from an National Institutes of Health (NIH)-funded research project aimed at understanding the role of assisted living in the aging-in-place process of frail older adults, conducted in rural Vermont as well as the Boston area, provide a glimpse of the experience I call "becoming at-home" in assisted living. Becoming at-home is important in the lives of all people, yet there are significant challenges for older adults who move and have to begin the process anew. Those challenges can compromise quality of life for the older person in assisted living or similar contexts. As the cases of Ted, Diana, and Rose indicate, becoming at-home is a holistic, continuous affair that varies by person, is both enjoyed and suffered, and includes the continuity of life before, during, and after the move. Unfortunately, becoming at-home in new residential contexts has not been adequately addressed in the gerontological literature to date. This is a surprising situation when one considers that becoming at-home is among the most significant of human experiences. To be at-home is to have the advantages and meanings that a positive relationship with home provides us: security, comfort, control, belonging, family, identity, and so on. This sought-after and cherished experience is difficult to understand. Part of the problem of understanding is the taken-for-granted character of becoming at-home. Another dimension is the complexity of the relationships at the heart of the experience. Yet another aspect is how to think about becoming at-home in a way that provides maximum insight for scholars and practitioners. Because in the early 21st century so many older people are moving to assisted living residences (also known as sheltered accommodation or residential care facilities) or similar types of homes, the question of how to work toward at-homeness in long-term care environments is of great relevance.

In this chapter, I reveal some of the most important dimensions and dynamics of becoming at-home for people who make this difficult transition late in life. The developing arena of assisted living research provides useful empirical clues about becoming at-home. Part of the journey is a conceptual synthesis in order to help us think more productively about the issue. Because of the particular theoretical orientation I bring to the problem, I emphasize becoming at-home as a never-ending effort that is central to happiness and life quality. How well the effort toward becoming at-home succeeds for older people is partially dependent on how older people and their care providers think about the process. It is also important to consider the role of persons who intervene to facilitate relocation to assisted living in old age. Thus, I will address the theoretical and the practical in this chapter in the hope of providing insights to both scholars and care providers.

HOME AS PLACE

There are various useful ways to understand the concept of home for those in later life, including sociological, anthropological, and psychological perspectives (Rowles & Chaudhury, 2005). While those disciplinary viewpoints are very useful, the experience of home is rooted most fundamentally in the geographical nature of home as place. Geographers have been concerned with the concept of place since antiquity, but modern geography only relatively recently regained this focus. For a certain type of modern geographer—the humanistic, phenomenological geographer—place is the most central of ideas. Place becomes the ontological basis of the everyday lifeworld and all that the lifeworld entails for emotional, cognitive, and pre-reflective meaning. Such importance in human experience suggests that place is worthy of significant and sustained inquiry. Moreover, this phenomenological position suggests that our relationship with place has both depth of meaning and characteristics that we can understand and use to make place more rewarding for experience. Place is saturated with both meaning and complexity, but this can be understood and used in practical ways.

But what of the concept of place as a way to understand home? I trust each reader of this chapter can agree that what she or he might call "home" also has the fundamental characteristics I have just ascribed to place. Yet another question arises. What do we consider to be "home"? Most often the term denotes the human-built structure in which we spend a significant proportion of our time and activity—time and activity that is uniquely work-related, restorative, familial, social, and personal. Other uses of "home" are possible, of course. We might consider our neighborhood, town, city, or country to be a component of home (Cuba & Hummon, 1991). The reason we consider each of those entities (places which exist at different geographic scales of experience) to be home is because of the feeling that each gives us. That feeling can be described as at-homeness. In the words of a phenomenological geographer, at-homeness is ". . . the usually unnoticed, taken-for-granted situation of being comfortable in and familiar with the everyday world" (Seamon, 1979, p. 70). Rowles (1983) has described the experience of at-homeness for older people using the related concept of "insideness" where the merging of self and place becomes significant for the experience of aging. Home, in other words, is *the* place of most significant attachment and meanings (Rowles, 1987). To be at-home, therefore, has much to do with the overall quality of life for all people, including older people. Those who are more vulnerable because of increasing frailty have even more at stake in at-homeness, because of that vulnerability.

PLACE TRANSITIONS AND HOME

Vulnerable or not, almost all people have to make at least one significant place transition during their lives; young and old alike move from one home to another. While there are many reasons for changing homes, including moves because of issues related to aging, all home transitions demand that an emplaced self must journey through displacement and back to emplacement (Chaudhury & Rowles, 2005). Such shifts into and out of home places can be wrenching, but not all are. Indeed, although the stability of home is often thought to be an important trait, the need to allow for movement and rest, as well as leaving home and coming home, are important aspects of experience and identity (Buttimer, 1980; Seamon, 1979). The displacement of self caused by a move appears to be a significantly distinct challenge for people who make place transitions.

The experience of place transitions, especially those that involve home, also should be considered within a broader context. Watkins and Hosier (2005) argue one's view of home is a life long process shaped by life long place relationships and social contexts. Furthermore, they argue that people use their personal view of home—shaped in part by their life course—to prepare for future life transitions. All people exist somewhere on a continuum of being at-home and being homeless (because of moves or potential moves), and one's state shifts over the life course. These insights about place transitions and home suggest that-home as place is not an objective, static thing. Home and the experience of it is a process that is both personal and social, intertwined with selfhood and with the larger social and historical contexts within which we live.

PLACE PROCESSES

It is commonplace to think of aging in terms of change of the individual, especially of her or his capacities. As we age, our bodies change and cause shifts in the processes that sustain well-being. As the body declines, other relationships to place that have often been noted in gerontology—such as place attachment or place identity—become more important (Rubinstein & Parmalee, 1992). Some scholars and practitioners appear to forget that aging in place should be equally concerned with change in place—change that is as powerful in shaping well-being as are bodily processes. Places are more than environmental contexts to be modified when one becomes frail—even if we include social and cultural elements as part of the environment. Places are holistic, dynamic, and meaningful entities with histories and evolutionary trajectories with which we have intimate relationships—and on which we depend. Various processes create those relationships and meanings, and among them are the way older adults negotiate change in place and change in their relationships with place (Heatwole Shank & Cutchin, 2010).

The move into a new place is a change that demands those relationships be recreated and negotiated. Rowles and Watkins (2003) suggested that in addition to the transference of belongings and their importance to symbolizing home and its meanings, the process involved in a successful move is even more complex. Inevitably, the older adult, family, and caregivers need to engage in place-making. Such place-making transforms a generic space into a place that has meaning for the older person and develops the "hearth" aspects of home. Rowles and Watkins (2003) also point to the need to reshape the habits tied to the old home via habituation into ones that fit the new home. These are valuable insights about becoming at-home in older age, and they are of relevance to the perspective I prefer to stress, place integration.

PLACE INTEGRATION

An alternative perspective on becoming at-home, "place integration" shares some traits with the aforementioned views. The basis for place integration is a combination of geographical theory and the philosophy of John Dewey, a meta-theoretical perspective we can call geographical pragmatism (Cutchin, 2001, 2008; Cutchin, Owen, & Chang, 2003). Focusing on the role of place as the social and physical medium of human experience, geographical pragmatism forms more of an action-based perspective on place experience. In this view, the continuity of person and place is paramount (Dewey, 1896/1998; Dewey, 1929/1989), and this means that the person-environment distinction is eschewed in favor of the relational unity of person and place (see Chapter 10). Also primary in this view is change, which is a continuing cause of challenges in the integrity or harmony of the person-place whole. Place integration emphasizes ongoing transactions that address instability and change (Garrison, 2001). For example, rather than thinking of the cross-sectional "fit" of person and environment by considering the key factors of each, the place integration perspective orients the researcher to the active process that connects person and place and continually transforms them and their relationship. Instead of asking how well an older adult fits with her new assisting living environment, place integration suggests we ask how the assisted living place (including social, symbolic, emotional, and aesthetic aspects) and person co-constitute each other in an ongoing way through constant change.

Dewey (1938/1986) suggested this transactional dimension of experience occurs as a process of inquiry and that the instabilities regularly faced in life were "undetermined" or "problematic" situations at the heart of such inquiry. Such situational challenges encourage imaginative thought and action by individuals or groups who experience them (Dewey, 1922/1957). The ideal result is the collaboration of people in activity that re-establishes positive relations in the situation (person-place whole). Such activity always entails morals and values, which are part of the meanings generated from the transformation of situational relations. Place integration is oriented toward an aesthetic vision or "end-in-view" that is part of new meanings created for those engaged in the situation.

It is worth noting that place integration is a process that describes various types of active, emerging relationships with place, from the community level (Cutchin, 1997) to the level of home in the traditional sense of residence (Cutchin, 2003). The need for some sense of being at-home necessitates a process of becoming at-home, which includes the outcomes of place attachment, insideness, hearth, and so on. Part of the story that follows portrays place integration as an ongoing process that is never complete, and not always successful, for those who enter assisted living. The important insight is that, if we can understand the structure and dynamics of the place integration process better, we can begin to devise better strategies for intervening to enhance attainment of a sense of becoming at-home and its associated well-being.

ASSISTED LIVING AND BECOMING AT-HOME

Assisted Living

A spectrum of residential care settings in the United States begins with independent living sites where few care services are offered and ends with nursing homes where 24-hour supervision and health care are provided (Leith, 2006). In the middle zone of this spectrum are assisted living residences (for a more detailed background and understanding of these places, see Golant & Hyde, 2008; Wilson, 2007). Assisted living offers key aspects of both ends of the spectrum. Those aspects include the provision of congregate housing and the availability of supportive services for functional, health, and social needs. Typically there are shared rooms and services for dining, exercise classes, and social activities. The common principles of assisted living include: (a) the provision of a homelike environment; (b) maximization of dignity, independence, autonomy, and privacy; (c) accommodation of residents' changing needs and preferences; and (d) minimizing required moves when needs increase (Wright, 2004). Interpretation of these principles and their implementation varies from state to state and site to site. Currently, more than 39,500 assisted living residences in the United States house more than one million older adults, and that population is expected to double by 2030 (Assisted Living Federation of America, 2009).

Some research has studied the characteristics of being at-home in settings similar to assisted living, such as congregate housing communities (Young, 1998) and life care and long-term care facilities (Hammer, 1999). Findings conveyed universal dimensions of feeling at-home in senior housing, such as autonomy, self-identity, close social relationships, mutual respect, comfort, involvement, and security. Leith (2006) studied the meaning of home for women who moved to congregate housing. She discovered that the meaning of home was expressed in three main themes: (a) as a reflection of a decision to make a new place, (b) as a deliberate result of the need to be "in place," and (c) as a reflection of the effort to stay placed after the move. Compared to the earlier research by Young (1998) and by Hammer (1999), Leith (2006) offered an emergent and fluid concept of home that was adjusted by older women in response to events and changes.

Others have pointed to the difficultly of becoming at-home in assisted living and similar settings (Cutchin, 2007a). Frank (2002, p. 17) argued that new assisted living residents typically experienced a state of "limbo," a "heightened sense of liminality," and a "suspended state" of transition that inhibited them from becoming at-home. I have also suggested (Cutchin, 2003) that the formation of home in assisted living reaches only an approximation of the previous state of being at-home. Some older persons perceive assisted living as a "way-station" on the route to a more institutional setting (Cutchin, 2004) and thereby are reluctant to form a homelike bond to the setting. Adding to the challenge of becoming at-home are ambiguities about what assisted living is, who it is for, and how people are to negotiate it. A common outcome is uncertainty for older adults and their families (Cutchin, 2004; Martin, Nancarrow, Parker, Phelps, & Regen, 2005). One reason for the ambiguity in assisted living comes from "blurring of boundaries" between home and institutional care (Dyck, Kontos, Angus, & McKeever, 2005; Milligan, 2006). While rules and regulations are necessary to the functioning of assisted living, those rules and regulations often run counter to the personal autonomy associated with home. Similar to this form of ambiguity, the blurring of private and public space is of concern. The result is a "semi-public" place (Milligan, 2006) where rules of private and public behavior and control are confounded.

Place Integration and Becoming At-Home in Assisted Living

As suggested above, assisted living does not necessarily offer an easy path to becoming at-home. The older person coming into assisted living has suffered displacement from a previous home with which deep attachment may have been formed. Transference of belongings from the old home to the new helps to begin a process of adjustment (Rowles & Ravdal, 2002), but transference is only a part of the larger process of place integration in assisted living. Place integration is more than a settling into place or finding an adequate person-place fit; it involves activities as a response to a new and changing situation. Those activities are almost always social, and therefore place integration should be considered primarily a social process. Integration also entails the creation of new meanings. Said most simply, integration is an ongoing process through which a meaningful relationship with place may be generated in assisted living (Cutchin, 2003; Cutchin, Owen, & Chang, 2003). In this section, we return to the cases of Ted, Diana, and Rose to more clearly understand that process.

Integration most distinctly involves the new assisted living place with which a person needs to develop a relationship. Integration may begin before any move is made, with a basis in whatever a priori knowledge or perceptions of a destination a person may hold, and it accelerates during displacement and transference as new information is gained. Ted's experience in assisted living was one in which much integration had been accomplished, yet Ted began the process by deciding to move at a time that seems to have been optimal for that integration—while he was still able to be actively engaged in place events. Ted's ability to maintain and develop active involvement in various affairs both inside (exercise classes, reading) and outside the assisted living residence (attending movies with friends, belonging to a Shakespeare society) was central to his integration with his assisted living place. Making friends was also helpful, but creating ongoing meaning in his life by being productive and involved with others appear to be most important to his integration process. Ted's engagement in his place, both inside and outside of his assisted living residence, maintained former aspects of place integration and helped develop others within the new setting. For Ted, more cohesive integration had taken time, but he had gotten better at it with practice.

Diana's integration process had worked somewhat differently. While we can say that she was partially integrated into her assisted living milieu, her restlessness and thoughts of moving were signs that her place integration process was not as successful as Ted's. Diana's conflicts with management and her view of some other residents as overly passive and resigned to dependence appeared to work as barriers to her integration. Diana was also active both outside and inside her assisted living environment, but she had not been able to make the place and her activities within it fully what she wanted them to be; and she had refused to bend her self-identity to fit the place. Ambivalence about her relationship with the assisted living residence was the result. Problematic aspects of place for Diana were related to her heritage and her expectations of what her new place should be. Trouble in negotiating and reshaping particularly difficult aspects of her relationship with her assisted living residence had reduced the success of her integration process.

Rose had experienced greater displacement, less transference, and less integration during her move to assisted living. The shock of her displacement from her former home and the lack of transferred meaning to her new residence echoed through her story of more than two years of the integration process. Whereas residents like Ted had been involved in social life and individual pursuits, Rose was stuck in perpetual recall of the move and its negative consequences. Rose was seemingly healthy in body, but in spirit she had not yet come to a happy relationship with her new residence. On the surface, Rose's experience suggests that if displacement is too severe and transference is too weak, then integration will never be as successful as it might otherwise be. That conclusion would be too simple. Rose spent little time trying to belong and participate in the affairs of her assisted living residence. While she regretted her lack of autonomy in the decision to move, she did not exert much agency in developing relationships with her new place. Her case starkly shows a principle of place integration that might be stated as follows: becoming engaged in the dynamics of place tends to foster becoming at-home. Becoming part of the dynamics of place in assisted living is not contingent on physical ability. Even older, frail adults can engage in social affairs and place making (McHugh & Mings, 1996) to integrate with place. Our findings suggest that the process takes some effort on the part of the older resident, but that residences can provide more or less successful opportunities and support for residents to become engaged.

Although not as displaced as Rose, an 89-year-old resident in a Boston assisted living residence, Phil, talked about how difficult it was to get used to his new setting. His comments speak to the process of integration.

> This is a different kind of place than what I've been used to . . . will I get to where I can [be comfortable in the setting]? I think so, but I wouldn't guarantee that prediction. . . . I've been to one or two of the lectures. . . . My guess is I'll begin to do more of that. Incidentally, I've thought about one of the pleasant changes of coming here. Just a few hundred yards down that way there is a little park where you can sit on the bench and see the boats on the river and the people on board; and on a Sunday afternoon, there are walkers, there are roller skaters, and that sort of thing.

Phil's statement points to the incremental and contingent nature of place integration. Phil's ability to find some type of engaged activity, even vicarious participation such as watching others boating and skating, became part of his integrative experience. As with Ted and Diana, Phil's active connections to the world outside the walls of his assisted living residence were an important complement to his place integration within the residence.

From the view of geographical pragmatism, the process of becoming at-home is a form of place integration. For all people, place integration never ceases. Everyone has to reintegrate with place on a continuing basis, because of the dynamics of the situation. As such, integration includes "the ongoing emergence of the person-place whole and the creative social effort to re-integrate the whole in a meaningful way when problems arise, compounded by an older adult's evolving situation" (Cutchin, 2003, p. 1079). Those problems need not be life-threatening to force integrative processes to occur. The range of challenges in becoming at-home includes minor to major issues. How capable one is in handling them, in terms of skills, self-efficacy, and support, makes all the difference in the level of integration accomplished.

EXTENSIONS AND PRACTICAL APPLICATIONS

Becoming at-home can be enhanced by understanding more about place integration and utilizing that knowledge within strategic interventions. Although place modification is an important aspect of such interventions, I want to emphasize here the role of skills, creative arts, and learning. Such an approach is consistent with Dewey's pragmatism and a place-integration approach.

Habits and Habitus in Becoming At-Home

Habit formation and habit reconstruction are important dimensions of becoming at-home in assisted living. For older persons, relevant habits range from calling assisted living "home," to developing a sense of belonging by using personal artifacts to make place a home (Rowles, 1987; Rowles & Ravdal, 2002), to the development of a rhythm of interactions in and out of place. In a thorough analysis of habits, Dewey (1922/1957) concludes that all human action is based on habits (Cutchin, Aldrich, Bailliard, & Coppola, 2008). Rather than view habits as mere automatic motor responses to environmental stimuli, he asserted that habits are socially constructed and acquired through exposure to "integrated systems of activity" (Dewey, 1957, p. 39) ubiquitous to the places in which we are born and live (Cutchin, 2007b). As we co-develop with these systems, we unconsciously internalize predispositions (habits) inherent to those social structures that guide our thoughts, values, and behaviors. Dewey also described habits as functions governing our continuous transactions with the world. The key point is that humans "functionally coordinate" with places through the development and use of habits (Campbell, 1995; Garrison, 2002). Dewey maintained that as individuals move through different situations, they adopt different habits that serve the coordinative purpose (Kestenbaum, 1977). We might think about the positive habits that are developed by older people in assisted living as providing the skills to get the most out of their situation by accomplishing or enjoying what they want and/or need.

Dewey also argued that places of experience shape habits of thought through the traditions and institutions in that place (Fesmire, 2003). Dewey added that people develop many minute forms of habits that work together in "configurations," specifically assembled for a particular situation. Such flexible configurations enable thought, movement, and other forms of action we need to survive and thrive. Dewey used the metaphor of "tools" when discussing habits because the more habits people have at their disposal, the more potential they have to respond to a situation and its emerging challenges. Because habits come from social participation in place, they are social tools that assist the functional coordination with place via action (Garrison, 2002). The employment of habits in coordinating with place is a central part of place integration, including the type we find in assisted living.

Because habits are always being shaped through our ongoing involvement in place, this provides the opportunity to develop or hone habits that are ever more useful for our relationship with place. The first principle of intervention, then, is to consider the habits that are useful to integrating with an assisted living residence. For instance, such habits might include those that are involved in particular schemes of action, such as social interaction, personally fulfilling projects, and activities of daily living. I do not mean to imply that the burden of habit development should be placed solely on the older resident in assisted living.

Bourdieu's (1998) concept of habitus aligns with Dewey's view. Bourdieu suggested that the "structuring structures" of a local society— such as staff, an organization, and symbolism in assisted living—have much to do with the internalization of habits in (older) people (Cutchin et al., 2008) and their relationship with home (Dovey, 2005). The lesson to be learned is that place integration can be facilitated by helping residents develop new habits of thought and activity—habits that will foster functional coordination with assisted living places. Encouraging older adults to utilize habits as tools to integrate with the new home must be accompanied by the development of assisted living culture, environments, and management that supports an integrative habitus. It is not a stretch to suggest that Diana and Rose would have fared better in their integrative process with better support of these types by their residences. Such support via staff action and policies would help to form habits of self-development, social being, and doing. Those habits are vital to generating better coordination and integration with place.

Imagination and Creative Place-Making

Habits of imagination also are essential in this process. Dewey's insight into habits is important with regard to imagination and how we handle novel situations. When faced with undetermined situations, like those that accompany a move to assisted living, an older person must assess the qualities of a situation and what, if anything, needs to change in order to feel more at-home. This call to deliberation forces one to use her existing stock of habits (thoughts/actions) as a form of imagination (Cutchin et al., 2008). Imagination in this sense is the ability to see possible new situational arrangements in light of the current situation (Fesmire, 2003). While much scholarly attention has been focused on the role of memories of older people in establishing a relationship with a new place, it is important to realize that the ability to see possible futures is equally, if not more, important.

Fesmire (2003) usefully portrays how Dewey understood the process. To imagine action in order to shape an undetermined situation, people must examine multiple mental images of what that situation might become through some action. To do so, they form images of possible actions and outcomes by putting together ideas—based on habits of thought they have at their disposal. Those images are framed and evaluated through one's moral and aesthetic sensibilities—other products of social customs and experience in different situations—to determine the best course of action to construct the new situation. That evaluation is a type of dramatic rehearsal of the possibilities, to determine which might be best. This process of inquiry is used continually in the ongoing course of action—by all people in all types of situations. The conclusion to be drawn is that better action—and thus better quality of life in particular situations such as assisted living—results from better imagination, which relies on the reservoir of habits one has to promote it.

Using this understanding of habits and imagination, we can begin to portray place-making as something more creative, especially place-making in congregate housing like assisted living. Because habits are the basis of creativity and place integration, place-making does not need to focus on creating a replica of the former home. Indeed, with the constraints of quasi-institutional settings and policies, the new place cannot be the old one. However, empowering an older person to make a new home in assisted living surely includes the use of artifacts and memories from the past.

The need for social problem solving/collaboration that builds and utilizes the habits and imagination of the older person is more important. The concept, therefore, is to stimulate or simulate interactions that focus on the practice and development of habits and imagination for place integration. Education, at its best, allows students to experience situations, learn new habits along the way, and develop their imaginative potential. Older adults moving into assisted living need to be guided through such experiences before and after the move so that this process can enhance their ability to enrich the place integration experience.

Practical Applications

The above ideas have potential to be translated into practical action (see Figure 5.1). I see three phases that assisted living residences could implement along those lines. First, the process could be started by the provision of educational material prior to the move, such as an *integration handbook* that begins the process of developing habits of thinking about the new place and how to best experience it. A handbook would offer principles of integration learned through the experience of residents, family, and staff connected to that particular site. Such a book would also begin the process of imagination about what and how the older person might engage in life in the new setting.

In a second phase, and perhaps even more useful, is the development of structures and systems of interactions in the assisted living context itself. Through group sessions and one-on-one mentoring, more experienced residents who have been successful in integration can share habits of thought/action that can open vistas on opportunities for action and allow residents and staff to see the current living assisting experience in light of the possible. Such interactions do not need to be artificial and classroom-like. Much of the shared learning can occur through informal interactions and events. Following the provision of material and resident mentoring, professional intervention may be warranted and is suggested as at least a standard and re-occurring checkup for all residents. Professionals who understand the principles of place integration and the role of participation and engagement in everyday life could assess each resident's integration process and provide advice and support. Occupational therapists

FIGURE 5.1 From Theory And Findings To Practical Applications

Assisted Living as Problematic Situation	Place Integration to Become at Home	Habits as Central to Place Integration	Practical Applications
Displacement	Engagement and Participation	Habits of Thinking and Doing That Functionally Coordinate Person With Place	Integration Handbook
Liminality in New Place	Social Relationships		Resident-to-Resident Mentoring
Ambiguities of Place	Remaking Place	Habits That Fund Imagination and Creative Action	Professional Assessment and Therapy
Uncertainty	New Meanings of Place		

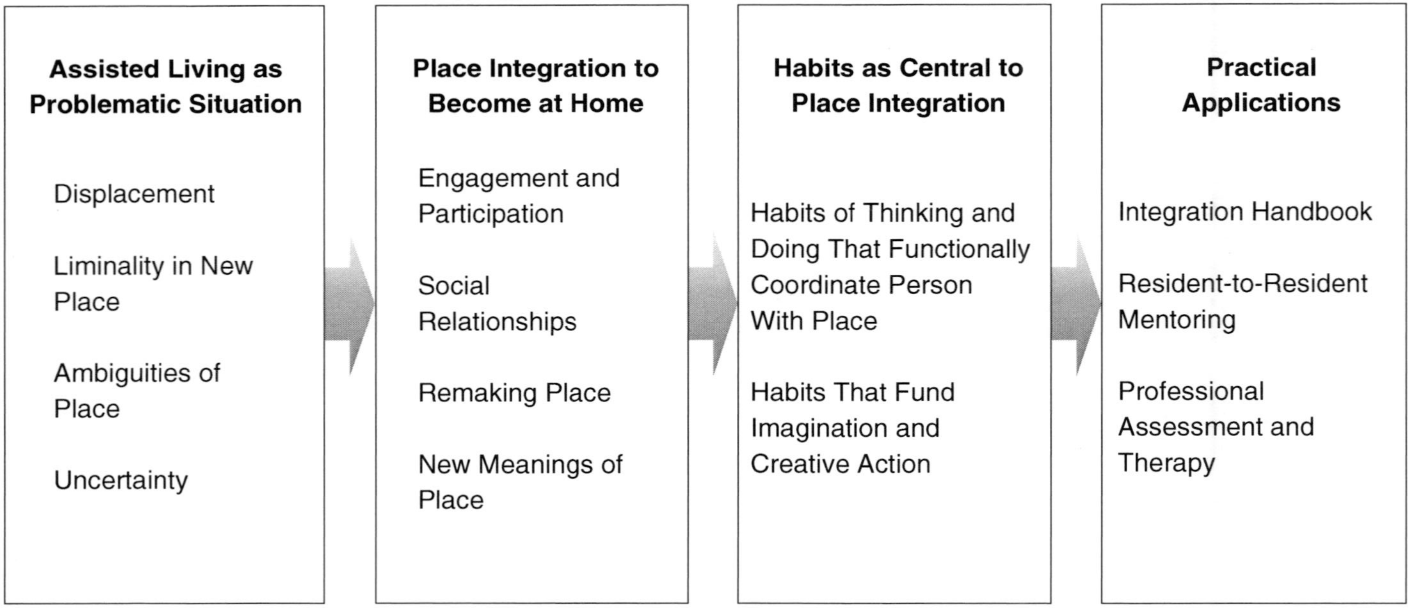

and social workers may be maximally suited to this work, and the concept would be to foster the development of integrative habits and practices so the older adult can maximize quality of life in assisted living on their own terms. An *integration handbook*, peer mentoring, and professional intervention could enhance each older person's ability to develop more meaningful person-place integration and thus a more meaningful and satisfactory process of becoming at-home.

CONCLUSIONS: LEARNING, GROWTH, AND THE FUTURE

The general approach I am advocating, based on evidence and the perspective of place integration, is one of ongoing education of those who will move and those who have moved to assisted living—or to any other setting that poses difficulties in becoming at-home. I do not suggest education in the sense of classroom-based continuing education. What I do suggest is the creative use of place integration principles to promote habits, imagination, and thereby ongoing learning by older people who wish to become at-home. Such education requires practice at solving various types of real-world problems in real-life settings; usually this means in collaboration with others in learning how to do so. This requires, first, recognition that older people are the same as younger people in their need for growth, enrichment, and empowerment. As Chaudhury and Rowles (2005, p. 13) note, "home experience provides the tools for both enduring and evolving possibilities of the self." Just as we all need to develop new skills and abilities in a changing world, so do those who intend to live in new residential settings that pose challenges for them. Becoming at-home is an ongoing process that depends on becoming better at coordinating with a new place, including all the dimensions of that place. Becoming at-home and place integration only cease upon death. Until that time, the need for integration is a constant in the attainment and maintenance of well-being. Those who want to improve well-being of their family members or care recipients can work with older adults to help them learn, develop appropriate habits, and become more at-home through various engaged activities with place. The employment of habits and imagination are important, but those must be put to work in meaningful pursuits—however the older person defines them. Settings such as assisted living are, as the name suggests, for living. And living can only be worthwhile by integrating with place and continuing to become at-home.

The research reported in this chapter was supported by the National Institute on Aging (R15 AG17028).

REFERENCES

Assisted Living Federation of America. (2009). *Overview of the assisted living industry*. Alexandria, VA: Assisted Living Federation of America.

Bourdieu, P. (1998). *Practical reason*. Stanford, CA: Stanford University Press.

Buttimer, A. (1980). Home, reach, and a sense of place. In A. Buttimer & D. Seamon (Eds.), *The human experience of space and place* (pp. 166–187). London, UK: Croom Helm.

Campbell, J. (1995). *Understanding John Dewey: Nature and cooperative intelligence*. Chicago, IL: Open Court.

Chaudhury, H., & Rowles, G. D. (2005). Between the shores of recollection and imagination: Self, aging, and home. In G. D. Rowles & H. Chaudhury (Eds.), *Home and identity in late life: International perspectives* (pp. 3–18). New York, NY: Springer Publishing Company.

Cuba, L., & Hummon, D. M. (1991). A place to call home: Identification with dwelling, community, and region. *Sociological Quarterly, 34*, 111–131.

Cutchin, M. P. (1997). Physician retention in rural communities: The perspective of experiential place integration. *Health & Place, 3*, 25–41.

Cutchin, M. P. (2001). Deweyan integration: Moving beyond place attachment in elderly migration theory. *International Journal of Aging and Human Development, 52*, 29–44.

Cutchin, M. P. (2003). The process of mediated aging-in-place: A theoretically and empirically-based model. *Social Science and Medicine, 57*, 1077–1090.

Cutchin, M. P. (2004). Using Deweyan philosophy to rename and reframe adaptation-to-environment. *American Journal of Occupational Therapy, 58*, 303–312.

Cutchin, M. P. (2007a). Therapeutic landscapes for older people: Care with commodification, liminality, and ambiguity. In A. Williams (Ed.), *Therapeutic landscapes: Advances and applications* (pp. 181–198). Aldershot, UK: Ashgate.

Cutchin, M. P. (2007b). From society to self (and back) through place: Habit in transactional context. *OTJR: Occupation, Participation, and Health, 27*, 50S–59S.

Cutchin, M. P. (2008). John Dewey's metaphysical ground-map and its implications for geographical inquiry. *Geoforum, 39*, 1555–1565.

Cutchin, M. P., Aldrich, R. M., Bailliard, A., & Coppola, S. (2008). Action theories for occupational science: The contributions of Dewey and Bourdieu. *Journal of Occupational Science, 15*, 157–165.

Cutchin, M. P., Owen, S. V., & Chang, P. F. (2003). Becoming "at-home" in assisted living residences: Exploring place integration processes. *Journals of Gerontology: Social Sciences, 58B*, S234–S243.

Dewey, J. (1957). *Human nature and conduct: An introduction to social psychology*. New York, NY: The Modern Library. (Originally published in 1922)

Dewey, J. (1986). *Logic: The theory of inquiry*. In J. A. Boydston (Ed.), *John Dewey, The later works, 1925–1953, vol. 12: 1938*. Carbondale, IL: Southern Illinois University Press. (Original work published in 1938).

Dewey, J. (1989). *Experience and Nature* (2nd ed.). LaSalle, IL: Open Court. (Original work published in 1929).

Dewey, J. (1998). The reflex arc concept in psychology. In L. Hickman & T. Alexander (Eds.), *The essential Dewey, vol. 2* (pp. 3–18). Bloomington: Indiana University Press. (Original work published in 1896).

Dovey, K. (2005). Home as paradox. In G. D. Rowles & H. Chaudhury (Eds.), *Home and identity in late life: International perspectives* (pp. 361–369). New York, NY: Springer Publishing Company.

Dyck, I., Kontos, P., Angus, J., & McKeever, P. (2005). The home as a site for long-term care: Meanings and management of bodies and spaces. *Health & Place, 11*, 173–185.

Fesmire, S. (2003). *John Dewey and moral imagination: Pragmatism in ethics*. Bloomington, IN: Indiana University Press.

Frank, J. B. (2002). *The paradox of aging in place in assisted living.* Westport, CT: Bergin & Garvey.

Garrison, J. (2001). An introduction to Dewey's theory of functional "trans-action": An alternative paradigm for activity theory. *Mind, Culture, and Activity, 8,* 275–296.

Garrison, J. (2002). Habits as social tools in context. *Occupational Therapy Journal of Research, 22,* 11S–17S.

Golant, S. M., & Hyde, J. (Eds.). (2008). *The assisted living residence: A vision for the future.* Baltimore, MD: The Johns Hopkins University Press.

Hammer, R. M. (1999). The lived experience of being at-home: A phenomenological investigation. *Journal of Gerontological Nursing, 25,* 10–18.

Heatwole Shank, K., & Cutchin, M. P. (2010). Transactional occupations of older women aging in place: Negotiating change and meaning. *Journal of Occupational Science, 17,* 4–13.

Kestenbaum, V. (1977). *The phenomenological sense of John Dewey: Habit and meaning.* Atlantic Highlands, NJ: Humanities Press.

Leith, K. H. (2006). "Home is where the heart is. . .or is it?" A phenomenological exploration of the meaning of home for older women in congregate housing. *Journal of Aging Studies, 20,* 317–333.

Martin, G. P., Nancarrow, S. A., Parker, H., Phelps, K., & Regen, E. L. (2005). Place, policy and practitioners: On rehabilitation, independence and the therapeutic landscape in the changing geography of care provision to older people in the UK. *Social Science and Medicine, 61,* 1893–1904.

McHugh, K. E., & Mings, R. C. (1996). The circle of migration: Attachment to place in aging. *Annals of the Association of American Geographers, 86,* 530–550.

Milligan, C. (2006). Caring for older people in the 21st century: Notes from a small island. *Health & Place, 12,* 320–331.

Rowles, G. D. (1983). Place and personal identity in old age: Observations from Appalachia. *Journal of Environmental Psychology, 3,* 299–313.

Rowles, G. D. (1987). A place to call home. In L. L. Carstensen & B. A. Edelstein (Eds.), *Handbook of clinical gerontology* (pp. 335–353). New York, NY: Pergamon.

Rowles, G. D., & Chaudhury, H. (Eds.). (2005). *Home and identity in late life: International perspectives.* New York, NY: Springer Publishing Company.

Rowles, G. D., & Ravdal, H. (2002). Aging, place, and meaning in the face of changing circumstances. In R. S. Weiss & S. A. Bass (Eds.), *Challenges of the third age: Meaning and purpose in later life* (pp. 81–114). New York, NY: Oxford University Press.

Rowles, G. D., & Watkins, J. F. (2003). History, habit, heart, and hearth: On making spaces into places. In K. W. Schaie, H-W. Wahl, H. Mollenkopf, & F. Oswald (Eds.), *Aging independently: Living arrangements and mobility* (pp. 77–96). New York, NY: Springer Publishing Company.

Rubinstein, R. L., & Parmalee, P. A. (1992). Attachment to place and the representation of the life course by the elderly. In I. Altman & S. Low (Eds.), *Place attachment* (pp. 139–163). New York, NY: Plenum Press.

Seamon, D. (1979). *A geography of the lifeworld: Movement, rest and encounter.* New York, NY: St. Martin's Press.

Watkins, J. F., & Hosier, A. F. (2005). Conceptualizing home and homelessness: A life course perspective. In G. D. Rowles, & H. Chaudhury (Eds.), *Home and identity in late life: International perspectives* (pp. 197–216). New York, NY: Springer Publishing Company.

Wilson, K. B. (2007). Historical evolution of assisted living in the United States, 1979 to the present. *The Gerontologist, 47*(S III), 8–22.

Wright, B. (2004). *An Overview of Assisted Living: 2004.* Washington, DC: AARP Public Policy Institute.

Young, H. M. (1998). Moving to congregate housing: The last chosen home. *Journal of Aging Studies, 12,* 149–165.

CHAPTER 6

Transforming Long-Stay Care in Ireland

Eamon O'Shea and Kieran Walsh

EDITORS' INTRODUCTION

*R*ecognizing *the importance of place in relation to well-being raises critical issues with respect to the consequences of relocation to an institutional setting and the design, operation, and ambiance of nursing facilities—a final residence for many people. Can an institutional setting ever be homelike or create even a semblance of home? How do we translate our growing knowledge of the manner in which older adults experience place and home into the creation of better long-term care environments? In this chapter, O'Shea and Walsh, consider the situation in Ireland, addressing this question in the context of the movement toward person-centered care. They note that the concerns described in literature critical of nursing facility environments, still remain in some long-stay facilities in Ireland. These include lack of privacy, the pervasiveness of routine, a culture of care minimizing autonomy, depersonalization, and limited opportunity for preserving a sense of self, and lack of connectivity to the outside world. O'Shea and Walsh describe how the "culture change movement" that is becoming normative internationally has yet to become as pervasive in Ireland. The consequences of this lagged development are far-reaching in terms of reducing the quality of life for so many people in their final months and days. There is a critical need revealed here, not just for an environment-sensitive culture of care, resident-friendly physical design of facilities, and an ethos of connectedness with the world beyond the facility—but also for accelerating the pace at which this must occur. We suspect that even in those nations that appear to have adopted a "culture of care" as the motif of their institutional long-term care, there still remain many facilities that remain unenlightened.*

In *The Wonderful Wizard of Oz*, L. Frank Baum suggests that "There is no place like home." The question is, does this principle still apply when you are an older person living in an institutional setting? In this chapter we explore the usefulness of the notion of home and its various associations and meanings when applied to institutional care settings in Ireland. We address the question of whether the creation of a more homelike environment in long-stay care leads to an improvement in the quality of life of residents. We draw on the international literature to present a review of the theoretical conceptualization of home and homelike and we interrogate these notions in the context of older adult institutional lives. We draw on a recent Irish data set to provide some empirical underpinnings to our analysis and to draw practice and policy implications from our deliberations. First, it is helpful to contextualize older adult care and institutional care in Ireland.

In Ireland, the large majority of the 11.7% of the population who are aged 65 years and over (just over a half million people) are healthy and live in their own homes in the community. Approximately 80,000 older people living at home require some form of care in the community, and this is mainly delivered by family and friends. By contrast, just over 21,000 older people live in institutional long-stay care settings, equivalent to 4% of the total elderly population (Department of Health, 2011). Institutional care in Ireland is delivered in public, private, and voluntary care settings, with the system evolving in recent years toward greater private provision. Private care in Ireland is generally referred to as nursing home care, while public and voluntary provision is usually termed extended care or residential care. The paradox is that nurse-resident staffing ratios are generally much higher in public residential care settings than in private nursing home settings. Typically, state-operated residential care has catered to more dependent residents than are found in private nursing homes. In addition, one of the difficulties of comparing long-stay care arrangements in Ireland with those in other countries is the different terminology used to describe the structure and location of care for older people across the care continuum from community-based provision to institutional care settings. There is, for example, no consensus on the definition of "institutional care"; the nomenclature, as well as the nature and scope of services, varies considerably (Mollica, 1998). In this chapter, we use the generic term "long-stay care" to refer to any form of institutional care provision in Ireland, whether provided in public, private, or voluntary settings.

At the policy level, there has been legislative controversy over the public entitlement of older people to free care in all types of long-stay care settings. Due to the shortage of public residential care beds, many older people eligible for means-tested public subvention have, in the past, had to be admitted to private nursing homes, thereby personally bearing a significant portion of the cost of care, which would have been much less had they received care in a public bed. In recent years, the state has been forced by the courts to retrospectively, and in many cases posthumously, compensate eligible older people who had been inappropriately charged for long-stay care in private nursing homes. A new funding scheme for long-stay care (the Nursing Home Support Scheme Act, 2009) was introduced in 2010 to bring consistency and uniformity into the funding of long-stay care in Ireland, whether provided in public, private or voluntary settings. This new scheme has itself been criticized due to increased cost-sharing arrangements for all older people and their families, particularly for those who might previously have avoided such charges by virtue of being eligible for care in a public residential care bed. Although the scheme was designed to simplify the system and make it fairer, it still incorporates out-of-pocket payments for the resident and a retrospective, albeit capped, posthumous means-tested payment to the state, based on the value of a person's housing assets.

There have also been high-profile cases of neglect and abuse in long-stay care settings in Ireland in recent years, particularly in relation to private nursing home care (Leas Cross Review, 2006; The Commission of Investigation, 2009). Although small in number, these cases have highlighted the vulnerability of older people in all types of long-stay care settings. They have also come to light at a time when broader concerns about quality of care, prioritization, and resource allocation in the older adult care sector are being actively debated (O'Shea, 2003; Murphy, O'Shea, Cooney, Shiel, & Hodgins, 2006; Walsh & O'Shea, 2010). Such controversies are not confined to Ireland, with similar sector-wide problems documented in the United Kingdom, the United States, and Canada (Spencer, Martin, Bourgeault, & O'Shea, 2010). Concerns with quality of care have also been noted in many countries (Ayalon, 2011; Gass, 2005; Olson, 2006; Stafford, 2003). New and comprehensive national quality standards for long-stay have now been introduced in Ireland to deal with some of these issues (HIQA, 2009). Together with the new funding scheme, the standards have increased the potential for a much more active role for older people and their families in the decision-making processes within long-stay care settings.

Despite these funding and legislative changes, most citizens in Ireland, as in other jurisdictions (Cangiano, Shutes, Spencer, & Leeson, 2009), regard institutional care as their least preferred option for care in later life, opting instead to be cared for in their own home (Williams, Hughes, & Blackwell, 2006). The current reality of an under-funded and fragmented community care system in Ireland means that such community-based preferences are difficult to realize without significant family involvement (Shutes & Walsh, 2012). Even though the vast majority of care for older people is still provided informally by family and friends (Callan, 2009), this will be less likely in the future. Current demographic and economic trends, including a reduction in the size of families and the increased labor participation of women, mean that the number of potential family caregivers is steadily decreasing. Moreover, notwithstanding preferences, and despite the best caring efforts of family and friends, many older people will require admission to long-stay care facilities because it is in such settings that they will receive the best care in relation to their needs.

One of the most important questions, therefore, is whether institutional care, either in public or private settings, can be a reasonable substitute for care in people's own homes. Given people's expressed preferences for care in their own homes, many factors are likely to influence the meaning and perception of home for older people relocated to long-stay care (e.g. personal characteristics, nature of the built environment, and the social meaning of the environment for residents). A deeper and more contested notion is whether or not it is feasible or desirable for long-stay care to ever be considered *home* or even *homelike* by older people? Home is a source of, and environment for, daily routines for older people, but it is also charged with symbolic meaning related to "the home of the mind" (Lewin, 2001), making it difficult for some residents to ever reconcile home and institutional care. These questions are well articulated in the international literature on the meaning of home within long-stay settings (de Veer & Kerkstra, 2001), and reflect broader concerns around the relationship between loss of competence and the meaning of home (Oswald & Wahl, 2005). These issues have also found practical expression in the United States, where federal and reimbursement agencies now tend to use the term "nursing facility" rather than "nursing home" to describe the place where older residents receive care (Stone, 2000). Debates in Ireland meanwhile have tended to focus less on terminology and the meaning of home in institutions, and instead have concentrated more on access to care, quality of care, and costs.

LONG-TERM CARE AND THE CONCEPT OF HOME

Research in a number of countries has focused on the broad determinants of quality of life within long-stay care settings (Ball et al., 2000; Edwards, Courtney, & O'Reilly, 2003; Kane, 2001, 2003; Murphy et al., 2006; National Council on Ageing and Older People, 2000; Tester, Hubbard, Downs, MacDonald, & Murphy, 2004). Findings emerging from this considerable literature, suggest that the following elements matter for quality of life: health of the older person; personal autonomy; choice and control; connectedness to residents, staff, family, and the outside community; the social and physical environment; and meaningful activities, all of which reflect in some way on the lived experience of residents in relation to their institutional surroundings. There is some evidence that older people living in long-stay care settings tend to have a better quality of life when they can replicate as closely as possible the life they would choose to live in their own home (Groger, 1995; Gubrium, 1975; Shields, 1988). Whether institutional care can ever encompass both the physical and mental attributes of home remains an open question, particularly in relation to the latter, in which feelings, relationships, experiences and memories are key. This is encapsulated in Rapoport's (1995) definition of home as a place where we feel *comfortable*, defined by *family and friendships*, where one finds *laughter and contentment*.

The distinction between home as an abstraction and home as a place where people live is critical to understanding life in residential care settings (Groger, 1995). People live in worlds of meaning, where a variety of meanings are interconnected and associated with their surrounding environment (Rubinstein, 1989; 1990). The greater the congruence between home as an abstraction, whatever the content and meanings of that subjective abstraction, and the physical space that functions as home, the more likely it is that older residents will be content in their surroundings (Groger, 1995). There is sufficient international literature to suggest that adapting to long-stay care can require significant compromise by residents (Kontos, 1998; Shield, 1988). If that compromise becomes so great and so pernicious that all concept of home is lost, then it is likely that quality of life, and its component elements of life satisfaction and well-being, will be diminished (Caouette, 2005; Groger, 1995). It is no wonder, therefore, that many people fear being admitted into long-stay care in later life, if that is the fate that awaits them. Both the well-publicized cases of abuse and the social meanings often associated with long-stay care, such as "you are sick" and "you are supervised" only serve to strengthen this fear (Robinson, 1985).

Home is a much-contested concept therefore, and the question of what constitutes home is still much debated (Oswald & Wahl, 2005). This is unsurprising, given that Somerville (1997) describes home, in both "real" and "ideal" forms, as being a construction of physical, psychological, and social dimensions. At its most fundamental, home is likely to be a source of experiential and emotional meaning for an older person (Kontos, 1998). In a description of the psychosocial processes linking a person to his or her home environment, Rubinstein (1989) suggests that meaning is attributed to home through a sociocultural order (related to social organization and operations within the home); the life course (expression of life course through home environments); and the body (the meaningful relationship of the body to environmental features). Further, given its embeddedness in a community setting, home embodies an important affirmation of a person's independence, freedom, and autonomy (Kontos, 1998) in both the individual and wider societal context. Home also embodies aspects of territoriality with respect to security, stimulation, and identity (Porteous, 1976).

This is in contrast to some of the existing literature on long-stay care facilities. Not surprisingly, the structured nature of the institutional environment and its connection or disconnection to the wider social community has inspired theoretical and applied questions around disassociation, segregation, identity loss, profit-driven care, and dependency (Baltes, Honn, Barton, Orzech, & Lago, 1983; Gubrium, 1975; Henderson & Vesperi, 1995; Laird, 1979; Mendelson, 1974; Olson, 2006; Townsend, 1971; Vladeck, 1980). In one of the first seminal works in this area, Goffman's (1961) concept of the "total institution" described how residents experience societal segregation, a set schedule of activities (batch living), institutional control (binary management), and a stripping of self-identity (identity stripping). While today these features may be more synonymous with penal rather than social care environments, increased need for care, loss of functional independence, and routine-driven activities remain intertwined with institutional life (Nay, 1995; Starck, 1992). The relevance of an individual's life course, and his or her accumulated material possessions, social roles, and community relations can be lost within the new and perhaps more confining boundaries of the care institution (Groger, 1995; Wilson, 1997). Research on life in long-stay care settings has also found that institutional routines and norms, and reduced interpersonal relationships, negatively influence psychological well-being, in terms of feelings of purposelessness and a lack of autonomy (Carpenter, 2002; Clarke & Bowling, 1990; Cohen-Mansfield et al., 1995; Fiveash, 1998; Gilbart & Hirdes 2000; Nay, 1995; Qassis & Hayden, 1990; Patel, 2003; Sidenvall, 1999).

Memories, attachments, status, and associations that stem from living and aging at home, which help to reinforce a sense of personal identity (Rowles, 1983), can be undermined by having to move to, and live in, an unfamiliar and regulated environment (Kontos, 1998). The centrality of home across a person's life course means that home, and its physical environmental reality, has the potential to serve as a "mnemonic anchor" for life events, even if those events are recollected through a co-production of memory and imagination (Chaudhury & Rowles, 2005). On the basis of this perspective, establishing home in a long-stay care setting may be very difficult, if for no other reason than the lack of experiential and life-course relevance that such an environment may have for an older person. Similarly, the link between developing a sense of home and broader socio-cultural environmental features, such as familiarity, history, community, and reciprocity, has been documented; as has the difficulty in creating these elements in an institutional setting (Shield, 1988).

There are a number of important counter-arguments. The first of these is that home, in the sense of lived experience of a physical environment, may, for some people, hold associations with distress and insecurity, or may in the mind of some people refer to the broader sense of belonging garnered from a place and not to an orthodox private dwelling (Russell, 2005). Second, Gott, Seymour, Bellamy, Clark, and Ahmedzai (2004) demonstrate that while older people in long-stay care settings perceive factors they associate with home (e.g., presence of friends and family) as crucial to a good death, they do not necessarily desire to be cared for at home, or see the realization of such factors as being unobtainable in their environmental settings. Third, Gubrium (1993) identified how the continuity of a person's life course, or at least elements of it, can be preserved and nurtured within nursing home environments. Johnson, Rolph, and Smith (2010), who revisited and reevaluated the work of Townsend (1962), argue that the notions of home and institutional care are not always mutually exclusive or contradictory in the lives of residents. Fourth and finally, Cutchin, Owen, and Chang (2003), in an exploratory study of assisted living facilities, found that *becoming at home* was more of a transactional integrative process rather than simply remaining living in the community. Indeed, aging in place has been suggested as an ongoing integrative process where a person creates new meanings as circumstances change (Cutchin et al., 2003; Rowles & Ravdal, 2002).

It is clear that home and the transferability of home are complex and multifaceted conceptions that certainly need to be interrogated in the context of institutional life. Of particular interest in this chapter is the possibility of creating more homelike places in long-stay care settings in Ireland as a means of improving the quality of life of residents. A vast number of interrelated factors help older people feel more at home in long-stay settings including: continuity, privacy, security, autonomy, involvement, choice, intimacy, belonging, and a sense of purpose. How these factors are experienced within long-stay care settings in Ireland was explored in a unique and comprehensive research study incorporating a national survey of long-stay care facilities combined with personal interviews with residents, relatives, and staff (Murphy et al., 2006). In this chapter, we rely mainly on further analysis of this data to explore how homelike long-stay care settings are for older residents in Ireland. First, we present a brief overview of the long-stay care sector in Ireland.

LONG-STAY CARE IN IRELAND

There are currently just under 23,000 beds available for the care of older people in long-stay care settings in Ireland (Department of Health, 2011); about two thirds of these are in the private sector. The vast majority of residents occupying long-stay care beds are aged 75 years or over, with 40% aged 85 years or over. Approximately 35% of all long-stay residents in Ireland are officially characterized as maximum dependency, defined by the Department of Health as older people whose independence is impaired to the extent that the person requires nursing care, is likely to be bed bound, to require assistance with all aspects of physical care, and may be ambulant but confused, disturbed, and incontinent. A further 30% of residents are defined as high dependency, while the remainder, equivalent to one third of all long-stay residents, are characterized as either medium or low dependency, prompting the question as to whether these people should be in long-stay care facilities at all.

The weakness of community care supports in Ireland has been instrumental in encouraging admission to long-stay care for people with low dependency, who could have been cared for in their own homes were appropriate support mechanisms in place. Public expenditure on long-term care in Ireland is low relative to other developed countries at about 0.5% of GDP, with institutional care accounting for the bulk of the available resources, especially when cash benefits are excluded (Huber, Rodrigues, Hoffmann, Gasior, & Marin, 2009). This has led to calls for an increase in public expenditure on long-term care in Ireland to move it closer to the Organisation for Economic Co-operation and Development (OECD) average, while simultaneously recalibrating the distribution of spending toward community-based care (National Economic and Social Forum, 2005). The bias toward institutional care is also a reflection of financial and tax incentives introduced in the early 1990s to encourage the building of private nursing homes which, in turn, led to a policy of ensuring these beds were occupied, mainly through public subvention of older people admitted to the new private facilities. Allied to this was an official policy of closing some public long-stay residential facilities, sometimes for good reason, given their antiquated nature, which has led to an even greater reliance on private nursing home care. A failure to invest in community-based services and facilities, while simultaneously providing tax incentives for the building of private nursing homes, has had the effect of engineering a systems bias toward private nursing home care. Moreover, one of the consequences of recent changes in the regulations guiding long-stay care in Ireland is that many public long-stay facilities now find it difficult to meet more stringent tests regarding design and physical infrastructure, mainly because they were built for other purposes and in a time when regulation was light touch and/or nonexistent. This, in turn, has led to an even greater reliance on the private nursing home sector.

The design and physical infrastructure tends to be better in private nursing home facilities, with many having been purpose-built for long-stay care (Murphy et al., 2006). Consequently, private nursing homes are more likely to provide accommodation in single or double rooms. In contrast, multi-bedded ward accommodation is much more prevalent in public residential care. The data also show that separate sitting and dining rooms are more prevalent in private facilities; 95% of private nursing homes have separate facilities for dining and sitting compared to just over half of public facilities.

IS RESIDENTIAL CARE IN IRELAND HOMELIKE?

The preceding overview suggests a far from homelike long-stay care sector in Ireland. Low levels of public expenditure and poor design, particularly in older public residential care settings, do nothing to reassure one that the maintenance and enhancement of quality of life of residents is central to the organization and structure of long-stay care. But, this may be to rush too quickly to conclusions based solely on quantitative data, without first interrogating the available evidence generated directly from residents within the system. Homelike care is not always dependent on aesthetics or staffing ratios. Very often it is staff attitudes and what might be termed "the culture of care" that determines the meaning that can be ascribed to "home" within long-stay care settings.

Fortunately, qualitative evidence from Murphy et al. (2006) helps shed light on whether long-stay care in Ireland can be characterized as homelike. Their findings, based on face-to-face interviews with residents (*n* = 101) and staff (*n* = 48), revealed three major themes affecting the potential for homelike care in long-stay settings: the care environment and ethos of care; expression of self and identity; and connectedness to family and community.

Care Environment and Ethos of Care

The care environment and ethos of care within any long-stay care setting determines how much control and autonomy residents have in relation to organizing various aspects of their life. The majority of residents in Ireland identified personal autonomy as important for quality of life and well-being. Autonomy included the capacity to make choices and to be included in decision making. Choices about the time residents were woken, had breakfast, went back to bed, had meals, what they wore, and what they did during the day, were identified as important. Only a small minority of residents perceived that they could shape their day as they wished and reported that they felt "at home" where they now lived and that they were able to continue to live their life as normal. For example, one woman living in a private nursing home reported positively on the autonomy she enjoyed with regard to making decisions on when to go to bed: when she said, "I don't go to bed until around 10. I can go to bed anytime that I like, but after 10 suits me."

This view was the exception rather than the rule: in most long-stay care settings, residents had to fit in to the routine of care which was designed primarily to fit the needs and schedules of staff. In general, people felt they had little option but to do what they were told as confirmed by this 77-year-old man living in a public long-stay care setting:

> You are woken at six and breakfast isn't until 10 past 8. It's a long day. So is there a routine here? There is. Yeah, and its every day the same, absolutely the same . . . the day is very long, boring.

There was a sense that residents had to "fit" their lives around the institution's routines and that they were effectively batch processed with little opportunity for independent decision-making. As one long-term resident in public residential care said, "It's just that it's like a school. It's very, how shall I say, regimented, you know." This view is reinforced by a director of nursing in public residential care who explained, "Because of our system and because of our staffing levels, and it's a huge issue, our staffing levels, things are done according to a routine."

In many cases, the emphasis on routine is linked to staffing constraints and roster structures, but not always. Mindset matters and, for many staff, this means the depersonalization of care where residents are treated more as objects than as residents. When care is routine it tends to focus mainly on the physical aspects of care, leaving the social and emotional needs of many residents unmet. Nurses and care staff do many things to and with residents, but in doing so do not always engage directly with them. Consequently, care relationships are familiar, in terms of frequency of interaction but, at the same time, can be distant and lack emotional meaning. While routine can have positive benefits for residents, particularly ones that mimic residents' previous personal routines (Brubaker, 1996; Jensen & Cohen-Mansfield, 2006; Tester et al., 2004), the pervasiveness of imposed routines designed to suit the work practices of staff ultimately tends to dominate, with negative consequences for residents.

The physical environment also matters in facilitating choice and homelike conditions within long-stay care settings. For some residents, the lack of a private room was a real problem, particularly for those people living in public residential care. Residents highlighted issues of privacy and the lack of choice in getting up and going to bed and accessing television or radio, while acknowledging the positive opportunities available in open-ward accommodation for greater levels of social interaction with fellow residents (Kayser-Jones, 1986). Poor physical facilities also meant that some residents, mainly in public facilities, spent a large part of each day by their bedside. Many reported that it was a struggle to have any kind of private life, as confirmed by this older woman, who had recently been admitted into public residential care, "I always had me own room till I came here. There's nowhere to get away on your own."

Even for those with a private room, privacy could still be a concern. Residents in private nursing homes reported that staff did not always knock when entering their room and tended in many instances to "barge" in. Having nowhere to take family and friends who visited was also a concern for people living in open accommodations, particularly when there were no communal meeting rooms where people could go and talk.

Maintaining a Sense of Self

Keeping a strong sense of self and maintaining identity was not easy. Residents in private nursing homes with a room of their own had a better opportunity to create personal space than residents in open wards, which were largely a feature of public facilities. In private nursing homes, people spoke about putting personal possessions on show in their own personal space, such as photographs, pictures, and favorite pieces of furniture. One resident mentioned having a wardrobe specially built in which to put all her belongings. Residents also sometimes organized their room themselves to make it more comfortable, for example, by positioning a chair near the window so as to take advantage of the light or for a better view of the outside. Similar findings in regard to self-expression and identity among residents in long-stay care settings have been documented in various ethnographic studies of nursing home life in both the United States and other countries (Gubrium, 1975, 1993; Johnson et al., 2010; Shield, 1988; Townsend, 1962).

By contrast, residents living in large open-plan public wards were very restricted in what they could bring with them. Space comprised a small locker and a single wardrobe. Despite space restrictions, many residents in open accommodation had a few personal items on display, usually photographs, ornaments or religious statues, and found great comfort in talking with fellow residents about them. Others would have chosen to bring more items with them had there been sufficient space. One recently arrived woman in a public long-stay care setting lamented:

> Sister said I will have to put them (books) down in the day room . . . Well, she said we will have to get rid of them. So I am slipping (them) out to me son every week . . . because some of them came from my own home.

Some residents brought very little with them into residential care and preferred it like that. Their rooms were less personal and more functional. Some with few possessions spoke a lot about "going home" and may have seen their stay as short-term, and so felt it was not worthwhile, or too painful, to personalize their room. In contrast to people who organized their space upon admission to long-stay care, these residents did not appear to have fully settled in their new surroundings and "home" remained their old home.

Photographs were greatly treasured by residents. They loved to talk around their photographs, speaking at length about the people or events depicted. Photographs provided a connection to a past life, prompted memories, and seemed to help maintain a sense of identity and individuality. Residents also used photographs to illustrate their life story, referring to photographs so that they could see what they looked like when their hair was brown or remember what their sons or daughters looked like. One very old man living in a private nursing home recounted his life in pictures as follows:

> And that is my picture, my relations, you know. And that is . . . and that was [Naming people and describing events.] And that's my wife and myself, and that's my son . . . that's my sister . . . that's my son and his wife . . . And that's my life story.

For some people, the photograph appeared more real than the life now lived. The impression sometimes given was that the image in the picture was closer to their true self than the regulated and truncated existence they now had within the long-stay care setting. The photograph may have been a convenient way of stepping outside current realities to a time when home and family were congruent and indistinguishable.

Another way in which residents expressed their individuality was through observance of their faith. Many participants spoke about the strength and comfort they derived from their religious belief which, for the majority of residents in Ireland, was Roman Catholic. In some facilities, residents had an opportunity to attend daily mass which they valued highly. Elsewhere, some residents reported that they had less opportunity to attend religious services than they would have liked. In some places, the decline in the number of priests made it more difficult to find one to lead the celebration of mass, particularly on Sundays, due to parish work. As one woman in a private nursing home remarked, "I'd like to have mass here more often. We only have mass here every month."

Residents who were not Roman Catholic sometimes had even more difficulty in finding ways to express their faith, particularly in rural areas. This comment from a care assistant working in a private nursing home reflects the difficulty for residents of being part of a minority religion within a long-stay care setting in Ireland:

> We have got two residents that are Protestants. I have never seen a reverend coming in while I have been here. I have seen the Catholic priests coming in and the mission priests and the nuns, but no minister.

For many female residents, how they presented themselves to the world was closely linked to their capacity for self-expression and positive self-esteem. Women liked to wear their own clothes and tended to have strong opinions on what they wanted to wear. They were equally concerned that their clothes were cared for properly. Women also enjoyed having their hair and nails looked after. The hairdresser's visit was a big event, creating a buzz of conversation about appointment times, hair color, and so on, as illustrated by this woman's comment:

> Oh yeah, the hairdresser comes in whenever I want, you know, get a perm, whenever I want it. I like a good shape on my hair, that's the way I like it.

Identity was also often intertwined with previous roles and staff who drew on residents' expertise or life experience in some way, for example by asking them to help out in the kitchen or sit on a committee, gave the message that they still had something to offer. Some places gave residents an opportunity to help with running the facility; for example, helping with the garden or setting up the altar. Unfortunately, most long-stay care settings did not see this as important and, therefore, did not encourage or invite participation. It was notable that residents living in care settings where no formal opportunities to help were available sometimes created opportunities themselves. This could be helping out another resident more disabled than they were, or fetching and carrying items for someone in a wheelchair. Clearly, volunteering and assisting others in some way was important for residents' self-identity and esteem. These findings are also reflective of the elements of community and reciprocity that Shield (1988) described as being essential to creating a sense of home. It also reinforced the view that life experience of the self is strongly influenced by interaction with an "other," meaning fellow residents, staff or the broader residential environment (Chaudhury & Rowles, 2005). When opportunities for this sort of participation are absent people notice, as is evident in the following comment from one female resident:

> Here you're not allowed in the kitchen. I went in to the kitchen after I came here to help. I said I'll give a bit of a hand. They said "What are you doing in here . . . you're not allowed in the kitchen " . . . . I miss all that.

Recognition of achievement was also important for residents. Such acknowledgment could be either formal or informal, and in many cases simply thanking older people or praising them for their help was enough. Some facilities made great efforts to acknowledge residents' accomplishments. For example, staff put their artwork on display or put up photographs of residents when on trips or at parties. In doing this, staff created an atmosphere that the older people living there were important and part of the social fabric of the institution. In contrast, other facilities placed little importance on the minutiae of residents' lives or on their current or past achievements. The atmosphere in these long-stay care settings was described as more like a hostel than a home; there was a sense that residents were transitory, even though many, in fact, had been there for a very long time.

Connectedness to Community and Family

Home offers the possibility of multiple connections to inside and outside worlds, most times mediated through family and friends in the form of regulated and unregulated interaction (Gott et al., 2004; Kontos, 1998; Rubinstein, 1989). These connections can be severely curtailed upon admission to long-stay care. Connectivity to the outside world depends on whether the institution adopts an "outward" or "inward" perspective to communication and relationship formation. The issue is whether residents are able to preserve a "temporal continuity" in their lives through participation in, and interaction with, the wider community (Rowles, Concotelli, & High, 1996). Where institutional permeability is weak, residents tend to be less connected externally and ties to the local community are likely to be weaker across a variety of dimensions.

In those long-stay care settings in Ireland where communication with the outside world is not encouraged, there is evidence to suggest that residents are more disconnected and have much less interest in what is happening externally. In conversation, they offered fewer opinions and, in some cases, their conversation was severely limited. Their lives appeared to revolve around the institution and its routine; the wider world had lost significance for them. The following quote, from a man living in a public long-stay care setting, reflects the frustration of being cut off from family and friends:

> I'm cut off. I feel cut off, you know, from all my friends. You see all the people here, they're very nice . . . but they are all strangers to me. I hate the idea of being so far from home, cos I lost my GP [General Practitioner], and my curate and all my friends, you know. I am not happy here.

Some residents emphasized the importance of "getting out" of the long-stay care setting as a way of keeping connected to the outside world. "Getting out" included doing simple things like going for a walk or shopping, visiting friends or family, attending outdoor events such as a barbeque, and having the opportunity to take day trips to places of interest. Unfortunately, most institutions were very cautious about allowing older people to leave the building, sometimes with good reason, as in the case of people with dementia, but sometimes too much caution was evident, as security and safety issues dominated decision-making. Long-stay care settings are uniformly risk-averse in relation to allowing even mobile cognitively intact residents to come and go as they please.

Residents value opportunities to chat with staff and were particularly pleased when staff shared personal information as opposed to care-related information only. This could be as trivial as what they did last night or other such gossip but, to residents, this was sometimes a sign that they had forged a "special" relationship. It is possible that by sharing even trivial information staff helped to equalize and normalize the care relationship, opening up the possibility of shared experience, reciprocity, and even friendship. It also demonstrated a mutual investment in the relationship and a mutual interest in sustaining and developing that relationship further. The care relationship not only shapes older residents' experiences of care but, because it is often one of the few sources of social interaction, it can also influence residents' sense of well-being and their quality of life (Bowers, Esmond, & Jacobson, 2000, 2003; Himmelweit, 1999). While person-centered care (McCormack & McCance, 2006) is very much the dominant culture of care nowadays in long-stay care in Ireland (Health Service Executive, 2010), the reality is that this philosophy has not permeated to all care facilities, particularly in places where staffing levels are low and time is a scarce resource. Nursing care staff are traditionally better at "doing" rather than "being," and time pressures mean that they rarely get an opportunity to develop the latter part of their skill set—the priority is always "to do" rather than "to be." This is reflected in the comments of one older man who observed that, "The staff are very, very busy here; you feel that you can't make more friendship with them."

Continuity of staff made it easier for residents to build a relationship as it provided more opportunities for friendships to be developed and sustained over a long period of time. Residents found it especially difficult to connect when there were high levels of staff turnover, while cultural differences between migrant staff and residents sometimes exacerbated communication problems, as has been documented elsewhere for Ireland (Walsh & O'Shea, 2010).

Opportunities for communication and connectivity among residents are affected by physical infrastructure and the design of buildings. Communication was easier to achieve when comfortable spaces existed where residents could congregate to chat or play card games, or engage in other such communal activity. Unfortunately, poor relationships were observed in some long-stay settings, particularly when design and space constraints prevented meaningful communication emerging, leading to frustration and anger among both residents and staff. As one nurse in a public facility remarked:

> Space is very limited. You bring them to the day room when everyone is in this little space with the table in front of them. Then you have to move three tables before you get to whom you want.

Residents, of course, differed in the extent to which they enjoyed the company of others. Some people preferred to be on their own, while others enjoyed socializing. People in the latter group frequently spoke about being lonely at home before admission to long-stay care; they enjoyed the companionship of the other residents and welcomed the opportunity to make new friends. Whether the older person was involved in the final decision to move into the facility mattered for how easy people found it to settle. Older people who had actively participated in the decision to enter found it easier to settle and make new friends. Those who had not been involved in the decision often responded very differently. They tended to withdraw into themselves and often described themselves as lonely and unhappy. This group spoke much more about going home and appeared to cope by considering their stay as short-term. As one older man in a private nursing home observed:

> Because at least the people who know they're coming, they've made the decision, they know they have to stay, and they get on with it. Whereas other people who are just brought in . . . they're on edge, they want to go home. They never give themselves the chance to settle down, whereas the other people do and they decide to just get on with it.

All residents enjoyed visits from family and friends. Visitors kept them updated on what was happening at home, brought gifts or other things that they needed, and sometimes helped out, for example, by doing their laundry. More importantly, visits from relatives made residents feel that they were still an integral part of family and community. Being consulted and included in family outings and events was viewed by residents as an indicator that they were still at the heart of the family. This woman, who lived in a private nursing home, clearly needs to feel connected to the locality and community where her family home is located:

> I make all the inquiries about what's happening, who dies and who lives! And what happens, and who's getting married, oh, I keep in touch with everybody!

Opportunities for residents and their visitors to have a private chat varied enormously. Those who had a room of their own were able to meet their visitors in private. For people without private rooms, the availability of a comfortable sitting room was crucial to encouraging visiting. Some private nursing homes, but almost no public residential care settings, had tea or coffee-making facilities in the sitting room, enabling residents to offer their visitors a cup of tea. When such facilities were available, they helped "normalize" the visit and made it feel more like visiting somebody in their home. Visiting people living in multi-bedded public wards was more problematic; there, visitors gathered around the resident's bed or in a corner of the day room and all interaction was in the public domain. The absence of child-friendly policies and facilities, such as play rooms and/or toys, is a feature of almost all long-stay care settings in Ireland. This can reduce the opportunities for interaction between residents and children, as emphasized by the testimony of this woman living in a private nursing home:

> No, well the nursing home doesn't like them (children), coming running around . . . I would like if I was allowed bring my youngest grandchildren in . . . but they (nursing home) don't seem to want that.

An interesting phenomenon within these facilities was the "generic" visitor, who visited everybody on the ward and not just their own relative or friend. Residents who had few or no visitors benefited greatly, as a "generic" visitor ensured that they had an opportunity to chat with somebody other than staff. Volunteers with no connection at all to any residents also play an important visitor role in some long-stay facilities, particularly in providing support to those residents whose family no longer visit, or to those who have no living relatives or viable contacts outside the facility. As one older woman remarked:

> Volunteers enhance the quality of life of people don't they. They do little things that no one else does . . . they develop personal relationships with individuals.

CREATING HOMELIKE ENVIRONMENTS IN LONG-STAY CARE SETTINGS

The data presented in the previous section provides insight into particular dimensions of residential care in Ireland that allow us to explore the importance and potential of creating homelike environments for people living in these settings. The findings in relation to the factors important for long-stay residents in Ireland are broadly supported by the international literature on quality of life within long-stay settings across countries (Bond & Corner, 2004; Hughes, 1990; Kane, 2001; Kane et al., 2003; Lawton, 1983; Tester et al., 2004). While the vast majority of older people in Ireland want to live in their own homes as they get older, irrespective of disability or dependency, a significant number of older people will always need to be admitted to residential care for short or long periods of time. For these people, aging in place means aging in a residential care environment, which feels and looks different from their own home. Admission to a long-stay care setting is always associated with major change and transition for an older person. Most of the time we tend to focus on the negative aspects of admission to residential care, ignoring any potential for improvement in the lives of residents (Savishinsky, 1991). What, therefore, can we do to ensure that older people living in long-stay care are provided with the best possible opportunities and facilities to maximize their capabilities and well-being in a setting that for some is freely chosen, but for the majority is far from a homelike environment?

The first requirement in the creation of a homelike environment is to move toward a care approach that emphasizes the personhood and the uniqueness of each and every resident. Unfortunately, long-stay care in Ireland is still dominated by rigid organizational routines, which limit expression of personal autonomy and choice for residents (Kane, 2001). Residents who feel disempowered are constrained by rules and routines. They perceive themselves to be "one of a number" rather than individuals, and this negatively affects their sense of self and personal identity. In contrast, a service that concentrates on the person, and those who support that person, is one that is based on consultation, autonomy, choice, individual care and participation in decision making (Clark, Hanson, & Ross, 2003; Davies, Laker, & Ellis, 1999; McCormack, 2003).

The "culture change movement," which originated in the United States, represents a systematic approach to the transformation of long-stay care toward person-directed values and practices where the voices of older people and those working with them are considered and respected. Core person-directed values associated with this movement are: choice, dignity, respect, self-determination, and purposeful living (Koren, 2010). Education and training for nurse managers can play a powerful role in shaping the philosophy within care facilities and in facilitating change toward the delivery of person-centered care (Kitson, 1991; Redfern, Hannan, Norman, & Martin, 2002; Wright & McCormack, 2001).

A second key influence on homelike care is the physical environment within which care is delivered. Public institutions in Ireland are older and often poorly designed for the purpose of caring for dependent older people. They are often extremely constrained in terms of space and design, thereby inhibiting internal communication between residents and staff and external connections between residents and communities. Residents who lived in large open-plan wards described their struggle to live a private life in a public space, and many expressed a desire for a room of their own. The absence of sitting rooms or homely social spaces in public long-stay facilities means that residents are often confined to spending their day by their bedside. This means limited opportunity for meaningful communication/contacts with other residents and participation in communal and/or physical activities. In contrast, private nursing homes in Ireland are relatively new and spacious, and have generally been designed for the specific purpose of caring for dependent older people in single or double rooms. While having a private room cannot necessarily be equated to living in homelike circumstances, and it carries dangers in relation to potential isolation, it seems to provide real autonomy for many long-stay residents.

Connectedness is the third key pillar for the creation of homelike conditions within institutional care. Some long-stay care settings are better than others in facilitating greater connectivity among residents, between residents and their families, and between the facility and the wider community. The latter may be easier to achieve in rural communities, based on the inherent social characteristics of these communities (Rowles et al., 1996), but it is worth exploring in all types of locations. Keeping people connected is more difficult, however, if they have very high levels of dependency, particularly if they have dementia, which tends to reduce the opportunity for peer group communication and interpersonal relationships (Walsh & Waldmann, 2008, 2010). Design issues need to be addressed to encourage family relationships and social relationships to be maintained, including the provision of private spaces, meeting rooms, and play areas for young children visiting the facility. The role of pets in contributing to a connected homelike environment in long-stay care may also be important, given what is known about their therapeutic impact on some residents (Galvin & De Roiste, 2005).

Fourth, the attitudes of staff need to change with respect to the balance between the private and the social within long-stay care settings. Nurses and care staff are, by definition, primarily concerned with individual care relationships rather than with broader holistic objectives that encompass the social world of the resident. But opportunities must also exist for residents to remain connected socially, both within and outside the long-stay care setting. The balance between risk and safety may need to be recalibrated in favor of the former, if residents are to remain connected to communities, both new and old. Older people in long-stay care settings sometimes attempt to create these sorts of community roles within institutional environments through voluntary work or reciprocal arrangements entered into with other residents. We need to take our cue from the example of these residents and, at the very least, recognize the importance of remaining active and socially engaged within residential care environments, even when there are risks attached.

Similarly, older people should be encouraged to spend time outside of the long-stay setting—for example, visiting friends in the community or socializing in the local area, whether in public houses (bars), restaurants, or through visits to the cinema or the theater. This would be real person-centered care, where normal risk is accepted and the resident's right to personal autonomy is guaranteed. Certainly when connectivity, reciprocity, and attachment are encouraged and protected, social relationships remain strong, and the potential for residential care to become a home away from home is enhanced. Changing the culture of nursing home life to one of greater acceptance of risk will be necessary, if not sufficient, to maximize social connection opportunities for residents.

Finally, we also need to reassess societal attitudes to long-stay care, and more specifically how much the stigmatization of long-stay care affects both the perception and reality of the care available to residents. There is some evidence that health-related stigma engender exclusionary mechanisms in certain care settings (Watkins & Jacoby, 2007). Certainly, public discourse within Ireland would indicate that such mechanisms may be influential in determining an almost universal negativity surrounding long-stay care and toward the facilities providing that care. Of course there are other mechanisms at work, not least some high-profile scandals in relation to physical and financial abuse within long-stay settings linked to subsequent negative media coverage of these events. This makes it all the more important to explore both process and outcomes in long-stay care. At the very least, there is a need to understand how home, and its various meanings, is conceptualized and/or transformed in long-stay care settings by older people and by providers of care. Ultimately, the goal is the more rapid diffusion of person-centered models of care for older people living in long-stay care settings and a more nuanced debate on optimal balance of care relationships that go beyond the "institutional care, bad—home care, good" dichotomy that currently prevails.

CONCLUSION

Admission to long-stay care in Ireland can certainly result in some erosion of people's independence, autonomy, belonging, and sense of self. Therefore, it is particularly important to promote a philosophy and culture of care that serves to counterbalance these negative effects, encouraging instead, as far as is possible, the creation of homelike conditions for residents. For that to happen, older people must be recognized as individuals in their own right, whole persons with a valuable contribution to make to life within the care setting and outside. Changing the ethos of care and the mind-set of management and staff to one of person-centered care is necessary for making progress toward the creation of homelike conditions in institutional settings. Although there is evidence to suggest that this has already happened in other countries, there is far from universal application of the model in Ireland. Public information, advocacy, and sustained education, and training programs for management and staff will be necessary to facilitate a move away from care models based on routine toward models based on maximizing the capabilities, self-expression, and personhood of residents.

Long-term care facilities should be at the center of communal activity, welcoming people from the outside through family visiting and intergenerational programs of activities. Connectedness can be improved by ensuring that the physical layout and design of institutions achieve the correct balance between private and communal space, as well as encouraging visiting from family and friends and facilitating the related social interaction. This will require significant new investment in Ireland to make buildings more enabling, drawing in and opening up contacts and relationships, rather than closing off opportunities for interaction. Residents must also be allowed to weigh up and decide on the level of risk they are willing to take in their own lives to maintain internal and external connections and relationships.

By maximizing choice, opportunity, and connectivity, care settings can become more like home and less like institutions. While it may be true that for many people "there is no place like home," it is possible to make all places a little more homelike. That would be a real achievement in relation to long-stay care, in Ireland and elsewhere.

REFERENCES

Ayalon, L. (2011). Abuse is in the eyes of the beholder: Using multiple perspectives to evaluate elder mistreatment under round-the-clock foreign home carers in Israel. *Ageing & Society, 31*(3), 299–520.

Ball, M. M., Whittington, F. J., Perkins, M. M., Patterson, V. L., Hollingsworth, C., King, S. V., & Combs, B. L. (2000). Quality of life in assisted living facilities: Viewpoints of residents. *Journal of Applied Gerontology, 19*(3), 304–325.

Baltes, M., Honn, S., Barton, E., Orzech, M., & Lago, D. (1983). On the social ecology of dependence and independence in elderly nursing home residents: A replication and extension. *Journal of Gerontology, 38*, 556–564.

Bond, J., & Corner, L (2004). *Quality of life and older people*. London, UK: Open University Press.

Bowers, B. J., Esmond, S., & Jacobson, N. (2000). The relationship between staffing and quality in long-term care facilities: Exploring the views of nurse aides. *Journal of Nursing Care Quality, 14*, 55–64.

Bowers, B. J., Esmond, S., & Jacobson, N. (2003). Turnover reinterpreted: CNAs talk about why they leave. *Journal of Gerontological Nursing, 29*, 36–43.

Brubaker, B. H. (1996). Self-care in nursing home residents. *Journal of Gerontological Nursing, 22*(7), 22–30.

Callan, A. (2009). The older adult health and social care sector. In K. Walsh & E. O'Shea (Eds.), *The role of migrant care workers in ageing societies: Context and experiences in Ireland* (pp. 14–24). Galway, Ireland: National University of Ireland.

Cangiano, A., Shutes, I., Spencer, S., & Leeson, G. (2009). *Migrant care workers in ageing societies: Research findings in the United Kingdom*. Oxford, UK: Centre on Migration, Policy and Society, University of Oxford.

Caouette, E. (2005). The image of nursing homes and its impact on the meaning of home for elders. In G. D. Rowles & H. Chaudhury (Eds.), *Home and identity in late life: International perspectives* (pp. 251–277). New York, NY: Springer Publishing Company.

Carpenter, B. D. (2002). Family, peer, and staff social support in nursing home patients: Contributions to psychological well-being. *Journal of Applied Gerontology, 21*(3), 275–293.

Chaudhury, H., & Rowles, G. D. (2005). Between the shores of recollection and imagination: Self, aging, and home. In G. D. Rowles & H. Chaudhury (Eds.), *Home and identity in late life: International perspectives* (pp. 3–17). New York, NY: Springer Publishing Company.

Clark, P., & Bowling, A. (1990). Quality of everyday life in long stay institutions for the elderly: An observational study of long stay hospital and nursing home care. *Social Science & Medicine, 30*(11), 1201–1210.

Clarke, A., Hanson, E., & Ross, H. (2003). Seeing the person behind the patient: Enhancing the care of older people using a biographical approach. *Journal of Clinical Nursing, 12*(5), 697–706.

Cohen-Mansfield, J., Werner, P., Weinfield, M., Braun, J., Kraft, G., Gerber, B., & Willens, S. (1995). Autonomy for nursing home residents: The role of regulations. *Behavioral Sciences & the Law, 13*(3), 415–423.

Cutchin, M. P., Owen, S. V., & Chang, P. J. (2003). Becoming "at home" in assisted living residences: Exploring place integration processes. *The Journals of Gerontology: Series B, 58*(4), S234–S243.

Davies, S., Laker, S., & Ellis, L. (1999). *Dignity on the ward: Promoting excellence in care. Good practice in acute hospital care for older people.* London, UK: Help the Aged.

Department of Health. (2011). *Long-stay activity statistics 2010.* Dublin, Ireland: Stationery Office.

de Veer, A. J., & Kerkstra, A. (2001). Feeling at home in a nursing home. *Journal of Advanced Nursing, 35*(3), 427–434.

Edwards, H., Courtney, M., & O'Reilly, M. (2003). Involving older people in research to examine quality of life in residential aged care. *Quality in Ageing – Policy Practice and Research, 4*(4), 38–43.

Fiveash, B. (1998). The experience of nursing home life. *International Journal of Nursing Practice, 4,* 166–174.

Galvin, C., & De Roiste, A. (2005). Living in care: Older persons' experiences of nursing homes. *Irish Journal of Applied Social Studies, 6*(1 Article 6), 77–95.

Gass, T. E. (2005). *Nobody's home: Candid reflections of a nursing home aide.* Ithaca, NY: Cornell University Press.

Gilbart, E. E., & Hirdes, J. P. (2000). Stress, social engagement and psychological well-being in institutional settings: Evidence based on the minimum data set 2.0. *Canadian Journal on Aging, 19*(2), 50–66.

Goffman, E. (1961). *Asylums: Essays on the social situation of mental patients and other inmates.* London, UK: Penguin Books.

Gott, M., Seymour, J., Bellamy, G., Clark, D., & Ahmedzai, S. (2004). Older people's views about home as a place of care at the end of life. *Palliative Medicine, 18*(5), 460–470.

Groger, L. (1995). A nursing home can be a home. *Journal of Aging Studies, 9,* 137–153.

Gubrium, J. E. (1975). *Living and dying at Murray Manor.* New York, NY: St. Martin's.

Gubrium, J. F. (1993). *Speaking of life: Horizons of meaning for nursing home residents.* New Brunswick, NJ: Aldine De Gruyter.

Health Services Executive (HSE). (2010). *Enhancing care for older people: A guide to practice development processes to support and enhance care in residential settings for older people.* Dublin, Ireland: Health Services Executive.

Henderson, J. N., & Vesperi, M. D. (Eds.). (1995). *The culture of long term care: Nursing home ethnography.* Westport, CO: Bergin and Garvey.

Himmelweit, S. (1999). Caring labor. *Annals of American Academy of Political and Social Science, 561,* 27–38.

HIQA. (2009). *National quality standards for residential care settings for older people in Ireland.* Retrieved November 2011, from http://www.hiqa.ie/publication/national-quality-standards-residential-care-settings-older-people-ireland

Huber, M., Rodrigues, R., Hoffmann, F., Gasior, K., & Marin, B. (2009). *Facts and figures on long-term care in Europe and North America.* Vienna, Austria: European Centre for Social Welfare Policy and Research.

Hughes, B. (1990). Quality of life. In S. Peace (Ed.), *Researching social gerontology concepts, methods and issues.* London, UK: Sage Publications.

Jensen, B., & Cohen-Mansfield, J. (2006). How do self-care routines of nursing home residents compare with past self-care practices? *Geriatric Nursing, 27*(4), 244–251.

Johnson, J., Rolph, S., & Smith, R. R. (2010). *Residential care transformed: Revisiting the last refuge.* Basingstoke, UK: Palgrave Macmillan.

Kane, R. A. (2001). Long-term care and a good quality of life: Bringing them closer together. *The Gerontologist, 41*(3), 293–304.

Kane, R. A. (2003). Definition, measurement and correlates of quality of life in nursing homes: Towards a reasonable practice, research and policy agenda. *The Gerontologist, 43*(2), 28–36.

Kane, R. A., Kling, K. C., Bershadsky, B., Kane, R. L., Giles, K., Degenholtz, H. B., . . . Cutler, L. J. (2003). Quality of life measures for nursing home residents. *Journal of Gerontology, 58A*(3), 240–248.

Kayser-Jones, J. S. (1986). Open-ward accommodations in a long-term care facility: The elderly's point of view. *The Gerontologist, 26*(1), 63–69.

Kitson, A. (1991). *Therapeutic nursing and the hospitalized elderly.* Middlesex, England: Scutari Press.

Kontos, P. C. (1998). Resisting institutionalization: Constructing old age and negotiating home. *Journal of Aging Studies, 12*(2), 167–184.

Koren, M. J. (2010). Person-centred care for nursing home residents: The culture-change movement. *Health Affairs, 29*(2), 312–317.

Laird, C. (1979). *Limbo: A memoir about life in a nursing home by a survivor.* San Francisco, CA: Chandler & Sharp.

Lawton, M. P. (1983). Environment and other determinants of well-being in older people. *The Gerontologist, 23*(4), 349–357.

Leas Cross Review. (2006). *Leas Cross Review.* Health Service Executive. Retrieved July 2009, from http://www.hse.ie/eng/Publications/services/Older/Leas_Cross_Report_.pdf

Lewin, F. A. (2001). The meaning of home among elderly immigrants: Directions for future research and theoretical development. *Housing Studies, 17*(3), 353–370.

McCormack, B. (2003). A conceptual framework for person-centered practice with older people. *International Journal of Nursing Practice, 9*(3), 202–209.

McCormack, B., & McCance, T. (2006). Development of a framework for person-centered nursing care. *Journal of Advanced Nursing Care, 56*(5), 1–8.

Mendelson, M. A. (1974). *Tender loving greed.* London, UK: Random House.

Mollica, R. L. (1998). *State assisted living policy: 1998.* Washington, DC: Office of the Assistant Secretary for Planning and Evaluation. Retrieved from http://aspe.os.dhhs.gov/daltcp/reports/98state.htm

Murphy, K., O'Shea, E., Cooney, A., Shiel, A., & Hodgins, M. (2006). *Improving quality of life of older people in long-stay care settings in Ireland.* Dublin, Ireland: National Council on Ageing and Older People.

National Council on Ageing and Older People. (2000). *A framework on quality on long-term residential care for older people in Ireland.* Dublin, Ireland: National Council on Ageing and Older People. National Economic and Social Forum. (2005). *Care for Older People* (Report #32). Dublin, Ireland: National Economic and Social Development Office.

Nay, R. (1995). Nursing home residents' perception of relocation. *Journal of Clinical Nursing, 4,* 319–325.

Nursing Home Support Scheme Act. (2009). No. 15 of 2009. Retrieved November 2011, from http://www.irishstatutebook.ie/pdf/2009/en.act.2009.0015.pdf

Olson, L. K. (2006). Book reviews: The inner world of nursing homes. *The Gerontologist, 46*(2), 293–297.

Oswald, F., & Wahl, H. W. (2005). Dimensions of the meaning of home in later life. In G. D. Rowles & H. Chaudhury (Eds.), *Home and identity in late life: International perspectives* (pp. 21–46). New York, NY: Springer Publishing Company.

O'Shea, E. (2003). Costs and consequences for the carers of people with dementia in Ireland. *Dementia: International Journal of Social Research and Practice, 2*(2), 201–19.

Patel, M. (2003). Death anxiety and psychological well-being among institutionalized and non-institutionalized aged. *Journal of Personality & Clinical Studies, 19*(1), 107–111.

Porteous, J. D. (1976). Home: The territorial core. *Geographical Review, 66*(4), 383–390.

Qassis, S., & Hayden, D. C. (1990). Effects of environment on psychological well-being of elderly persons. *Psychological Reports, 66*(1), 147–150.

Rapoport, A. (1995). A critical review of the concept of 'home'. In D. N. Benjamin, D. Shea, & D. Saile (Eds.), *The home: Words, interpretations, meanings and environment* (pp. 25–52). Aldershot, UK: Avebury.

Redfern, S., Hannan, S., Norman, I., & Martin, F. (2002). Work satisfaction, stress, quality of care and morale of older people in a nursing home. *Health and Social Care in the Community, 10*(6), 512–519.

Robinson, J. W. (1985). Architectural settings and the housing of older developmentally disabled persons. In M. P. Jaricki & H. M. Wisniewski (Eds.), *Aging and developmental disabilities: Issues and approaches* (pp. 391–400). Baltimore, MD: Brookes.

Rowles, G. D. (1983). Place and personal identity in old age: Observations from Appalachia. *Journal of Environmental Psychology, 3*, 299–313.

Rowles, G. D., Concotelli, J. A., & High, D. M. (1996). Community integration of a rural nursing home. *Journal of Applied Gerontology, 15*(2), 188–201.

Rowles, G. D., & Ravdal, H. (2002). Aging, place, and meaning in the face of changing circumstances. In R. S. Weiss & S. A. Bass (Eds.), *Challenges of the third age: Meaning and purpose in later life* (pp. 81–114). New York, NY: Oxford University Press.

Rubinstein, R. B. (1989). The home environments of older people: A description of the psychosocial processes linking person to place. *Journal of Gerontology, 44*, S45–S53.

Rubinstein, R. L. (1990). Personal identity and environmental meaning in later life. *Journal of Aging Studies, 4*(2), 131–147.

Russell, C. (2005). Home, identity, and belonging in later life: The perspectives of disadvantaged inner-city men. In G. D. Rowles & H. Chaudhury (Eds.), *Home and identity in late life: International perspectives.* (pp. 237–249). New York, NY: Springer Publishing Company.

Savishinsky, J. S. (1991). *The end of time: Life and work in a nursing home.* New York, NY: Bergin and Garvey.

Shield, R. R. (1988). *Uneasy endings: Daily life in an American nursing home.* Ithaca, NY: Cornell University Press.

Shutes, I., & Walsh, K. (2012). Negotiating user preferences, discrimination, and demand for migrant labour in long-term care. *Social Politics.* doi:10.1093/sp/jxr025

Sidenvall, B. (1999). Meal procedures in institutions for elderly people: A theoretical interpretation. *Journal of Advanced Nursing, 30*(2), 319–328.

Somerville, P. (1997). The social construction of home. *Journal of Architectural and Planning Research, 14*(3), 226–245.

Spencer, S., Martin, S., Bourgeault, I., & O'Shea, E. (2010). *The Role of Migrant Care Workers in Ageing Societies: Report on Research Findings in the United Kingdom, Ireland, Canada and the United States.* IOM migration Research Series, Report no. 41, International Organization for Migration.

Stafford, P. B. (Ed.). (2003). *Gray areas: Ethnographic encounters with nursing home culture.* Santa Fe, NM: School of American Research Press.

Starck, P. L. (1992). The management of suffering in a nursing home: An ethnographic study. In P. L. Starck & J. P. McGovern (Eds.), *The hidden dimensions of illness: Human suffering.* New York, NY: National League for Nursing.

Stone, R. I. (2000). *Long-term care for the elderly with disabilities: Current policy, emerging trends and implications for the twenty first century.* New York, NY: Milbank Memorial Fund.

Tester, S., Hubbard, G., Downs, M., MacDonald, C., & Murphy, J. (2004). Frailty and institutional life. In A. Walker & C. Hennessy Hagan (Eds.), *Growing older quality of life in old age.* Berkshire, UK: Open University Press.

The Commission of Investigation. (2009). *The Leas Cross Commission: Final Report June 2009*. Department of Health and Children, Dublin. Retrieved July 2009, from http://www.dohc.ie/publications/leas_cross_commission.html

Townsend, C. (1971). *Old age: The last segregation*. New York, NY: Grossman Publishers.

Townsend, P. (1962). *The last refuge: A survey of residential institutions and homes for the aged in England and Wales*. London, UK: Routledge and Kegan Paul.

Vladeck, B. (1980). *Unloving care: Nursing home tragedy*. New York, NY: Basic Books.

Walsh, K., & O'Shea, E. (2010). Marginalized care: Migrant workers caring for older people in Ireland. *Journal of Population Ageing, 3*, 17–37.

Walsh, K., & Waldmann, T. (2008). The influence of nursing home residency on the capacities of low dependency older adults. *Ageing & Mental Health, 12*(5), 528–535.

Walsh, K., & Waldmann, T. (2010). Exploring the impact of nursing home life: Routines, dependency and measurement. *Irish Journal of Anthropology, 13*(2), 13–21.

Watkins, F., & Jacoby, A. (2007). Is the rural idyll bad for your health? Stigma and exclusion in the English countryside. *Health & Place, 13*, 851–864.

Williams, J., Hughes, G., & Blackwell, S. (2006). *Attitudes towards funding of long-term care of the elderly*. Dublin, Ireland: Economic and Social Research Institute.

Wilson, S. A. (1997). The transition to nursing home life: A comparison of planned and unplanned admissions. *Journal of Advanced Nursing, 26*, 864–871.

Wright, J., & McCormack, B. (2001). Practice development: Individualized care. *Nursing Standard, 15*(36), 7–42.

CHAPTER 7

Developing a Physical Environmental Evaluation Component of the Dementia Care Mapping (DCM) Tool[1]

Habib Chaudhury, Heather Cooke, and Krista Frazee

EDITORS' INTRODUCTION

*A*s *we become more sensitive to the influence of the physical environment on well-being, the need for research and assessment-related instruments to measure subtle dimensions of this relationship is becoming increasingly apparent. In this chapter, the authors report on developing a potential supplement to Dementia Care Mapping (DCM), an increasingly widely employed dementia care evaluation tool. Their work reminds us once again that different population subgroups, not only persons with dementia, experience their environment in unique ways and that it is important to recognize such diversity and to design and use physical settings in ways that maximize the potential of each user to sustain the highest possible quality of life. The chapter also reveals the critical role of observational approaches in assessing the experience of the environment for those who cannot themselves verbalize this experience. Of course, we can never be certain that the inferences we make from observation of a person with a dementing illness accurately reflect their phenomenological experience; but, as we develop increasingly sophisticated observational measures, it may be possible to use outcomes such as lowered levels of agitation, improved socialization, and reduced wandering behavior as proxy measures of success in improving our sensitivity to the environmental needs of sub-populations that cannot speak for themselves.*

The physical environment is an important contributor to psychosocial, behavioral, and health outcomes of people with dementia in institutional environments (e.g., Calkins, 2001; Lawton, 2001; Sloane et al., 2002). It is increasingly recognized that the environment—both interpersonal and physical—plays an important role in fostering or impeding how well the individual with dementia retains existing capabilities and functioning (O'Connor et al., 2007). Such recognition is the underlying rationale behind the Press-Competence Model (Lawton & Nahemow, 1973), which states that while each individual maintains a certain level of competence, the surrounding environment can exert more or less press on that individual and can create potentially negative outcomes. Further development of this model led to the creation and development of the Progressively Lowered Stress Threshold Model (Smith, Gerdner, Hall, & Buckwalter, 2004), incorporating individuals with cognitive impairment and suggesting that cognitive decline associated with dementia can decrease the cognitive threshold of an individual to process environmental stimulation. The progressive nature of dementia can, therefore, create a heightened sensitivity to stimulation and subsequent negative outcomes, such as anxiety and agitation. Such theoretical foundations have generated a growing body of research and suggestions on how aspects of both the physical and social environments can influence the well-being (positively or negatively) of individuals at any stage of cognitive decline. This has led to the emergence of care units designed specifically for people with dementia (e.g., Schwarz, Chaudhury, & Tofle, 2004; Zeisel et al., 2003).

Several environmental assessment tools have been developed for use in long-term care settings. A well-known tool in group residences for older adults is the Multiphasic Environmental Assessment Procedure (MEAP) (Moos & Lemke, 1994). This tool has four primary rating instruments addressing resident and staff characteristics, physical and architectural features, policies and services, and the social climate of sheltered care environments. The MEAP is the first comprehensive tool that includes a major component on the physical environment, emphasizing its importance, as well as having the flexibility of application in long-term care and supportive housing facilities. Although the tool is comprehensive in addressing several aspects of a facility environment, it does not address environmental or organizational issues related to people with dementia.

Cohen and Weisman (1991) outlined eight therapeutic goals (TGs) of the physical environment in a dementia care setting: maximize safety and security, support functional abilities, maximize awareness and orientation, facilitate social contact, provide privacy, regulate stimulation, provide opportunities for personal control, and facilitate continuity of the self. Subsequently, various physical environmental assessment tools have been developed to evaluate these goals. Among these, two instruments have been well validated and used extensively in both stand-alone and integrated dementia care facilities. These two instruments are the Therapeutic Environmental Screening Survey (TESS-NH) (Sloane & Mathew, 1990; Sloane et al., 2002) and the Professional Environmental Assessment Protocol (PEAP) (Weisman, Lawton, Sloane, Calkins, & Norris-Baker, 1996). The TESS-NH examines 84 discrete items and one global item that cover multiple environmental domains, including exit control, maintenance, safety, orientation/ cueing, privacy, lighting, cleanliness, odors, physical appearance, noises, plants, outdoor areas, resident appearance, and access to public toilets from main areas. TESS-NH data provide a descriptive quantitative profile of the care environment, which is useful in comparing multiple facilities or in a pre-post assessment of renovation of a particular facility.

The PEAP examines the eight global dimensions of the built environment outlined by Cohen and Weisman (1991) by using a five-point rating scale. PEAP was designed to supplement TESS-NH by providing a holistic evaluation of the built environment in terms its potential for behavioral outcomes, whereas TESS-NH was designed to evaluate qualities of discrete environmental features. Another instrument: the Nursing Unit Rating Scale (NURS) (Grant, 1996), is based on six environmental dimensions: separation, stimulation, stability, complexity, control/tolerance, and continuity for people with dementia. Although this tool is useful to assess policy and program features on dementia care units, it falls short in evaluating the built environmental features in an effective way as the dimensions overlap between physical environmental and organizational aspects of the care setting. Other notable environmental evaluation tools include the Environmental Indices (Cutler, Kane, Degenholtz, Miller, & Grant, 2006), the Stirling Environmental Audit Tool (SEAT) (Fleming, 2009) and the Environmental Audit Tool (EAT) (Fleming, 2009).

There are two general limitations of these evaluation instruments. First, these walk-through environmental observation tools focus *solely* on the physical environment and do not explicitly account for any *observed* resident behaviors or resident-staff interactions in the care environment. Observed characteristics of the built environment are ranked or evaluated based on their predicted potential to support or hinder behaviors in people with dementia. The foundation or premise of this linkage between objective quality of the environment and its ability to support individual and group behaviors is primarily based on previous literature and expert opinion. The missing data in these evaluations are any observed resident behaviors; these remain implicit and assumed in the use of these evaluation tools.

Second, existing tools do not explicitly address the quality of the physical environment from the perspective of the person with dementia. With the increasing focus on person-centered dementia care in recent times, this is an important gap in the current approaches to environmental evaluation of dementia care settings. The psychosocial and behavioral manifestations of the condition of dementia vary across individuals and are influenced by several factors, including the type of disease, stage in the disease progression, physical frailty, and personality. Current evaluation tools are based on generalizations in understanding built environmental aspects and behavioral associations, which overlook personal characteristics and the resultant variability in individual interrelationships with the environment. In order to address these issues, we developed an environmental evaluation component designed to function along with a well-known dementia care evaluation tool: Dementia Care Mapping (DCM).

DEMENTIA CARE MAPPING

Dementia Care Mapping (DCM) is a well-established tool originated by Tom Kitwood of the Bradford Dementia Group in the United Kingdom. Used by staff to examine and record components of quality of care and quality of life for residents with dementia in residential care facilities (Brooker & Surr, 2005; Innes & Surr, 2001; Kitwood & Bredin, 1992), the DCM has gained international popularity and acceptance in the last ten years as a standardized assessment measure as well as for practice development (Brooker, 2005; Brooker, Foster, Banner, Payne, & Jackson 1998; Sloane et al., 2007). The tool has been used in various settings and contexts that include: comparing quality of care and quality of life across facilities (Chung, 2004; Kuhn, Kasayka, & Lechner, 2002; Potkins et al., 2003), evaluating the impact of an intervention for people with dementia (Bredin, Kitwood, & Wattis, 1995), group reminiscence (Brooker & Duce, 2000), and intergenerational programs (Jarrott & Bruno, 2003). DCM is conceptually grounded in a person-centered care approach that advocates maintenance of personhood in people with dementia in the face of cognitive decline (Brooker, 2004; Kitwood, 1997). A person-centered care approach moves beyond the traditional biological model of care and incorporates psychological and sociological perspectives on dementia (Brooker, 2007). DCM is a tool that measures the extent to which the person-centered care approach is a reality for people with dementia (Innes, 2003; Innes & Surr, 2001).

Conventional or suggested use of DCM involves six continuous hours of observation or *mapping* of five to eight persons with dementia. In every five-minute time period, Behavioral Category Codes (BCCs) and associated Well/Ill Being (WIB) values are recorded. Although work on the DCM began in the early 1990s, an updated and revised version was released in 2007, which made significant changes and developments in the protocol. Support for the validity and reliability of DCM is mixed; this can be attributed to the limited number of appropriately designed studies; we need additional research to effectively identify limitations in the current version of the tool which, in turn, would suggest areas for improvement (Cooke & Chaudhury, 2012). One current drawback of the tool is that it does not explicitly evaluate or incorporate possible influences of physical environmental features of the care setting on observed BCCs. The newly developed environmental evaluation component addresses this limitation, as well as providing an opportunity for environmental gerontologists to systematically link the built environment and behaviors of people with dementia in real time.

FRAMEWORK FOR A PHYSICAL ENVIRONMENT EVALUATION COMPONENT FOR DCM

The physical environment evaluation component is composed of two key coding schemes: Environmental Category Codes (ECCs) and Therapeutic Goals (TGs). The 20 ECCs (see Table 7.1) represent key environmental aspects and features of a dementia care setting. These are based on architectural features (e.g., orientation cues, walking paths), interior design features (e.g., furniture-type/arrangement, personally meaningful objects) and sensory attributes (e.g., auditory stimulation, glare). The ECCs have been identified by the authors as the recurring environmental features that affect behaviors of people with dementia and are drawn from existing literature on physical environment in dementia care settings (e.g., Brawley, 2006; Briller, Proffitt, Perez, Calkins, & Marsden, 2001; Day, Carreon, & Stump, 2000; Zeisel et al., 2003). In particular, environmental features and concepts from two validated and widely used environmental evaluation tools, the TESS-NH (Sloane & Mathew, 1990; Sloane et al., 2002) and the PEAP (Weisman et al., 1996), were used to develop the new tool's codes and goals. In order to be consistent with the format/structure of the DCM tool, the ECCs were constructed in a similar manner to those of the DCM's BCCs such

TABLE 7.1 Environmental Category Codes

Environmental Category Code (ECC)	Memory Cue	General Description of Category Code
EA	Auditory stimulation	Presence of auditory stimulation
EC	Cues (way finding)	Presence of environmental cues for navigation around unit
ED	Décor	Presence & degree of home-like décor
EE	Exits	Visibility of unit exits
EF-T	Furniture-type	Institutional vs. home-like furniture
EF-A	Furniture-arrangement	Arrangement of furniture that would support or impede participation in group activity or social interaction
EG	Glare	Presence of glare
EH	Handrails	Presence of handrails along main hallways
EK	Corridor length	Length of primary hallway on unit
EL	Lighting	Type of lighting in terms adequacy, brightness, and institutional/residential appearance
EM	Meaningful objects	Presence of personally or culturally meaningful objects in the context of the resident's culture and preference
EO	Outdoor space	Presence of/access to outdoor space adjacent to unit
ER-S	Room-size	Size of common living/dining spaces
ER-C	Room-configuration	Configuration of common areas
ES	Smell	Odor on unit
ET	Tactile stimulation	Presence of everyday objects/activity props
EU	Unfamiliar hallway clutter	Hallway clutter
EV	Visual stimulation	Presence of visual stimulation
EW	Walking path	Presence of walking path
EZ	Zero effect	No perceived environmental effect, i.e., absence of any possible previously identified items

Full description and explanation of the ECCs is beyond the scope of this chapter and is part of the training materials to be available to DCM environment tool users.

that there is a code for almost every letter of the alphabet. The letter "E" is placed in front of each code to indicate that the code is part of the environmental evaluation tool.

In the same way a BCC is linked with a Mood and Engagement Value (ME Value) in the DCM tool, each ECC is linked with a positive or negative ECC Value (+1 or –1), depending on whether it appears to positively or negatively influence a resident's behavior, mood and/or engagement. For example, the category EF-A (Furniture arrangement) refers to the arrangement of furniture that facilitates conversation and social interaction among residents (e.g., placing chairs at right angles to

FIGURE 7.1 Example of ECC and Related ECC Values—EF-A (Furniture Arrangement)

ECC Value +1   ECC Value –1

one another, creating conversational groupings with seating and coffee, or end tables). Furniture that is arranged in a conversational pattern would be ascribed a +1 value, whereas furniture that is arranged around the periphery of the room and is therefore not supportive of easy visual and verbal contact would be assigned a –1 value (see Figure 7.1). As mapping data are collected at different times of day, it is possible that the same space may have either a +1 or –1 value, depending on any reorganization or movement in the furniture arrangement.

The ECCs are identified in association with the observed BCCs. Trained observers (or *mappers*) position themselves as unobtrusively as possible within the care setting (but with clear sight lines to the residents being observed), and use a mapping table (see Table 7.2), to record the appropriate BCC, along with up to two ECCs and their associated value (i.e., +1/–1). The policy allowing a mapper to record up to two ECCs associated with one BCC acknowledges the potential influence of more

TABLE 7.2 Sample Mapping Table for Physical Environment Evaluation Tool

Participant	Time	10:00	10:05	10:10	10:15	10:20	10:25
Helen	BCC	B	A	A	E		
	ME	+1	+3	+3	+3		
	ECC	ER-C	EO	EO	EL		
	ECC Value	+1	+1	+1	+1		
Judith	BCC	K	K	A	W		
	ME	+1	+1	+1	–3		
	ECC		ER-C	EE	EF-T		
	ECC Value		+1	–1	–1		

Instructions: Record up to a maximum of two Environmental Category Codes (ECCs), along with their respective value (e.g., EFA –1, EA –1) every 10 minutes. BCC = Behavioral Category Code. ME = Mood and Engagement Value.

than one environmental feature on an observed behavior. For example, furniture arrangement of the activity (positively or negatively) and noise from other residents/staff interaction in the activity room (negatively) may both affect a resident's observed behavior. While the BCCs are mapped every 5 minutes as per the DCM rules, related ECCs are mapped every 10 minutes, in order to reduce burden on the observer. The 10-minute mapping interval also reflects the fact that ECCs are less likely to change as frequently as the BCCs. Data collected from the ECC observations can be used to generate both Individual and Group Environmental Category Profiles and Environmental Category Value Profiles (see Pilot Study section for illustration). These profiles can in turn be used to identify physical environmental features of the care setting that foster or hinder person-centered care practice and lead to recommendations for positive environmental modifications.

The second coding scheme associated with the environmental evaluation tool is based on the eight outcome-oriented TGs identified earlier by Cohen and Weisman (1991) and other researchers (Calkins, 1988; Lawton, 1986; Moos & Lemke, 1994; Regnier & Pynoos, 1992). The TGs, which serve to connect the ECCs with the notion of personhood, are described in Table 7.3. In the environmental evaluation tool, each TG is associated with multiple related ECCs, as well as with what we term an Environmental Enhancer (EE) and an Environmental Detractors (ED). By recording EEs and EDs in conjunction with the ECCs, it is possible to identify the environmental characteristics that appear to facilitate or undermine the personhood and well-being of a person with dementia. For example, the TG of "Maximize Awareness and Orientation" refers to environmental characteristics that enable residents to orient themselves to space, time, and activity. The related ECCs include Cues (EC), Corridor Length (EK), Room Configuration (ER-C), Tactile Stimulation (ET), and Unfamiliar Hallway Clutter (EU). The EE for this TG includes physical features that assist residents in orienting themselves to space, time, and activity—for example, small unit size, cluster-style floor plan, physical landmarks, familiar objects, contrasting colors, unique activity spaces, and furnishings unique to specific areas (lounge vs. dining). In contrast, the ED for this TG includes physical features that limit residents' ability to orient themselves to space, time, and activity—for example, large unit size, long double-loaded hallways (hallway with rooms on both sides), large multipurpose common areas, and unfamiliar institutional equipment (lifts, laundry carts, commodes). The photographs in Figure 7.2 illustrate several environmental features that serve as EEs and EDs of this TG.

TABLE 7.3   Description of Therapeutic Goals (TGs)

Therapeutic Goal	General Description
Maximize safety and security	Environmental characteristics that maximize resident safety and security of self.
Support functional abilities	Environmental characteristics that enable residents to function as independently as possible and support their continued use of everyday skills.
Maximize awareness and orientation	Environmental characteristics that enable residents to orient themselves to space, time, and activity.
Facilitate social interaction	Environmental characteristics that facilitate and enable meaningful interaction with others (i.e., resident-resident, resident-staff, resident-family).
Provision of privacy	Environmental characteristics that facilitate residents' choices in various levels of privacy through regulation of visual and auditory stimuli.
Regulate of stimulation	Environmental characteristics that contribute to an appropriate quantity and quality of sensory experience.
Provide opportunities for personal control	Environmental characteristics that enable residents to exercise choice and personal preference about their everyday life and care circumstances. Such characteristics influence how, what, where, and with whom, the residents spend their time.
Provide continuity of the self	Environmental characteristics that help preserve or support residents' past activities, preferences, and beliefs.

FIGURE 7.2   Example of an Environmental Enhancer (EE) and Environmental Detractors (ED) to Awareness and Orientation

Awareness and Orientation EE—Small unit size, cluster-style floor plan, familiar objects, furnishings unique to specific areas

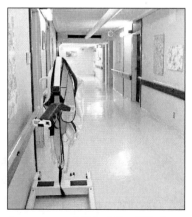

Awareness and Orientation ED—long, double-loaded hallway, unfamiliar institutional equipment

USING THE ENVIRONMENTAL EVALUATION TOOL:
A PILOT STUDY

Pilot testing of the newly developed physical environment evaluation tool was conducted over a three-month period in five dementia care units in Vancouver, British Columbia, Canada. The units were selected based on their varied physical environments (e.g., a newly built free-standing dementia care facility, a Special Care Unit housed in a larger facility, and a renovated dementia care unit). At each facility, five residents, selected by administration and care staff, were mapped for three observation periods over the course of one week. Each observation period lasted 120 to 140 minutes, such that each resident was mapped for approximately 6 to 7 hours. All observations took place in the public areas of the unit. A BCC and accompanying ME Value were documented every five minutes during the observation period, as per DCM protocol. Up to two ECCs and their associated ECC Values were recorded every 10 minutes. The focus of the pilot study was to assess the appropriateness and functionality of the ECCs as the primary environmental coding mechanism. The secondary coding scheme with EEs and EDs were not explicitly recorded. However, the resultant ECCs and their associated ECC Values can provide some indication of related EEs and EDs.

The majority of the 25 pilot-study participants were female residents. All participants experienced difficulties with short- and long-term memory and displayed impaired daily decision-making. Most of the residents were independent with regard to bed mobility, transfers, locomotion on the unit, and eating; however, many of them required extensive assistance (or were totally dependent) in terms of dressing and personal hygiene.

Case Study

Drawing on the results from one of the participating facilities, Cedarwood Manor (a pseudonym, as are all proper names in this chapter), this section illustrates how the physical environment evaluation tool can be used. Observations at Cedarwood Manor were conducted on the 18-bed dedicated dementia care unit. Figure 7.3 depicts the floor plan of the unit: the lounge area is situated on the left, with the dining area on the right. A small kitchen area is located in the upper right corner of the diagram. The arrows denote the camera angle of the photographs displayed in Figures 7.4 through 7.6.

FIGURE 7.3   Unit Floor Plan—Cedarwood Manor

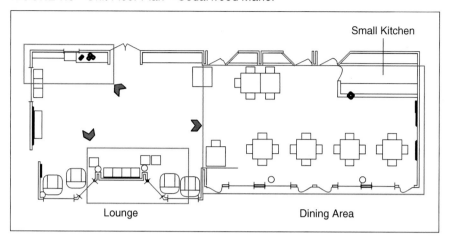

Small Kitchen

Lounge

Dining Area

FIGURE 7.4   Unit Dining Area at Cedarwood Manor

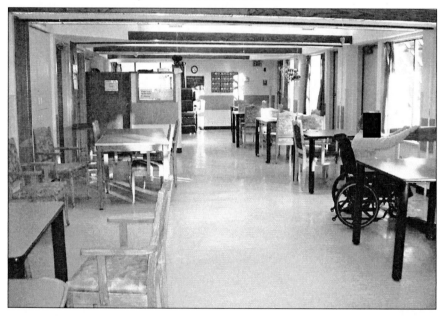

As part of the DCM based observation data, Figure 7.7 outlines the Group Behavior Category Profile for the five participating residents at Cedarwood Manor. The most frequently observed BCCs were **K** (Kum/Come and Go—walking, standing, or moving independently), **A** (Articulation—interacting with others verbally or otherwise), and

FIGURE 7.5   Lounge Area at Cedarwood Manor

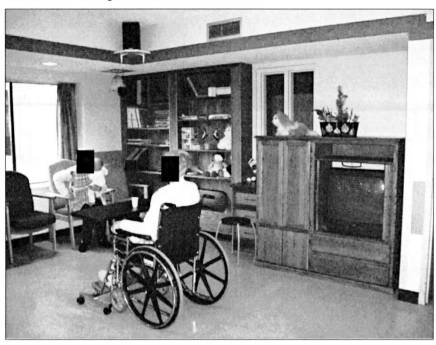

FIGURE 7.6   Lounge Area Seating at Cedarwood Manor

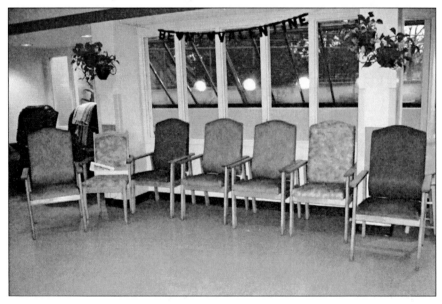

FIGURE 7.7   Group Behavior Category Profile

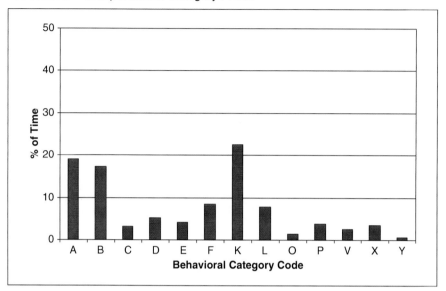

B (Borderline—being engaged but passively watching), which accounted for 22.6%, 19.1%, and 17.3% of the time, respectively.[2]

In terms of mood as assessed through the main DCM tool, more than 75% of the time, residents exhibited either a neutral mood (i.e., +1), in which they were alert and focused on their surroundings and displayed brief or intermittent engagement; or a considerably positive mood (i.e., +3), in which they were content and relaxed and displayed considerable engagement. Approximately 15% of the time, residents exhibited small signs of negative mood (i.e., −3).

The environmental coding data were used to produce the Group Environmental Category Profile as displayed in Figure 7.8. During the observation period, all but two of the 20 ECCs were used to account for the potential influence of the environment on resident behavior, and ME. EA (Auditory stimulation), EF-T (Furniture-type), EF-A (Furniture-arrangement), and ER-C (Room configuration) were the most commonly observed ECCs, accounting for 22%, 15.4%, 17.8%, and 9.7% of the data points, respectively. It should be noted that, as observers can record up to two ECCs per 10-minute time frame, the point of reference for the ECCs is percentage of data points as opposed to percentage of time.

As can be seen in Figure 7.9, auditory stimulation (EA) and furniture arrangement (EF-A) were observed to have a predominantly positive influence on behavior, while furniture type (EF-T) and

FIGURE 7.8   Group Environmental Category Profile

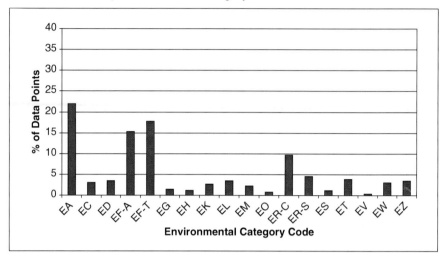

FIGURE 7.9   Group Environmental Category Value Profile

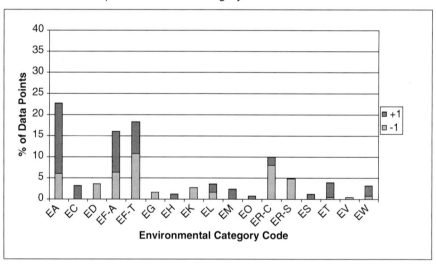

room configuration (ER-C) were observed to have a predominantly negative influence. In terms of auditory stimulation, staff were diligent in choosing appropriate television and radio programming and residents appeared to experience a great deal of enjoyment in listening and watching musical, dance, and nature programs. While the recliners located in alcoves adjacent to the lounge area appeared comfortable, offered a non-institutional appearance and an opportunity for residents to sit and observe an activity or people without actively being part of that activity, at times their location detracted from residents' ability to see, converse with others, or participate in social activities. This was especially the case when wheelchairs were present. Due to the arrangement of chairs around the lounge's periphery, residents in wheelchairs could only be accommodated by being placed directly in front of other residents. With the exception of the recliners, the majority of lounge seating was quite institutional in appearance and was not conducive to sitting for any length of time. In terms of room configuration, considerable distance existed between the lounge/dining area and residents' bedrooms, and there was no visual access to the washrooms from the lounge/dining area.

Similar graphs can be generated for individual residents. For example, Figures 7.10 through 7.12 summarize the BCCs, ME Values, ECCs, and ECC Values for one of the female residents, Cecilia. As is evidenced in Figure 7.10, Cecilia spent most of her time passively engaged (B), walking around the unit (K), talking with other residents or staff (A), and eating and drinking (F). For the most part, her ME was either neutral (+1) or considerably positive (+3). As shown in Figure 7.11, furniture type (EF-T) and arrangement (EF-A) were the ECCs most commonly noted as influencing her behavior and ME. While the comfortable recliner in which she sat (i.e., EF-T) was given an ECC Value of +1 (see Figure 7.12), the chair was set back in an alcove (i.e., EF-A), behind other residents

FIGURE 7.10   Individual Behavior Category Profile—Cecilia

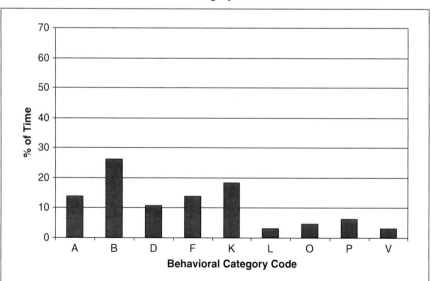

FIGURE 7.11 Individual Environmental Category Profile—Cecilia

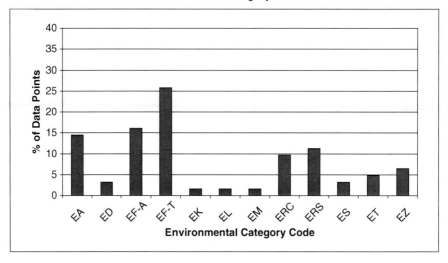

FIGURE 7.12 Individual Environmental Category Value Profile—Cecilia

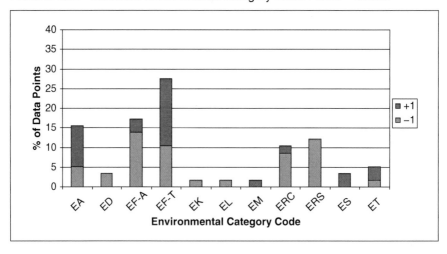

(see left side of photograph in Figure 7.6), which resulted in a –1 rating. Although Cecilia is a social person, the placement of the recliner appeared to limit the opportunity for her to engage with others and to be included in group activities. The –1 ECC Value associated with furniture type reflected the times when Cecilia rested in the less comfortable chairs along the room's perimeter. Cecilia appeared to enjoy listening to the music playing through the television, which resulted in the positive ECC Value ascribed to auditory stimulation (EA).

As evidenced here, use of the physical environment evaluation tool, along with existing DCM, offers insight into the influence of the surrounding built environmental characteristics on both individual resident's behavior and group behavior and highlights areas for potential improvement in the physical environment.

APPLIED IMPLICATIONS

Evaluation of the built environment in a dementia care setting has let us make notable progress in conceptualizing the goals of a therapeutic environment with associated psychosocial outcomes. However, existing validated evaluation tools lack observation of real-time objective behavioral data and resident-level assessment of the care environment. The newly developed environmental evaluation component embedded within the well-recognized DCM tool provides an opportunity to systematically gather environmental data linked with observed resident behaviors. It is, we believe, a useful addition to the field of dementia care evaluation.

The new addition to the DCM offers an important opportunity for staff in dementia care settings and for design professionals involved in the planning and design of dementia care environments. Currently, DCM is used by staff in several countries as an evaluation and practice development tool for systematically observing and recording residents' behaviors and the quality of staff-resident interactions. With use of the environmental coding schemes presented in this chapter, staff members will be able to account for potential physical environmental influences on residents' behaviors. The new environmental data will provide an opportunity to identify areas for environmental modifications and/or renovations. Some of these interventions could be fairly modest—for example, rearrangement of a furniture grouping to help residents better engage in activities/conversations or the introduction of color contrast in appropriate areas to increase visual cues of environmental features. Environmental interventions of larger scale can also be identified, such as the need for toilets that are easily accessible from activity spaces and direct access to safe and secure outdoor spaces. Undertaking the environmental training program (to be offered for the environmental evaluation tool users) and using the new tool would also increase the environmental sensibility of staff and equip them with an understanding of the importance of physical environmental features in positively or negatively contributing to residents' behaviors and mood.

The second group of practitioners who can benefit from this tool is design professionals, for example, architects, and interior designers.

In post-occupancy evaluations of a facility, in this case a dementia care setting, design professionals typically conduct observations utilizing the kinds of standardized environmental evaluation tools discussed earlier. Our new tool would provide them with *evidence-based data* based on real-time "environment-behavior" interactions, leading to individual or group targeted intervention strategies that are likely to be more meaningful and effective compared with the traditional methods of making design decisions. Moreover, the standardized coding schemes of the DCM environment component provide an opportunity to compare care environments in multiple facilities in a valid and reliable manner.

The purpose of this chapter has been to provide a descriptive overview of a newly developed environmental evaluation tool as an addition to the existing DCM tool. The primary component of this new addition allows DCM users to systematically link built environmental features (i.e., ECCs) with residents' observed behaviors (Behavior Category Codes or BCCs) in long-term care settings. The secondary coding scheme provides an opportunity to cluster similar ECCs in order to identify Environmental Enhancers (EEs) or Environmental Detractors (EDs). Together, these make possible the identification of built environmental features that are supportive of, or contribute negatively to, behaviors of people with dementia. This new environmental evaluation tool will be further refined, based on the recently completed pilot study, to enhance its conceptual rigor, increase ease of mapping, and refine data analysis procedures. Future plans also include formal incorporation of this environmental evaluation component with a version of the DCM tool alongside the development of an environmental training module that will be available as part of DCM training programs. As we further recognize the importance of person-centered dementia care approaches, it is critical to take into account the role of the physical environment and make appropriate environmental design decisions, informed by a more meaningful assessment of both environment and behavior.

NOTES

1. The "environmental evaluation component" is a proposed sub-tool to work in tandem with the existing Dementia Care Mapping (DCM) tool. This sub-tool is being revised, refined, and pilot-tested in consultation with the Bradford Dementia Group at the University of Bradford, UK.
2. Other categories are: C: Cool (being disengaged or withdrawn); D: Doing for self (Self-care); E: Expressive (Expressive or creative activities); F: Food (eating or drinking); L: Leisure (leisure, fun or recreational activities); O: Objects (displaying attachment to or relating to inanimate objects); P: Physical (receiving practical, physical, or personal care); V: Vocational (work or work-like activity); X: Excretion (episodes related to excretion); and Y: Yourself (interaction in the absence of any observable other).

REFERENCES

Brawley, E. (2006). *Design innovations for ageing and Alzheimer's: Creating caring environments.* Hoboken, NJ: John Wiley and Sons.

Bredin, K., Kitwood, T., & Wattis, J. (1995). Decline in quality of life for patients with severe dementia following a ward merger. *International Journal of Geriatric Psychiatry, 10,* 967–973.

Briller, S., Proffitt, M., Perez, K., Calkins, M., & Marsden, J. (2001). *Maximizing cognitive and functional abilities. Vol. 2: Creating successful dementia care settings.* Sydney, Australia: Health Professions Press.

Brooker, D. (2004). What is person-centred care for people with dementia? *Reviews in Clinical Gerontology, 13,* 215–222.

Brooker, D. (2005). Dementia care mapping: A review of the research literature. *The Gerontologist, 45*(Special Issue), 11–18.

Brooker, D. (2007). *Person-centred dementia care: Making services better.* London, UK: Jessica Kingsley Publishers.

Brooker, D., & Duce, L. (2000). Well-being and activity in dementia: A comparison of group/reminiscence therapy, structured goal-directed group activity, and unstructured time. *Aging & Mental Health, 4,* 354–358.

Brooker, D., & Surr, C. (2005). *Dementia care mapping: Principles and practice.* Bradford, UK: Bradford Dementia Group.

Brooker, D., Foster, N., Banner, A., Payne, M., & Jackson, L. (1998). The efficacy of dementia care mapping as an audit tool: Report of a 3-year British NHS evaluation. *Aging and Mental Health, 2*(1), 60–70.

Calkins, M.P. (1988). *Design for dementia: Planning environments for the elderly and the confused.* Owings Mills, MD: National Health Publishing.

Calkins, M.P. (2001). The physical and social environment of the person with Alzheimer's disease. *Aging and Mental Health, 5*(Suppl. 1), 126–130.

Chung, J.C.C. (2004). Activity participation and well-being in people with dementia in long-term care settings. *OTJR: Occupation, Participation and Health, 24*(1), 22–31.

Cohen, U., & Weisman, G. (1991). *Holding on to home: Designing environments for people with dementia.* Baltimore, MD: Johns Hopkins University Press.

Cooke, H., & Chaudhury, H. (2012). An examination of the psychometric properties and efficacy of dementia care mapping. *Dementia: The International Journal of Social Research and Practice.* doi:10.1177/1471301212446111

Cutler, L.J., Kane, R.A., Degenholtz, H.B., Miller, M.J., & Grant, L. (2006). Assessing and comparing physical environments for nursing home residents: Using new tools for greater research specificity. *The Gerontologist, 46*(1), 42–51.

Day, K., Carreon, D., & Stump, C. (2000). The therapeutic design of environments for people with dementia: A review of the empirical research. *The Gerontologist, 40*(4), 397–416.

Fleming, R. (2009). *The use of environmental assessment tools for the evaluation of Australian Residential Facilities for people with dementia.* Sydney: Australia: Hammond Care.

Grant, L. (1996). Assessing environments in Alzheimer special care units. *Research on Aging, 18*(3), 275–291.

Innes, A. (Ed.) (2003). *Dementia care mapping: Applications across cultures.* Baltimore, Maryland: Health Services Press.

Innes, A., & Surr, C. (2001). Measuring the well-being of people with dementia living in formal care settings: The use of dementia care mapping. *Aging and Mental Health, 5*(3), 258–268.

Jarrott, S. E., & Bruno, K. (2003). Intergenerational activities involving persons with dementia: An observational assessment. *American Journal of Alzheimer's Disease and Other Dementias, 18,* 31–37.

Kitwood, T. (1997). *Dementia reconsidered: The person comes first.* Buckingham, UK: Open University Press.

Kitwood, T., & Bredin, K. (1992). Towards a theory of dementia care: Personhood and well-being. *Ageing and Society, 12,* 269–287.

Kuhn, D., Kasayka, R.E., & Lechner, C. (2002). Behavioral observations and quality of life among persons with dementia in 10 assisted living facilities. *American Journal of Alzheimer's Disease and Other Dementias, 17*(5), 291–298.

Lawton, M.P. (1986). *Environment and aging.* Second printing (orig. 1980). Albany, NY: Center for the Study of Aging.

Lawton, M.P. (2001). The physical environment of the person with Alzheimer's disease. *Aging and Mental Health, 5* (Suppl. 1), S56–S64.

Lawton, M.P., & Nahemow, L. (1973). An ecological theory of adaptive behavior and aging. In C. Eiserdorfer, & M.P. Lawton (Eds.). *The psychology of adult development and aging* (pp. 657–667). Washington, DC: American Psychological Association.

Moos, R.H., & Lemke, S. (1994). *Group residences for older adults.* New York, NY: Oxford University Press.

O'Connor, D., Phinney, A., Smith, A., Small, J., Purves, B., Perry, J., . . . Beattie, L. (2007). Personhood in dementia care: Developing a research agenda for broadening the vision. *Dementia: The International Journal of Social Research and Practice, 6*(1), 121–142.

Potkins, D., Myint, P., Bannister, C., Tadros, G., Chithramohan, R., Swann, A., . . . Margallo-Lana M. (2003). Language impairment in dementia: Impact on symptoms and care needs in residential homes. *International Journal of Geriatric Psychiatry, 18,* 1002–1006.

Regnier, V., & Pynoos, J. (1992). Environmental interventions for cognitively impaired older persons. In J. Birren, B. Sloane, & G. Cohen (Eds.), *Handbook of mental health and aging* (pp. 763–792). New York, NY: Academic Press.

Schwarz, B., Chaudhury, H., & Tofle, R.B. (2004). Effect of design interventions on a dementia care setting. *American Journal of Alzheimer's Disease and Other Dementias, 19*(3), 34–43.

Sloane, P., Brooker, D., Cohen, L., Douglass, C., Edelman, P., Fulton, B.R., . . . Zimmerman S. (2007). Dementia care mapping as a research tool. *International Journal of Geriatric Psychiatry, 22,* 580–589.

Sloane, P. & Mathew, L. (1990). The therapeutic environment screening scale: An observational screening instrument to assess the quality of nursing home environments for residents with dementia. *American Journal of Alzheimer's Disease and Dementia, 5,* 22–26.

Sloane, P. D., Mitchell, C. M., Weisman, G., Zimmerman, S., Foley, K. M. L., Lynn, M., . . . Montgomery R. (2002). The therapeutic environment screening survey for nursing homes (TESS-NH): An observational instrument for assessing the physical environment for institutional settings for persons with dementia. *Journal of Gerontology: Social Sciences, 57B*(2), S69–S78.

Smith, M., Gerdner, L. A., Hall, G. R., & Buckwalter, K. C. (2004). History, development, and future of the progressively lowered stress threshold: A conceptual model for dementia care. *Journal of the American Geriatrics Society, 52*(10), 1755–1760.

Weisman, G., Lawton, M.P., Sloane, P.S., Calkins, M., & Norris-Baker, L. (1996). *The professional environmental assessment protocol.* Milwaukee, WI: School of Architecture, University of Wisconsin at Milwaukee.

Zeisel, J., Silverstein, N.M., Hyde, J., Levkoff, S., Lawton, M.P., & Homes, W. (2003). Environmental correlates to behavioral health outcomes in Alzheimer's special care units. *The Gerontologist, 43*(5), 697–711.

PART IV

Public Spaces

CHAPTER 8

Mobility in Outdoor Environments in Old Age

Susanne Iwarsson, Agneta Ståhl, and Charlotte Löfqvist

EDITORS' INTRODUCTION

*T*his chapter represents a transition to consideration of older adults'
use of outdoor environments. Synthesizing insights from research in
different European countries conducted over more than a decade, a nuanced
perspective is provided on the complex issue of older adult mobility. The chapter is an exemplar of the use of mixed methods and longitudinal perspectives
in probing the underlying explanation of changing patterns of outdoor mobility. A particular focus is on the use of mobility assistance devices to compensate for declining physical capability. Framed from a broader perspective
than is provided by the traditional person–environment interaction lens, the
chapter explicitly incorporates the theme of the nature of human activity as a
variable influencing adaptive behavior. There is strong reinforcement of the
importance to older adults of walking and continuing everyday participation in outdoor environments. Of particular significance are insights on the
longitudinal process of utilizing mobility assistance devices, including the
transition from reluctant adoption to creative dependence on such devices
as a normative and integral component of everyday life. The chapter is also
important in exploring the notion of the "usability" of outdoor environments.
The authors illustrate how both physical barriers (poor design and environmental obstructions) and social barriers (stigmatization and limited social
acceptance) serve as constraints on the potential for creating outdoor settings that maximize the participation of older adults in community life. Both
empirical evidence and the persuasive writing of the authors emphasize the
need for translating growing awareness of the wish of older adults to utilize
the outdoor environment for as long as possible into practical interventions
to maximize their participation in spaces beyond the threshold. Active user
participation, not only in research but also in the process of implementing
such interventions, will be essential to ensure the success of such initiatives.

Since mobility is a fundamental aspect of daily life, preserving mobility and participation in society is a critical part of maintaining function and an active life during the process of aging (Mollenkopf et al., 2004; Schootman et al., 2006; Shumway-Cook et al., 2002). Mobility is an observable physical, spatio-temporal process of moving across space and over a period of time from one point to another. It may involve walking, using a bicycle, or travel by train, bus, or car. Mobility is usually regarded as a natural and important part of people's everyday life (Rosenkvist, Risser, Iwarsson, & Ståhl, 2010). Mobility in public environments is a prerequisite for the accomplishment of various activities, such as shopping and social visits (Wessels, de Witte, Jedeloo, van den Heuvel, & van den Heuvel, 2004). Synthesizing 15 years of methodological and empirical interdisciplinary research on outdoor mobility in the Nordic countries, this chapter presents a knowledge base with potential for practice implementation in societal planning, for example in health and social care, and urban planning.

Functional decline is an inevitable consequence of aging, and multiple health problems are common in the older population (Karlamangla et al., 2007). Older persons generally experience a gradual decline in physical capacity, manifest in functional limitations including, but not limited to difficulties in moving, in bending and kneeling, and in maintaining balance. In order to compensate for functional decline, the use of mobility devices such as canes, rollators (wheeled walkers, usually with four wheels and brakes), and wheelchairs often plays an important role in daily life in old age. Such devices help older people to remain independent in everyday activities, feel safe, and participate in society (see, for example, Wressle & Samuelsson, 2004). Given the complexity of functional decline and dependence on mobility devices, the occurrence of accessibility problems in outdoor environments and public places is evident; indeed, older people often experience usability and safety problems when moving in outdoor environments (Shumway-Cook et al., 2002). Consequently, well-designed pedestrian environments and public transportation systems are important prerequisites for older people to be able to travel and conduct their everyday activities independently and safely (Leslie et al., 2005).

In order to come up with efficient solutions to support outdoor mobility in old age, there is a need for research generating a knowledge base with potential for transfer to practice contexts. The grand challenge is to increase our understanding of the complexity of the transactional relationship between the person, the environment, and the tasks and activities forming daily life.

CONCEPTS, THEORY, AND METHODOLOGY

At the outset of research, it is necessary to define the core concepts involved. Theoretical models and conceptual frameworks that illuminate the relationship between the individual's capacity and the demands of the environment emphasize that both activity limitations and participation restrictions arise in the relationship between the individual and the environment; such an emphasis is the focus of the International Classification of Functioning, Disability, and Health (World Health Organization, 2001). The theoretical model most often referred to in connection with issues of accessibility for people with functional limitations is Lawton and Nahemow's well-known ecological theory of aging (1973) (see Chapter 1). This theory, as well as related empirical research, supports a definition of the term *accessibility* as the relationship between the individual's functional capacity and the demands of the physical environment (Iwarsson & Ståhl, 2003). Accessibility is thus a relative concept comprising two components: a personal component and an environmental component. This definition was operationalized in the Enabler Concept (Steinfeld et al., 1979), serving as a starting-point for the development of assessment instruments (Iwarsson & Slaug, 2010). In the Enabler Concept, the personal component describes functional limitations and the extent of dependence on mobility devices, while the environmental component describes environmental barriers in great detail. In this context, *accessibility* might be considered objective, since assessment of the personal and environmental components is performed by professionals using reliable methods. Most important, the environment is described on the basis of established guidelines and standards (Preiser & Ostroff, 2001).

A term that often occurs together with the concept of accessibility in planning and building legislation and policy documents is *usability*. This is based on the individual's own perception and on cultural and social norms (Steinfeld & Danford, 1999). Usability incorporates people's own assessments of the extent to which desired activities can be performed in a given environment and thus comprises not only the personal and environmental components but also a third component—activity. Whereas accessibility can be rated objectively by professionals, usability is based on the user's own perception and is therefore subjective by nature (Iwarsson & Ståhl, 2003). This perspective is congruent also with theories emphasizing human activity and the relationship between the individual and the environment as described within occupational therapy (see, for example, Townsend & Polatajko, 2007).

Safety and security are essential human needs (Maslow, 1954). As suggested by Wretstrand (2003), safety is a state without danger while security is a state without intentional danger. It is generally accepted that perceived safety and security are composed of two dimensions: a cognitive dimension, concerning the perceived probability of potential incidents, and an emotional dimension, concerning fear and anxiety related to potential incidents. Beaulieu, Dubé, Bergeron, and Cousineau (2007) suggested a third dimension: a behavioral dimension referring to behaviors of avoidance or protection. "Fear of falling" is a safety-related term frequently used in the field of public health research. Minimizing this fear entails "perceived self-confidence at avoiding falls during essential, relatively non-hazardous activities" (Kressig et al., 2001, p. 1457). A security-related term is "fear of crime," which is defined as "a feeling expressed by avoidance or protection behaviors, an abstract fear when being in a perceived threatening environment, or a concrete evaluation of the risk of being the victim of personal or personal-property attack" (Beaulieu et al., 2007, p. 338). In the context of outdoor mobility, Rantakokko et al. (2009, p. 634) used the phrase "fear of moving outdoors" as "an emotional condition that can lead to avoidance of outdoor activities that are well within a person's functional health capacity," which relates both to safety and security.

With respect to methodology, since the mid-1990s we have developed an applied methodology including quantitative, qualitative, and mixed-methods approaches. With the ecological theory of aging (Lawton & Nahemow, 1973) as a foundation, and based on the principles of the Enabler Concept (Steinfeld et al., 1979), many of our studies target accessibility, as defined above. The fundamental methodological principle for such studies is the structured and objective analysis of both the individual's functional limitations and the demands of the environment, followed by an analysis of the person–environment relationship. When it comes to studying mobility in old age, it is crucial to also capture perceived aspects of person–environment-activity transactions. For example, usability can be captured by means of participatory techniques (Patton, 2002) such as participant observation combined with critical incident analysis (Carlsson, 2004; Flanagan, 1954), research circles (Härnsten, 1994), and case studies (Yin, 2003). Research circles are a practice-oriented, structured method developed as a means to engage practitioners and researchers in a joint effort to develop or collect knowledge that has not previously been recognized. Research circles are led by researchers, but involve participants with different backgrounds. The method aims to nurture engagement and communication among people with different perspectives but with core interests in common, ultimately resulting in joint agreements for practical actions to change their own situation. The most common way of studying safety is by using official accident data and/or injury data from hospitals (Berntman, 2003). To capture individual perceptions of safety and security, the use of questionnaires is the most common technique (Wennberg, Ståhl, & Hydén, 2009; Wennberg, Hydén, & Ståhl, 2010). As exemplified in studies published by Rantakokko et al. (2009, 2010a, 2010b), knowledge can also be generated by utilizing data at hand in longitudinal databases, comprising data originally collected for other purposes but lending themselves to secondary data analyses.

SYNTHESIS OF EMPIRICAL STUDIES

When planning for this chapter, we reviewed more than 30 original publications emanating from several major research projects, and some PhD student projects focusing on different aspects of mobility in old age that we have been involved in during the past decade. A subset of the empirical publications was used to produce a synthesis of the findings.

The largest database utilized emanates from the European project "Enabling Autonomy, Participation, and Well-Being in Old Age: The Home Environment as a Determinant for Healthy Ageing" (ENABLE-AGE) (Iwarsson et al., 2007). The main objective of this project was to examine the home and neighborhood environment and its importance for major components of healthy aging. The target group was community-residing, very old, single-living inhabitants in Sweden, Germany, the United Kingdom (UK), Hungary, and Latvia ($N = 1,918$). This group was involved in survey studies, in-depth interviews, and observational studies, applying a longitudinal approach (Hovbrandt, Fridlund, & Carlsson, 2007; Hovbrandt, Ståhl, Iwarsson, Horstmann, & Carlsson, 2007; Löfqvist, Nygren, Széman, & Iwarsson, 2005; Löfqvist, Nygren, Brandt, Oswald, & Iwarsson, 2007).

SIZE (life quality of senior citizens in relation to mobility conditions) is another European project, where perceived problems among older people in the traffic environment in eight European countries were studied. The SIZE project also addressed the question of why measures known to be efficient and effective with respect to the outdoor mobility of senior citizens are often not implemented (Risser, Haindl, & Ståhl, 2010). Focus group interviews, personal interviews, quantitative surveys, and workshops were carried out within this project.

The other projects used were carried out in Sweden, or in collaboration with researchers in other Nordic countries. The "Let's Go for a Walk" project was a before and after study in a medium-sized town (79,000 inhabitants) in southern Sweden, running over a 5-year period. This outdoor environment-intervention project included several substudies applying different methodologies. It involved older inhabitants in three adjacent residential areas as well as public actors and stakeholders (municipality representatives from health and social care and the highway department, estate owners, public transport authorities, etc.) engaged in the urban planning of outdoor environments (Hovbrandt, Ståhl et al., 2007; Ståhl, Carlsson, Hovbrandt, & Iwarsson, 2008; Ståhl, Horstmann, & Iwarsson, 2012).

Another database utilized is the project "Screening and Counseling for Physical Activity and Mobility in Older People" (SCAMOB), conducted in Jyväskylä, Finland (Leinonen et al., 2007), where we were involved in studies based on data collected with the control group recruited for a controlled trial investigating the effects of physical activity counseling in community-living older people (Rantakokko, Mänty, et al., 2009; Rantakokko, Iwarsson, Hirvensalo, et al., 2010; Rantakokko, Iwarsson, Kauppinen, et al., 2010).

"Walking in Old Age" is a PhD student project focusing on accessibility and usability for older pedestrians in two Swedish municipalities, one in the south and one in the north, representing a year-round perspective on accessibility. This involves removal of physical barriers in outdoor environments in bare-ground conditions (i.e., differences in level, uneven surfaces, drainage grooves, and curbs at zebra crossings [crossings marked with stripes for pedestrian crossing]) (Wennberg et al., 2009, 2010). The aim was to examine the implementation process in municipal planning and assess the effects of measures taken. Older pedestrians' perceptions in terms of usability, mobility, and perceived safety, as well as municipal employees' views in a year-round perspective, were captured by means of a mixed-method approach. Using a sequential design, qualitative methods were followed by quantitative ones. First, we used focus group interviews and participant observation to identify physical barriers in the outdoor environment. Subsequently, the qualitative findings were used to formulate relevant questions for a questionnaire-based study (Creswell & Plano Clark, 2006). Such an exploratory mixed methods approach, with qualitative findings helping to develop and inform the quantitative method, was useful in terms of pre-screening potential respondents and their perceptions, as well as discovering local preconditions regarding the study districts.

With respect to older people's visits to public facilities, use of mobility devices in old age, and aspects of user satisfaction, PhD student projects undertaken in Sweden (Hedberg-Kristensson, Dahlin Ivanoff, & Iwarsson, 2007; Valdemarsson, Jernryd, & Iwarsson, 2005) and Denmark (Brandt, Iwarsson, & Ståhl, 2003, 2004) were also incorporated within our synthesis. In addition, a methodological project involving therapists and users of mobility devices in the five Nordic countries (Denmark, Sweden, Norway, Iceland, and Finland), delivered important insights on the complexity of use of mobility devices as related to everyday activity and participation (Brandt et al., 2008).

The Synthesis Process

From the original papers, parts of the results sections considered relevant for this book chapter were extracted into one large document. First, two of the authors (AS and SI) completed a crude categorization of the content into three categories: mobility devices; mobility/ activity; mobility/urban planning. In a next step, a text extraction procedure concentrating on the category "mobility devices," was completed. After an attempt to synthesize the results of the category "mobility/activity," because of considerable overlaps with mobility/urban planning, we subsequently went into these parts of the text more inductively. This approach resulted in a new set of tentative categories, and subsequently, during an iterative process of text reduction, a core category and three subcategories emerged. We titled the core category "A transactional perspective on outdoor mobility in old age," and the subcategories 1) functional limitations, age, sex, and psychological factors' influence on mobility; 2) the role of mobility devices in supporting or restraining outdoor mobility, and 3) the influence of physical environmental barriers and traffic dynamics on outdoor mobility. The first author (SI) then compiled a raw version of the findings. Finally, the second (AS) and third (CL) authors read the findings and suggested further refinement. After joint discussion and further text revision involving all three authors, the final version was agreed upon.

FINDINGS

A Transactional Perspective on Outdoor Mobility in Old Age

In all of the studies underlying this synthesis, a key point is that to a greater or lesser extent, the importance of maintaining independent performance of daily activities came through as the main priority for older people when discussing outdoor mobility. Outdoor mobility is connected to necessary daily activities such as shopping, running errands, visiting health care facilities, visiting relatives and friends, and engaging in leisure time activities (cinema, theater, countryside journeys, gardening), or traveling (taking a walk, biking). Older people also emphasize their involvement in taking care of other older people or children, or doing other voluntary jobs. Such types of activity are important sources of self-acceptance (feeling important and useful), and thus, important sources of motivation for mobility. Religion (religious activities) also plays a role as a motivation factor. "Keeping on doing as before" is an important element of taking part in the outside world, and older people are very interested in continuing to perform activities they have done for most of their lives. They describe how they use the environment to carry on their interests as they wish, for example, exercising, visiting the library, or shopping for groceries as usual. For more or less all such activities, outdoor mobility is a necessary but complex prerequisite.

Regarding motivation and reasons for going out, older people claim that staying at home results in passivity, with less participation in social life and/or less physical exercise. Immobility may enhance depression, lack of motivation, and fear or loneliness, while being mobile is considered to be important in order to enjoy life. For instance, walking, including walking with friends or walking the dog, is mentioned as being connected to fun and to joyful activities. Having the chance to go to a park is experienced as enjoyable, and getting out into the countryside can be a momentous occasion, a special event.

Personal factors including functional limitations, age, sex, and psychological factors such as motivation and feelings of fear or insecurity strongly influence mobility. Overall, more functional limitations, higher age, being a woman, and having feelings of fear and anxiety about moving outdoors have a negative influence on mobility. Mobility devices represent a supportive solution for many older people, but there are some potentially negative aspects. There are psychological hindrances to overcome, in terms of stigmatization and non-acceptance, but also practical issues to deal with such as possibilities for training and availability of services. Most important, mobility devices not only support mobility, they to a great extent also restrain mobility, not the least outdoors and in public facilities where the mobility device can be difficult to manage due to high curbs (Figure 8.1) or stairs, and not the least due to steep slopes, both sideways and along pedestrian roads.

Once the older person has accepted the fact that she or he has to use a mobility device, it is often said to be indispensable. Gradually, the use of the device develops from being only a walking support to becoming embedded in the performance of various daily activities. For example, for kitchen work, making use of the rollator seat as support when lifting food out of the oven, and using the rollator basket to transport various items during home maintenance may become normative.

The transactional character of mobility in old age is very obvious, since successful activity performance depends heavily on the interplay between the person, the mobility device, and the environment. Physical environmental barriers and various dynamic factors in traffic (i.e., sudden unevenness or slopes on surfaces, different curb heights, weather conditions, combined bicycle and pedestrian paths, construction work) certainly have an influence on mobility, but in the person–environment interaction, social aspects and perceptions of safety and security also play important roles. For example, older people point out feelings of being unsafe and insecure when moving outdoors, causing mobility-restricting behaviors, especially during the evening and at night. Often, there is no clear-cut differentiation among the multitude of factors perceived as obstacles or barriers. Barriers to outdoor mobility mentioned

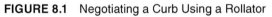

FIGURE 8.1   Negotiating a Curb Using a Rollator

Photo courtesy of Charlotte Löfqvist

by older people are personal characteristics (e.g., fears, perceived lack of stamina, cautious attitudes toward novelty), social preconditions (e.g., the need for social support, friends, and other contacts), environmental barriers (e.g., differences of elevation and slopes, lack of benches, long distances, shared pedestrian-bicyclist areas), and legal or policy preconditions (e.g., separating pedestrians from bicyclists, enforcement of speed limits, one-way streets). The assessment of one's own outdoor mobility is connected to modes of transportation available, to the type of settlement where one lives (city, suburban area, rural) and to individual features like physical and psychological fitness. Such factors also have an influence on the frequency of outdoor mobility.

In terms of frequency of mobility, overall, older people are quite satisfied. Still, it should be noted that when asked about frequency of going outdoors and of activity performance, older people often would like to increase their mobility. In fact, as much as one third report that they do not participate as much as they would like to in various activities. Environmental factors identified as negative increase the probability of unmet physical activity aspirations, in particular in those already experiencing difficulties in walking outdoors.

Functional Limitations, Age, Sex, and Psychological Factors' Influence on Mobility

One theme identified under this subcategory is different types and combinations of functional limitations and their influence on outdoor mobility in old age. Such limitations affect frequency of going outdoors, autonomy, and independence in activities of daily living. Another theme centers around variation related to demographic characteristics such as age and sex, and living situation. A third theme comprises personal psychological factors, for example, coping and adaptation, and issues of fear and anxiety.

Numerous examples of how different types of functional limitations are related to perceiving problems in the outdoor environment come up. Different types of physical environmental barriers cause usability problems, in particular for study participants with severe loss of sight or difficulties in bending and kneeling. Usability problems depend on the occurrence of functional limitations and use of mobility devices. Some people with severe loss of sight and/or reduced perception/cognition state that environmental barriers such as signs, posts, or advertisement displays in pathways cause problems. For example, there are significant differences among subgroups of older people with different profiles of functional limitations, with respect to their frequency of activity. That is, older people without any functional limitations and those with only perception/cognition-related functional limitations, report a higher frequency of activity than those with movement-related functional limitations. Even though the frequency of activity overall is rather high, as much as one third of older people report that they are not engaged in activities outside their home as much as they would like to be. As to satisfaction with frequency of activity, it is lower among older people with more complex combinations of functional limitations. It is also common that large proportions of older people are willing to increase their physical activity level, but do not perceive that they have opportunities to do so.

Regarding factors influencing frequency of activity, anxiety and fear seem to be important. When it comes to avoiding moving outdoors because of fear, there often is a marked difference between the sexes: up to two thirds of women report such reactions, compared to less than one third of men. People who report fear of moving outdoors are more likely to be women, to have less education, to be in a poorer financial situation, to live alone, to have musculoskeletal diseases and slower walking speed, and to report the presence of poor street conditions, noisy traffic, and hills in their environment. Over time, women are more than four times as likely to report fear of moving outdoors as men, and this fear of moving outdoors increases with age. In addition to fear, other psychological and personal factors of importance for outdoor mobility are the ability to adjust, cope, and adapt to the current and changing situation, especially when it is necessary to use mobility devices in everyday activities. Strategies and adaptive behavior develop over the years when people strive to maintain participation; they may develop altered ways of performing daily activities, planning well in advance to deal with environmental demands, or an acceptance of the way things have to be done due to changing and sometimes constrained circumstances.

With only a few exceptions, women report more usability problems when moving outdoors, but they also use mobility devices to a greater extent than men. At the same time, among rollator users, being a woman as well as living alone appear to indicate dissatisfaction with the mobility device, for example concerning simplicity of use, multi-purposefulness, effort required, transportation, and professional maintenance of the mobility devices. As to perceived environmental barriers, "no snow at bus stops" is far more important for women than for men and, regarding appraisal of environmental measures taken, women tend to express a higher level of concern than men, in particular with respect to crossing time at traffic signals. Concerning differences based on age, the oldest age groups consider environmental barriers more important than do their younger counterparts.

The Role of Mobility Devices in Supporting or Restraining Outdoor Mobility

This subcategory comprises three themes, namely issues of acceptance/ non-acceptance and satisfaction related to mobility devices, perceived obstacles and barriers when using mobility devices, and changes in use of mobility devices over time.

In the Nordic countries, the rollator is the most common mobility device used by older people, and often the users are fully satisfied. Still, when asking about specific characteristics, not all people are fully satisfied. Complaints are often reported, such as the weight of the device, the effort required, and the comfort of using it. Users who do not always use their rollator are more likely to be dissatisfied with their device.

Need and use of mobility devices causes mixed feelings. For example, the device itself and other people's reactions cause stigma. Further, the acceptance or not of mobility devices is based on experiences of problems performing everyday activities. Some older people readily accept using a mobility device when independence in daily activities is at stake, while others do not immediately accept the fact that they should use such a device. For some, participation in the community with mobility devices is experienced as a great step to take, and other people's opinions have an influence on the process of acceptance. Participants who accept that they have to use mobility devices report positive feelings such as increased independence, security, and confidence when regaining the opportunity to make decisions about desired activities. A mobility device such as a rollator is something one may have to accept using, but it is also a constant reminder of one's limitations. Another attitude described is to consider the device as a possibility to remain active and to manage everyday activities; as such, it becomes embedded with other aspects of everyday life. Successively and over time, the mobility device is perceived as necessary and mostly positive and has an influence on how daily activities are being performed, rather than whether new or extended activities are initiated.

Using mobility devices in everyday activities implies experiences of various kinds of obstacles and barriers. Along with gradual functional decline, environmental barriers become harder to overcome when using mobility devices. In fact, the mobility device is often referred to as a limitation on mobility. For example, it is perceived as difficult to walk on paving stones, because the rollator shakes or gets stuck in between stones. Weak wrists and pain in the arms cause problems, as do limitations in balance and walking. When using a rollator or two sticks, both hands are occupied; in such situations it is impossible to lean on any handrail. Regarding type of mobility device, low curbs are considered more important by wheelchair users than they are for rollator and cane/crutch users, and similar differences are found concerning curbs at zebra crossings (marked pedestrian crossings) and ramps at shop entrances. Shops with entrance steps, high counters, lack of parking places for mobility devices, and insufficient clearance of snow and ice are also described as barriers.

Other obstacles expressed by users of mobility devices concern lack of training about how, for example, to lift heavy mobility devices, and concerns that their device is poorly adapted for outdoor use. Users of mobility devices also express a fear of leaving them at entrances or outside shops because of the risk of theft. With respect to powered wheelchairs, the need to recharge the battery is also a limitation. Help from relatives, friends, or social services also influences the way mobility devices are used over time. Fluctuating factors such as weather conditions and health status are crucial, as are technical details of the devices (weight, size, safety aspects).

Over time, different ways of using mobility devices enable outdoor mobility and control over daily routines to be maintained, even though functional limitations increase. Combinations of different types of mobility devices are essential for optimizing their use, such as a walking stick in combination with more supportive devices like a walking frame or rollator. Dependence on the device also changes in character over time, from facilitating walking and providing safety when moving around in the environment, to being a prerequisite and support for activity performance when performing everyday activities.

The Influence of Physical Environmental Barriers and Traffic Dynamics on Outdoor Mobility

The four themes comprising this subcategory are environmental barriers outdoors and in public facilities, traffic dynamics, seasonal variations, and problem solutions suggested by older people themselves.

The picture of older people's perceptions of environmental barriers outdoors and in public facilities is quite consistent: pedestrian walkways, high curbs, uneven and irregular walking surfaces, and narrow sidewalks with severe inclines, represent barriers to mobility.

Additional environmental barriers are the lack of places to sit down and rest and benches of a poor design (too low, without armrests), as well as long distances to bus stops and public facilities. Older people describe how the absence of a bench where they could pause and rest might prevent them from taking a walk. Steps at entrances are the most common problem perceived for entering public facilities, and if there are steps, banisters are important. The lack of seating possibilities inside shops and department stores, difficulties in picking merchandise from shelves, and narrow aisles in department stores are problematic for quite a few, as are heavy doors and narrow entrances. Another barrier often described as problematic is the lack of toilets in public spaces.

Since the studies constituting the empirical base for this synthesis of findings were conducted in countries with marked seasonal variations, problems related to the winter situation are prominent. Such environmental barriers include poor snow clearance (Figure 8.2) and icy pedestrian walkways. Older people emphasize that heaps of snow

FIGURE 8.2 Snow: A Barrier to Outdoor Mobility

Photo courtesy of Hanna Wennberg

often block pavements and crossings, creating difficulties for rollator and wheelchair users. Problems also occur on narrow streets where the ploughing vehicles cannot get through. The importance of snow removal increases with increasing age. Seasonal variations also influence the use of powered wheelchairs, resulting in lower frequencies of use in the winter, in particular for activities such as going for a ride and moving around in the garden.

Traffic dynamics that cause problems most often concern bicycles and mopeds ridden on shared pedestrian and bicycle pathways and on sidewalks. The problems highly ranked by older people are frequently related to the behavior of other road users, or to the behavior of other persons more generally, such as inconsiderate car drivers, and are also related to negative attitudes toward older people. It is also common for older people to want more traffic signals at pedestrian crossings and to want such signals to provide more time for crossing the road.

Older people themselves suggest solutions to some of these problems, both in terms of what they themselves could do and what society could provide. For example, they report that they try to explain to cyclists that they should not use the pavement, but they are often met with a negative and non-understanding attitude. Older people emphasize the benefits of maintaining outdoor mobility in old age, but still the cyclists suggest that older people should stay indoors in bad weather. Apart from limiting such mobility-restricting behaviors, participants also suggest more pro-active strategies. For example, they recommend using mobility devices as well as spikes underneath the shoes and a pair of walking poles to facilitate safe walking. Walking more slowly and carefully with great attention to the pavement surface, as well as support by a companion, are further suggestions. Older people would also like to encourage the highway departments in their municipalities to enforce speed limits, to improve public transportation, both with respect to infrastructure and vehicles, and to improve the maintenance of pedestrianized roads. Measures to support a sense of security and safety among older people (more police in the streets), as well as improvements to accessibility in housing and public facilities, are also emphasized.

Case Study: Elisa

In order to exemplify and contextualize the findings described under the core category and the subcategories, a case study was used, applying a transactional perspective to person–environment-activity. The case study was based on one of the original publications from the ENABLE-AGE Project, exploring how very old single-living Swedish women experience the use of mobility devices over time in relation to everyday activity and participation (Löfqvist, Nygren, Brandt, & Iwarsson, 2009). The case study used an exploratory strategy and a combination of quantitative and qualitative data sources (Yin, 2003), gathered on three different occasions over five years. The case of "Elisa" was purposefully selected from single-living women, 80 to 89 years of age at baseline, living in ordinary housing, who had recent and varied experience in using mobility devices. In addition to survey assessments and interviews, a participant observation approach called the "experiential walk" was conducted. This walk targeted typical everyday activities involving use of the mobility device chosen by the informant, and asked what kind of activity and how, why and where it was performed. The interviewer went along, guided by the informant, while she talked about and performed the activity.

Elisa—a Swedish woman, aged 94 at the time of data collection, who lived alone—had been a rollator user for more than six years. This type of mobility device is common in the Nordic countries (Brandt et al., 2003). Over the years, Elisa found that her dependence on a rollator gradually increased due to reduced walking ability and loss of stamina. Elisa had lived in the same apartment for many years, on the outskirts of a Swedish town. She had two children and grandchildren living nearby, which was the reason for moving there when she became a widow many years ago. Many of her former friends had died and nowadays she sometimes socialized with her single-living neighbors. She valued very highly her ability to manage everyday activities, and being able to keep up daily habits and routines independently was crucial, as she had been a housewife all her life. She declared that everyday activities nowadays were more time-consuming and straining than before, with the result that only the most important everyday activities such as personal care, cooking, and light housework were performed. She began to use assistive devices for personal care (for showering, toiletry, etc.) five years previously and, at that time, she also began to receive support with everyday activities from social services and from special transportation services (STS).

Elisa was still independent in most activities of daily life, but experienced difficulties in an increasing number of activities. Indoors she moved around mostly without any mobility device but with support from walls and furniture, since she felt that the rollator was clumsy. At night, when feeling weaker, she sometimes used the device. When leaving her apartment to do laundry or take out the garbage, she always used the rollator with its basket. Due to her lack of strength, she was no longer able to open the heavy doors in her yard that led to these facilities. She found this very frustrating, since she really struggled to be independent.

When the rollator was initially provided, it gave more support and security than the walking stick she had used before: it made walking and transportation easier, and facilitated her activity performance. Gradually, the rollator had become indispensable for outdoor walks and to manage shopping and going to the dentist and bank. Some years ago she received a lighter rollator, intended for indoor use, but, nowadays, she preferred to use it outdoors too. Outdoor walks had become rarer over time since poor balance, pain, and loss of strength were more prominent. Outdoor mobility in relation to local bus transportation had gradually become more demanding. Bringing the rollator onto the bus was hardly possible nowadays since the lifting and handling had increased the pain in her arms and shoulders. Five years ago, Elisa used to take the bus to the city center on a regular basis to do shopping (instead of using the STS). This happened very seldom nowadays, mostly due to lack of stamina but also due to what she perceived as the risk of falling and the feeling of insecurity while trying to move around and manage stairs, steps, curbs, and heavy doors. In addition, not daring to leave the rollator outside shops with steps, because of the risk of theft, implied a limitation in choice of shops to visit.

Dependence on a mobility device has had an impact on Elisa's life situation, in both a positive and a negative way. She says, "I wouldn't get out without the rollator but I hate to be dependent on it." The experience of being a rollator user in public places was described as problematic, both for her and for other people. Elisa felt that she was in the way and took up too much space, always making other people adjust or asking them for help. Therefore she avoided some activities and avoided socializing in public: "It's troublesome with the rollator. I can get where I want to but I think it's troublesome for other people—there's always someone who has to step aside to make way for the rollator." The convenience and familiarity of the surroundings could be crucial for the decision to attend an event, and affected her view of whether the rollator was perceived as an obstacle or not. Elisa felt that it was much easier to go to a center for older people than to a more public club or event, being confident about getting a helping hand there if needed, and meeting with and being more comfortable with others in the same situation.

The case of Elisa illustrates that, even though it was more time-consuming, the use of mobility devices in combination with adaptive strategies made it possible to maintain everyday activities in spite of decreased physical mobility and difficulties in undertaking them. Increased functional limitations changed the conditions for mobility. Elisa's dependence on mobility devices had changed over time, from facilitating mobility and everyday occupations to becoming indispensable for support and security. Diversified use of mobility devices had evolved over the years and also during the day due to her changing health conditions. When encountering environmental barriers and functional limitations, the need to adapt the activity performance and adjust to different environmental situations increased, and it sometimes created dependence on help from others. Visiting well-known environments was therefore preferred. Using the rollator in public places sometimes implied the need to make other activity choices due to feelings of inconvenience for others.

FROM KNOWLEDGE TO PRACTICE

Based on the findings and experiences from our empirical studies, two of the projects underlying this book chapter also aimed at practice implementation. That is, since the "Let's Go for a Walk" (Ståhl et al., 2008) and "Walking in Old Age" (Wennberg et al., 2009, 2010) projects also included a pre-post research design, we were able to study effects on outdoor mobility in old age after the implementation of tangible changes to outdoor environments (Figure 8.3).

FIGURE 8.3 Pre-Implementation of Environmental Measures: No Sidewalk (Pavement)

Photo courtesy of Marie Grönvold

After implementation of concrete environmental measures in the "Let's Go for a Walk" study area (Figure 8.4), the overall satisfaction among the older people participating in the project was moderately to highly positive, as was the evaluation of each of the specific environmental measures taken. Women evaluated the overall environmental measures taken higher than did men ($p = 0.013$), as did those with better perceived health ($p = 0.025$). Multivariate regression models for each of the specific measures implemented showed that only use of a rollator was significantly related to the appraisal of need for more even pavements ($p = 0.049$), while for separation of pedestrians and cyclists, use of rollator, as well as better perceived health, resulted in significantly more positive appraisal ($p = 0.012$ and 0.018, respectively). As to lowered curbs, they were more appreciated by older people ($p = 0.002$) and rollator users ($p = 0.035$). Regarding longer green time at crossings with traffic lights, being a woman was significantly related to appreciation ($p = 0.006$). As concerns change in difficulty of walking, in activity in the town overall, and in activity in the residential area as a pedestrian, no sub-group differences were found.

In the "Walking in Old Age" project, older people were more satisfied with outdoor environments within the study district in general ($p = 0.049$), as well as with outdoor environments nearby their residences

FIGURE 8.4   Post-Implementation of Environmental Measures: A New Sidewalk (Pavement)

Photo courtesy of Lars Glantz

(p = 0.025), after implementation of environmental measures. As to specific measures, satisfaction with orderliness (p = 0.041), removal of graffiti and litter (p < 0.0001), and clear separation between pedestrians and cyclists (p = 0.017) increased. No difference in the frequency of walking was found after implementation. However, fewer respondents cited barriers in the outdoor environment (p = 0.023) or snow and ice on pedestrian roads (p = 0.008) as reasons to avoid walking outdoors after implementation. A fact worth considering is that in both studies referred to, the evaluation took place 1.5 to 3 years after implementation. How sustainable and long-term the perceived improvements will be remains to be evaluated.

CONCLUDING REMARKS

A major finding in our studies is the importance for older people of maintaining independent performance of activities in daily life, and that outdoor mobility is essential to maintain participation. Based on a decade of research in several European countries, we have described the types of environmental barriers that impede outdoor mobility in old age. Differences in curb levels, irregular walking surfaces and steep inclines along walking paths, lack of benches, and long distances to bus stops all constrain outdoor mobility. In addition, a lack of understanding from other road users or fear of crime can create fear of moving outdoors. The most vulnerable groups are very old women and people using mobility devices. A striking finding that warrants further research attention is the fact that mobility devices can be seen as both supportive and restrictive of outdoor mobility. In contrast to the goal of provision of this type of assistive technology, under some circumstances the mobility device can even be regarded as a constraint on outdoor mobility. In other words, the mobility device is not always optimally designed for outdoor use, taking into account the design and maintenance of outdoor environments and traffic dynamics. It should be noted that reasons for this are also related to the individual, often in terms of stigma or functional decline.

Even so, there are solutions available. In several of our studies, older people themselves suggested solutions, both regarding what they themselves could do and what highways departments could provide to improve outdoor mobility. A couple of our intervention studies provide guidance on how to successfully bring "knowledge to practice" and show that measures taken in the environment do have a positive impact on problems associated with walking, as well as on older people's general levels of satisfaction with their outdoor mobility.

Turning to issues of concepts and theoretical background, we conclude that studying outdoor mobility in old age requires a transactional approach, which takes into consideration the complex relationships of functioning, disability, and health. Theories based on the notion of person–environment fit draw our attention to how individual capacity interacts with environmental barriers. However, when studying outdoor mobility in old age, we need theories with the capacity to nurture our understanding of the transactional dynamics of the aging person, the different dimensions and demands of the environment, and the tasks and activities of daily life. As to methodological experiences, the research synthesized in this chapter demonstrates the necessity and value of adopting longitudinal designs and multi-method or mixed-method approaches: given the complex nature of the dynamics under study, there is much to gain from studying phenomena in different ways and over time.

In conclusion, our results display the transactional and complex character of outdoor mobility in old age and highlight the fact that performance of daily activities plays a paramount role. It is evident that personal factors of different character strongly influence outdoor mobility and the satisfaction with frequency of activities. Environmental barriers and mobility devices play important roles, but not in isolation from personal factors. In order to understand outdoor mobility in old age, research needs to be based on valid and well-defined concepts and should utilize multi-method approaches.

REFERENCES

Beaulieu, M., Dubé, M., Bergeron, C., & Cousineau, M. M. (2007). Are elderly men worried about crime? *Journal of Aging Studies*, 21(4), 336–346.

Berntman, M. (2003). *Consequences of traffic casualties in relation to traffic-engineering factors—An analysis in short-term and long-term perspectives* (Doctoral thesis). Lund, Sweden: Department of Technology and Society, Lund University.

Brandt, Å., Iwarsson, S., & Ståhl, A. (2003). Satisfaction with rollators among community-living users: A follow-up study. *Disability and Rehabilitation*, 25(7), 343–353.

Brandt, Å., Iwarsson, S., & Ståhl, A. (2004). Older people's use of powered wheelchairs for activity and participation. *Journal of Rehabilitation Medicine*, 36(2), 70–77.

Brandt, Å., Löfqvist, C., Jónsdottir, I., Sund, T., Salminen, A. L., Werngren-Elgström, M., & Iwarsson, S. (2008). Towards an instrument targeting mobility-related participation: Nordic cross-national reliability. *Journal of Rehabilitation Medicine*, 40(9), 766–772.

Carlsson, G. (2004). Travelling by urban public transport: Exploration of usability problems in a travel chain perspective. *Scandinavian Journal of Occupational Therapy*, 11(2), 78–89.

Creswell, J. W., & Plano Clark, V. L. (2006). *Designing and conducting mixed methods research*. Thousand Oaks, CA: Sage Publications Inc.

Flanagan, J. C. (1954). The critical incident technique. *Psychological Bulletin, 51*(4), 327–358.

Härnsten, G. (1994). *The research circle: Building knowledge on equal terms*. Stockholm, Sweden: Swedish Trade Union Confederation (LO).

Hedberg-Kristensson, E., Dahlin Ivanoff, S., & Iwarsson, S. (2007). Experiences among older persons using mobility devices. *Disability and Rehabilitation: Assistive Technology, 2*(1), 15–22.

Hovbrandt, P., Fridlund, B., & Carlsson, G. (2007). Very old people's experience of occupational performance outside the home: Possibilities and limitations. *Scandinavian Journal of Occupational Therapy, 14*(2), 77–85.

Hovbrandt, P., Ståhl, A., Iwarsson, S., Horstmann, V., & Carlsson, G. (2007). Very old people's use of the pedestrian environment: Functional limitations, frequency of activity and environmental demands. *European Journal of Ageing, 4*(4), 201–211.

Iwarsson, S., & Slaug, B. (2010). *Housing enabler—A method for rating/screening and analysing accessibility problems in housing. Manual for the complete instrument and screening tool* (2nd ed.). Lund & Staffanstorp, Sweden: Veten & Skapen HB och Slaug Enabling Development.

Iwarsson, S., & Ståhl, A. (2003). Accessibility, usability and universal design—positioning and definition of concepts describing person–environment relationships. *Disability and Rehabilitation, 25*(2), 57–66.

Iwarsson, S., Wahl, H-W., Nygren, C., Oswald, F., Sixsmith, A., Sixsmith, J., . . . Tomsone, S. (2007). Importance of the home environment for healthy aging: Conceptual and methodological background of the European ENABLE-AGE Project. *The Gerontologist, 47*(1), 78–84.

Karlamangla, A., Tinetti, M., Guralnik, J., Studenski, S., Wetle, T., & Reuben, D. (2007). Comorbidity in older adults: Nosology of impairment, diseases, and conditions. *Journal of Gerontology, 62A*(3), 296–300.

Kressig, R. W., Wolf, S. L., Sattin, R. W., O'Grady, M., Greenspan, A., Curns, A., & Kutner, M. (2001). Associations of demographic, functional, and behavioral characteristics with activity-related fear of falling among older adults transitioning to frailty. *Journal of the American Geriatrics Society, 49*, 1456–1462.

Lawton, M. P., & Nahemow, L. (1973). Ecology and the aging process. In C. Eisdorfer & M. P. Lawton (Eds.), *The Psychology of Adult Development and Aging* (pp. 619–674). Washington, DC: American Psychological Association.

Leinonen, R., Heikkinen, E., Hirvensalo, M., Lintunen, T., Rasinaho, M., Sakari-Rantala, . . . Rantanen, T. (2007). Customer-oriented counseling for physical activity in older people: Study protocol and selected baseline results of a randomized-controlled trial (ISRCTN 07330512). *Scandinavian Journal of Medicine & Science in Sports, 17*(2), 156–164.

Leslie, E., Saelens, B., Frank, L., Owen, N., Bauman, A., Coffee, N., & Hugo, G. (2005). Residents' perceptions of walkability attributes in objectively different neighborhoods: A pilot study. *Health and Place, 11*(3), 227–236.

Löfqvist, C., Nygren, C., Brandt, Å., & Iwarsson, S. (2009). Very old Swedish women's experiences of mobility devices in everyday occupation: A longitudinal case study. *Scandinavian Journal of Occupational Therapy, 16*(3), 181–192.

Löfqvist, C., Nygren, C., Brandt, Å., Oswald, F., & Iwarsson, S. (2007). Use of mobility devices and changes over 12 months among very old people in five European countries. *Aging Clinical and Experimental Research, 19*(6), 497–504.

Löfqvist, C., Nygren, C., Széman, Z., & Iwarsson, S. (2005). Assistive devices among very old people in five European countries. *Scandinavian Journal of Occupational Therapy, 12*(4), 181–192.

Maslow, A. H. (1954). *Motivation and personality*. New York, NY: Harper & Row.

Mollenkopf, H., Marcellini, F., Ruoppila, I., Széman, Z., Tacken, M., & Wahl, H-W. (2004). Social and behavioural science perspectives on out-of-home mobility in later life: Findings from the European project MOBILATE. *European Journal of Ageing, 1*(1), 45–53.

Patton, M. Q. (2002). *Qualitative evaluation and research methods* (3rd ed.). Newbury Park, USA: Sage Publications.

Preiser, W. F. E., & Ostroff, E. (Eds.). (2001). *Universal design handbook*. New York, NY: McGraw-Hill.

Rantakokko, M., Iwarsson, S., Hirvensalo, M., Leinonen, R., Heikkinen, E., & Rantanen, T. (2010). Unmet physical activity need in old age. *Journal of the American Geriatrics Society, 58*(4), 707–712.

Rantakokko, M., Iwarsson, S., Kauppinen, M., Leinonen, R., Heikkinen, E., & Rantanen, T. (2010). Quality of life and barriers in the urban outdoor environment in old age. *Journal of the American Geriatrics Society, 58*(11), 2154–2159.

Rantakokko, M., Mänty, M., Iwarsson, S., Törmäkangas, T., Leinonen, R., Heikkinen, E. & Rantanen, T. (2009). Fear of moving outdoors and development of outdoor walking difficulty in older people. *Journal of the American Geriatrics Society, 57*(4), 634–640.

Risser, R., Haindl, G., & Ståhl, A. (2010). Barriers to senior citizens' outdoor mobility in Europe. *European Journal of Ageing, 7*(2), 69–80.

Rosenkvist, J., Risser, R., Iwarsson, S., & Ståhl, A. (2010). Exploring mobility in public environments among people with cognitive functional limitations—challenges and implications for planning. *Mobilities, 5*(1), 131–145.

Schootman, M., Andresen, E.M., Wolinsky, F.D., Malmstorm, T.K., Miller, J.P., & Miller, D.K. (2006). Neighborhood conditions and risk of incident lower-body functional limitations among middle-aged African Americans. *American Journal of Epidemiology, 163*(5), 450–458.

Shumway-Cook, A., Patla, A. E., Stewart, A., Ferrucci, L., Ciol, M. A., & Guralnik, J. M. (2002). Environmental demands associated with community mobility in older adults with and without mobility disabilities. *Physical Therapy, 82*(7), 670–681.

Ståhl, A., Carlsson, G., Hovbrandt, P., & Iwarsson, S. (2008). "Let's go for a walk!": identification and prioritization of accessibility and safety measures involving elderly people in a residential area. *European Journal of Ageing, 5*(3), 265–273.

Ståhl, A., Horstmann, V., & Iwarsson, S. (in press). A five-year follow-up among older people after an outdoor intervention. *Transport Policy*.

Steinfeld, E., & Danford, G. S. (Eds.). (1999). *Enabling environments: Measuring the impact of environment on disability and rehabilitation*. New York, NY: Kluwer Academic/Plenum Publishers.

Steinfeld, E., Schroeder, S., Duncan, J., Faste, R., Chollet, D., Bishop, M., . . . Cardell, P. (1979). *Access to the built environment: A review of the literature*. Washington, DC: Government Printing Office.

Townsend, E., & Polatajko, H. (2007). *Enabling occupation II: Advancing an occupational therapy vision for health, well-being & justice through occupation*. Ottawa, ON: COAT Publications ACE.

Valdemarsson, M., Jernryd, E., & Iwarsson, S. (2005). Preferences and frequencies of visits to public facilities in old age—a pilot study in a Swedish town center. *Archives of Gerontology and Geriatrics, 40*(1), 15–28.

Wennberg, H., Hydén, C., & Ståhl, A. (2010). Barrier-free outdoor environments: Older peoples' perceptions before and after implementation of legislative directives. *Transport Policy, 17*(6), 464–474.

Wennberg, H., Ståhl, A., & Hydén, C. (2009). Older pedestrians' perceptions of the outdoor environment in a year-round perspective. *European Journal of Ageing, 6*(4), 277–290.

Wessels, R. D., de Witte, L. P., Jedeloo, S., van den Heuvel, W. P. M., & van den Heuvel, W. J. A. (2004). Effectiveness of provision of outdoor mobility services and devices in the Netherlands. *Clinical Rehabilitation, 18*(4), 371–378.

World Health Organization (WHO). (2001). *International Classification of Functioning, Disability and Health, ICF*. Geneva, Switzerland: WHO.

Wressle, E., & Samuelsson. K. (2004). User satisfaction with mobility assistive devices. *Scandinavian Journal of Occupational Therapy, 11*(3), 143–150.

Wretstrand, A. (2003). Wheelchair passengers and local public transport vehicles: Perceptions of safety and comfort (Dissertation, Bulletin 220). Lund, Sweden: Lund University, Department of Technology and Society.

Yin, R. K. (2003). *Case Study Research: Design and Methods* (3rd ed., Vol. 5). Thousand Oaks, CA: Sage Publications Inc.

CHAPTER 9

Older People's Use of Unfamiliar Space

Judith Phillips

EDITORS' INTRODUCTION

A primary focus of aging/environment research has been the manner in which people develop attachment to familiar environments as they transform spaces into places. This chapter provides an important contrast by considering how older adults experience unfamiliar out-door environments. A key issue concerns the way in which, over time, unfamiliar spaces become familiar and comfortable places as they are utilized in potentially different ways by visitors, new residents, and long-time residents. Utilizing site visits, simulated visits in a reality cave, and participant commentaries, Phillips identifies aspects of public spaces in two British towns (Swansea and Colchester) that facilitate the development of familiarity. Understanding this process and its implications for design is critical. It is argued that planners need to become increasingly sensitive to the kinds of environmental cues and features that facilitate place attachment and identification and the creation of meaning in unfamiliar public spaces. This process of making meaning is facilitated by the attractiveness of the place as well as its accessibility and ease of mobility. Phillips notes that first impressions are crucial, that there is a need for the preservation of historic buildings and landmarks that make outdoor spaces both memorable and easy to negotiate, that it is important to consider street ambiance and provide spaces for social interaction, and that the provision of adequate signage is a prerequisite for making both newcomers and long-time residents comfortable in community spaces. The argument here echoes and reinforces the contentions of Sheila Peace with respect to environmental complexity (see Chapter 2). In particular, it suggests the need for achieving an appropriate balance between the complexity and ambiguity that make

*for a rich visual, auditory, and somatic environment and the legibility,
negotiability, and clarity of design that makes outdoor space immediately interpretable and negotiable by first-time visitors. Achieving this
balance, not only for older adults but for all populations, is an essential aspiration if we are to combat the potential for exclusion of certain
groups in less sensitively planned environments.*

Studies of the ways in which "place" conditions and contributes
meaning to everyday life have tended to focus on people's relationship with familiar spaces. This is particularly relevant in studies of
older people's attachment to places where meaning and a sense of
place have developed through a lifetime of memories and associations
(Hay, 1998; Rowles & Watkins, 2003). Increasingly, older people are
experiencing the unfamiliar—either through traveling as tourists and
visitors to other towns and cities or through redevelopment of urban
centers. What was familiar can also become unfamiliar through cognitive decline. This raises questions such as: How do older people make
initial sense of unfamiliar outdoor environments and create meaning in
them? What particular features of the environment convey a sense of
meaning to older people? What are the lessons for planners in designing public outdoor spaces, such as positioning of signage or location of
parks where older people can feel comfortable, secure, and confident as
well as included?

This chapter addresses these questions by drawing first on the literature on the meaning of place and space as it relates to outdoor public
environments. This literature, mainly from within environmental gerontology, indicates clearly that familiarity over time is crucial in developing a sense of place and meaning. A sense of place is a feeling of identity
with place or, as Wiles (2005) describes it, it is the human experience
of space with meaning attached. Second, drawing on a research study
of Older People's Use of Unfamiliar Space (OPUS), the chapter investi-
gates how older people develop a sense of place and meaning in relation
to unfamiliar space. The study involved 44 older people exploring their
experiences of familiar and unfamiliar spaces, together with interviews
with planners and local residents. The study found that the attractiveness of the built and physical environment, conveyed through distinctive and historic buildings, as well as the ease with which a town or city
is accessible, were two crucial features in developing a sense of place.
The key issues for planners, addressed in the final section of the chapter,
point to the importance of preserving heritage and historic town fabric

while also making the townscape accessible and pleasant, enabling older people to participate fully as citizens, consumers, tourists, and residents. Although this chapter draws on material from the exploration of two towns in the United Kingdom (UK), the ideas are applicable to urban areas as a whole, including suburban areas, and also apply to rural areas.

UNFAMILIAR SPACES—FAMILIAR PLACES: CREATING MEANING FOR OLDER PEOPLE

Public urban spaces take on a distinctive sense of place when they create meaning for people using them. What gives place an identity and how people attach meaning to space are key geographical questions addressed by much of the literature on place and space over the last 30 years. Creating meaning and distinctiveness in town and city centers is increasingly important to spatial planners, as many town centers tend to become replicas of each other. Relph (1976) refers to this standardization or uniformity as *placelessness*. Meaningful places are also important to people's quality of life and identity, as they become part of who we are and how we understand ourselves and others (Lewicka, 2005). Public space is also important to older people's psychological and physical well-being and their positive experience of aging and place (Holland, Clark, Katz, & Peace, 2007; Newton, Ormerod, Burton, Mitchell, & Ward-Thompson, 2010; Smith, 2009; Wiles et al., 2009; WHO, 2007).

In creating meaning, the spatial planning literature highlights particular aspects that each city or town center should possess, such as a unique sense of place, an attractive environment, and safety and security (British Retail Consortium, 2010). How people experience place is diverse and not necessarily only through the visual but through other perceptions—smell, taste, touch, and hearing. Seamon (1980) also refers to "body awareness": an implicit physical familiarity with an environment, stemming from repeated use, that allows the individual to transcend conscious awareness. Such routines and actions in a familiar environment can also transform that environment into a place with a unique dynamic and character (Seamon, 1980). Others' perceptions of space and place may also influence meaning. One of the most influential contributors to the literature, Yi-Fu Tuan (1977), argues that the social and the spatial are inseparable. To develop a sense of place, one has to be intimately involved with that space and to know it emotionally, he argues. Seamon (1980) connects the importance of what people do in places to their experience of places. He suggests that people are attached to place and create meaning both bodily and emotionally, and says this is associated with the regularity and routine of everyday activity. Smaldone, Harris, and Sanyal (2008) consider the processes by which these meanings and attachments develop, and the importance of life course and age as places become marked with experiences, personal relationships, and life agendas. Such aspects of creating meaning all suggest that familiarity over time is essential.

In addition, how older people make sense of their environment is crucially important for identity, competence, mobility, and quality of life (Burholt, 2006; Peace, Wahl, Mollenkopf, & Oswald, 2007). Only recently in the United Kingdom has this focus turned to outdoor public spaces; much of the literature, as detailed in this volume, has concentrated on private indoor space. Outdoors, policy and planning in relation to older people has focused primarily on environment, activity, and well-being (the UK government's focus is on nurturing active, sociable living spaces) and on interaction, safety, and cohesion (a feature of sustainable communities); it also has addressed social exclusion (lifetime neighborhoods; lifetime homes; see Chapter 2). A limited number of studies (such as Aspinall et al., 2010; Holland et al., 2007; Sugiyama, Ward Thompson, & Alves, 2009) look at older people's use of space outside the "home" environment.

Environmental gerontology has focused attention on concepts such as "aging in place" and "place attachment," particularly in assessing the suitability of places in which to age (Keating & Phillips, 2008; Smith, 2009). Such concepts relate to familiar places and are often linked with where people reside or where they have lifetime associations. "Attachment to place" is normally associated with lengthy periods of exposure to a place (Rowles, 1978; Smith, 2009), "with memories of smells and sounds of communal activities and homely pleasures acquired over time" (Tuan, 1977, p. 159). Although such romantic images of the sense of "home" and place can be artificial, attachment to place has contributed significantly to how we conceptualize later life and give meaning to the spaces inhabited and used by older people over their life course (Phillipson, Bernard, Phillips, &, Ogg, 2001; Scharf, Phillipson, & Smith, 2003).

A key element in the relationship between aging and place is familiarity which comes with a period of time. This is reinforced by the literature on place and aging. For example, Smith (2009) looked at deprived neighborhoods where older people were at risk in both the United Kingdom and Canada, and found that the key factors influencing this relationship were: physical attachment and place knowledge; social attachment; historical attachment; religiosity and spirituality;

and the life history or life course of the older person. Living in the same location for a number of years was also associated with establishing strong social and support networks and a sense of "physical insideness" (Rowles, 1983; and see Chapter 1), all of which are important markers of social capital for older people. Spending time in one location led to familiarity with the social and physical environment. Familiarity is also one of the recurring key themes in research on dementia-friendly environments (see Chapter 7)—unfamiliarity prevents or limits older people with dementia from going out, thus reducing the physical extent of their activity as well as interactions with others (Blackman, Van Schaik, & Martyr, 2007; Duggan, Blackman, Martyr, & Van Schaik, 2008). In addition "homeliness," a term inextricably linked with familiarity, is recommended when designing spaces to retain access to the outdoors (Day, Carreon, & Stump, 2000). This body of literature confirms the importance of the temporal dimension in attachment to place and, consequently, familiarity with the rhythms and routines of life within that locality.

By contrast, only a few studies (mainly on tourism) look at *unfamiliar* public space in urban centers (Rojek & Urry, 1997) and older people's use of such unfamiliar spaces, in locations where they may not have longtime associations and may not have developed any roots or any feelings of attachment to the place. Yet, focusing on the unfamiliar is increasingly important for a number of reasons. First, larger numbers of older people are traveling as tourists to new places:

> In 2006 slightly more than two-thirds of women and men aged 50 and over in England said that they had gone on a day trip in the last year. Fifty-eight percent of women and men aged 50 and over had holidayed in the UK in the last year and about half of women and men of this age said that they had gone abroad on holiday in the last year. (Office of National Statistics, 2011, p. 6, www.statistics.gov.uk)

Older people are also being encouraged to use the outdoors for recreation and for physical exercise—walking in particular (Diehr & Hirsh, 2010; Sugiyama & Ward Thompson, 2007).

Second, urban regeneration has transformed many town and city centers in the United Kingdom. In redesigning and retrofitting many places, understanding how people create meaning in such new and unfamiliar spaces will be of increasing importance to planners. As Wiles (2005) argues, places are "dynamic, negotiated, contested, contextual, and complex processes" (p. 105), not just locales for specific activities. Change of function and form is part of every place. Consequently, as places change there will be an element of unfamiliarity within them.

Third, unfamiliarity can lead to insecurity, disorientation, fear over personal safety, social exclusion, and loss of independence (see Chapter 2). Such factors can severely limit activity for older people as they retreat to the familiar and comfortable known places of a community. Increased anxiety and disorientation can lead to falls and public embarrassment (Baragwanath, 1997), and both are more likely to be experienced in unfamiliar environments; so, it is crucial that we look at how the unfamiliar can become more familiar.

Fourth, the familiar can become unfamiliar as a result of cognitive decline. Worldwide, 35 million people are currently estimated to have dementia, with 4.6 million new cases diagnosed each year, a number forecast to rise rapidly as the population ages (www.alzheimersresearch. org.uk). People with dementia are increasingly excluded from "familiar" neighborhoods through a lack of consideration given to the outdoor environment by planners (Mitchell & Burton, 2006). In combating such exclusion, design can be used therapeutically with people with dementia. Exploring how to enable the unfamiliar to take on meaning is also important. Research from the United States and United Kingdom shows that the lives of people with dementia can be significantly improved by making changes to their environment that support a sense of meaning and purpose, such as eliminating unnecessary clutter, increased lighting, and allowing views to give orientation to the time of day and season (Day et al., 2000). In making outdoor environments dementia-friendly there needs to be a consideration of how the environment, which might be experienced as unfamiliar, can become safe and secure and enable people with dementia to participate in their local neighborhood. This has implications far wider than for those with dementia, as many people without dementia become disoriented in public places or get confused about where they are (Blackman et al., 2007).

Finally, as successive generations become more mobile, there will be fewer people putting down roots in familiar places, more people identifying with multiple locales and, consequently, challenges to the goal of "aging in place" as a policy objective. The experience of place over a life course may be superficial, with fewer people having a feel for a place beyond just knowing what amenities the place offers. As Tuan (1977, p. 184) states, "attachment is seldom acquired in passing."

Unfamiliarity is often associated with "placelessness" (Augé, 1992; Relph, 1976). The work of Relph through *Place and Placelessness* (1976) has continued to be significant in questioning the role of "place" in human experience. He argues that an overriding concern with efficiency and kitsch has undermined the significance of place, replacing a sense of place with "anonymous spaces and exchangeable environments" (p. 143). Globalization may have reduced our sense of the uniqueness of each place, yet we are continually creating carbon copies to re-establish our sense of familiarity and create the spirit of place: shopping malls with identical brand names or shop frontages. To create continuity and a sense of what we know, color, ambience, and layout are preserved and replicated from places that are familiar to us. Figure 9.1 illustrates this "universal public space" with brand name shops that could be found anywhere in the United Kingdom or United States, often providing a "comforting familiarity," predictability and reassurance for the traveler to an unfamiliar environment.

Unfamiliarity is also defined in terms of time and activity; that is, something that is not part of the daily routine. If the definition by Buttimer (1980, p. 171) is adopted, "One's sense of place is a function of how well it provides a center for one's life interest." This suggests that places and spaces that are unfamiliar are not part of the daily routine and are not places where our actions become almost automatic (Burholt, 2006). As Tuan (1977, p. 6) comments, "What begins as undifferentiated space becomes place as we get to know it better and endow it with value." In other words, as Tuan remarks later, "when space feels thoroughly familiar to us, it has become place" (p. 73). Familiarity therefore is a key concept in exploring "attachment to place," "aging-in-place," and "place identity."

FIGURE 9.1 Universal Public Space

This suggests that the unfamiliar cannot immediately take on meaning and distinctiveness, and it leaves two crucial questions: What are the time frames in which the unfamiliar can take on meaning? What characteristics are important to create meaning for people in unfamiliar spaces? In relation to the first question, for Tuan (1977) it is the quality and intensity of experience that matters more than simply its duration. Intense experiences of a short duration that are memorable may give a place its meaning and distinctiveness (Tuan, 1977). For example, a day trip and tour of Oxford, a famous university town with distinctive architecture conveying a sense of learning, may leave a lasting impression. In relation to the second question, Kevin Lynch (1960), in *The Image of the City*, highlights how "imageability" is important in giving cities meaning: the extent to which the city or town makes an impression on the person. This he linked to objects that featured in people's mental maps such as paths, edges, nodes (strategic meeting points), landmarks, and districts (distinct places with "some recognizable character"); all these would be clearly identifiable in a memorable place. Drawing on environmental images to make sense of our everyday environments is important when looking at unfamiliar places. Lynch (1960) argues that our mental map of the environment gets updated when we venture into an unfamiliar environment; once sufficient information is gleaned, then our mental map can relate to this new information, and it conditions the way we behave, based on existing information.

How older people make use of unfamiliar space will depend on the factors above, but also on their biography, who they travel with to such spaces, and whether they explore alone (Diehl & Willis, 2004; Rubinstein & De Medeiros, 2004). Older people who have intimate childhood memories of a place may have patterns of use and attachments that differ from those of the visitor who shops in the town on an irregular basis, the casual traveler passing through, or someone who has only a "formal" knowledge of a place, achieved from reviewing a brochure. Exploring the concept of unfamiliarity is therefore a useful way in to understanding how to create meaning in spaces. Moreover, changing environments to support a sense of meaning and purpose can enhance the lives of older people, particularly those with dementia (www.sensorytrust.org.uk).

METHODOLOGY

I turn now to findings from a study conducted in two urban centers in the United Kingdom: one center in South Wales (Swansea) familiar to the forty-four participants in the study, and one unfamiliar urban center in Eastern England (Colchester). The overall aim of the study was to investigate how older people used, and consequently gave meaning to, spaces and places that were unfamiliar to them. We were interested in their ability to cope with unfamiliar environments; what factors they associated with worrisome environments; how often, why, with whom, and how they traveled to unfamiliar places; and the extent to which unfamiliar environments curtailed their independence and led to social (and environmental) exclusion. Additionally, we engaged with spatial planners in discussing forms of environmental design that facilitated older people's use of space and learning about place, with a view to producing a pocket guide to "planning with older people."

Initially, forty-eight people over the age of 60 were recruited into the study from the University of the Third Age (U3A) and Network 55+, two voluntary/community groups consisting of older people from Swansea. Forty-four were interviewed to collect both quantitative and qualitative data (of the 48, one was a wheelchair user, one withdrew, one was younger than 60, and one interview had technical difficulties). Participants were asked to complete a questionnaire, detailing demographic information. In addition, the questionnaire covered cognitive functioning through the Cognitive Abilities Screening Instrument— CASI (Teng et al., 1994), which was originally developed to make cross-cultural comparisons of dementia; it makes a quantitative assessment on a scale of 0–100 of a person's abstraction, language, memory, and visual abilities. Sense of direction was explored through the Santa Barbara Sense of Direction Scale (SBSOD) (Hegarty, Richardson, Montello, Lovelace, & Subbiah, 2002). The SBSOD is a 15-item self-report scale adapted from previous measures of environmental spatial abilities and social networks (Antonucci, 1986). Participants place network members in three concentric circles, according to feelings of closeness. Structural characteristics are asked about the first ten people listed, followed by further questions about the supportiveness of various close relationships. Navigational ability was assessed through basic physical spatial orientation tests within a room, and participants were classified qualitatively on the basis of either needing assistance or not. The questionnaire also included questions about visits to familiar and unfamiliar towns; dealt with the frequency of such visits and modes of transport used; elicited open-ended themes about why people visit, how they prepare, what they do, how they navigate and avoid getting "lost," the usefulness of signage and presence of obstacles, situations, and places to be avoided, as well as general impressions and experiences of familiar places.

Following the questionnaire, 2D images of the familiar (Swansea) and unfamiliar (Colchester) urban centers were displayed in a "reality cave" (see Figure 9.2) and a 30-minute walking route was projected in the cave setting. Participants were asked to comment on general impressions and distinctive features in the environment—for example the use of signage, confusing and helpful cues, color, lighting, and how confident or not they felt while undertaking the 30-minute walk. The data was collected in the form of oral narratives.

In addition, focus groups were held with participants following a real-time street audit in which they assessed the quality of the street environment, including quality of design and ambience of the familiar urban center. The tools used in the street audit included the Senior Walking Environment Assessment Tool-Revised—SWEAT-R (Michael & McGregor, 2005) and the Urban Design Quality index—UDQ (Ewing, Clemente, Handy, Brownson, Winston, 2005; Ewing, Handy, Brownson, Clemente, Winston, 2006). The first of these has been developed as a quantitative measure of the "walkability" of urban environments, recording information about such physical characteristics as pavement width, curb height, and the presence of controlled crossing facilities. The second captures information about the quality of urban spaces, including such items as the range of building uses

FIGURE 9.2 Participant in the Reality Cave

and the presence of amenity places, such as playgrounds and planting. The UDQ in particular, captures emotional responses to the aesthetics and structure of the built environment. One section of the UDQ relates to the memorability of a locality and covers features such as historic buildings and landmarks that can make a lasting impression, provide imageability, and evoke feelings, as well as the visual richness of places, including items related to the diversity of the physical, built, and social environments (designated as "complexity"). Other sections cover a sense of enclosed space, such as the amount of observable sky ("enclosure" and "transparency"), and items that match the sizes and dimensions of people, such as potted plants and street furniture ("human scale"). Using this measure in conjunction with the SWEAT-R and the oral narratives from the reality cave enabled us to look at what key features created meaning for older people in an unfamiliar town landscape, in comparison with a familiar landscape. Together, these provided a quasi-objective assessment of the condition and ambience of the urban environment along the route screened in the reality cave.

Finally, a site visit by the Swansea participants in the study to the unfamiliar Colchester town center allowed the opportunity for a smaller group ($n = 10$) to follow the route "for real" with a "walk around town" with older residents. They also met as a focus group with the same ten older residents (recruited through a day center) and with spatial planners in the "unfamiliar" town (the spatial planners had suggested the assigned route for viewing in the cave). Qualitative data were collected through participants recording their experiences in notes and through the focus groups.

A final set of interviews were conducted with planners from the East of England ($n = 3$) and community development and tourism officers ($n = 2$) to explore the extent to which older people's voices were heard and taken into account when planning and regenerating places; what processes were necessary to engage older people; and how planners factored age into the design, spatial layout, signage, and ambience of community environments to make places more older-person-friendly. As a consequence, the research led to the identification of policy and practice implications for making unfamiliar environments safe and accessible for older adults, some of which are detailed in the conclusion to this chapter.

CREATING MEANING IN UNFAMILIAR PLACES

The findings reported here center on the open questions in the pre-cave survey, oral narratives in the cave, the street audit, and focus groups with Swansea and Colchester town residents and Colchester planners. Despite the small sample size, a diversity of oral narratives and accounts were produced. All older participants were aged over 60, mobile, and had no pre-existing diagnosis of cognitive impairment. Most enjoyed living as long-time residents in their neighborhood and had knowledge of their local place as pedestrians and car drivers as well as users of public transportation.

The majority of the 44 participants were car drivers (86%, $n = 38$) or had access to a car and traveled considerably within their local place (63%, $n = 28$). They traveled to a familiar town center, mainly to shop, at 30 minutes or more away from home, once or twice a week, and they rarely visited unfamiliar places (59%, $n = 26$). When they did, nearly half said they drove themselves (41%, $n = 18$). This created particular issues for many of our participants in negotiating new roads and finding available car parks. One 70-year-old male participant, who experienced some difficulty with driving, noted in the questionnaire that:

> If driving, I try and avoid complicated one way systems and roads with several lanes with traffic moving at high speed. It is difficult for the newcomer to make split second decisions.

Another 69-year-old driver explained:

> If I'm driving I find that road signs do not always continue to every road intersection and lane directions do not give you time to adjust before the crossroads, corners, and so on. Many towns have their directions written by people familiar with the place, and so knowledge is often assumed, and a stranger can take a wrong turning very easily.

The purpose of visiting a "new" town was primarily for leisure, that is trips for shopping, sightseeing, and to visit family and friends; to sightsee while on holiday; or to visit shops that provided something different to those at home. Only two participants said they traveled for business or a conference to an unfamiliar place. Several also considered themselves as adventurous and traveled to new places out of interest to gain new experiences.

Nearly all (91%, $n = 40$) people planning to visit unfamiliar places said they prepared by looking at a map (from the Internet or map book) to familiarize themselves with the new place, particularly if they were driving and needed to find a car park. A couple of participants (5%, $n = 2$) went into more depth, deciding in advance on specific buildings to visit or routes to follow around the town and checking the opening hours of places they wanted to visit. With respect to the physical environment, two key themes emerged in the analysis of the interviews as crucial in developing a sense of place: the attractiveness of the place and the ease of accessibility.

Attractiveness of the Place

The aesthetics of the place were very important in establishing people's first impressions of the town center. In our pre-cave questionnaire we asked participants "When you arrive, what sort of places do you like to see and visit?" Overwhelmingly, there was interest in the historical built environment (91%, $n = 40$) of participants said churches, historic buildings, and museums) and in attractive physical environments such as parks and gardens or canal walks. Alongside this, a majority of people preferred the old town, old streets, cobbled streets, quaint, "olde worlde," idiosyncratic, original, and unaltered streets; streets with character and distinctive buildings. The presence of historic and distinctive buildings was central to people's perceptions, expectations, and first impressions of the town center. Our data suggest that such buildings and landmarks are pivotal characteristics of the town landscape for navigation and for making sense of a place. To avoid getting lost, the majority of participants also said they always looked for identifying landmarks: "By choosing a very high building as a central point and making a mental note of certain shops as you pass" (Swansea male, aged 73) or "Fixing certain landmarks or street names in our minds so that we can retrace our steps, especially the way back to the car park" (Swansea male, aged 80).

In the reality cave, our older participants followed the 30-minute circular walking route from the station to the shopping center and made sense of their new surroundings as pedestrians, as the quotations below demonstrate. Distinctive landmarks and historical buildings were again key factors in both navigation and in establishing first impressions and expectations:

> There's a red brick building with what looks like a series of three turrets on it, so that is a very handy landmark, would be pretty recognizable. (Swansea female, aged 65)

> The building on my right with the tower again looks a place of historical interest. I am beginning to get more interested. (Swansea male, aged 75)

We are now passing columns with something carved on the top and they would be worth pausing at to look at, and what looks like a very old pub on the right: cycle stands for the cyclists; more pedestrian crossings, plenty of those and plenty of bus stops; hanging baskets and a balustrade, wrought iron; above the shops some very interesting architecture; a bright yellow building which would be a definite landmark and especially as it is on the corner of Museum Street, which suggests there is something to explore there; and attractive old buildings, the white ones with a bow window above the functional shop fronts. (Swansea male, aged 76)

We are coming to another building of interest on the right, and pass what seems to be a war memorial now, yes, roughly half way down High Street, with an attractive open space and a beautiful old building beyond and this would be a very good landmark, and what seems to be an open space, possibly a park. (Swansea female, aged 80)

There's a building that catches my eye on the left hand side with a clock on the top, it is hexagonal in shape, and it probably is something of interest, going back through the centuries, there could be something very important about that. (Swansea male, aged 76)

Imageability (a measure of UDQ) covered features such as historic buildings and landmarks that can make a lasting impression; it was a key feature in creating meaning for older people visiting unfamiliar places. Several buildings such as the castle, and landmarks such as the water tower, captured people's attention and gave a sense of uniqueness to the town as well as a point of orientation; the high proportion of historic buildings in the street also made this a memorable place.

In comparison, what made a place distinctive to those who were familiar with the town also revolved around the historical significance of place. Memories of events and associated emotions created meaning for older people familiar with the place. Events during the war, previous employment locations, and famous marketplaces were all recalled as significant. This sense of history led our participants to go beyond the immediate image in the reality cave to provide more detailed narratives of the wider place. The physical-psychological and emotional components of place, together with a temporal dimension, are critical in these accounts in creating meaning (see also Chapter 2).

For some participants who were unfamiliar visitors to Colchester and who did the "walk around town" for real, the lack of historic and attractive buildings was disappointing, and the character of the town was judged on what they first saw on arrival at the train station, an impression that for some did not change. These first impressions were of crucial importance in conveying a sense of place, as the quotations from Swansea residents below indicate:

> Yes, tends to be, look a little down market. . . . That's a not a particularly inspiring view from coming out of the station. (Swansea female, aged 76)

> Cars parked on the roads, nothing very attractive so far about this. (Swansea female, aged 67)

> As a stranger, to me it is not terribly appealing so far. (Swansea male, aged 78)

> I don't particularly like the frontage to the station, bit mishmash. (Swansea female, aged 76)

> I wasn't particularly impressed by the railway when the train came into the station, looks a bit run down I think, the frontage much better. (Swansea female, aged 65)

> What I've seen at the moment there is not a lot going for this part, nothing pretty to see, just a few shops here and there. There is nothing much of interest at the moment, just keep on walking, see what happens: car parks, ah now we are getting somewhere. (Swansea male, aged 69)

> Very busy road—buses, lorries, many cars: I hope there is something more interesting to see in this town. (Swansea female, aged 67)

Conversely, unattractive spaces can also create distinctive places; run-down derelict areas, boarded up or monotonous shop frontages, and empty premises were seen to be places to be avoided. Even greenery can be seen as a nuisance if it is not kept tidy or is found growing out of derelict buildings. If this forms part of the first impression, then it can convey an unintended and negative message to the visitor that the urban center is unwelcoming, run-down, and boring.

Our older participants clearly identified that it was this imageability that established the first and lasting impression through which they would create a "sense of place." An emphasis on the importance of preserving the cultural heritage of many town centers and their entry points, such as rail and bus stations, is therefore central in conveying a sense of purpose and meaning to visitors unfamiliar with a town.

Whether familiar or unfamiliar, it is here that both local residents and visitors can make meaning of a place through shared histories (such as World War II) or shared architectural narratives linked to specific buildings. Stories were told with fondness of past uses of civic buildings such as banks, and of particular events that were held, linked to the history of the town.

Accessibility and Ease of Mobility

A further factor that helped create a sense of place was the ease with which people could navigate their environment. Street maps, hand held or on display boards, as well as street signs, were used to navigate the new town and to find specific buildings. Most participants said they relied totally on street signs or visited the local tourist information center. Participants in the cave commented:

> I park the car and hope to find a map or a signpost—or ask someone along the way. (Swansea female, aged 76)

> I look for street signs, bus names or underground maps. If this isn't helping me then I ask for directions. (Swansea male, aged 76)

The simplicity of the route, with clear signs (also indicating distance), was of great importance to those in unfamiliar places, whereas street signs were of very limited use to the resident. The conditions of pavements, roads, and the presence of street furniture and clutter, all affected how people perceived the new place:

> There is poor access here and evidence of more stands; they don't give the pedestrians much room here, even with the bus stops there, poor waiting areas and obstructions. (Swansea female, aged 65)

> Looks as if we've come through a more appealing area, I wasn't too impressed with the town itself, a mishmash of old buildings and new and poorer road arrangements and hazards. (Swansea female, aged 76)

> They certainly love putting things on pavements, not the most attractive town I must admit, it's not the easiest access. (Swansea female, aged 69)

A few participants preferred streets that were well-lit, clean, well laid out, and tree-lined. They avoided dirty, dark, isolated streets, narrow alleyways, extremely congested places, and roads that were crowded and busy with traffic. Most did not like billboards or rubbish/ garbage bins outside cafes, where it was unclear where the pedestrian could walk. Having clear rules of engagement also extended to negotiation with traffic and shared spaces. Although most people recognized the importance of car access to shops and historic sites in the town, most felt this detracted from the ambience of the center and contributed to a "sensory overload" of smells, sight, color, and noise; pollution; and dangerous walking conditions. This was particularly acute for the group of ten Swansea residents who visited Colchester town center:

> For a town center the pavements are very narrow with a lot of people having to walk out onto the road to get past; pavements a bit uneven, he's going to be run over, standing in the middle . . . There are very uneven pavements. (Swansea female, aged 70)

> Yes, yes, it is quite appealing now, but not being able to judge walking distance it probably took me too long to get there, longer than I had prepared, was prepared for. I can't say it is a town I would visit a second time, it is just a typical smallish market town; the history part which isn't totally obvious when you walk along. (Swansea male, aged 80)

> More street signs there which could be useful but then again the writing looks very small. (Swansea male, aged 70)

> A rubbish bin on the street, which if you weren't looking where you were going you could walk into. (Swansea female, aged 78)

> I think if you were new to the city you could have a problem finding your way . . . there are so many crossroads or crossing places that looks similar, so one of these navigation devices might be a quite a good idea. (Swansea male, aged 80)

> Coming down towards the outskirts of town, I think there are people about, few shops, fewer cars parked, road signs on the pavement that's in a dangerous position. (Swansea female, aged 78)

> Got no signs, no street signs here at all. (Swansea female, aged 78)

> Cars coming up onto the pavement to park off road which cause problems for pedestrians. (Swansea male, aged 78)

> Rubbish in the road, trees in the middle of pavements. You've got to be very careful there, oh look at that, oh yes with the uneven surface

around there; you can fall down there quite easily . . . now we've got bollards in the way. I wonder why they're there but, keep walking, awful lot on this pavement isn't there, a lot of obstructions on that pavement but we're crossing the road. Another post is on the road . . . cars on pavements, they should not be there. (Swansea female, aged 81)

Although few people commented on the character of the place in relation to the people, our respondents avoided large crowds and troublesome-looking people, if on foot. The social aspect of place is affected by the physical environment and cannot be ignored; it is intertwined with the physical and psychological, despite its not being at the forefront of our participants' narratives.

Many of these findings are applicable to all generations, not just older people, but they particularly support previous work in relation to environmental issues concerning people with dementia (Mitchell & Burton, 2006). In a study by Brorsson, Öhman, Lundberg, and Nygård (2011), people with dementia relied on familiar and well-tested routes and were uncomfortable when they lost their way; this occurred when there were complex street layouts. Participants were also startled by sudden noise, heavy vehicles passing, or by emergency vehicle sirens, which left them disoriented and confused, a finding supported through design guidance on the importance of minimizing sensory overstimulation (Day et al., 2000). Cues that signaled the use of buildings were important, and designs that were recognizable helped understanding of the place where they were located. Clear use and function were keys to success in navigating the environment.

In relation to the OPUS study, participants on the real "walk about town" regularly looked for landmarks in the environment, including buildings, structures, places of activity, or particular aesthetic features such as green spaces and street furniture. Making the streetscape interesting as well as simple, clutter-free, and with clear signage, good lighting, and even, non-slip surfaces was extremely important. Designing towns and city centers to be inclusive is a further challenge to planners.

KEY IMPLICATIONS FOR DESIGN OF PUBLIC SPACES

A neighborhood is at first a confusion of images to the new resident; it is blurred space "out there." Learning to know the neighborhood requires the identification of significant localities, such as street corners and architectural landmarks, within the neighborhood space. (Tuan, 1977, p. 18)

The OPUS study found that developing a sense of history and ensuring older visitors have easy access to the most attractive places of a town will enable them to create meaning and a sense of place within a short period of time, even if they are unfamiliar with the location. Both the OPUS study and a growing volume of literature suggest that the meaning (as well as use) of space is important to older people. Many older people are interested in the histories of buildings, routes, and landscapes, the stories around them, and the emotions attached to them, which can be created and recorded by local residents. Preserving memories of spaces and places is also important in relation to the regeneration of towns and city places for locals as they "age in place." For spaces to become places then, emotion and meaning have to be embedded in such spaces. Older people come with a variety of experiences and knowledge of places to which planners need to pay attention if places are to become attractive, safe, and walkable.

To fully facilitate use and the development of meaning, a place has to be easily accessible and enable outdoor mobility for a diverse group of people. This provides planners with a challenge in preserving the historical while ensuring routes and buildings are accessible: How, for example, does one reconcile the cobbled street with its historic charm with the need for a smooth surface to enable older people to walk safely? And how do we provide spaces for pedestrians that are separate from bicycle paths and bus routes where there is shared space?

In conclusion, the key messages for urban planners revolve around five issues. *First impressions* are crucial at entrance points and routes into a town such as the railway station where, on arrival, people need to orient themselves and quickly develop an understanding of the kind of place they are visiting. This goes beyond just factual information, and could include stories or narratives from different times in history and from local residents. As Tuan (1977, p. 174) notes, "An old town or city has a rich store of facts on which successive generations of citizens can draw to sustain and re-create the image of place." Collective understandings of place, through powerful stories and mythologies, can shape the physical journey into unfamiliar space for the visitor. "Attachment to place" for the resident is also tied into such collective memories (Burholt, 2006), as older people act as a reference point for stability and continuity in such environments (ODPM, 2006).

Second, is the need to *preserve historic buildings and attractive landmarks*. Detailing the history and associated stories of buildings and landmarks can help create meaning in unfamiliar places. Distinctive buildings and features in the landscape are also useful for navigation and orientation. They provide older visitors (and younger ones too) with an immediate sense of place, particularly if they feature churches, museums, towers, pubs, and public buildings. High streets need to create and maximize the inherent advantages of such heritage features, as well as green spaces, to draw the eye of the older visitor. Creating distinctiveness is important for locals and visitors alike; it alleviates the monotony of repetitive streets and shop frontages.

Third, planners should *consider ambience in the street landscape*, particularly to avoid sensory overload by creating spaces that have too many cues for orientation or too many functions: bus stations with busy shops alongside, narrow pavements that are crowded with cars, bollards, and street furniture. Pedestrian routes need to be wide enough for mobility scooter use, of good quality, well lit, and maintained. Despite the use of tactile features, people may be forced off the pavement as surfaces become uneven and this can lead to disorientation. Developing and maintaining an attractive environment is crucial to the success of a town, whether the function be for trading, recreation and leisure, or transportation. Additionally, a key feature of creating such ambience may well be establishing a balance between negotiability and interpretability of the urban landscape and the need for a level of complexity and ambiguity that stimulates continued interest. As Rapoport and Kantor (1967) note, people prefer some degree of ambiguity and complexity in their visual field and see these as important to creating a "good" environment.

Customers, employees, and businesses must feel main town routes are safe, welcoming, and clean and well designed. Once in place, the public realm needs to be maintained to very high standards. Streets must be kept clean and people deterred from littering or anti social behavior (British Retail Consortium, 2010). People's perceptions of place are crucial in shaping the way they behave in that space— environmental cues of litter and graffiti may suggest it is unsafe and hostile to older people.

Fourth, *effective signage* is crucial to aid accessibility. Signage that is too high with small print is not suitable for the older visitor; it also needs to show direction and distance to be useful. Street signs should be appropriate in terms of the amount and position of information so that older people are able to remain safely on the pavement. People with multiple needs in relation to sight and hearing should be consulted on the positioning of signs on the pavement; older drivers, unfamiliar with the place, also need to have a voice in relation to directions and signage. Designers and architects, along with spatial planners, should plan street and townscapes with the unfamiliar visitor in mind. This includes having clear visual rules for visitors in their use of shared space to aid mobility and safety and give confidence to older visitors; the experiment of "tourist sidewalks" or "lanes" could be one feature to be considered, as in Portland, Oregon, and Manhattan, New York in the United States (Amira, 2010).

Nonvisual cues may also be important alongside signage for those who need auditory cues at crosswalks or crossings. Similarly, olfactory cues such as the smell of a bakery may signify particular places to people who are visually impaired. Such features in the design of public spaces can lead to a sense of place, making them meaningful, interesting, stimulating, and memorable.

Finally, opportunities for *social interaction are important.* A town center is not just about buildings; there need to be places for social interaction that are comfortable and safe for older people. What can look placeless to the eye can, however, be the hub of social action. As Buttimer (1980, p. 178) comments, "It is the style of life associated with place which is still far more important . . . than its external forms." Our participants rarely commented on the social interaction observed in the reality cave (this may have been a limitation of the method used) although the small group who experienced the "walk around town" did comment on the friendliness and social activities they observed, which added to the positive experiences of the town.

CONCLUSION

People's lives and everyday activities are carried on in a range of familiar places that are important to them (Holloway & Hubbard, 2001). How we imbue such places with meaning will depend on how we perceive our environment and make sense of space and place. The conceptualization of place depends on the theoretical perspective to which one subscribes. In environmental gerontology, concepts such as "aging in place," "place attachment," and "person-environment fit" (Lawton & Nahemow, 1973) have dominated our thinking and governed policy initiatives. In relation to psychological dimensions, our emotional attachment to place is also a key factor in determining how we develop meaning and make sense of different places. Similarly, there is a temporal dimension and, for older people, a lifetime of memories and experiences will develop a sense of meaning and attachment to particular locales. Increasingly, social change and the homogenization of globalization are challenging this notion of attachment to one place; as older people more frequently travel the world, unfamiliar places take on increasing importance.

Exploring the concept of unfamiliarity is becoming increasingly important as older people identify with multiple locales as they age, whether these are real or virtual. How the unfamiliar takes on a "sense of place" concentrates on the temporal dimension in environmental gerontology, as advocated by Golant (2003). The OPUS research study indicates that there are some immediate features within a townscape that can convey meaning and a sense of place to the older visitor. Consequently, our conceptualization of place needs to take on multiple dimensions and not be fixed solely on the long-term resident.

There are suggestions that unfamiliarity creates "placelessness," yet older people who are unfamiliar with environments can make initial sense and create meaning in them if the environment is accessible and distinctive. As towns and cities become ever more similar in their design and architecture, this creates challenges for planners following an inclusive agenda in designing places where older people can feel comfortable, secure, and confident as tourists and visitors, pedestrians, and car drivers. This leaves key questions for practice. What tools can we develop to aid navigation for older visitors? To what extent can distinctiveness be built into measures of urban design? How do we balance the needs of the unfamiliar visitor with the needs of traffic, retail, and business? How do we conceptualize the familiar, given changing demographics and social support networks? If cities and towns are to be planned with inclusion as a guiding principle and with "sense of place" as a key feature, then a diversity of approaches is necessary, with the older visitor at the forefront of consideration in tracing design implications.

This chapter highlights the importance of planning for the resident, the newcomer, and the visitor with respect to the creation of meaning. For the long-time resident, the meaning of place is strongly tied to environmental experience and to a history of engagement with the setting. At the other extreme is the visitor, the person passing through, who needs to obtain an immediate sense of spatial orientation as well as be inculcated with an image of a meaningful place. But a third group, the newcomers, when they move to a new place will transition from being visitors to being residents through a process that involves learning about place—in other words, the visitor gradually becomes the resident. This has implications for design of open spaces that support the resident, appeal to the visitor, and facilitate the process of the visitor's becoming the resident.

ACKNOWLEDGMENTS

I thank the New Dynamics of Ageing Programme (NDA) for funding the OPUS study (Grant number RES-352-25-0003), as well as the other members of the OPUS team: Nigel Walford, Ann Hockey, Nigel

Foreman, Mike Lewis, Edgar Samarasundera, Martin Spaul, Mark Delaguila.

Thanks also to all the people who took part in the study in both Swansea and Colchester.

REFERENCES

Amira, D. (2010). Tourist sidewalk lanes actually not a bad idea. *New York Magazine* (http://nymag.com/daily/intel/2010/05/tourist_sidewalk_lanes_actuall.html).

Antonucci T. C. (1986). Hierarchical mapping technique. *Generations: Journal of the American Society on Aging, 10*, 10–12.

Aspinall, P. A., Ward Thompson, C., Alves, S., Sugiyama, T., Brice, R., & Vickers, A. (2010). Preference and relative importance for environmental attributes of neighbourhood open space in older people. *Environment and Planning B: Planning and Design 37*(6), 1022–1039.

Augé, M. (1992). *Non-Places: Introduction to an anthropology of supermodernity*. London, UK: Verso.

Baragwanath, A. (1997). Bounce and balance: A team approach to risk management for people with dementia living at home. In M. Marshall (Ed.), *State of the art in dementia care* (pp. 102–106). London, UK: Center for Policy on Ageing.

Blackman, T., Van Schaik, P., & Martyr, A. (2007). Outdoor environments for people with dementia: An exploratory study using virtual reality. *Ageing and Society, 27*(1), 811–825.

British Retail Consortium. (2010). 21st Century high streets: A new vision for our town centres. Retrieved from brc.org.uk

Brorsson, A., Öhman, A., Lundberg, S., & Nygård, L. (2011). Accessibility in public space as perceived by people with Alzheimer's disease. *Dementia, 10*(4), 587–602.

Burholt, V. (2006). 'Adref': Theoretical contexts of attachment to place for mature and older people in rural North Wales. *Environment and Planning A, 38*, 1095–1114

Buttimer, A. (1980). Home, reach and the sense of place. In A. Buttimer & D. Seamon (Eds.), *The human experience of space and place* (pp. 166–187). London, UK: Croom Helm.

Day, K., Carreon, D., & Stump, C. (2000). The therapeutic design of environments for people with dementia: A review of the empirical research. *The Gerontologist, 40*(4), 397–416.

Diehl, M., & Willis, S. (2004). Everyday competence and everyday problem solving in aging adults: The role of physical and social context. In H. W. Wahl, R. Scheidt, & P. Windley (Eds.), *Aging in context: Socio-physical environments* (pp. 130–166). New York, NY: Springer Publishing Company.

Diehr, P., & Hirsh, C. (2010). Health benefits of increased walking for sedentary, generally healthy older adults: Using longitudinal data to approximate an intervention trial. *Journals of Gerontology Series A, Biological Sciences and Medical Sciences, 65A*(9), 982–989.

Duggan, S., Blackman, T., Martyr, A., & Van Schaik, P. (2008). The impact of early dementia on outdoor life. *Dementia, 7*(2), 191–204.

Ewing, R., Clemente, O., Handy, S., Brownson, R. C., & Winston, E. (2005). *Identifying and measuring urban design qualities related to walkability—final report*. Princeton, New Jersey: Robert Wood Johnson Foundation.

Ewing, R., Handy, S., Brownson, R. C., Clemente, O., & Winston, E. (2006). Identifying and measuring urban design qualities related to walkability. *Journal of Physical Activity and Health, 3*, S223–S239.

Golant, S. M. (2003). Conceptualizing time and space in environmental gerontology: A pair of old issues deserving new thought. *The Gerontologist, 43*(5), 638–648.

Hay, R. (1998). Sense of place in developmental context. *Journal of Environmental Psychology, 18*(1), 5–29.

Hegarty, M., Richardson, A., Montello, D., Lovelace, K., & Subbiah, I. (2002). Development of a self-report measure of environmental spatial ability. *Intelligence, 30*, 425–447.

Holland, C., Clark, A., Katz, J., & Peace, S. (2007). *Social interaction in urban public places.* York: Joseph Rowntree Foundation.

Holloway, L., & Hubbard, P. (2001). *People and place: The extraordinary geographies of everyday life.* London, UK: Prentice Hall.

Keating, N., & Phillips, J. (2008). A critical human ecology perspective on rural aging. In N. Keating (Ed.), *Rural ageing: A good place to grow old?* Bristol, UK: Policy Press.

Lawton, M. P., & Nahemow, L. (1973). Ecology and the aging process. In C. Eisdorfer & M. P. Lawton (Eds.), *Psychology and adult development and aging* (pp. 619–674). Washington, DC: American Psychological Association.

Lewicka, M. (2005). Ways to make people active: The role of place attachment, cultural capital, and neighbourhood ties. *Journal of Environmental Psychology, 25*(4), 381–395.

Lynch, K. (1960). *The image of the city.* Cambridge, UK: MIT Press.

Michael, Y., & McGregor, E. (2005). *Training manual: Senior walking environmental assessment tool—revised (SWEAT-R).* Portland, OR: Oregon Health & Science University.

Mitchell, L., & Burton, E. (2006). Neighbourhoods for life: Designing dementia-friendly outdoor environments. *Quality in Ageing-Policy, Practice and Research, 7*, 1.

Newton, R., Ormerod, M., Burton, E., Mitchell, L., & Ward-Thompson, C. (2010). Increasing independence for older people through good street design. *Journal of Integrated Care, 18*(3), 24–29.

Office of the Deputy Prime Minister. (2006). *A sure start to later life.* London, UK: Social Exclusion Unit.

Peace, S., Wahl, H-W., Mollenkopf, H., & Oswald, F. (2007). Environment and ageing. In J. Bond, S. Peace, F. Dittman-Kohli, & G. Westerhof (Eds.), *Ageing in society* (pp. 209–234). London, UK: Sage & BSG.

Phillipson, C., Bernard, M., Phillips, J., & Ogg, J. (2001). *The family and community life of older people: Social networks and social support in three urban areas.* London, UK: Routledge.

Rapoport, A., & Kantor, R. (1967). Complexity and ambiguity in environmental design. *Journal of the American Institute of Planners, 33*(4), 210–221.

Relph, E. (1976). *Place and placelessness.* London, UK: Pion.

Rojek, C., & Urry, J. (1997). *Touring cultures: Transformations of travel and theory.* London, UK: Routledge.

Rowles, G. D. (1978). *Prisoners of space: Exploring the geographical experience of older people.* Boulder, CO: Westview Press.

Rowles, G. D. (1983). Geographical dimensions of social support in rural Appalachia. In G. D. Rowles & R. J. Ohta (Eds.), *Aging and milieu: Environmental perspectives on growing old* (pp. 111–130). New York, NY: Academic Press.

Rowles, G. D., & Watkins, J. F. (2003). History, habit, heart and hearth: On making spaces into places. In K. W. Schaie, H.-W. Wahl, H. Mollenkopf, & F. Oswald (Eds.), *Ageing independently: Living arrangements and mobility.* New York, NY: Springer Publishing Company.

Rubinstein, R., & de Medeiros, K. (2004). Ecology and the aging self. In H.-W. Wahl, R. J. Scheidt, & P. G. Windley (Eds.), *Aging in context: Socio-physical environments* (pp. 59–84). New York, NY: Springer Publishing Company.

Scharf, T., Phillipson, C., & Smith, A. (2003). Older people's perceptions of the neighbourhood: Evidence from socially deprived urban areas. *Sociological Review Online, 8*, 4.

Seamon, D. (1980) Body-subject, time-space routines, and place ballets. In A. Buttimer & D. Seamon (Eds.), *The human experience of space and place* (pp. 148–165). London, UK: Croom Helm.

Smaldone, D., Harris, C., & Sanyal, N. (2008). The role of time in developing place meanings. *Journal of Leisure Research, 40*(4), 479–504.

Smith, A. (2009). *Ageing in urban neighbourhoods: Place attachment and social exclusion.* Bristol, UK: Policy Press.

Sugiyama, T., & Ward Thompson, C. (2007). Older people's health, outdoor activity and supportiveness of neighbourhood environments. *Landscape and Urban Planning, 83*, 168–175.

Sugiyama, T., Ward Thompson, C., & Alves, S. (2009). Associations between neighborhood open space attributes and quality of life for older people in Britain. *Environment and Behavior, 41*(1), 3–21.

Teng E. L., Hasegawa, K., Homma, A., Imai, Y., Larson, E., Graves, A., . . . White, L.R. (1994). The Cognitive Abilities Screening Instrument (CASI): A practical test for cross-cultural epidemiological studies of dementia. *International Psychogeriatrics, 6*, 45–58.

Tuan, Yi-Fu. (1977). *Space and place: The perspective of experience.* Minneapolis, MN: University of Minnesota Press.

WHO (World Health Organization) (2007). *Global age-friendly cities: a guide.* Geneva, Switzerland: Author.

Wiles, J. (2005). Conceptualizing place in the care of older people. *International Journal of Older People Nursing, 14*(8b) 100–108.

Wiles, J., Allen, R. E., Palmer, A. J., Hayman, K. J., Keeling, S., & Kerse, N. (2009). Older people and their social spaces: A study of well-being and attachment to place in Aotearoa, New Zealand. *Social Science & Medicine, 68*(4), 664–671.

CHAPTER 10

Intergenerational Pathways for Building Relational Spaces and Places

Leng Leng Thang and Matthew S. Kaplan

EDITORS' INTRODUCTION

This chapter provides a counterpoint to the motif of age segregation that has characterized western society for more than half a century. Picking up on Lewis Mumford's (1956) plea for generational integration rather than segregation in age-specific environments, Thang and Kaplan argue for public spaces that not only accommodate the needs of multiple generations, but also are designed to be conducive to interaction among generations. A key point here is that it is not enough to create universally designed spaces; rather, it is important to create spaces that actually promote intergenerational exchange and nurture a sense of community. In exploring what it means to create public places and spaces that are conducive to intergenerational engagement and cooperation, Thang and Kaplan provide an important perspective on how our increasing knowledge of the manner in which individuals and groups experience environments can actually be employed to enhance quality of life by fostering a sense of belonging and participation among all population groups. By providing a series of international exemplars of environments designed to foster intergenerational collaboration and engagement, and by presenting a series of design and planning guidelines to accomplish this, Thang and Kaplan provide the outlines of a prospectus for creating public spaces that facilitate the synergistic celebration of life and community by people of all ages.

The following is an e-mail that the organizer of an online conference on Creating Aging-Friendly Communities (held in 2008) sent to the listserv group of conference participants:

I received an email from a 75-year-old woman who read about the conference and wanted me to pass along her thoughts and message to

225

the conference for us to keep in mind as we learn more about how to make our communities more aging-friendly.

I live in a gated senior community with all the amenities one could dream of; workshops, handicrafts, exercise, etc., you name it we have it.

. . . And yet I am longing, longing, to walk to the corner coffee shop, to hear the sound of children playing, dogs barking. I want to eat at the corner cafe, see young people in love, walk to the library, catch the BART [Bay Area Rapid Transit] into the city, watch mothers with their children in the park, young families, teenies in the latest, wildest outfit.

. . . Yes, I'm lucky to have what I do and I never forget that. But, I am excluded from the mainstream of life. I have a graduate education. Staying with it was my style. But there is no longer a place in the mainstream that I can afford or feel safe. I am not elderly and never will be, my mother never was and she died at 92.

. . . Please consider in your conversations, that there are many of us who do not want to be maintained. We want to belong, not only to each other, with whom we may have only one common denominator, age, but to society. We want to be "just like everyone else." Instead of a multi-million dollar resort where every need is met, and everything is planned for the generic aging American, think up something daring, something challenging, something creative. After all, the end of segregation by race began only a few years ago. Think about how this country can put an end to the insulting mentality of segregation by age.

When I needed this supportive environment was when I was a single parent, raising children, educating myself, working every day. Think about building communities that are whole. We need each other, we can learn to care about each other, support the young and the old, give what we have the energy to do, not what society has assigned to. I would volunteer in a day care center to help out moms like I used to be, work to find alternatives to kids coming to empty homes after school. Be "on call" for parents caught in traffic who can't get home for dinner. Be there for sick friends, young or old. Take classes of course, stimulating ones about what wasn't known when I was in school, not just with old guys who love to pontificate on WWII. [Quote from Anne Leitch; reprinted with permission]

This woman's letter is a testament to the need to think about environment and housing for older adults as more than providing safe, secure, and financially affordable places to live. For many, the lifestyle they desire has not changed with age: they desire to remain in the mainstream of life and to feel a belonging to society through active engagement with the lives of other community residents.[1]

This chapter is about what it means to create public places and spaces that are conducive to intergenerational engagement and cooperation. These are places such as parks, playgrounds, shopping malls, community centers, and purpose-built age-integrated centers where the generations can readily meet, interact, and develop relationships with one another. Such places are also rich in psychological meaning; they provide inhabitants with opportunities for gaining a cognitive understanding and an emotional appreciation of age diversity and intergenerational communal experience.

The aspiration for such age-integrated environments is certainly not a new endeavor. More than half a century ago Lewis Mumford (1956), in his seminal commentary "For older people—not segregation but integration," published in the journal *Architectural Record*, noted the significance of age integration both in family settings, as with three-generation family living arrangements, and in the context of neighborhood development and relationship building. He recommended more integration of older adults' dwellings in neighborhoods, and more older adult involvement in activities which resemble three-generation family arrangements such as baby sitting. In his earlier work (1949), he explored the need for an "organic conception of city planning" that deals with all the phases of life in a balanced manner, where to restore balance within the urban community, "one must think of establishing balance in time through inter-relationship between the phases of life . . . which can be well served only when the co-ordinate needs of other age groups are taken into account" (p. 16). However, as evidenced from Anne Leitch's letter about living in a gated senior community, such aspirations for age-integrated environments contrast significantly with the trend toward age-segregated spaces and places, especially during the second half of the 20th century (Grant, 1970; Laws, 1993).

Our focus on creating intergenerational environments thus reflects an effort to revisit and extend the earlier work of scholars such as Mumford, while at the same time attempting to reframe current environmental planning and design deliberations that have a monogenerational focus. Our concern is that when community development efforts treat the age groups separately, with distinct interests, abilities, and needs (as noted in Henkin, Homes, & Greenburg, 2003; Raynes, 2004), it can be difficult to recognize areas of overlap that exist between the goals of developing *child and youth-friendly* environments and *aging-friendly* environments.

Van Vliet (2009), in noting that there are characteristics of child-friendly cities that overlap with those of elder-friendly cities, makes the argument that there should be synergistic efforts to create livable cities for all ages:

> There is much overlap in how livability issues impact children, youth, and elders, particularly those with low incomes and limited support systems. All benefit from neighborhoods that are safe and walkable and housing that is affordable and near shops, neighbors, and services, with easy access to public spaces for social interactions. Likewise, all benefit from the availability of healthy foods at local markets, Mercados [traditional Mexican grocery stores], and community gardens within neighborhoods. Schools that serve as community centers and senior centers that offer child care and after-school programs can simultaneously provide for the physical and social needs of both elders and children and youth. Similarly, both populations also need reliable, safe, and affordable public transportation to support independent mobility and access to the resources of the city. (p. 21)

We contend that the challenge of creating an environment that meets the needs of an aging population should be considered in the context of a broader effort to meet the needs of all generations that will use that environment in some way. With recognition of the importance of not losing sight of the distinct needs of each population age group, we suggest that programs, policies, and places could be developed in ways that take advantage of areas of overlapping needs, interests, and patterns of behavior.

As an illustration, Ghazaleh, Greenhouse, Homsy, and Warner (2011) describe an example of a community planning process driven by the area's agency on aging, which originally focused on issues faced by older adults, but which broadened its agenda and inter-agency organizing efforts to also focus on the needs and assets of other generations.

> As part of the 2020 Community Plan on Aging in the Charlottesville, Virginia, area, planners decided to be intentionally age inclusive. High school students were recruited as members of the planning committee. They acted as ambassadors to other young people through focus groups and student surveys. In the end, the students wrote a chapter of the plan titled "Strengthening Intergenerational Connections" with recommendations that included: recruiting students as health care workers; encouraging alternative transportation options; promoting intergenerational volunteering to bring together seniors and youth in meaningful service; and educating youth on the need for lifelong financial planning. Another outcome of this intergenerational planning process was a program that recruited more than 20 seniors to volunteer in seven elementary schools to help tutor reading, math, and languages as well as provide library and landscaping assistance. (p. 9)

Our orientation for weaving an intergenerational perspective into environmental design is informed by the conceptual framework provided by Kaplan, Haider, Cohen, and Turner (2007, p. 89):

> Environmental design cannot be exercised independent of context. There is a need for integration between curriculum or program models, organizational policies and objectives, social values, *and* environmental design. In other words, the environment of an intergenerational program should reflect: programmatic, organizational, socio-cultural, political, and economic goals and realities.

Accordingly, we view the task of creating an effective intergenerational setting as not just a matter of good environmental design, but rather as an exercise in aligning what is proposed to be built with institutional and community policies for using this space and the programs that will be conducted in this space. If, for example, a community organization wants to diversify and expand its intergenerational theater arts program, a decision might be made to build a larger multi-use amphitheater to ensure that all groups in the community have access to the facility, and they might need to establish a multi-agency task force to handle the scheduling of this amphitheater space.

After brief clarification of key terms and concepts relating to what we refer to as an *intergenerational perspective*, we explore the applications of such an orientation through our proposed conceptual framework in community settings that serve a variety of purposes, including education, social services, and recreation. We draw from both Asian and Western experiences as portrayed in the literature and from our own fieldwork to provide a critical assessment of the extent to which these applications meet the goals of designing spaces to facilitate intergenerational engagement. Finally, we discuss the main issues and challenges faced in such a framework, including a review of environmental design issues to be considered when developing new intergenerational settings in the community.

INTERGENERATIONAL SETTINGS, PRACTICE, AND PERSPECTIVE

What does it mean to create an environment that "brings different generations together?" To begin to answer this question, it is necessary to draw a distinction between *intergenerational* and *multigenerational* settings. When setting out to create a colocated cross-generational facility, from an environmental design point of view, the term *multigenerational* alludes to a focus on designing the facility to accommodate the physical and psychological needs of people across the age and ability spectrum. Calls for "universal design" and "inclusive design" fit into this framework (Carr, Francis, Rivlin, & Stone, 1992; Christensen & O'Brien, 2003). An *intergenerational* perspective takes the design concept one step further. Here the design goal is to create environments that are not only appropriate for multigenerational groups of users, but are also conducive to intergenerational interaction: environments that afford opportunities for meaningful engagement among members of different generations. "Shared sites" or "age-integrated facilities" are terminologies usually used for such settings in which "multiple generations receive ongoing services and/or programming at the same site, and generally interact through planned and/or informal intergenerational activities" (AARP, 1998, p. v). It is important to note that the intergenerational domain deals with the "relational"—that is, the communication and relationships among individuals of different generations.

To embrace the many dimensions involved in creating an intergenerational setting, we allude to terms such as "intergenerational practice," defined by the Beth Johnson Foundation in the United Kingdom as follows (n.d.):

> Intergenerational practice aims to bring people together in purposeful, mutually beneficial activities which promote greater understanding and respect between generations and contribute to building more cohesive communities. Intergenerational practice is inclusive, building on the positive resources that the young and old have to offer each other and those around them.

Under this definition, intergenerational practice includes: formal programs of intervention (as found in a wide variety of settings, including schools, community organizations, residential communities, hospitals, and places of worship); cultural traditions with a distinct intergenerational engagement component; policies designed to facilitate intergenerational exchange (e.g., tax policies to provide financial assistance for families supporting older relatives at home); and environmental design practices aimed at facilitating intergenerational exchange. The literature on intergenerational practice has roots in many academic disciplines, including child development, education, gerontology, social work, psychology, sociology, family studies, social policy, community development, and anthropology.

We also use the term "intergenerational perspective" to refer to a distinct way of thinking about and going about constructing public settings and basic institutions. Drawing from the literature that highlights intergenerational program development principles and considerations (including, for example, Brabazon & Disch, 1997; Bressler, Henkin, &

Adler, 2005; Henkin & Kingson, 1998/99; Kaplan, Henkin, & Kusano, 2002; MacCallum et al. 2006; Newman, Ward, Smith, & Wilson, 1997), an "intergenerational perspective" encompasses the following propositions:

- The "longevity revolution" is seen as *an opportunity* rather than a crisis.
- Focus is on *more than one population*, and on the *interaction* among age groups.
- Emphasis is on *building lines of mutual support* among the generations.
- Focus is on creating *inspiring opportunities for lifelong learning* (teaching, learning from, and learning with people of other generations).
- Focus is on creating *inspiring opportunities for life enrichment* (for self and others).
- Emphasis is on energized civic engagement.

Before we move on to explore how, and the extent to which, such a perspective has been realized in intergenerational settings, we clarify how the terms "space" and "place" are used in this chapter. While space in environmental terms has specific dimensions, we are concerned with the conversion of a space into *place*. In contrast with space, place constitutes a psychological component; a space may remain a space, but it may also become a place as defined by one's emotional feeling and a sense of belonging to the space. The concepts of "place identity" and "place attachment," drawn from the literatures of environmental psychology and community psychology, provide further understanding of the distinction. "Place identity" is defined as consisting of dimensions "of the self that develop in relation to the physical environment by means of a pattern of beliefs, preferences, and transforms through lived experience" (Manzo & Perkins, 2006, p. 337). "Place attachment" refers to people's affective bond with the places with which they are most familiar (Altman & Low, 1992). Both place attachment and one's sense of place identity can be achieved for different generations together through intergenerational activities providing participants with shared experiences in their local environment (Larkin, Kaplan, & Rushton, 2010).

As illustrated below, intergenerational programs that involve an environmental design or community participation component (e.g., Kaplan, 1997; Lawrence-Jacobson, 2006) provide another layer of shared experiences in participants' local environments. The process of working together to assess and develop recommendations to improve the character of jointly used *space* engages adults and children in a process of creating a shared sense of *place*.

Intergenerational Spaces and Places Devoted to Education

Schools where children and youth congregate are generally appropriate spaces and places for intergenerational interaction in a community. In the United States, many examples can be found of multipurpose schools which function as *multigenerational* facilities (in which distinct space and programs are set aside for older adults) and/or *intergenerational facilities* (where the focus is more on the school functioning as a center for intergenerational engagement). As noted by Sullivan (2002), Abramson (2007), Van Vliet (2009), and others, there are many reasons to support such facilities, including: increased support for public education, enriched learning experiences for children and adults, enhanced health for older adults, reduced financial expenditure, and the creation of a hub of activity in the community. Below, we provide diverse examples of shared site schools in the United States.

The Intergenerational School

The Cleveland, Ohio, intergenerational school opened in August 2000 as a community or charter school, with 31 children and 5 full-time staff. It is located at the Fairhill Center, which assists senior citizens, including those suffering from Alzheimer's disease. The school was created with the explicit goal of challenging the traditional age segregation found in most schools. As noted by Catherine Whitehouse, principal and executive director, the school enables "people of different ages to come together around learning" (Sullivan, 2002, p. 4). At the school, the learning goes both ways. Students gain academic skills and they excel on standardized tests; the school has been rated by the Ohio Department of Education as a high-performing urban school. With help from the students, the older adults gain computer skills, which they apply in various ways, including receiving job retraining and job search assistance and taking part in cognitive training software programs. The participants also learn alongside one another, as is the case with the school's new nature-based science curriculum, which brings both generations together for experiential learning activities in the parklands and watersheds surrounding the school (George, Whitehouse, & Whitehouse, 2011).

Fellowship and Lifelong Learning at Waialae School

The FELLOWS (Fellowship and Lifelong Learning at Waialae School) program is based in Waialae Elementary School (in Honolulu, Hawaii). This program takes a "senior center within a school" approach to cultivating senior adults as educational resources, with local senior volunteers based in a classroom that became vacant due to the declining population of local children. The FELLOWS Center serves as a magnet for recruiting and training senior adult volunteers to perform a variety of functions at the school, including basic tutoring, participating in special school events, mentoring, and engaging the students in discussion about the local community and issues of citizenship. Program partners include Older Adults Actively Volunteering in Education and the Hawaii Intergenerational Network.

Swampscott Multigenerational School

The multigenerational school facility at Swampscott, Massachusetts, was built to contain both a high school and a senior center.[2] The primary driver was financial, that is, to save on building costs, operations, and land use. However, there was a growing recognition that building a shared site would provide substantial benefits for the youth and older adults of Swampscott. As described by Donna Butts (2011, p. 5), Director of Generations United:

> The city of Swampscott, Massachusetts, faced a serious financial decision. Two of the community's assets, both about one hundred years old, needed to be replaced. Would the town council choose to build a new high school or would they lean towards their older citizens and replace the senior center? With strong leadership, creativity, and much dialogue, the city decided to combine the two into an intergenerational shared site and built the Swampscott High School and Senior Center. The resulting "green" building is larger and has more amenities than a single age focused facility would have encompassed. As the programs mature, the informal interactions between generations are enhanced by planned, intentional opportunities. For example when filming a history of the high school, the students interviewed seniors who had gone to the school in its early years. When the library was threatened with closure two days a week because of a budget shortage, the older adults stepped up, received training, and organized themselves to staff the library and keep it open.

In Japan too, as a result of demographic changes, it has become increasingly common in the last two decades for senior services to be placed within schools. Colocating aging services such as day care centers and centers for older adults in the school compound had been almost impossible before 1990, as schools come under the purview of the Ministry of Education while senior welfare belonged to the Ministry of Health and Welfare. Sharing spaces was only made possible from the early 1990s, due to a shortage of space for senior services with the rapid aging of the population, coupled with more vacant classrooms in schools as student numbers declined in association with a persistently low birth rate. It is common for schools that incorporate older adults to relate to the "community school" movement, started in the 1930s in the United States (Kurauchi & Suzuki, 1998, p. 121), even though the "opening up" of schools to outsiders may have been more of a pragmatic response to the changing demographics.

The Kodaira Second Elementary School

This school, situated in Tokyo, is one such integrated location, where a center for older adults in the community was built out of remodeled empty classrooms. The space, set up in 2001 and called the "interaction room," was framed as a place for older persons living in the community to drop in as and when they liked for activities among themselves as well as to interact with the children. When the first author conducted fieldwork at the center in mid-2001, there were 73 members, ranging from 60 to 91 years old, almost 90% of whom were women. Between five and ten older adults visit the center in a day; some come by every day, while others visit once a week. The center is open from 10:00 am to 3:30 pm on days when the schools are open. Volunteers—many of whom are older adults themselves—help to coordinate the activities and serve as instructors for activities such as dance, painting, handicrafts, and cooking. The within-school setting allows for spontaneous as well as planned intergenerational interactions. A few students can be seen strolling in the center during recess time in morning breaks and lunch; they may just come and take a look at the handicrafts on display, chat with the older adults there, or even play traditional games with them. Teachers and school administrators interact with the older adults in creating opportunities and implementing plans for them to visit the classrooms as "instructors" for lessons such as arts and crafts, history, and social education (Thang, 2008). Over the years, the interaction has expanded to include having meals together, joining in the singing group, and senior participation in school ceremonies such as first day of school and graduation.

The "Suku Suku School"

The "suku suku[3] school" is another "open school" program, spearheaded by the Edogawa district in Tokyo. Instead of colocating schools with senior centers, the schools in this district encourage volunteers in the community to initiate activities they would like to have with the children after school hours on the school grounds. These include programs relating to school subjects, science experiments, traditional cultural classes, and sports. In an observation conducted in one of these schools (by the first author in April 2009), there were several retirees among the volunteers who actively interacted with the school children through classes and other activities they proposed. The school teacher noted how such intergenerational interactions have promoted a sense of community identity among the children with the senior volunteers staying in the neighborhoods.

At the outset, we argued that intergenerational settings do best (in terms of facilitating intergenerational engagement) when there is alignment across efforts to develop institutional policies, programs, and the built environment. In this section, examples from the United States and Japan have shown the significance of policy and program support in enabling intergenerational interaction in varied forms, such as older adults volunteering in teaching, youth supporting older adults in their learning pursuits, and joint (intergenerational) learning, civic engagement, and recreational activities within and beyond the school environment. In some cases, particularly when the decision to establish an age-integrated school facility is initially driven by fiscal considerations, intergenerational policy and program initiatives come later, after the participants, staff, and community stakeholders begin to recognize the benefits that meaningful intergenerational interactions provide for the young and older users of the facility. Each of the sites described in this section is unique, with the trajectories of activity development influenced by local educational policies and practices, as well as community- and culture-specific values and notions with regard to school-community integration.

Intergenerational Spaces and Places Devoted to Social Services: Age-Integrated Childcare and Adult Care Facilities

The combination of childcare and older adult care facilities provides another form of shared site arrangement, widely known to be effective in promoting intergenerational interaction (Generations United, 2006; Heyman, Gutheil, & White-Ryan, 2011; Jarrott, Gigliotti, & Smock, 2006). The forms of combination vary for each shared site; we have observed various design settings, ranging from colocation of services within the same building, through the use of different buildings in the same compound, to bringing together members from different facilities under one roof for regular joint activities. It is useful to describe examples of such age-integrated social services.

The Tiny Tigers Intergenerational Center (TTIC)

Based in Marshfield, Wisconsin, this center brings together children from a child care center (ranging in age from 6 weeks to 12 years), students from the Marshfield High School Human Service Academy, and adults from an adult day care center (the Companion Day Services program serves people of advanced age who have irreversible dementia/Alzheimer's, developmental disabilities, and physical disabilities) to regularly interact under one roof. The facility aims to provide outstanding care and education to children, students, and older adults while actively engaging them in activities designed to provide cognitive stimulation, physical exercise, spiritual development, recreation, and socialization opportunities.

The Tampines Three-in-One Center

This center in Singapore consists of adult day care, childcare, and before-and-after-school care programs for children of ages 7 to 12, all within a facility that stretches through the ground floor level of three blocks of high-rise public apartments. The three components of the Center are situated short distances from each other, are linked by covered walkways, and all face a courtyard that has a landmark clock tower, a basketball court, benches for the residents, and a covered playground. The courtyard is also where morning exercises are held for Center members as well as for residents of the wider community. All three components of the Center come under the same management, which emphasizes intergenerational interaction, where regular intergenerational activities are held to bring together the young and the old.

Kotoen Age Integrated Facility

In Japan, shared social services sites are increasingly seen following the success of pioneer age-integrated facilities such as Kotoen, situated in Tokyo. As described in detail in Thang's (2001) ethnography, this three-level shared site is composed of a special nursing home for the aged on the top level, a home for ambulant older adults on the second level, an adult day care center for older adults from the community (also on the second level), and childcare services on the first level. The Kotoen building is unique for its large open space on the ground floor, which functions not only as an open hall for activities, morning exercises, children's playground, and assembly hall, but also for its potential to serve as a "big bedroom" for the children's afternoon naps once the curtains are drawn and the floor is laid with portable mattresses (Figure 10.1a and b). The center is closely linked with older adults living in the

FIGURE 10.1   Kotoen, Japan. (a) Open Hall Concept Gives Flexibility to Merge Activities of Different Generations. (b) Intergenerational Activity.

(a)

(b)

surrounding community, through offering services for those living in their own homes, such as day services, a short stay service for bed-ridden older adults, rehabilitation, and bath services and seminars for caregivers in the community.

Intergenerational interaction at Kotoen occurs on a daily basis for children and the older adults. Interaction begins with informal interaction during morning exercises together, followed by other informal contact, including older adults helping the children to put on and get out of their sleepwear during the afternoon nap session and various programs such as joint activities in arts and crafts, story-telling, and once a month joint care sessions, where adults from the older adult residential part of the facility join in for a day's activities with the children (Figure 10.2). At the beginning of spring, the babies and toddlers new to the center will be babysat by the older adults and given individual attention. All generations are involved in various events held at the center, such as birthday celebrations for the older adults, childcare graduation and opening ceremonies, sports day, various cultural events, and memorial ceremonies for those who have died. Childcare teachers are often seen bringing the children for a walk on the second and third level to greet and meet with the older adult residents.

Kotoen endorses the concept of intergenerational interaction through the model of "a big family," where it aims to achieve a lively and bright big family, a facility where children and older adults live together. Visually, Kotoen resembles a huge three-generation family with children as the young, the staff as the middle generation, and the older adults living in the institution and attending the day services at the institutions as the older generation. Moreover, the "big family" concept also embraces values such as mutual caring and sharing of cultural traditions common within the three-generation family.

Intergenerational interaction is fostered through a committee set up across the services to propose and evaluate the various intergenerational programs planned for the children and older adults. Kotoen is flexible in the creation of responsive spaces; when the plan for a large open space on the ground floor was rejected by the government authorities, who reasoned that children and older adults needed their own spaces and uninterrupted privacy, they compromised by having a removable sliding wall, which has not been set up since. The open space is a crucial space for intergenerational interaction, affording both planned activities and casual contacts, as older adults are often seen sitting at the side, watching the children play in the space and joining them as they wish.

Kotoen shows that success in achieving age-integration lies in the clear articulation of a common goal among the different social services to promote interaction across generations. The common goal is more

FIGURE 10.2 Intergenerational Learning

easily achieved when the services for different generations are placed under the same administration, which takes care to train and equip all staff with some knowledge of intergenerational practice. Although putting services into age-integrated settings contributes to opportunities for intergenerational interaction, there are also ample examples showing that colocation does not automatically result in close intergenerational interaction, as factors such as differing goals among social services (particularly if they are under different administrative structures) and the lack of staff knowledge of intergenerational programming practices may hinder interaction, even if the services are colocated (Thang, 2001, 2002).

Intergenerational Spaces and Places Devoted to Recreation

Even though public spaces and places for leisure and recreation do not formally restrict access to an individual based on age there are, nonetheless, various purpose-built spaces such as playgrounds and sports fields, which tend to be occupied by certain age groups. How can an intergenerational framework be applied to such spaces so that they can be opened up as places that promote intergenerational interaction? Such places, when built with equipment for different generations, may become either multigenerational or intergenerational, depending on whether the design promotes or hinders interaction across generations. The following are some examples.

Intergenerational Community Centers

In Germany, there are over 500 Multigenerational Houses (Mehrgenerationenhäuser), funded by the German Ministry of Family, Older Adults, Women, and Youth. They serve many functions, including those associated with a multiservice center, an open community drop-in center, and a meeting point (or café), typically run mostly by volunteers (including teenagers, parents, and older adults). Heid and Liebenberg (2007) note that in the facility in Nürnberg, there are various dimensions to intergenerational interaction and support, including older adults providing homework assistance for youth and helping families with childcare. Each center receives 40,000 euros per year for 5 years and, after that, it is expected to be self-sufficient. This has stimulated an entrepreneurial element in many programs. For example, Kreativhaus Center (in Berlin) runs a café, a rental service for theater costumes, and they conduct a range of fee-for-service creative and educational programs (Figure 10.3).

Parks and Playgrounds

In Singapore, playgrounds at the public housing estates are increasingly built with multigenerational populations in mind, with children's playgrounds built side-by-side with exercising equipment for older adults and adults, such as pebble paths for foot reflexology and a simple range of exercise stations (Figure 10.4 a and b). On a typical day, older adults can be seen doing their exercises on one side while children play

FIGURE 10.3   Kreativehaus Center (Berlin)

FIGURE 10.4 Mixed Use Open Space. (a) Children's Playground in Singapore with Exercise Equipment for Older Adults in the Background. (b) Exercise Equipment for Older Adults with Children Participating and Older Adults Sitting at the Side Chatting.

(a)

(b)

and run on their own playground next to it. Although such a design would readily be categorized as a *multigenerational* site, it is not necessarily intergenerational, as different generations are more likely to be engaging in activities side by side, and do not necessarily interact with each other.

In another common multigenerational setting, a community park has children's playground equipment on one end of the playground and seats for adults at the other end. In Japan, Kihara (1995) has termed such arrangements, where older adults in wheelchairs spend time in the background, as a form of volunteering. While the presence of children and their laughter contribute to a sense of generational inclusiveness for older adults, older adults are also said to be "volunteers" by being near the children, as they benefit the children with a secure feeling of being watched over by older adults. This concept of "communication by watching" was initially regarded by non-Japanese observers as undesirable: from the perspective of intergenerational communication dynamics, communication is expected to be direct and overt. Eventually though, these cultural differences in mode of communication, and the likelihood of psychosocial benefits associated with older adults getting to know and develop relationships with local young people through indirect communication, are now recognized and acknowledged (Kaplan, Kusano, Tsuji, & Hisamichi, 1998). Nonetheless, the extent of intergenerational interaction in such public playground settings also depends on one's perception of safety within the community. Safety concerns about pedophiles and inappropriate behavior between generations, including older adults being hassled by teenagers, may be a real concern, especially in the United Kingdom and United States; this means that communities may be reluctant to engage in environmental designs that increase the potential for such concerns to become manifest. That said, with increasing attention being paid to how shared play experiences can serve as a bridge between generations, intergenerational design ideas for recreation-oriented public places and spaces should be explored further (Generations United, 2008; National Toy Council, 2008).

Whether speaking about shared site facilities or shared outdoor places such as parks, plazas, and other community gathering places, intergenerational practitioners are significant in making these shared places come alive with intergenerational interaction; their development of some provocative strategies for promoting intergenerational conversations about place and place identity contribute toward an active intergenerational community. For example, Community Celebration of Place, a nonprofit organization in the United States, has established a variety of methods for using arts such as music, photography, videography, and graphic design to help multigenerational groups document their communities, organize festivals, and conduct other community celebration projects (e.g., using photo essays, music, or video CDs).[4] Such activities can contribute to mutual understanding and a shared sense of community across generations.

DISCUSSION

Snapshots of age-integrated settings in schools, social services, and public spaces like playgrounds, indicate that these are complex settings that afford many benefits for those who use them. Such facilities tend to have community-building properties insofar as they provide community focal points for service delivery and, depending on the model, they can stimulate and nurture various types of nonfamilial intergenerational relationships, with the potential outcome of promoting well-being across generations.

There are also various challenges associated with advocating, planning, and operating intergenerational facilities. For organizations and agencies interested in embarking on intergenerational programming endeavors, it is not uncommon to face obstacles from bureaucracies, which often work in silos and fail to see the benefits of overlapping services from different ends of the life continuum. Organizations serving different generations also, typically focus on representing the interests of the population they serve without a broader perception of how cross-generational collaboration, through well planned programs and activities, may ensure greater benefits for all (Van Vliet, 2009).

It is also important to consider intergenerational dynamics in the surrounding community before efforts are exerted to plan, develop, and build age-integrated facilities. In communities with patterns of intergenerational conflict and tension, such as some multiethnic communities in the Netherlands that have histories of conflict with regard to how, when, and by whom public spaces are used (as noted by Mercken, 2003; Penninx, 1996), it may be especially challenging to persuade local residents to embrace new schemes for the intergenerational use of local facilities.

Another challenge comes in the form of working in communities where the generations appear to be "naturally" age-segregated in the ways they access and use public spaces. For example, Holland, Clark, Katz, and Peace (2007) describe a study of Aylesbury, a small market town in South East England, where it was found that different age groups tended to avoid contact with each other in public spaces such as shopping centers, parks, and public squares, usually by occupying different parts of the same space (see Chapter 2). Although this minimizes conflict, it also hinders opportunities to interact and can perpetuate the separation of the generations. Whether the identification of a public space as appropriate only to certain generation or population groups is intentional or unintentional, planners need to understand this dynamic before embarking on large-scale community development and revitalization projects that might violate local patterns of intergenerational engagement, and that local residents might reflexively resist.

The development of successful intergenerational settings, such as many of the age-integrated facilities highlighted in this chapter, is not a simple, linear process. While the close proximity of programs serving different age groups is conducive to developing and implementing intergenerational activities, the extent to which colocation will maximize interaction and lead to meaningful relationships across generations depends on other conditions. To begin with, not all shared sites are equally committed to promoting intergenerational connections; they vary in terms of philosophy, funding constraints, administrator, and front-line staff interest and support, and in the structures established to facilitate intergenerational contact, communication, and cooperation. While Kotoen in Japan serves as an excellent model, with careful and supportive planning across different social services to optimize intergenerational connections within a single space, we have observed other purpose-built age-integrated settings in which the different service components merely coexist side by side, with little interaction. Sometimes, the administrators of one setting (providing services for children) may not be keen to interact with older persons because of a misguided notion that older adults may carry disease and are unhealthy. There may also be objections from parents who do not understand the benefits of letting their children interact with older adults. At times, administrators of senior care services may limit interaction for fear that children are too active and may hurt the older adults (Thang, 2001). Such attitudes signal the need for a comprehensive, inclusive approach to staff training as well as to program planning and environmental design.

A focus on staff training and development is consistent with one of the conclusions provided by Hayes (2003) after evaluating the Community Programs Center in Long Island (New York): a shared site facility with childcare and learning programs for children, a program for pregnant women and families with infants, toddlers, and preschoolers, and an adult day services program serving frail older adults and their caregivers. Hayes noted, "You can't just throw [children and elders] into a room and think intergenerational programming is going to work, it takes tremendous time and effort, it requires a special group [staff] that is willing to make the effort" (p. 125).

The benefits of taking an intergenerational perspective are increasingly recognized in the United States and in some parts of Europe, but equipping staff with intergenerational skills and expertise remains an area requiring improvement. Rosebrook & Larkin (2003) have outlined a set of standards that have been influential in framing the discussion about what is considered exemplary performance. They include: the ability to draw upon knowledge of human development across the lifespan in planning mutually beneficial intergenerational programs; skills in facilitating effective communication and collaboration between partnering agencies; the ability to utilize and integrate the knowledge base from a variety of relevant fields, including psychology and sociology; and the ability to employ appropriate evaluation techniques. We would add two items to this list of vital skills and areas of knowledge that intergenerational practitioners need: design literacy and cultural sensitivity. By design literacy we are referring to the need to understand behavior—including intergenerational communication and cooperation—in the context of the physical, designed environment. Intergenerational practitioners for the most part tend to have low design literacy skills, as do most human service professionals who have been trained in the helping professions, and this leaves them in a somewhat dependent role when seeking assistance from design professionals to build or modify facilities. The second item is cultural sensitivity. Training of staff and designing of activities requires sensitivity to cultural appropriateness and expectations in intergenerational communication. This includes sensitivity toward cultural norms in terms of touch, humor, dealing with illness, and loss.

This relates to the importance of paying close attention to the values and implicit, culturally constructed meanings and expectations that people (including designers and users) have with regard to intergenerational dynamics and how they evolve across cultural and social contexts. In Asian societies such as Japan and Singapore, it is common to evoke the three-generational family ideal in positioning intergenerational interaction within the community, where children simply address older adults as "grandpa" and "grandma," just as they would address their own grandparents. Such familial interactions allow for older adults, regardless of gender, to perform "homely" tasks such as helping the children to dress and undress and putting the toddlers to sleep as in the case of Kotoen. However, when scenes such as a "grandpa" undressing a little girl were shown to non-Asians, it attracted questions on the need for segregation of the older adults from children to avoid sexual harassment, reflecting different cultural expectations and values.

It is also important to keep in mind that there are policy differences across countries in terms of how public facilities are built and regulated. While Japan has somewhat relaxed its bureaucratic divide to accommodate the colocation of facilities for different generations, in most other countries shared sites struggle with sometimes conflicting regulations surrounding childcare and elder care facilities.[5] This spells out the need for bureaucracy to change alongside sociodemographic changes and increasing needs for intergenerational connection.

Toward a Conceptual Model of Intergenerational Spaces and Places

In the literature on intergenerational practice, various concepts and values associated with intergenerational community living are invoked, such as "inclusiveness" (Granville & Hatton-Yeo, 2002); "civic engagement" (Lawrence-Jacobson, 2005), "caring communities" (Eheart, Power, & Hopping, 2003); and "communities for all ages" (Henkin, 2004). It is not always clear how to implement such key concepts—that is, to translate them into environmental design practices in real-world settings. As illustrated in this chapter, there is no single notion or design plan for creating an intergenerational school, social services facility, or recreational facility. That said, it is possible to lay out a conceptual framework that can provide direction in working with and making decisions about intergenerational spaces. With this goal in mind, we introduce a series of recommendations, drawn from the literature on intergenerational practice, that we feel are useful in approaching the challenge of creating intergenerational settings.

Recommendation 1

Keep in mind that environmental design cannot be exercised independent of context; we reiterate the importance of working to align environmental design, policy, and programming. A "weak link" within any of these dimensions could compromise an overall effort to operationalize desired values (e.g., "normalized living," providing options for intergenerational engagement, etc.) in the creation and day-to-day operations of an intergenerational setting.

Recommendation 2

Ensure that participants with a wide range of physical and mental abilities have access to and within the site. Where appropriate, "universal design" principles should be incorporated when developing indoor sites and outdoor spaces to ensure that buildings, products, and environments are usable and effective for everyone. Examples of universal design features include: smooth ground surfaces of entranceways (without stairs), wide interior doors and hallways, lever handles for opening doors rather than twisting knobs, light switches with large flat panels rather than small toggle switches, clear lines of sight (to reduce dependence on sound), and buttons and other controls that can be distinguished by touch.

Recommendation 3

Design the environment to be responsive to the way that people across the lifespan perceive and use space. It is useful to ask, for example, if a design of a community park accommodates children's needs for creative play and mutual (multigenerational) needs for safety and exploration.

Recommendation 4

Provide opportunities for spontaneous meetings and informal interaction as well as planned, structured interaction. There are various ways to create spaces that are conducive to intergenerational encounters. One outdoor example would be the ground-level water fountains at a popular plaza in Rotterdam (the Netherlands), which invite impromptu gatherings by providing opportunities to play with water. An indoor example would be the nooks and alcoves strategically placed around the Intergenerational Center at Providence Mount St. Vincent, a shared site in Seattle that includes assisted living, long-term care, adult day care programs for older adults, and an early childhood education program. These stimulate spontaneous intergenerational gatherings and informal conversation outside of the formal activity hubs of the facility (Kaplan et al., 2007).

Recommendation 5

Provide cues in the environment that convey positive messages about people in various age groups and that suggest certain modes of interactive behavior. Such cues are communicated via murals, photographs, notices, brochures, and regulations that are posted in the facility or program area. Related questions to be considered include: Are design elements included that provide welcoming messages for *all* who enter and use the setting? Is care taken to avoid stereotypical cues that convey negative inferences about people of a certain age group?

Recommendation 6

Plan and organize spaces in ways that facilitate interaction without violating people's need for privacy. Shared site facilities with active intergenerational programs should include some space where people can go to congregate and engage one another. There should also be opportunities to disengage. In residential settings that provide long-term care to residents, for example, building "escape routes" (additional exits) into spaces used for congregate meetings is one way to protect residents from what they might perceive as too much (or overly forced) intergenerational engagement.

Recommendation 7

Incorporate enough flexibility in the design to accommodate a wide range of intergenerational exchanges and other social behaviors that might change as participants' interests, relationships, and abilities evolve. One way to build flexibility into the design is to limit the use of stationary/fixed structures and materials that predetermine and constrain usage.

Many of these themes have been emphasized by the creators and stewards of the intergenerational settings described in this chapter as well as elsewhere in the literature that examine colocated cross-generational facilities (e.g., Jarrott, 2007; Steinig, 2005, 2006). Whether it is in an environment within the confines of social services or schools situated within the community or in the larger setting of the neighborhood or community as a whole, the mainstream of life extends beyond the confines of monogenerational interaction, as the testament from Anne Leitch, the woman quoted at the beginning of this chapter, reminds us. Public places and spaces need to be relational spaces that encourage and enable multiple generations to coexist and interact. Hence, the application of an intergenerational framework is called for, where good environmental design aligns with institutional and community policies for using space, and design is enhanced with programs and activities to be conducted in that space.

NOTES

1. For more information about the Creating Aging Friendly Communities conference and its ancillary web-based resources and workshops, see: http://www.icohere. com/agingfriendly/index.htm.
2. To see a video clip that provides additional detail with regard to the background and operation of the Swampscott High School and Senior Center facility, go to: http://www.youtube.com/watch?v=m95u_1DQDUs
3. Suku suku in Japanese means children growing healthily and steadily.
4. The organization posts some of its work on its website; see: http://www. communitycelebration.org
5. See Steinig (2005), particularly the chapters by Goyer and Turner, for a review of policy and regulation issues related to licensing, accreditation, and building design in the United States.

REFERENCES

AARP. (1998). *Intergenerational shared site project: Final report.* Washington, DC: AARP.

Abramson, P. (2007). Schools should be part of their community. *School Planning and Management, 46*(6), 90.

Altman, I., & Low, S. (1992). *Place attachment. Human behavior and environments: Advances in theory and research* (Vol. 12). New York, NY: Plenum Press.

Beth Johnson Foundation (n.d.). *Definition of intergenerational practice.* Stoke on Trent, UK: Centre for Intergenerational Practice. Retrieved from http://www.centreforip.org.uk

Brabazon, K., & Disch, R. (1997). *Intergenerational approaches in aging: Implications for education, policy and practice.* New York, NY: Haworth Press.

Bressler, J., Henkin, N., & Adler, M. (2005). *Connecting generations, strengthening communities: A toolkit for intergenerational program planners.* Philadelphia, PA: Center for Intergenerational Learning, Temple University.

Butts, D. (2011). Existing framework for dialogue and mutual understanding across generations: Family, community, educational institutions and workplace. United Nations Expert Group Meeting. March 8–9. Doha, Qatar.

Carr, S., Francis, M., Rivlin, L., & Stone, A. (1992). *Public space.* Cambridge, UK: Cambridge University Press.

Christensen, P., & O'Brien, M. (Eds.). (2003). *Children in the city: Home, neighborhood and community.* London, UK: Routledge Falmer.

Eheart, B. K., Power, M. B., & Hopping, D. E. (2003). Intergenerational programming for foster-adoptive families: Creating community at Hope Meadows. *Journal of Intergenerational Relationships, 1* (1), 17–28.

Generations United (2008). *Play is forever: The benefits of intergenerational play.* [Factsheet.] Washington, DC: Author.

Generations United (2006). *Intergenerational shared sites: Making the case.* Retrieved from http://gu.org/LinkClick.aspx?fileticket=iMXIx4uF5nI%3d&tabid=157&mid=606

George, D., Whitehouse, C., & Whitehouse, P. (2011). A model of intergenerativity: how the intergenerational school is bringing the generations together to foster collective wisdom and community health. *Journal of Intergenerational Relationships, 9*(4), 389–404.

Ghazaleh, R. A., Greenhouse, E., Homsy, G., & Warner, M. (2011). *Multigenerational planning: Using smart growth and universal design to link the needs of children and the aging population.* Chicago, IL: American Planning Association. Retrieved from http://www. planning.org/research/family/briefingpapers/multigenerational.htm

Grant, D. P. (1970). An architect discovers the aged. *The Gerontologist*, 10(4), 275–281.

Granville, G. and Hatton-Yeo, A. (2002). Intergenerational engagement in the UK: A framework for creating inclusive communities. In M. Kaplan, N. Henkin, and A. Kusano (Eds.), *Linking lifetimes: A global view of intergenerational exchange* (pp. 193–208). Lanham, MD: University Press of America.

Hayes, C. (2003). An observational study in developing an intergenerational shared site program: challenges and insights. *Journal of Intergenerational Relationships*, 1(1), 113–131.

Heid, S., & Liebenberg, A. (2007). Multigenerational House Nürnberg. EAGLE Case Study: Germany. FIM–New Learning, University of Erlanen, Nuremberg, Germany.

Henkin, N. (2004). Beyond programs: Moving toward age-integrated communities. Presentation conducted at the Second Biennial Conference of the International Consortium for Intergenerational Programmes, June 3–5, 2004, Victoria, British Columbia, Canada.

Henkin, N., Homes, A., & Greenburg, B. R. (2003). *Communities for all ages: Youth and elders as allies in neighborhood transformation. Position paper.* Baltimore, MD: The Annie E. Casey Foundation.

Henkin, N., & Kingson, E. (Eds.). (1998/99). Keeping the promise: intergenerational strategies for strengthening the social compact [Special issue]. *Generations*, 22(4), 6–9.

Heyman, J. C., Gutheil, I. A., & White-Ryan, L. (2011). Preschool children's attitudes toward older adults: comparison of intergenerational and traditional day care. *Journal of Intergenerational Relationships*, 9(4), 435–444.

Holland, C., Clark, A., Katz, J., & Peace, S. (2007). *Social interactions in urban public spaces.* Bristol, UK: The Policy Press. Retrieved from http://www.jrf.org.uk/sites/files/jrf/2017-interactions-public-places.pdf

Jarrott, S. E. (2007). *Tried and true: A guide to successful intergenerational activities at shared site programs.* Washington, DC: Generations United.

Jarrott, S. E., Gigliotti, C. M., & Smock, S. A. (2006). Where do we stand? Testing the foundation of a shared site intergenerational program. *Journal of Intergenerational Relationships*, 4(2), 73–92.

Kaplan, M. (1997). The benefits of intergenerational community service projects: implications for promoting intergenerational unity, community activism, and cultural continuity. *Journal of Gerontological Social Work*, 28(1/2), 211–228.

Kaplan, M., Haider, J., Cohen, U., & Turner, D. (2007). Environmental design perspectives on intergenerational programs and practices: an emergent conceptual framework. *Journal of Intergenerational Relationships: Programs, Policy, and Research*, 5(2), 81–110.

Kaplan, M., Henkin, N., & Kusano, A. (Eds.). (2002). *Linking lifetimes: A global view of intergenerational exchange.* Lanham, MD: University Press of America.

Kaplan, M., Kusano, A., Tsuji, I., & Hisamichi, S. (1998). *Intergenerational programs: Support for children, youth and elders in Japan.* Albany, NY: SUNY Press.

Kihara, K. (1995). *A volunteer just by being present.* Tokyo Shine Video: Federation of National Old-age clubs.

Kurauchi, S., & Suzuki, M. (Eds.). (1998). *The basics of lifelong learning (In Japanese).* Tokyo: Gakubunsha.

Larkin, E., Kaplan, M., & Rushton, S. (2010). Designing brain healthy environments for intergenerational programs. *Journal of Intergenerational Relationships: Programs, Policy and Research*, 8(2), 161–176.

Lawrence-Jacobson, A. (2006). *Recreating the common good: Intergenerational community action* (unpublished doctoral dissertation, Social Work and Sociology). University of Michigan, Ann Arbor, Michigan.

Laws, G. (1993). "The land of old age": society's changing attitudes toward urban built environments for elderly people. *Annals of the Association of American Geographers*, 83(4), 672–693.

Manzo, L. C., & Perkins, D. D. (2006). Finding common ground: the importance of place attachment to community participation and planning. *Journal of Planning Literature*, 20(4), 335–350.

MacCallum, J., Palmer, D., Wright, P., Cumming-Potvin, W., Northcote, J., Brooker, M., & Tero, C. (2006). *Community building through intergenerational exchange*. Report from the (Australian) National Youth Affairs Research Scheme (NYARS).

Mercken, C. (2003). Neighborhood-reminiscence. *Journal of Intergenerational Relationships*, 1(1), 81–94.

Mumford, L. (1949). Planning for the phases of life. *The Town Planning Review*, 20(1), 5–16.

Mumford, L. (1956). For older people—not segregation but integration. *Architectural Record*, 119, 109–116.

National Toy Council (2008). *Intergenerational Play*. [Factsheet.] London: Author.

Newman, S., Ward, C. R., Smith, T. B., & Wilson, J. (1997). *Intergenerational programs: Past, present and future*. Bristol, PA: Taylor & Francis.

Penninx, K. (1996). *The Neighborhood of all ages: Intergenerational neighborhood development in the context of local social policy*. Utrecht, Netherlands: Dutch Institute for Care and Welfare.

Raynes, N. (2004) Where we are now with intergenerational developments? An English perspective. *Journal of Intergenerational Relationships*, 3(4), 187–95.

Rosebrook, V., & Larkin, E. (2003). Introducing standards and guidelines: a rationale for defining the knowledge, skills, and dispositions of intergenerational practice. *Journal of Intergenerational Relationships*, 1(1), 133–144.

Steinig, S. (Ed.). (2005). *Under one roof: A guide to starting and strengthening intergenerational shared site programs*. Washington, DC: Generations United.

Steinig, S. (2006). *Intergenerational shared sites: Troubleshooting* (Occasional Paper #2: To Encourage and Expand Intergenerational Shared Site Development). Washington DC: Generations United.

Sullivan, K. J. (2002). *Catching the age wave: Building schools with senior citizens in mind*. Washington, DC: National Clearinghouse for Educational Facilities. Retrieved from http://www.edfacilities.org/pubs/agewave.pdf

Thang, L. L. (2001). *Generations in touch: Linking the old and young in a Tokyo neighborhood*. Ithaca, NY: Cornell University Press.

Thang, L. L. (2002). Intergenerational initiative in Singapore: Commitments to community and family building. In M. Kaplan, N. Henkin, & A. Kusano (Eds.), *Linking lifetimes: A global view of intergenerational exchange* (pp. 119–134). Lanham, MD: University Press of America.

Thang, L. L. (2008). Engaging the generations: age-integrated facilities. In F. Coulmans, H. Conrad, A. Schad-Seifert, & G. Vogt (Eds.), *The demographic challenge: A handbook about Japan* (pp. 179–200). Leiden: Brill Publisher.

Van Vliet, W. (2009). *Creating livable cities for all ages: Intergenerational strategies and initiatives*. Working Paper CYE-WP1-2009. Children, Youth and Environments Center, University of Colorado. [Paper prepared for UN-Habitat's Global Dialogue on Harmonious Cities for All Age Groups at the World Urban Forum IV, Nanjing, November 3–6, 2008. Jointly published with UN-Habitat.] Retrieved from http://www.cudenver.edu/Academics/Colleges/ArchitecturePlanning/discover/centers/CYE/Publications/Documents/CYE-WP1-2009%20website%20verson.pdf

CHAPTER 11

Creating Homelike Places in a Purpose-Built Retirement Village in the United Kingdom

Bernadette Bartlam, Miriam Bernard, Jennifer Liddle, Thomas Scharf, and Julius Sim

EDITORS' INTRODUCTION

*T*his chapter addresses the issue of the degree to which it is possible to create home and the experiential essence of "being at home" through planning and environmental design. We now know that environment has a key impact on human experience, and we are becoming increasingly knowledgeable about the manner in which the human/environment relationship evolves over the life course. Based on this growing awareness, an implicit premise that it is possible to manipulate environment in a manner that supports wellbeing has underlain the process of developing special environments for older people for several decades. Yet, as Bartlam and her colleagues suggest, experiential dimensions of home and the manner in which home is created have not been fully internalized by those who build and manage environments for older adults. The story of Denham Garden Village tellingly points out that those who would be the best judges of success in this endeavor, the residents, are seldom appropriately consulted during the development process or in the operation of such facilities. The critical issue here pertains to the distinction between house and home (see Chapter 1). Despite the deceptiveness of real estate industry advertising, one cannot move into a "home," because this is something that has to be created or recreated by each resident. On the other hand, good environmental design and sensitive management of facilities can create the kind of environment that facilitates the making of home by developing a "homelike" context. The quest is to develop homelike contexts that enable older adults to support their changing needs.

Dramatic expansion of the world's aging populations will have a profound impact on "all aspects of individual, community, national and international life; and every facet of humanity will be affected: social, economic, political, cultural, psychological and spiritual" (Zelenev, 2008, p. 5). There have been a variety of policy responses across the globe to this demographic shift. Underlying such responses is an acknowledgment that providing sustainable environments capable of supporting individuals in realizing their potential, and which will allow them to participate actively and contribute to their communities throughout their lives, is an urgent policy matter and is key to enhancing quality of life as we age (World Health Organization [WHO], 2011). In line with this is the shift away from traditional housing for older people—generally provided within a framework that fosters dependency—toward more flexible and inclusive approaches designed to provide choice and promote autonomy (Bernard, Bartlam, Biggs, & Sim, 2004). Purpose-built retirement villages are one example of such innovation, and are contributing to the transformation of housing options in later life (Bernard, Liddle, Bartlam, Scharf, & Sim, 2012; Streib, 2002). Fundamental to these developments are notions of "aging in place" and "homes for life."

In this chapter, we ask whether purpose-built retirement villages can be places that residents can call "home" and, if so, whether they do indeed offer homes for life. We begin by examining key theories that inform understandings of "home" and the significance of the concept in relation to well-being. We then turn to findings from our 4-year project entitled LARC (Longitudinal Study of Ageing in a Retirement Community). Taking a case study approach, we explore the vision behind the development of a particular village, the extent to which that vision has translated into an environment allowing residents to engage successfully in the process of "home-making," and the consequences for their ability to age well in place. We conclude with discussion of broader implications of our findings for policy and service provision. In particular, we ask how those involved in developing and providing this particular form of accommodation for older people might continue to identify and meet the needs of growing, and increasingly diverse, populations. We suggest that crucial to such provision is an understanding of the complexity and importance of home as we age.

ENVIRONMENT AND AGING

Exploring the relationship between individuals and the environment(s) in which they live requires a range of perspectives and approaches in order to begin to capture its complex, multi dimensional nature. It is a relationship that reaches across time and space; one that is located culturally and embodied within structures that frame everyday lives, from built through to virtual environments (Rapoport, 2005). Among the first to highlight such complexity was Rowles (1978), who identified the interdependency of four key modalities in the relationship between the individual and their environment: action (nature, frequency); orientation (knowledge of place, with home as the fulcrum); feeling (emotional attachments and responses); and fantasy (vicarious immersion in places displaced in space and/or time as a component of the construction and reconstruction of biography and personal identity).

Homes are central structures within which these four domains are created, and played out, in an iterative process. Taking the notion that home relates to microenvironments, Wiles (2005, p. 86) argues that homes be considered both as "material objects and symbolic entities" that "are shaped and reshaped by their occupants over time in response to changes in the individual's life course and the social context within which they are set." Since we tend to spend more time in our home environment as we grow older, it follows that home contributes increasingly to maintaining, or not maintaining, our health and quality of life (Sixsmith & Sixsmith, 2008). This intimate relationship is reflected in the fact that, as O'Bryant (1983) notes, lay and subjective meanings attached to home have been found to be more powerful predictors of residential satisfaction than expert measures of the physical quality of housing. In a study exploring the features that older people themselves saw as signifiers of home, she identifies four components:

- *Social relationships*: In addition to being the stage on which important social events are enacted, the home has significance as a storage facility for memories and mementos relating to family or other key attachment figures; it also serves as the embodiment of, and contemporaneous link to, such important individuals when they might not be present physically.
- *Cost versus comfort trade-off*: One's immediate environment becomes more of a home when the resources required to maintain it are outweighed by the benefits; if this balance is reversed, independence and autonomy can be threatened.
- *Home ownership*: In many cultures, home ownership is accorded high status, and is an aspiration for many people.
- *Environmental competence*: The extent to which the familiarity afforded by one's home allows one to retain independence and autonomy, notwithstanding any physical or mental declines, is also a key factor in determining the degree of attachment one feels (pp. 38–40).

Healthy Aging

Notions of well-being and active aging are embedded within the literature on the importance and function of home. Notwithstanding its potential to medicalize aging (Higgs, Hyde, Wiggins, & Blane, 2003), here we use the phrase "healthy aging" as an umbrella term to capture the differing concepts of health and quality of life. In their recent review of the literature on conceptualizations of healthy aging, and differences between lay and academic perspectives, Hung, Kempen, and Vries (2010) recommend the use of this term, arguing that it is more widely understood at both a lay and expert level than others such as "successful aging," "active aging," or "positive aging." In particular, they note that lay definitions place greater emphasis on independence, being in control, and being responsible for one's own life, and include other independence-related domains such as family, adaptation, financial security, personal growth, and spirituality. Such prominence is in keeping with Maslow's (1943) hierarchy of needs, and with Higgs et al.'s (2003) conceptualization of quality of life (from a Maslovian perspective) in relation to four domains: control, autonomy, self-realization, and pleasure. Control is defined in terms of an individual's ability to intervene in his or her environment, whereas autonomy is freedom from unwanted interference from others. Higgs et al. (2003, p. 245) argue that "once these requirements (control and autonomy) have been met," individuals are in a position to use them to "pursue the reflexive process of self-realization through activities that make them happy." The capacity to engage with this process of self-realization is indicative of one's degree of ontological security. This theoretical argument has been operationalized in a needs-based quality of life measure—CASP-19—encompassing these four domains, which has been used both in the English Longitudinal Study of Ageing (Hyde, Wiggins, Higgs, & Blane, 2003) and in the LARC surveys, and has been found to be an effective measure when used with older populations (Sim, Bartlam & Bernard, 2011; Wiggins, Netuveli, Hyde, Higgs, & Blane, 2008).

Home and the (Re)creation of "Self"

The notion that the home provides a microenvironment for the ongoing expression and (re)construction of the self highlights its importance in facilitating self-realization in later life. Here we use the term "self" as a proxy for identity, since it conveys a more holistic concept across both physical and mental domains. In line with Maslow (1943), evidence from Rowles (1978) and Higgs et al. (2003) suggests that the self can be understood as a combination of different phenomena, grouped into four components (Ramachandran, 2003): continuity (an awareness of one's past, present, and future); embodiment (connection to one's physical being and environment); agency (feelings of autonomy and choice); and coherence (this last notion is generated when the other three components coalesce). This sense of coherence can also be understood in terms of a complex social construction that links together life events and changing circumstances—including environments—through the generation of a meaning-forming narrative. It is this "self-narrative," placing what might otherwise be haphazard events within a meaningful context, that creates a sense of coherence and direction in one's life (Gergen & Gergen, 1993), in effect leading to self-realization. Thus, the places in which we live are imbued with meanings that are contingent on a process of "complex, symbolic and social construction" (Andrews & Phillips, 2005, p. 7). As Rubinstein and Parmelee (1992, p. 147) note: "Place and things are important symbols of the self, cues to memories of significant life experiences, and a means of maintaining, reviewing, and extending one's sense of self." The extent to which the environments we live in allow for the (re)production and (re)enactment of our "self-narrative" determines the degree to which we are "at home" in them.

From these theoretical perspectives it follows, first, that our sense of self is constructed by the meanings we apply to life events, and to the circumstances and the places in which we find ourselves. Second, this sense of self is under constant revision in terms of our changing relationship with each other, and with events and places—including our homes—over the life course. Third, since our homes play an intimate role in the (re)construction of the self, they are a crucial factor in our capacity to engage with the process of self-realization and thus with healthy aging.

Aging in Place

Perhaps unsurprisingly, then, there is a wealth of literature that suggests that most of us would prefer to stay in our own home as we age (e.g. Lawton, 1985; Means, 2007; Mesch, 1998), and the ability to age in place has been highlighted as a major factor in promoting overall well-being in later life (Rowles, 1978; Rowles & Chaudhury, 2005). It is considered to be of particular importance when health is an issue for, as Rowles (1993, p. 26) notes, ". . . older people, particularly as they grow more frail, are able to remain more independent by, and benefit from, aging in environments to which they are accustomed." Environmental familiarity can help develop compensatory strategies in the face of declines in physical and/or mental capacity, such that the more individuals know their environment, the more independent they can be, whatever their level of physical and mental competence (Lawton, 1985). Aging in place is also recognized as the most economical way of providing support to people with care needs; it is cheaper than nursing home or residential care (Organisation for Economic Co-operation and Development [OECD], 2005).

Emphasis on aging in place is not without its critics; it has been argued that such policies have resulted in the transfer of care from institutional settings to community-based and home-care services for older people, leaving families with little choice but to provide informal care in the home (Williams, 2002). Moreover, there is increasing concern over the tendency to equate aging in place with happiness (Means, 2007), not least because many older people live in impoverished conditions without access to the services and support necessary for aging well *in situ* (Best, 2009; Nair, 2005; Osgood, 1982; Scharf & Bartlam, 2008; Scharf, Phillipson, Smith & Kingston, 2002).

Many people do relocate in later life and there is a growing body of literature documenting the process, together with the reasons for doing so (e.g. Longino & McLelland, 1978; Osgood, 1982; Phillips, Bernard, Biggs & Kingston, 2001; Sim, Liddle, Bernard, Scharf & Bartlam, 2012; Warnes & Williams, 2006; Warnes, 2007). Emerging from this is an awareness of the importance of "elective belonging"—that is, forging attachments to new environment(s) as key to the process of successfully moving and (re)creating home, such that individuals generate a meaning-making narrative that explains their choice. The meaning-making narrative is contextualized within their life-course biography and contributes to their sense of self (Dupuis-Blanchard, Neufeld & Strang, 2009; Peace, Holland, & Kellaher, 2006; Phillipson, 2007; Savage, Bagnell, & Longhurst, 2005). At a practical level, it is also clear that where the built environment is age-friendly, people are more likely to remain independent as they age, even if experiencing reduced mental and/or physical functional ability (Bartlett & Peel, 2005; Lawton, 1985; Rowles, 1993). Purpose-built retirement villages claim to provide precisely such age-friendly environments.

Purpose-Built Retirement Communities

Purpose-built retirement communities, well established in the United Kingdom, Europe, and North America, are increasingly popular, and can now be found across the globe. Evans (2009) cites work by Webster (2002), which shows that they now account for approximately 11 percent of all new housing in the United States of America, with an estimated 12 percent of the older population living in these developments. Comparable figures for the United Kingdom are hard to come by, not least because there are no nationally collated statistics specifically related to this trend (Croucher, Hicks & Jackson, 2006). At the time of writing, the Elderly Accommodation Counsel lists 95 purpose-built communities on its website. In doing so, it notes the lack of any clear definition in the United Kingdom, and says that these communities can range from a modest development with little choice of accommodation type through to a full-size village consisting of various housing options, sometimes with recreation facilities and a care home (www.housingcare.org/elderly-uk-retirement-villages.aspx).

We have explored the challenges posed by such lack of clarity elsewhere, not least its effect on meeting the expectations of residents (Bernard et al., 2012). While some developers such as Anchor Trust, the ExtraCare Charitable Trust, and the Joseph Rowntree Housing Trust have been generous in both funding research and giving access to researchers, there is still a paucity of evidence about the experience of living and aging in such environments (Bernard, Bartlam, Sim, & Biggs, 2007, Bernard et al., 2012). What evidence there is suggests that purpose-built retirement communities have the potential to address present UK policy objectives around promoting independence, reducing demand on institutional facilities, providing a "home for life," reducing social isolation, and promoting a better quality of life for residents (Croucher et al., 2006, p. 19). Yet there is also evidence to suggest that they may not be the panacea they might at first seem.

We have outlined previously a number of questions around these kinds of developments (Bernard et al., 2004, 2007), one of which concerns whether they can achieve a balance between independence and interdependence over time, especially as residents age and potentially become frail. We ask this because retirement communities generally badge themselves as homes for life, in which people are encouraged to be active and to participate as fully as possible. It seems to us that these two aspirations may generate tensions, particularly when people become more dependent and/or develop conditions such as dementia. Linked to this question is the challenge of balancing the cost of services, and in particular staffing, where the evidence suggests that staff are not especially well qualified or well trained, and where it is difficult to recruit and retain personnel. Furthermore, while these environments are generally marketed as supporting independent living, there is an emerging body of work that questions the degree to which residents in a tenant-landlord—or a leasehold[1]—relationship are indeed able to exercise control and autonomy (Bevan, 2010; Gamliel & Hazan, 2006). These questions—and the extent to which they affect residents' ability to re-create home and, in doing so, support their capacity for healthy aging—are now the focus of our attention.

LONGITUDINAL STUDY OF AGEING IN A RETIREMENT COMMUNITY (LARC)

The LARC study took place over four years in Denham Garden Village (DGV), a purpose-built retirement community in Buckinghamshire, 19 miles north-west of London (Figure 11.1). The study was funded by Anchor Trust, the owner of the site and one of the foremost providers of housing and care for older people in England. As a mixed-method longitudinal study, LARC has drawn on a range of quantitative and qualitative approaches. In this chapter we focus on some of the qualitative data, specifically those drawn from two focus groups conducted with staff (n = 10) and one-to-one interviews with 16 stakeholders involved in creating the original vision and developing the village. Eleven of these interviews were with Anchor/DGV senior personnel (past and present) and five were with individuals from the Licensed Victuallers' National Homes (LVNH) organization[2] and from the architectural practice, estate agents, and marketing agencies working on the redevelopment. In what follows, these interviewees are identified as K1 to K16.[3] We also draw on selected data from residents, including interviews (n = 18), diaries (n = 6), directed writing responses (n = 82), and

FIGURE 11.1 Denham Garden Village 2009 after Redevelopment

Source: LARC archive.

photographs, in particular those produced by residents and submitted as part of a photography competition titled "DGV—My Home" (*n* = 30), as well as our own field notes. Taking the Maslovian framework outlined earlier (Higgs et al., 2003), thematic content analysis of these data sources in relation to the four domains of control, autonomy, self-realization, and pleasure forms the basis of the following discussion. The quotations chosen throughout are those that best illustrate and summarize common responses.

The Historical Environment of DGV

To understand the environmental and cultural context in which residents of DGV are creating their homes, it is helpful to consider how the present village came into being. When first opened by the LVNH in 1958, the village consisted of 188 single- and two-bedroom semi-detached bungalows (i.e., single-story buildings) available to rent, and included staff accommodations (Figure 11.2). Part of a wider national network of accommodation available to ex-publicans and their partners upon retirement from the licensed trade, DGV was unique in its range

FIGURE 11.2 The Old Village

Source: LARC archive.

of facilities, which extended beyond the provision of accommodations to include a shop, a public house,[4] a concert-cum-dance hall and a 100-bed on-site nursing home. Financial market changes during the 1980s and 1990s saw major decreases in funding for the LVNH, and by the late 1990s severe pressures were building up in terms of essential maintenance and modernization costs. These pressures ultimately led the LVNH management board to seek alternative strategies to support its housing stock and residents and resulted in Anchor Trust assuming ownership in 2001.

The Contemporary Environment of DGV

The agreement between the LVNH and Anchor Trust was for maintenance and modernization of all housing stock nationally, and for a major redevelopment of DGV. This redevelopment consisted of demolishing the existing village in three phases between 2001 and 2009 and replacing it with a variety of housing options: a total of 326 detached and town houses, new bungalows, and apartments comprising a mix of leasehold and rented accommodation. The commitment was to re-house all existing tenants on site and to make the remaining accommodations available to a range of new residents, beginning in 2006. There is now a gym, swimming pool, health spa, hairdresser and shop, and a café-bar has replaced the more traditional public house. The on-site nursing home—including its annex for those with dementia—has been replaced with domiciliary and support services delivered in "homes for life," that is, accommodation built to UK Lifetime Homes Standards (Department for Communities and Local Government, 2008). There is now also a health center housing two primary care teams serving the needs of both village residents and people living in the local community; the latter also have access to the other on-site facilities. The redevelopment represented a major change in the village environment, both micro (home) and meso (neighborhood), and formed a major theme within the research. To understand the effects of this redevelopment on the capacity of residents to (re)create home, we turn first to an analysis of data around the vision for the village.

The DGV Vision and the Creation of Home

It appears that the vision for DGV was not finalized at the outset, but rather the details developed through a "very collaborative process" (K11), led by key senior personnel who gathered a team around them and worked closely with individuals in the LVNH and with the architects to bring their ideas to fruition. From the outset, the planning team was keen to incorporate three themes in the redevelopment of DGV. First, was awareness that the original village had itself been innovative; there was a determination to continue in that spirit. Second, in order to sustain this sense of innovation, the challenge was to create a development based on a blend of the best of what was originally there and creative ideas and practice from elsewhere in the world, which would also draw in people from the wider community: "We were determined that it would be a community within a community, and that we would look out" (K6). "Looking out" was part of an intention to move away from a gated community, with its potential to emphasize traditional age-segregation:

> I think the concern from Anchor was that they didn't want an old person's ghetto. And I remember somebody using that exact term of, you know, you have to have a sentry on the gate and a bar to get through, and you get through here and everyone's of a certain age. (K12)

Third, there was a philosophy of offering choice not only in terms of types of accommodation but also in support and lifestyles:

> Choice is what you've got. You can choose to have a handyman, you can choose to have a nurse, you can choose to have none of the above. You can choose a one-bedroomed apartment, you can choose a two-bedroomed house, you can choose a three-bed-roomed detached bungalow. (K13)

This emphasis on choice was in keeping with UK national policy directions at the time, and included a strong emphasis on maintaining independence and the personalization of services—"Care would go to people rather than people go into care" (K12)—together with an awareness of the need to move toward greater engagement with health promotion. Such emphasis brought new challenges in terms of how to appeal to diverse groups with differing needs while maintaining a positive marketing image:

> When we were putting the marketing materials together, we deliberately didn't talk about care. Care comes quite late in the marketing stuff, so the marketing materials talk about lifestyle, and they focus on the pool and the café bar, and the life that you can have. And towards the end, they, sort of, vaguely refer to ". . . and if you need a bit of help." And I think, actually, many of the people I talk to, know

that they need a bit of help. It's actually quite difficult to say, "think I need . . ." (K5)

Such ambivalence was reflected in a lack of clarity about how the care framework would develop over time:

I suppose at some point we'll need to re-think that. I think if people age *in situ,* and require nursing care, then we can think about how we would do that. (K1)

Moreover, there was recognition that while Lifetime Homes Standards (Department for Communities and Local Government, 2008) were being applied in building the accommodation, these might not be sufficient to allow residents to age in place regardless of their circumstances, despite what the marketing material for the village might suggest: "what you cannot do is create a single location that meets everyone's needs, because it simply doesn't" (K13). There were implications to this apparent ambivalence for village identity as a whole, not least in terms of staffing, but also in terms of marketing.

It was also clear that the organization was keen to inculcate its own culture of aspiration around aging into the redevelopment by in-house appointments of staff tasked with delivering the vision. With hindsight, it was felt this might not have been the most innovative way forward: "So I think perhaps we should have been a bit braver about saying 'there are some different skills we need here . . . Let's go and find people with good attitudes and values that fit with our organization, but with different skill sets'" (K5).

In addition, there was a *post-hoc* realization of the scale of disruption and change faced by existing residents, which was not incorporated into the development stage:

We've got some great people there, but, I think there's times when we've taken our eye off the ball sometimes, around the relationships, and the importance of this [the moving process] is as emotionally upheavaling [sic] as moving into a care home. And if somebody moves into a care home, they've got a huge, huge amount of support around them for their first couple of weeks . . . We've tried to do that, but it's not been an overriding priority, I don't think. I think we've wanted to make sure the curtains were up and they were in, and they were okay, you know. (K5)

More specifically, in terms of support, we know that residents in age-segregated communities can experience a particular intensity around issues of death and dying, simply because of the concentration of older people in one place (Bernard et al., 2004). Unsurprisingly, therefore, this reluctance to engage with the broader psychosocial issues around moving extended to the issues of death and bereavement. In response to a question about any strategies in place to support residents and the community in such circumstances, posed by the research team early on in the study, the reply from a member of staff was: "We don't do death." A further example from the field highlights this tension. A member of staff was observed informing other staff of the death of a resident; during the subsequent discussion, one staff member's suggestion to post a notice to let residents know was rejected by a more senior staff member, who pointed out: "this is not the message we want"; instead it would be better to have "a word with a few, select" residents (Field notes, October, 2008). By contrast, a more senior member of the Anchor team, when asked to express a view on DGV, replied:

> Fun, community . . . peace of mind. I guess the only negative I can see around it is . . . I'm trying to find the right word for this, having to choose your friends all the time, because people pass on, whereas if you live in the community you've got all ages. This is a community of older people . . . you have that sense of remembering your mortality as well. (K9)

As part of working up the vision for the village and developing a community, consultation with both residents and nonresidents at the planning stage was seen as key. As one of the architects reflected when asked, the sense of community was seen as something that that the built environment could facilitate and that would evolve once people had moved in or been rehoused: "I suppose in a sense you can't create communities really, but you can put in place structures that maybe encourage that" (KI2). It also appears that there were limitations to the level of user engagement, and residents were not included in any review of the development process:

> There has been . . . an informal review process, and what we did is when we finished Phase One, we sat down with the builders and the design team and brought all the operational people and the marketing people together and said: "What could we have done differently?" (K9)

As these quotations indicate, it was clear from the interviews that the overarching vision behind the initial redevelopment of DGV was to incorporate all that was best in the existing village within an innovative new development that would have control, autonomy, self-realization, and pleasure at the center of its ethos. Such a development corresponded closely to the organization's broader strategic direction at the time, and those involved were highly committed. However, the lack of a detailed vision—perhaps inevitable in an organization itself undergoing significant change—meant that resources were not always available in a timely fashion and that challenges were often unforeseen:

> There was a genuine buzz, and that was both in terms of a very close-knit central team who were very much supporting the leadership of Anchor in terms of its growth strategy, but also I think genuinely there was also a buzz at the operational level because it was . . . a new development. Which I think in hindsight actually took a lot more resources than people had understood, in terms of the planning, the relationship building both with the residents as well as the local authority, the planning department. (K7)

What is striking from the interviews is the paucity of emphasis on the psychosocial aspects of the microenvironment, including a lack of awareness of any need to support residents in (re)creating home-like spaces. Although stakeholders were not specifically asked about this, one would have expected it to emerge as a theme in the discussions. To understand the implications of this, we now explore residents' perspectives. All names used in subsequent sections are pseudonyms.

Residents' Efforts to Re-create Home

Residents spoke of their expectations of living at DGV in terms of: being independent; being safe; having opportunities to engage socially; and gaining reassurance that care would be available should it be needed. As Violet Dixon noted:

> My main expectations were to live in a warm comfortable home safely, to meet new friends, to have a hot meal without having to cook, to be able to get to the shops independently, to be able to swim every day, to be assured of care and support twenty-four seven.

Physical design was a significant feature in such expectations for many residents. Vincent Brennan, for example, saw the potential for the property he viewed to be adapted to his future needs as a major deciding factor in purchasing the house, particularly because of the possibility to convert his attached garage to a ground-floor bedroom (Field notes, January 2007) (Figure 11.3). Indeed, previewing their house offered the first opportunity for residents to identify with their new dwelling, to begin the process of exerting control, to be autonomous with respect to the changed environment, and to enjoy their home—in essence, to become attached:

That is where I'm going to put my, um, cupboard with all my glasses . . . I can imagine myself doing the cooking in here . . . I like that . . . There's quite a lot of cupboards, even with my dishwasher . . . (Doreen Evans, on viewing her new apartment for the first time)

FIGURE 11.3 Meeting Future Needs

Source: DGV—My Home.

Not all residents felt they had a choice when it came to deciding on their accommodation. This particularly applied to some of the LVNH residents who were being re-housed. Their lack of choice appears linked to a sense of disempowerment and isolation:

> I don't think a lot of people did have a choice . . . well, we didn't certainly. I know Muriel didn't. I wouldn't have chosen this for the outlook . . . it is very lonely. (Nettie Gray)

Kathleen Lee found it difficult to invest emotionally in her new accommodation after the death of her husband. But with time she has found herself identifying with her house and spoke of the process of forging new attachments:

> At that time I wasn't too sure it really felt like 'home'. However, I have put a lot into this place to make it into our—my—home and it is now beginning to feel a bit more like home.

Unsurprisingly, for residents confined through ill health to their accommodation, the prospect for social engagement and the pleasure that might bring could be very limited. As Muriel Harris noted: "Unless you go out, you don't see anybody . . . apart from seeing the carers who are very good . . ." Conversely, residents who were more mobile but living in the enclosed environment of the apartment blocks had greater freedom all-year round:

> That's why I like it in these flats. I don't have to go out in the rain and the snow. In the summer I can sit out there and have my fresh air. (Lillian Martin)

In order to create the "richly encoded and materially complex worlds" that constitute homes (Peace, Holland, & Kellaher, 2005, p. 201), some residents went to great lengths to redesign their residence including: knocking two houses or apartments into one; removing internal walls; converting bedrooms into studies, or dining rooms into bedrooms; creating storage cupboards; and building conservatories. In addition to exercising control in redesigning their dwelling, residents realized autonomy through internal decoration and furnishing.

> Prior to moving we had our carpets and curtains fitted, so all we had to do on the day was to move our furniture in. One of the first things

we found that there was a lack of storage space, but we soon adjusted to that. (George Hughes)

Often, particularly for new arrivals in the village, the process of moving had involved downsizing and reducing their possessions to one degree or another (Morris, 1992). While for some residents this involved buying entirely new furniture to suit their new accommodation, for others it meant being able to transfer only those items that had most meaning. As in the processes of redesigning and decoration, retaining such objects clearly contributed to the ongoing creation and maintenance of identity and to generating a sense of authority over, and ownership of, the microenvironment. An additional element in the creation of a home was using it as a means of maintaining family and social contacts. Consequently, having space to accommodate overnight guests was seen as important:

You can certainly make a life for yourself, which I have to do. And then look forward to the family coming and that sort of thing, you know. And I have lots of phone calls . . . I've got two lovely sisters and they come and see me two times a year and stay with me for a few days . . . and take me out. (Nettie Gray)

This sense of home as a connector to absent loved ones also mattered on a more metaphysical level, as Glenys Robertson, a widow, noted when she described how glad she was that she had moved to the village with her late husband before he died. Because he had shared their home in the village with her before his death, she now feels that "he is here with me," and in a way that he would not be if she had moved after he had died. Linked to this need to foster connections, it was evident that residents used their homes as a means of storing and displaying mementos relating to family, key attachment figures, and significant events and places in their lives. As Buber (2004, p. 18) notes, "Objects subsist in time that has been" (Figure 11.4).

Participants took care to define the boundaries of their home beyond the brick walls that physically constituted their residence, and to differentiate this space clearly from surrounding public/shared spaces. This territorial marking around liminal spaces was evident through a range of strategies, most particularly through placing plants in pots outside apartments or creating hedges outside bungalows and houses. Despite the fact that in many areas of the village, the green spaces had been designed as "open" spaces, residents also commonly erected small

FIGURE 11.4 Objects in Time That "Has Been"

Source: DGV—My Home.

areas of fencing and trellising and attempted to stretch the boundaries of their properties by beginning to garden in the flowerbeds nearby—in effect taking unofficial ownership of communal areas (Figure 11.5). Such boundary-marking functioned on various levels: strengthening a sense of control over their home and exercising autonomy, in addition to giving pleasure. This demarcation of the boundary between the micro-environment of home and the meso-environment beyond was also an important part of creating privacy and ensuring that the home was a sanctuary from the wider community.

While residents generally appeared to exercise autonomy and control within their home environment, and for many moving to the village represented a positive new phase in their lives, the relationship with Anchor Trust as the landlord was not without its tensions. Members of staff, too, were aware of this relationship and the possible effects on residents, as one staff member noted in the focus group discussions:

> You might see it as not living independently; you're then part of . . . Denham Garden Village and perhaps [people] wouldn't feel that it was really their own place, like you would if you had a house outside of the village.

FIGURE 11.5 Boundaries in the Making

Source: DGV—My Home.

A key part of the sense of diminished control over the home environment was related to worries about possible increases in maintenance and care charges, over which residents felt they had little say. There was a sense for some residents that they were not listened to in a meaningful way, and that there was a covert culture of ageism operating in the village. This was demonstrated in Ida Hopkins's report of an encounter with a staff member (in which the staff member remarks on something Ida was purchasing): "What do you want with [buying] that? You're old." Ida was left feeling very upset and said that she felt unable to challenge the retort because, if she did, perhaps the help and support she was receiving would diminish or be withdrawn. Such vulnerability was echoed by others, including Vera Poole, who reported the story of her carer arriving and arguing about the start time: "[She] arrived at ten past eleven, but insisted it was eleven and

I had to sign otherwise, what do you do? She left without making the bed." Opportunities to discuss such issues and concerns and to exercise control and autonomy at a broader level were limited. There was a Residents' Association in the village and a monthly "Village Forum" meeting with DGV staff to which all residents were invited, and where minutes were taken. These meetings were seen by residents as important in obtaining responses from Anchor that might not be forthcoming through other channels:

> There seems to be nobody to go to over anything. You phone a number and you go, it gives you, always says please leave a message, which you do. But it's seldom that you get any real feedback, except at the monthly meeting. (Joyce Wade)

In 2009, the meetings were stopped unilaterally by management. Instead, an informal quarterly coffee morning was introduced, where management staff would chat with residents who had any concerns. Tensions created through the lack of consultation exemplified by this move existed regardless of whether one was a tenant or a leaseholder. Such tensions sometimes came as a surprise to those home owners who had never encountered a leasehold arrangement before or were unaware of its implications. As Gladys Ashton put it: "I can't understand why 'bright' people could move in and not have realized [the] implications of lease holding . . ." Five months later, the Village Forum meetings were reinstated at the behest of residents, albeit on a quarterly rather than a monthly basis.

In its marketing literature, DGV does not explicitly position itself as offering a "home for life." In common with other such villages, it offers a range of support services from housekeeping to personal care and the administration of medication on the basis of 24-hour service provision. Generally, residents were clear that their accommodation could not be viewed as providing the resources necessary to age in place regardless of physical or mental decline, even for those who were positive about the care they were receiving. Perceptions of the training and expertise of the care staff played a large part in this:

> I said if ever he [husband] becomes ill I would not bother to phone these carers up. Because they come over, they look at you and they decide whether you should go to hospital or not. If they can't give you an injection . . . how can they be trained enough to know that you are ill? . . . Then if you need it, if they decide you need it, they phone up North somewhere to the headquarters. The headquarters

then phones the ambulance service and then you get it. That to me, that's . . . half an hour's wasted. You could be dead in half an hour. (Lillian Martin)

There was also considerable concern about staffing levels within the village, as Joyce Wade noted:

They're so overstretched that, believe me, if I had a fall, if I had any problem at all in future, I wouldn't push my buzzer to my carer. I just wouldn't do it. They don't come.

While most residents and those involved in planning the village understood that DGV could not provide a "home for life," this appeared to be less clear among staff functioning at an operational level, as an episode observed by a member of the research team indicates:

Overheard phone conversation that a member of staff was having with a potential purchaser. Started out talking about how properties were designed for wheelchair access, stair lifts, ceilings strong enough for hoists, etc. if they were needed in the future, then followed by: "Most people are not going to move from here. The village can support people no matter what." (Field notes, June 2009)

Most residents were highly appreciative of the practical support available in the village. For some, though, there was a sense of frustration with the standards and quality of the service received, which itself could lead to lowered well-being. O'Bryant (1983) refers to this as the "cost versus comfort trade-off," such that when the balance between resources required to maintain one's home and the benefits becomes unfavorable, independence and autonomy can be threatened. Comments by Rex Shepherd illustrate this predicament:

With so many problems . . . I am despondent and wish I could move from here. But I can't because I've spent so much money on my house . . . I was so happy but now I'm despondent.

Nonetheless, alternative types of accommodation were seen so negatively that, for one person at least, death was viewed as preferable to having to move:

You only have to press your red button; you've always got somebody here, even during the night . . . I do tend to think, well, I am all right while I can do things for myself. But, if I became that I couldn't do, you would have to go into a nursing home . . . You'd have to move and I don't think I would like that. So I hope that it goes the other way. (Muriel Harris)

MAKING A PLACE THAT IS HOME

Findings from our analysis of data on the vision of those responsible for planning the village, and the experiences of residents as they seek to re-create home, confirm and extend the research literature and evidence outlined at the beginning of the chapter. In particular, our research points to a discordance in understandings of the importance and function of "home" in the lives of older people, with professionals tending to focus almost exclusively on broader notions of community, while limiting their engagement with the micro-environment to its built dimensions. It may be that this is so because they fail to appreciate the significance of the home in identity re-formation and in supporting ontological security. Residents, on the other hand, clearly articulate their awareness of the physical, psychological, and emotional importance of home, not just verbally but through the ways in which they visibly engage with creating homelike spaces. It appears from this that there are a number of key issues—both strategic and practical—to be addressed in order for planners, designers, and service providers to develop a greater understanding of the importance of home for older people, particularly in the context of purpose-built retirement villages.

Understanding the Importance of Home

Key to understanding the role and function of home is staff training, part of which requires a continuing process of raising awareness of ageism and ageist practices. Such awareness will lead to improved services centered on transparency and user engagement. Understanding the importance of the home from the subjective stance of users highlights its role in acting as a connector to people and times past and present. This throws up challenges to planners and developers in how best to meet the desires of people to downsize, while at the same time providing sufficient space for them to create "home." A very common complaint among residents in this development—as in our previous work (Bernard et al., 2004)—was the lack of space, and in particular storage space.

To support people in forging attachments with their environments, close attention needs to be given to improved support during the moving-in period, for example through individualized care plans that take into account personal biography, reasons for moving, expectations and needs (health and psychosocial), and which explore possible losses and gains in the transition. Regular postoccupancy consultations to review the situation should be implemented according to individual need. In addition, thought should be given to developing frameworks for informal support, such as befriending schemes. Such schemes, while not costly, nonetheless require resourcing in terms of dedicated staff time to support those residents acting as friends. In line with this, consideration should be given to how best to support residents who are also carers in creating "home." It is important to ensure that their well-being is not damaged by their caring responsibilities and that opportunities for breaks and for psychosocial support are identified. At a broader level, there is a need for close auditing of levels of care and care needs so that community change over time is clear, and the implications of such change for individual residents—and for their sense of home—can be investigated.

Clarity of Vision

An essential part of effectively developing environments that offer residents the opportunity to re-create home is clarity of vision. Those involved in planning the redevelopment of DGV were committed to raising expectations and aspirations around accommodation in later life, and to creating an environment in which residents would achieve well-being through fostered independence. The end result was to be an environment that was nurturing and that would allow residents choice over lifestyle and support options.

Yet, the predevelopment vision lacked implementation details, not least around how the increased expectations for the residents in relation to independence would be resourced and managed and, as a result, it failed to address important inherent tensions. For example, there was clearly an awareness of the importance of creating an "outward-looking" village, which would have permeable boundaries, allowing it to be part of the local community "rather than an alien imposition on the local landscape" (Rowles, Concotelli & High, 1996, p. 199) and, in doing so, creating opportunities for residents to continue contributing on a wider social level. The extent to which this was or is communicated to DGV residents remains debatable, with many voicing resentment over the use of village facilities by the local community, viewing it solely as a money-making endeavor on the part of the organization. In addition, the vision lacked clarity over care and how this would be supplied. There was a clear intention that domiciliary care would replace the old nursing home, yet how this would be made operational was much vaguer and was based on a sense that any future needs of residents for nursing care was something that would be addressed when the time came. No audit took place on the potential effects of closing the nursing home and its dementia care unit.

Organizations operating at the forefront of their fields are by definition dynamic and in a state of flux. Consequently, having a clear, strategic, and evolving vision can be challenging. It requires development with all stakeholders (existing and prospective residents included) and the identification of immediate, medium-term, and long-term goals. Preplanning focus groups with stakeholders that are followed up with implementation and, subsequently, evaluation/reflection workshops might offer a useful way forward. The vision needs to be transparent to all involved and should be reflected in an honest representation of the development and what the village can, and cannot, offer. This transparency begins at the initial point of contact with prospective residents, with clarity as to the strengths and limitations of the development and an explanation of whom it suits and whom it does not. This also means that service providers need to be unambiguous about how they are positioning themselves along the spectrum of social versus medical or health-related care. In particular, clarity is needed on how changing and diverse care needs can be met over time, for example around dementia. This is important so that individual residents can maintain maximum autonomy and control for as long as possible; lack of clarity means that residents will inevitably experience a reduction in these domains as they struggle to have their expectations met.

Meaningful Engagement with Residents

Meaningful engagement is also crucial to supporting maximum autonomy and control, and is essential in order to avoid tokenism on the part of staff and professionals involved in this work. Such engagement is also critical in recognizing, supporting, and unlocking individuals' potential as they age (Peace, 2010), and in creating sustainable communities. Engagement is a reciprocal relationship that can be of benefit to all partners; it needs to be based on a position of mutual respect. It requires: Clear roles and responsibilities; Clear and realistic expectations;

accessible information; and appropriate staff training. It is an evolving process that requires resourcing in terms of developing skills and capacity in communication and mediation, as well as time, transportation, and remuneration.

It is essential that staff appreciate and understand the diversity of the population within a retirement village, in terms of age, gender, health status, biography, and living arrangements (alone or with someone else). Such diversity offers opportunities in terms of creativity and innovation, and can contribute to a dynamic and vibrant community. Part of capturing and exploiting such diversity is to ensure that the voices of those who are less visible within the community—whether through disability or personality—are also heard and included appropriately and sensitively. This extends to a transparency around death and dying, not least in planning and preparing for end-of-life issues. Addressing these issues, and incorporating them into existing training for staff, is crucial to ensuring that residents feel valued and respected, in turn fostering confidence and autonomy.

Failure to address the issues outlined above leads, as we have seen, to some residents having their capacity to re-create home severely limited or, indeed, to their being unable to do so at all. In not having the necessary degree of control and autonomy, they experience significant reduction in both satisfaction and pleasure. Some residents clearly experience ontological insecurity as a result, which carries with it serious consequences for their health. In addition, it is important to note that there remains a paucity of research within these particular environments and, more specifically, a lack of longitudinal research mapping the changing needs of residents over time and how these needs are—or are not—met. There is also a dearth of information about residents who leave these developments and their reasons for doing so. Central to these endeavors is the inclusion of the views of older people themselves which, as this and other work has shown, tend to be significantly different from the views of experts and professionals. This work is essential before we can genuinely claim to understand whether developments such as purpose-built retirement communities can indeed be places that we can ever call home.

NOTES

1. Leasehold is a form of property tenure where one party buys the right to occupy land or a building for a given length of time. As lease is a legal estate, leasehold estate can be bought and sold on the open market and differs from a rental tenancy where a property is let on a periodic basis such as weekly or monthly. Until the end of the lease period (often measured in decades; a 99 year lease is quite

common) the leaseholder has the right to remain in occupation as an assured tenant paying an agreed rent to the owner. Terms of the agreement are contained in a lease, which has elements of contract and property law intertwined. www. websters-online-dictionary.org

2. The LVNH was a national charitable organization serving the needs of retired members of the licensed trade—that is, those employed in the selling of alcoholic drinks.
3. For reasons of anonymity, no further details about these respondents are provided in this chapter.
4. A UK term for an establishment that sells alcoholic drinks for consumption on the premises.

REFERENCES

Andrews, G. J., & Phillips, D. R. (2005). Geographical studies in ageing: Progress and connections to social gerontology. In G. J. Andrews & D. R. Phillips (Eds.), *Ageing and place: Perspectives, policy, practice* (pp. 7–12). Abingdon, UK: Routledge.

Bartlett, H., & Peel, N. (2005). Healthy ageing in the community. In G. J. Andrews & D. R. Phillips (Eds.), *Ageing and Place: Perspectives, Policy, Practice* (pp. 98–109). Abingdon, UK: Routledge.

Bernard, M., Bartlam, B., Biggs, S., & Sim, J. (2004). *New lifestyles in old age: Health, identity and well-being in Berryhill retirement village.* Bristol, UK: Policy Press.

Bernard, M., Bartlam, B., Sim, J., & Biggs, S. (2007). Housing and care for older people: Life in an English purpose-built retirement village. *Ageing and Society, 27*(4), 555–578.

Bernard, M., Liddle, J., Bartlam, B., Scharf, T., & Sim, J. (2012). Then and now: Evolving community in the context of a retirement village. *Ageing and Society, 32*(1), 109–129.

Best, R. (2009). Why retirement housing deserves priority. *Housing, Care and Support, 13*(4), 8–9.

Bevan, M. (2010). Park-home retirement living in England. *Ageing and Society, 30*(6), 965–985.

Buber, M. (2004). *I and Thou,* (3rd ed.). London, UK: Continuum International Publishing Group.

Croucher, K., Hicks, L., & Jackson, K. (2006). *Housing with care for later life: A literature review.* York, UK: Joseph Rowntree Foundation.

Department for Communities and Local Government. (2008). *Delivering lifetime homes, lifetime neighbourhoods: A national strategy for housing in an ageing society.* Retrieved from www.communities.gov.uk/publications/housing/housingageingsociety

Dupuis-Blanchard, S., Neufeld, A., & Strang, V. R. (2009). The significance of social engagement in relocated older adults. *Qualitative Health Research, 19*(9), 1186–1195.

Evans, S. (2009). *Community and ageing: Maintaining quality of life in housing with care settings.* Bristol, UK: Policy Press.

Gamliel, T., & Hazan, H. (2006). The meaning of stigma: Identity construction in two old-age institutions. *Ageing and Society, 26*(3), 355–371.

Gergen, M. M., & Gergen, K. J. (1993). Narratives of the gendered body in popular autobiography. In R. Josselson & A. Lieblich (Eds.), *The Narrative study of lives* (pp.191–218). Newbury Park, CA: Sage.

Higgs, P., Hyde, M., Wiggins, R., & Blane, D. (2003). Researching quality of life in early old age: The importance of the sociological dimension. *Social Policy and Administration, 37*(3), 239–252.

Hung, L. W., Kempen, G. I. J. M., & de Vries, N. K. (2010). Cross-cultural comparison between academic and lay views of healthy ageing: A literature review. *Ageing and Society, 30*(8), 1373–1391.

Hyde, M., Wiggins, R. D., Higgs, P., & Blane, D. B. (2003). A measure of quality of life in early old age: The theory, development and properties of a needs satisfaction model (CASP-19). *Aging and Mental Health, 7(3)*, 186–194.

Lawton, M. P. (1985). The elderly in context: Perspectives from environmental psychology and gerontology. *Environment and Behavior, 17*(4), 501–519.

Longino, C. & McLelland, K. (1978). *Age Segregation and social integration in midwestern retirement communities.* Miami, FL: University of Miami.

Maslow, A. H. (1943). A theory of human motivation. *Psychological Review, 50*(4), 370–396.

Means, R. (2007). Safe as houses? Ageing in place and vulnerable older people in the UK. *Social Policy & Administration, 41*(1), 65–85.

Mesch, G. S. (1998). Social ties, environmental perception and local attachment. *Environment and Behavior, 30*(4), 504–519.

Morris, B. R. (1992). Reducing inventory: Divestiture of personal possessions. *Journal of Women and Aging, 4*(2), 79–92.

Nair, K. (2005). The physically ageing body and the use of space. In G. J. Andrews & D. R. Phillips (Eds.), *Ageing and place: Perspectives, policy, practice* (pp. 110–117). Abingdon, UK: Routledge.

O'Bryant, S. (1983). The subjective value of 'home' to older homeowners. *Journal of Housing for the Elderly, 1*(1), 29–43.

Organisation for Economic Co-operation and Development (OECD). (2005). *Ensuring Quality Long-term Care for Older People.* Retrieved from www.oecd.org/dataoecd/53/4/34585571.pdf [2011, 01/29]

Osgood, N. J. (1982). *Senior settlers: Social integration in retirement communities.* New York, NY: Praeger Publishers.

Peace, S. (2010). Introduction: Reflecting on user-involvement and participatory research. In S. Peace & J. Hughes (Eds.), *Reflecting on user-involvement and participatory research* (pp.1–5). London, UK: Centre for Policy on Ageing/Open University.

Peace, S. M., Holland, C., & Kellaher, L. (2005). Making space for identity. In G. J. Andrews & D. R. Phillips (Eds.), *Ageing and place: Perspectives, policy, practice* (pp. 188–204). Abingdon: Routledge.

Peace, S. M., Holland, C., & Kellaher, L. (2006). *Growing Older: Environment and Identity in Later Life.* Maidenhead: Open University Press.

Phillips, J., Bernard, M., Biggs, S., & Kingston, P. (2001). Retirement communities in Britain: A 'third way' for the third age? In S. Peace & C. Holland (Eds.), *Inclusive housing in an ageing society* (pp. 189–213). Bristol, UK: Policy Press.

Phillipson, C. (2007). The 'elected' and the 'excluded': Sociological perspectives on the experience of place and community in old age. *Ageing and Society, 27*(3), 321–342.

Ramachandran, V. S. (2003). The emerging mind. BBC Radio 4, Reith Lectures, http://www.bbc.co.uk/radio4/reith2003/lecturer.shtml.

Rapoport, A. (2005). On using "home" and "place." In G. D. Rowles & H. Chaudhury (Eds.), *Home and identity in late life* (pp. 343–360). New York, NY: Springer Publishing Company.

Rowles, G. D. (1978). *Prisoners of space? Exploring the geographical experience of older people.* Boulder, CO: Westview Press.

Rowles, G. D. (1993). Elderly migration and development in small communities. *Growth and change, 24*(4), 509–538.

Rowles, G. D., & Chaudhury, H. (2005). Leaving home. In G. D. Rowles & H. Chaudhury (Eds.), *Home and identity in late life* (pp. 379–386). New York, NY: Springer Publishing Company.

Rowles, G. D., Concotelli, J. A., & High, D. M. (1996). Community integration of a rural nursing home. *Journal of Applied Gerontology, 15*(2), 188–201.

Rubinstein, R. L., & Parmelee, P. A. (1992). Attachment to place and the representation of life course by the elderly. In I. Altman & S. M. Low (Eds.), *Place attachment* (pp. 139–163). New York, NY: Plenum Press.

Savage, M., Bagnell, G., & Longhurst, R. (2005). *Globalization and belonging*. London, UK: Sage.

Scharf, T., & Bartlam, B. (2008). Ageing and social exclusion in rural communities. In N. Keating (Ed.), *Rural Ageing: A Good Place to Grow Old?* (pp. 97–108). Bristol, UK: Policy Press.

Scharf, T., Phillipson, C., Smith, A. E., & Kingston, P. (2002). *Growing older in socially deprived areas: Social exclusion in later life*. London, UK: Help the Aged.

Sim, J., Bartlam, B., & Bernard, M. (2011). The CASP-19 as a measure of quality of life in old age: Evaluation of its use in a retirement community. *Quality of Life Research, 20* (7), 997–1004.

Sim, J., Liddle, J., Bernard, M., Scharf, T., & Bartlam, B. (2012). Home from home? A mixed-methods study of relocation within a purpose-built retirement community. *Journal of Housing for the Elderly, 26*(4), 373–395.

Sixsmith, A., & Sixsmith, J. (2008). Ageing in place in the United Kingdom. *Ageing International, 32*(3), 219–235.

Streib, G. F. (2002). An introduction to retirement communities. *Research on Aging, 24*(1), 3–9.

Warnes, A. T. (2007). Migration, older people and social policy. In K. Clarke (Ed.). *Social Policy Review 19* (pp. 297–320). Bristol, UK: Policy Press.

Warnes, A. T., & Williams, A. (2006). Older migrants in Europe: A new focus for migration studies. *Journal of Ethnic and Migration Studies, 32*(8), 1257–1281.

Webster, C. (2002). Property rights and the public realm: Gates, green belts and gemeinschaft. *Environment and Planning B, 29*(3), 315–326.

Wiggins, R. D., Netuveli, G., Hyde, M., Higgs, P., & Blane, D. (2008). The evaluation of a self-enumerated scale of quality of life (CASP-19) in the context of research on ageing: A combination of exploratory and confirmatory approaches. *Social Indicators Research, 89*(1), 61–77.

Wiles, J. (2005). Home as a new site of care provision and consumption. In G. J. Andrews & D. R. Phillips (Eds.), *Ageing and place: Perspectives, policy, practice* (pp. 79–97). Abingdon: Routledge.

Williams, A. M. (2002). Changing geographies of care: Employing the concept of therapeutic landscapes as a framework in examining home space. *Social Science and Medicine, 55*(1), 141–154.

World Health Organization (WHO) (2011). *Our ageing world*. Retrieved from: www.who. int/ageing/en/ [2011, 02/08]

Zelenev, S. (2008). The Madrid Plan: A comprehensive agenda for an ageing world, *Regional Dimensions of the Ageing Situation*. United Nations, New York. Retrieved from www.un.org/esa/socdev/ageing/documents/publications/regional-dimensions-ageing.pdf

PART V

Challenges of Application

CHAPTER 12

Past, Present, and Future in Designing Private and Public Environments for Creating and Sustaining Place

Miriam Bernard and Graham D. Rowles

> It was good to be back in my flat, even for just a night . . . I wandered round the rooms in my flat, marvelling at how empty they felt compared to May's, how light and spacious, though measurement for measurement that's probably not true. What these rooms are empty of is memories. That, maybe, is the crucial difference, more important than wooden floors versus thick carpets, blinds versus crimson velvet curtains, and so on. May's house is choked with memories. I'm constantly aware of the life lived within the walls for the last—what?—fifty-odd years. I see her as she was when I was a small child, a little bustling figure, forever rushing around busily putting things to rights, vigorously polishing her best bits of furniture or dusting her many ornaments. And now her belongings hardly know her—they seem to own her instead of May owning them. She can't polish or clean effectively any more, or do a host of small things that would stamp her authority on the place. I've tried to do it for her, but she doesn't want me to. "Leave it," she said, when I began picking up her Toby jugs on the mantelpiece to clean them. She couldn't bear to see me taking over. I have to know my place.
>
> —Margaret Forster *Isa and May* (2011, pp. 88–89)

Acclaimed British author Margaret Forster's most recent novel concerns a young woman, Isamay, who is writing her thesis about grandmothers in history while, at the same time, trying to come to terms with the secrets and intrigues her own two grandmothers (Isa and May) have been keeping from her. Here, Forster once again lays bare the realities of aging, old age, and family relationships in all their intricate and often uncomfortable complexity, as she has done before in novels such as *Mother Can You Hear Me?* (1979) and *Have the Men Had Enough?* (1989); and in her poignant memoirs, *Hidden Lives* (1995), and *Precious Lives* (1998).

Fictional though *Isa and May* is, the quotation has been chosen because it graphically encapsulates key themes and issues in our own book: the importance of the environments in which we live for maintaining identity and supporting social activity and interaction; the ways in which older people transform the spaces of their life into places that sustain meaning and enhance well-being; and how older people maintain their connections with their families, their communities, and the wider "public" environment beyond the immediate confines of their apartment, their house, their home.

Our aims and objectives for this concluding chapter are threefold. First, we provide a synthesis of the research findings and current thinking our contributors have drawn upon in their individual chapters and from their differing disciplinary perspectives, experiences, and cultural contexts. Second, we present a set of guiding principles to facilitate effective translation of research findings on the meaning of place in old age into practical applications for the design of both residential and public spaces. Finally, the chapter reflects on developing environmental gerontology along a path toward greater integration of theoretical insight and applied research findings.

RESIDENTIAL ENVIRONMENTS AND PUBLIC SPACES: RESEARCH FINDINGS

As our contributors have shown, the environments in which people live out their later lives are crucially important. Expanding knowledge in environmental gerontology and a rapidly proliferating literature provides an ever more sophisticated view of the use and meaning of place in old age and of the older person's changing relationship with environment. Against this background, our contributors have helped us to look at two environmental domains: contemporary residential environments and public spaces.

In Part I of the book, we briefly examined theoretical and conceptual underpinnings of environmental gerontology. Rather than solely reiterate what has been ably accomplished or advocated elsewhere (Pastalan, 2012; Phillipson, 2004; Scheidt & Windley, 2006; Schwarz, 2012; Wahl & Weisman, 2003), our focus was on a stream of thought and research within this emergent field that focused on the experience and meaning of places, both private and public, in old age. Chapter 1 set the scene by discussing the emergence and history of environmental gerontology under the leadership of pioneers such as Frances Carp, M. Powell Lawton, Sandra Howell, Eva Kahana, Leon Pastalan, Robert Rubinstein, and Anthony Warnes. We noted the more recent contributions of Sheila Peace, Malcolm Cutchin, Habib Chaudhury, Susanne Iwarsson, Chris Phillipson, Hans-Werner Wahl, and others, and presented our own perspective on the lived experience of the older person/environment transaction that provides the lens through which we approached compiling this volume. Focusing on the older person's experience of residential environments, we articulated an array of interwoven ideas that reflect the deepening understanding of the older person-environment relationship that has occurred in recent years. We considered the process by which people transform the spaces of their life into the places of their life through the habituation of their everyday activities and by imbuing these patterns of use and "dwelling" with meaning. We explored the notion of "home" and the experience of "being at home." We described what is known about the manner in which older adults adjust to environmental and personal changes, at first through environmental accommodation within their familiar setting and, when that is no longer possible, through relocation. Key to this experience, we noted, was an array of concerns regarding the stresses of relocation, "breaking up home" and giving up possessions and treasured artifacts to accommodate to more limited space. Modeling the translational and applied focus of this book, we considered what is known about ways in which older adults and their families may be supported through environmental design, human service programs, and policy, in the process of making and remaking place that is the inevitable consequence of relocation. Finally, we considered the key issue of community integration and continuing environmental engagement as a key underlying motif in the contribution of environmental gerontology to enhancing the quality of life of older adults, wherever they may be living.

Our opening chapter was complemented by Sheila Peace's (Chapter 2) conceptual synopsis of environment, identity, and the relationships between older people and the public spaces and places they frequent in their everyday lives. She considered issues such as connectivity with place, intergenerational interaction in public space, and integration of the meaning of public and private space in maintaining person-environment fit in later life. The chapter makes a convincing case for recognizing environmental complexity and bringing the physical/material, social, and psychological dimensions together—alongside recognition of the diversity that exists among older people over the latter part of the life course: a period which may now span 40 years or more.

Parts II and III of the book focused on residential environments, looking first at private residences (Chapters 3 and 4) and then at long-term care environments (Chapters 5, 6, and 7). Frank Oswald and Hans Werner-Wahl (Chapter 3) present their developmental framework for understanding person-environment processes as they play out in the immediate home environment. By emphasizing two key dimensions, belonging and agency, and by drawing on empirical data from the European ENABLE-AGE project, they show how these psychological processes are fundamental elements of people's lived experience of housing in later life (Wahl, Oswald, Schilling, & Iwarsson, 2009). Their analysis also demonstrates the importance of uncovering the complex and multifaceted nature of person-environment interactions if we are to be able to reconcile an objective analysis of housing issues with sub-jective constructs such as meaning, belonging, and agency. They point to important gaps in our research when it comes to thinking about and understanding the roles of agency and belonging for demented and cognitively impaired older adults, issues that are picked up by Habib Chaudhury and his colleagues in their consideration of long-term dementia care environments (Chapter 7).

Chapter 4, by Kate de Medeiros and colleagues, turns attention to the meaning of home for older women. In contrast with Margaret Forster's fictional grandmothers, the women in this chapter are child-less. This adds a new dimension to our discussion by exploring the notion that, for single older women with no children, traditional mean-ings of home as grounded in family (and specifically children) no longer apply. It also makes explicit the critical idea of "environmental positioning" whereby we are asked to acknowledge that one's place—or position—in the home environment or society may be intentional or unintentional and is not necessarily fixed. Instead, "environmental position" captures the dynamic and changing relationship between a person and an environment, in which meanings have to be viewed as relational, fluid and sometimes contradictory.

The universality of "at homeness," and the meaning of becoming and being at home, are explored further by Malcolm Cutchin (Chapter 5) in the context of moving into assisted living environments. The com-plexity of this transition, and the process of trying to establish a rela-tionship with the new home through "place integration," is highlighted. We are also reminded that "place" has to be seen as more than just the physical environment—it includes social and cultural elements—and that "place integration" is incremental, contingent, and not just reliant on memory, but also on the ability of individuals to envisage possible futures. Cutchin shows how public and private space in assisted living facilities are blurred, and how the rules and regulations necessary to operate an institution often run counter to the personal autonomy we conventionally associate with being "at home."

From assisted living in the United States we move, in Chapter 6 (O'Shea and Walsh), to institutional care settings in Ireland. Here, notions of "connectedness" and "connection pathways" are keys to understanding residents' ties to home and place. Evidently, some of the issues raised in this chapter—around residents' rights, autonomy, and independence—are still problematic in Ireland, and person-centered care appears to be especially important for helping people to feel "at home" in these settings. O'Shea and Walsh also see community engagement as an essential opportunity for reducing the separation of residents from the community when they enter a nursing facility, thus bridging the gap between the "private" aspects of institutional living and the "public" world outside.

A further chapter on institutional living, by Habib Chaudhury and his colleagues (Chapter 7), focused on long-term dementia care environments, completes Part III of the book. Here again there is an emphasis on person-centeredness—this time in relation to design—and on the input of people with dementia into design considerations. The chapter set out to explicitly describe the development and piloting of an environmental addition to the Dementia Care Mapping (DCM) tool (Kitwood & Bredin, 1992). In so doing, it underlines the therapeutic potential of place-biography and how important it is to involve older people themselves in the creation of responsive physical environments for dementia care.

Having explored private microenvironments of home and the more communal environments of institutional living in which the private and public are blurred, Part IV of the book then turned to an examination of macro public spaces. We are becoming increasingly aware that the configurations and meanings of public and shared spaces can help older people maintain connections with their communities. We also know that barriers to participation in public and shared spaces involve far more than physical accessibility. How older people experience such environments was therefore central to all four chapters in this part of the book. Like Oswald and Werner-Wahl, Suzanne Iwarsson and her colleagues (Chapter 8) draw on findings from the multicountry ENABLE-AGE study to explore issues around the design of the physical environment and, in particular, older people's mobility and access in public spaces (Iwarsson et al., 2007). Their findings highlight environmental barriers to mobility experienced by older people and raise crucial questions about what needs to be done, design-wise, to make mobility aids nonstigmatizing.

In Chapter 9, Judith Phillips presented findings from her study of older people's use of unfamiliar spaces, to show clearly how the physical-psychological and emotional components of (outdoor) place(s), together with the passage of time, are critical in creating meaning. There are suggestions that lack of familiarity creates "placelessness" (Relph, 1976), yet her findings demonstrate that older people who are introduced to an unfamiliar environment can make initial sense of it and create meaning if that environment is accessible and distinctive. She draws distinctions in this respect among the resident, the visitor, and the newcomer: the meaning of place for the long-time resident is strongly tied to familiarity and environmental experience; the visitor, by contrast, needs to rapidly access images of a meaningful place in order to orientate to the new environment; while the newcomer transitions from being a visitor to being a resident through a process of learning about place.

While the chapters thus far have concentrated on older people, Leng Leng Thang and Matt Kaplan (Chapter 10) stimulate our thinking on creating spaces for intergenerational integration and communication. Using examples from sites in Japan and Singapore as well as Western Europe, their discussion provides a much needed counterpoint to the trend of the past few decades to separate the generations through the creation of age-segregated environments (in, for example, age-segregated housing and retirement communities for older adults). They stress that in order to meet the goal of designing both public and private spaces to facilitate intergenerational engagement, we have not only to consider design issues but also the values and policies that underlie the creation of such spaces.

Finally, Bernadette Bartlam and colleagues (Chapter 11) use their considerable experience of undertaking research in retirement communities to explore complex issues of transforming so-called purpose-built environments from spaces into places through processes of creating and re-creating a sense of home. They also show how the trend toward stronger integration of these kinds of "housing with care" developments within the community in which they are located is emerging as an important theme in contemporary planning and community design. While it is effectively an age-segregated facility, the retirement village they focus on in this chapter is also attempting to look outwards and integrate within the local community. In this sense, new retirement communities are illustrative of how the distinction between residential and public environments discussed in this book is one that is increasingly blurred: many residential environments include essentially public spaces and many public spaces provide opportunities for privacy. This juxtaposition of private and public space has been evident throughout the contributions and leads us to consider now how these scholarly insights and empirical findings might best be translated into practical applications.

TRANSLATING RESEARCH INTO PRACTICAL APPLICATIONS: GUIDING PRINCIPLES

This book has explored the ways in which older people transform the spaces of their life into places that sustain meaning and enhance well-being. All the contributors have provided suggestions and indications for how their research might contribute to, enhance, and inform practice in a number of related professional and policy fields, including architecture, urban and rural planning, health and social care provision, transportation planning, environmental design, and the emergent field of gerotechnology. Translating what we know from recent theoretical and empirical insights and from older peoples' lived experiences of space and place into recommendations of value to policy makers, planners and designers, is no simple undertaking. It requires embracing principles, values, skills, and knowledge that we consider to be fundamental underpinnings of practice if environmental gerontology is to sustain its relevance to policy. Below, we attempt to capture these in a set of guiding principles, which draw on the rich discussions from our contributors.

The need for initiatives that translate growing knowledge of the manner in which older people experience both private and public environments into concrete recommendations and actions arises from a number of factors. First, in simple demographic terms, older people are ever more visible in all of the societies and countries referred to throughout this book. Old age and aging is not necessarily synonymous with ill health and disability but, much as a youth-oriented culture would seek to deny it (Jacoby, 2011), the older we get, the more likely we are to experience physical and psychological limitations that may require help, support, and modifications to our environments in order to sustain an acceptable quality of life. It is precisely these oldest sectors of our populations that have grown most markedly over the last century and are predicted to continue doing so (U.S. Bureau of the Census, 2011). Second, and somewhat paradoxically, the demographic visibility of a growing elderly population is coupled with a marked invisibility of older people in many of the policy and practice decision-making arenas that directly affect their lives—not least in those that have environmental dimensions. Reasons for this are many and varied, they may be culturally contingent, and they vary from country to country. The fact remains that older people are still often seen as unproductive and therefore incapable of contributing to these debates and discussions. Entrenched ageism and the impact this has on how older people are treated has to be resisted and challenged. Third, as our contributors lucidly demonstrate, knowledge and research about older people and the environments in which they live has proliferated over recent decades. We now know far more about the complex relationship between people and their environment and the manner in which this relationship evolves over the life course, and especially in old age. Yet much of this research and knowledge has still to reach and be internalized by older people themselves, policy makers, and front-line workers in ways that would make a real difference to older people's lives. This book, and its varied contributions, is a modest step toward bridging the research-practice gap.

While we would not wish to be overly prescriptive, six guiding principles are articulated here. They emphasize desired ways of working with older people in professional capacities and are underpinned by values that we, and those of our colleagues who regard themselves as critical (environmental) gerontologists, have espoused in previous work (Bernard, 2001, 2006, 2008; Bernard & Phillips, 1998, 2000; Bernard & Scharf, 2007; Ray, Bernard, & Phillips, 2008; Rowles, 1978, 2001, 2008; Zanjani & Rowles, in press). These values include the right of older people to have control over their lives; to maintain independence and autonomy; to be fully involved in decisions that affect their lives; to be accorded the respect and dignity they deserve; and to be recognized and embraced as full citizens. Articulating a value base and a set of guiding principles is a political act: it acknowledges that translational work cannot be a detached or value-free undertaking (Holstein & Minkler, 2007), but involves working with policy makers, practitioners, and older people in effective partnerships to change things for the better (Phillipson & Walker, 1987; Townsend, 2007; Estes, Biggs, & Phillipson, 2003; Ray, Bernard, & Philips, 2008).

The guiding principles we propose are recognition and commitment to understanding the diversity of older people, their needs and aspirations; research-informed practice and practice-aware research;

person-centered practice and research; a focus on inclusive design of spaces; development of a critical (environmental) gerontological sensibility; and interdisciplinary, interagency, and interprofessional collaboration.

Understanding Diversity

Understanding the diversity of older people, their needs and aspirations, entails acknowledging that aging is a multidimensional and multifaceted experience. Working with a group of people who, chronologically, may span some 40 or more years and whose origins, life histories, and current circumstances may be completely different from one another is challenging. But explicit recognition of this diversity is an essential counter to the view that older people's lives and needs are essentially homogeneous: that a "one size fits all" solution is appropriate when it comes to concrete strategies and approaches to human service provision, environmental design, and community planning.

Conscious recognition of diversity also encourages us to think about underrepresented or marginalized groups. Several of our contributors emphasize the need to consider the environmental sensitivity and environmental needs of special populations, including cognitively impaired older adults (see Chapters 3 and 7), older women in general (Chapter 8), and older childless women in particular (Chapter 4). These groups are in danger of being overlooked when it comes to thinking about and understanding the roles of, for example, agency and belonging (Chapter 3) or familiarity and unfamiliarity (Chapter 9) in place integration and in making and remaking place in different settings (Chapters 5, 6, 9, and 11). At the risk of developing a "shopping list" of special groups, we would also add here the importance of attending to the environmental needs and aspirations of physically impaired older people; older people with different sexual orientations; and those with differing cultural backgrounds and expectations (Chapter 10).

Research-Informed Practice and Practice-Aware Research

A second guiding principle is the need for mutual exchange between research and practice so that each can inform and enhance the other to the benefit of both. This book is testament to the fact that in environmental gerontology there is currently a gap between research and practice that reflects a separation from the strongly applied focus that characterized the origins of the field (see Chapter 1). The reasons for this are many and varied. They include an implicit hierarchy in contemporary academic circles, which has tended to value certain kinds of research above others; applied and evaluative research has assumed less importance and, it has to be said, has attracted fewer resources. While some of this has changed in recent years with the emphasis on re-engagement with users, on the involvement of older people in research (Ray, 2007), and on the "impacts" of our research, applied and policy-oriented translational research has still been undervalued.

From the perspectives of frontline workers or policy makers, there are also issues about how research is presented: research publications and reports are often not user-friendly or practitioner-friendly, and therefore are essentially inaccessible. Equally, practitioners may not in fact have the skills to evaluate the quality of research and, in the context of a busy—often excessive—workload, may have little time or inclination to engage with research findings, especially if those findings challenge cherished and established ways of working. Consequently, this principle contains within it a direct challenge to researchers like us and the contributors to this volume to develop more effective ways of communicating our research findings.

Person-Centered Practice

Person-centeredness has been a critical component of long-term care (Chapters 6 and 7) and other areas of health and welfare provision for many years, but is perhaps less used or applied in fields such as design or planning. Simply, and perhaps very obviously, it is about ensuring that irrespective of their individual circumstances or difficulties, older people's involvement and participation is central to any considerations about what is or is not needed to support them (Ray, Bernard, & Phillips, 2008). A person-centered approach aims to counter the tendency to construct older people in negative and dysfunctional ways, to avoid labeling them as, for example, "frail," "at risk," "dependent" or "demented," or characterizing them as "problems" and passive recipients of care and support (Grenier, 2007, 2012). Indeed, in the United Kingdom it was Tom Kitwood who, in the early 1990s, challenged the dominance of bio-medical perspectives and proposed that personhood should be central to the care of people with dementia, rather than allowing the label of "dementia" to subsume everything that the person had been and now is (Kitwood, 1993, 1997). Others have sought to develop person-centered care practice further and, as in Chaudhury et al.'s contribution (Chapter 7), have gone on to develop and refine tools to assist practitioners in its implementation and evaluation.

A concomitant of person-centered practice is that it recognizes, and builds on, the strengths and resources of an older person: it values what older people value and takes proper cognizance of older people's subjective experiences. In particular, person-centered practice values the temporal depth of lives and seeks to understand older adults not simply as they appear on the surface to us today, but rather through the lens of the historical experiences that molded their persona and shaped their cultural and social values. For example, to have been raised during the Great Depression of the 1930s provided a distinctive perspective on home, family, community, independence, dependence, and interdependence that for many of today's older adults still conditions expectations. Understanding this biographical context and seeking a deeper level of appreciation of the complexity of lives is an important ingredient of creating environments that are truly attuned to people's needs. At the same time, in relation to our current considerations, person-centered practice also emphasizes the importance of being attuned to the potential of older adults for continuing societal engagement. While the past is important, the large majority of older adults, whatever their circumstances, live and wish to continue living in the present. Indeed, as the 75-year-old woman quoted by Thang and Kaplan (Chapter 10) so poignantly and eloquently points out, "there are many of us who do not want to be maintained. We want to belong, not only to each other, with whom we may have only one common denominator, age, but to society. We want to be just like everyone else." Thus, it is important that our practices be directed toward stimulating and supporting older adults' continued engagement in their current environments through nurturing and facilitating the unique life-course-generated propensity for creating a sense of being in place that we explored in Chapter 1. Person-centeredness is about meaningful engagement and being reflective, proactive, anticipatory, and preventative, not just reactive. At a more macro level, this principle also aligns with what Sheila Peace (Chapter 2) notes are wider policy agendas concerning social inclusion and exclusion, community cohesion and the growing movement around developing age-friendly cities and environments (Abbott, Carman, Carman, & Scarfo, 2009; Bevan & Croucher, 2011; Liu, Everingham, Warburton, Cuthill, & Bartlett, 2009; World Health Organization, 2007).

Inclusive Design

The past few decades have seen an increased tendency toward the daily and sometimes long-term separation and geographical segregation of generations. While the multigenerational family of history was in fact never as prevalent as romantic mythology suggests, there has been a growing trend toward generational and cultural Balkanization, manifest in the increasing segmentation of lives. This trend has been reinforced not only by evolving lifestyles but also by environmental design. For example in Peoria, Arizona, Senior Citizen Overlay Zoning requires that at least one householder be over 45 and no person under 18 years of age can remain in residence for more than 90 days (City of Peoria, 2012). Such large-scale generational segregation is complemented by the proliferation of age-exclusive retirement communities, the development of social-resource-rich apartment complexes for young singles, and the daily temporal and spatial segregation of daycare. People of different generations appear to be spending less and less time together. One consequence of this is generational estrangement.

We shape our residential environments and public spaces; in turn, they shape us. By the way we design spaces, we make a political statement; we can reinforce separation or encourage engagement among generations. Here, we are concerned with far more than universal design and the potential for the creation of spaces that can be adapted to changing individual needs as the person grows older and his or her environmental needs change. Rather we are concerned with the potential for the creation of inclusive environments such as those described by Thang and Kaplan (Chapter 10) that proactively embrace intergenerational communication by creating spaces designed to encourage the process (see, also Goltsman & Iacofano, 2007). Sometimes the process can be as simple as providing places for older adults to sit where they can watch children or even interact with them as they play. While we are not suggesting that environments should never be designed for a specialized population, age inclusiveness should become an accepted criterion in assessing environmental design options and the creation of both private and public spaces.

Critical Environmental Gerontology

A fifth principle is the need to ensure that our translational work in tracing the practice and applied implications of insights into the older person's experience of place is guided by a critical (environmental) gerontological sensibility. There is not room here to go into a detailed explanation of the development of critical gerontology. We, and others, have contributed accounts of its evolution since Phillipson and Walker (1987) defined it some 25 years ago as a value-committed approach concerned with understanding how aging and old age is socially constructed and how we can best challenge and, importantly, change the experience for the better. Grenier's (2012, p. 22) book includes an overview of critical perspectives on aging and late life where she draws together approaches from critical gerontology, humanistic gerontology, and cultural gerontology. To our mind, these approaches resonate strongly with the concerns and orientations expressed by the environmental gerontologists who have contributed to this volume. Consider, for example, one of Grenier's (2012, pp. 34–35) concluding contentions:

> What emerges from the analysis of critical approaches to ageing and the life course is a shared desire to understand the interplay of structures, history, context and experience. Key to this is paying attention to the challenges of linking the macro and the micro, implementing envisaged ideals into the context of research and practice, and addressing diversity.

This encapsulates what we, and our contributors, are trying to achieve in our research and is an approach, and a principle, that provides an essential critical edge not only to research, but to knowledge exchange and translational work.

Interdisciplinary, Interagency, and Interprofessional Collaboration

Our final guiding principle arises out of the other five; it is the need for interdisciplinary, interagency, and interprofessional collaboration. One of the threads that has wound its way implicitly and explicitly throughout this book is the tendency for research, policy, and practice to work in separate silos, and for each of these areas to also have unhelpful internal divisions and hierarchies. Thang and Kaplan (Chapter 10) point to this in the context of creating intergenerational spaces, where it is apparent that those responsible for designing and program development for older adults tend to have little to do with those who are planning parallel developments such as playgrounds or other spaces for children. Many of the concrete strategies and approaches suggested by our contributors require interdisciplinary, interagency, and interprofessional collaboration to be successful. Such an approach also has implications for educating and training practitioners and policy makers. Our experience of running academic and vocational programs in gerontology for over 20 years, together with our involvement in training gerontologists, social workers, psychologists, and health care practitioners (including physicians, physician assistants, pharmacists, nurses, rehabilitation specialists, and occupational therapists), suggests that there are few opportunities for these groups to come together with trainee architects, planners, or designers. It would be beneficial if this guiding principle could therefore be applied to the knowledge translation that is, or should be, an integral part of professional training and educational activity.

The broad principles outlined here apply across the range of environments considered in this volume. How they play out in practice in these different settings and in different cultures will necessarily vary. With these guiding principles as a foundation, we conclude this chapter by considering how the strategies and approaches suggested by our contributors can be related back to, and integrated with, the theory and methods from environmental gerontology.

ENVIRONMENTAL GERONTOLOGY: INTEGRATING THEORY AND APPLIED RESEARCH FINDINGS

Environmental gerontology as considered in this volume is, first and foremost, a field of study. It is not, in itself, a profession or a domain of public service. Consequently, the onus is on us to communicate how the environmental gerontology findings and insights provided in these pages might best be applied in practical and policy contexts. It is also important to reflect on how some of the conceptual and theoretical insights might help develop the field further. Across the contributions, there is evidence of advancement and refinement in our conceptual and theoretical understandings since the historical foundations of environmental gerontology discussed in Chapters 1 (Rowles and Bernard) and 2 (Peace). Oswald and Werner-Wahl (Chapter 3) have spent many years championing the importance of theory in environmental gerontology and here they have built a convincing case for close examination of the roles of "agency" and "belonging" in the person-environment fit model. To help us better understand the interactions between people and their environments, other contributors also elaborate helpful notions, such as "environmental positioning" (de Medeiros et al., Chapter 4); "connectedness" and "connection pathways" (O'Shea and Walsh, Chapter 6); "place integration" (Cutchin, Chapter 5), and "familiarity/unfamiliarity" (Phillips, Chapter 9). Beyond the individual psychological aspects of motivations and needs associated with person-environment fit, we have though, as Cutchin (Chapter 5) argues, to look at place, at our attachments to place, and at our understandings of what place means in people's lives, as more than just the environment: it includes social, cultural, and structural elements of the manner in which people's lives are grounded in the settings where they reside. We cannot simply characterize these relationships and interactions in objective terms but have, instead, to acknowledge the subjective dimensions of many of these concepts. Between them, these chapters demonstrate what we (Chapter 1) and Sheila Peace (Chapter 2) are advocating: a more nuanced approach and theoretical frameworks that recognize environmental complexity and bring the physical/material, social, and psychological dimensions together.

Theoretical and conceptual refinement has also to be seen in tandem with, and informed by, the kinds of applied findings that have arisen from the empirical analyses presented by our contributors. A number of shared suggestions have emerged across these chapters with respect to practical applications arising from the research reported. Thematically, there are common calls for built environments—from the micro spaces of private/domestic homes to the macro public spaces of urban centers—that take cognizance of the needs of a wide spectrum of older and disabled people. Issues of safety and security; adaptable and flexible design; walkability and accessibility; reliable and affordable public transportation; physically and socially accessible amenities and facilities; and the widespread availability of adequate information all recur as important themes across the chapters. Synthesizing contributors' practical suggestions reveals a set of applications that might usefully be grouped into four overarching areas: physical alterations and the preservation of environments; communication and information; monitoring and evaluation; and education, training, and learning.

Physical Alterations and the Preservation of Environments

Physical alterations and the preservation of environments are, arguably, the most obvious and well-understood ways in which findings from research can be translated into practical outcomes of use to planners and architects in particular. A number of our contributors revisit and reinforce this, showing how, in the case of outdoor environments, things like lowered curbs, longer times at signals/crossings, clear separation between pedestrians and bicyclists, the provision of benches along routes and routes that are wide enough for the use of mobility devices, the removal of graffiti and litter, the provision of good quality and well-maintained lighting, and adequate signage can all help to enhance older people's access to, and mobility around, the environment

(Chapters 8, 9, and 11). Spaces and places that provide opportunities for social interaction are also important. Furthermore, Phillips' research (Chapter 9) underlines how valuable preserving historic buildings and attractive landmarks can be, not just as a means of providing tourist attractions, but also because such features serve as important visual cues for navigation and orientation in environments that may be undergoing regeneration. She suggests too, that the stories, memories, and emotions attached to particular places and landmarks might be recorded by local residents and either used in strategic places and/or be part of aural town trails. Olfactory cues—the smell of a bakery, for example—are additional ways in which people may be helped to orient and relate to their environment.

With respect to the design of private spaces (residences and institutional settings), physical alterations and the preservation of place might also be considered as essential elements of good design. There are a plethora of emergent options. These include interior home modifications (using principles of universal design or the technologies of smart homes) to facilitate aging in place (Chapter 1). Physical alterations to reinforce interior mobility can ease the use of the rollator (Chapter 8). Design of residences and institutional settings can routinely incorporate display spaces for treasured artifacts and identity-reinforcing photographs (Chapter 1). Both facilitative design and institutional policies might also be employed to extend identification with, and possession of, home space as territory through the placement of potted plants and other markers on and just beyond the threshold (Chapter 11). The development of effective counseling strategies and provision of assistance with downsizing may well become routine (Chapters 1 and 11). These are but a few of a proliferating array of alternatives that are likely during the next decade to make it increasingly easy for older adults to maintain, create, and recreate home and reinforce engagement in place.

Communication and Information

Across the chapters, the need for good communication and information at all levels—for older people and professionals alike—has been reiterated. For example, Bartlam and colleagues (Chapter 11) show how, in creating a purpose-built retirement village, a failure to clearly communicate the developers' vision can lead to misunderstandings about expectations. They suggest that preplanning focus groups with stakeholders/developers and potential residents would be one avenue through which expectations about, for example, engagement with the wider community and the use of village facilities by "outsiders" might be conveyed.

Another concrete suggestion is the potential for developing printed materials and handbooks of various kinds. Cutchin (Chapter 5) makes the case for a simple and easily comprehended "Integration Handbook" for those moving to assisted living facilities. Importantly, this would be based on the experiences of residents, staff, and family and would show how an older person might begin to live in such a new setting, and thus would begin the process of place integration. It does not take a great leap of imagination to see the transferability of such an idea to other settings, be they monogenerational or intergenerational.

Handbooks that include research-based "design principles" for professionals such as architects and planners provide another practical option. Such user-friendly manuals, including the latest findings from research on the environmental experience of diverse groups of older people, would be especially useful as a resource for working with marginalized and historically excluded populations.

Monitoring and Evaluation

These kinds of practical suggestions beg the question "How do we know if they work?" It is also important then that adequate monitoring and evaluation take place. For some contributors, this involves the development, modification, and application of existing research tools. Chaudhury and colleagues' environmental addition to the DCM tool is probably the clearest demonstration of this (Kitwood & Bredin, 1992). Since its development in the United Kingdom, the DCM has been used by practitioners and researchers for a number of years in many countries. This observational tool enables trained staff in institutional care settings to systematically watch and record residents' behaviors and the quality of staff-resident interactions. The newly proposed environmental coding scheme will, it is argued, assist staff to identify areas where environmental modifications or renovations might be needed, ranging from simple rearrangements of furniture, through the provision of increased visual cueing, to the facilitation of direct access to safe and secure outdoor spaces.

In other settings, increased emphasis on postoccupancy evaluations is needed to assess the degree to which these environments are effectively meeting the needs of older people. As Bartlam and colleagues (Chapter 11) point out, this has to involve meaningful engagement with residents rather than reliance on externally imposed, traditional, and generally superficial and inadequate management-implemented satisfaction surveys. Post-occupancy assessment teams that involve and include residents and draw on the wider support and advice of partner/academic organizations represent an important direction forward in developing environments for older people that are consonant with their lived experience.

Education, Training, and Learning

Underlying all of these suggestions are concerns with education, training, and learning. We have already highlighted the need for interprofessional education and training. This applies both to initial professional training and to the continuing professional education of health and social care practitioners, planners, designers, architects, and the administrators and managers of facilities and institutions. Clearly there are staff training needs to be met if, for example, they are expected to use tools such as the environmental addition to the DCM (Chapter 7), either to assess residents' interactions with their environment or to engage in postoccupancy evaluations of a facility. Professional interventions such as the standard and recurring checkup for assisted-living residents suggested by Cutchin (Chapter 5) and the regular postoccupancy consultations for retirement village dwellers suggested by Bartlam and colleagues (Chapter 11) require specific training if staff are to fully understand and appreciate how they can best assess each resident's processes of place integration and establishing a sense of being in place. Such training would facilitate a deeper level of understanding of the older adult and as a result would facilitate the provision of sensitive and optimally tailored advice and support.

Ongoing staff training in the form of workshops that sensitize participants to the experience of older people is suggested by a number of contributors. These range from general awareness-raising about the process of aging and the specific needs of older people, through tackling associated concerns about ageism and ageist practices, to more specific recommendations about the need to inculcate what Thang and Kaplan (Chapter 10) call "design literacy" and "cultural sensitivity." Such training should include activities designed to improve sensitivity toward diverse cultural norms with respect to appropriate touch, use of humor, and dealing with issues of illness, loss, and bereavement. While a primary focus might be on educating professional and human service practitioner groups, there is also considerable potential for the involvement of community residents and groups of older people in seminars, workshops, and focus groups that would increase awareness of environmental gerontology themes. For example, sessions instilling in facility staff an appreciation of the importance to residents of "home," including the role of possessions and personal artifacts in making a residence into a home (Chapters 1, 5, and 11), are likely to significantly increase mutual understanding. Cutchin (Chapter 5) extends this to suggest that peer support and one-to-one mentoring also has a vital role to play in enabling older people to go on learning from one another as well as demonstrating to staff how the skills accumulated over a lifetime can be honed, how new skills can be developed, and what might be needed to support people to get the most out of their situations. It is important to recognize that these kinds of interactions and shared learning opportunities can also occur beyond formal classroom settings, in the context of informal interactions and social events.

CONCLUSION

As with other branches of gerontology, environmental gerontology has undergone periods when it has developed rapidly and others where it has languished. It is commonly regarded as having "come of age" in the 1970s with the seminal work of Powell Lawton (Kendig, 2003; Scheidt & Windley, 2006); in the twenty-first century, the field is undergoing something of a resurgence in interest, as evidenced by the contributions to this volume. This interest has extended beyond fledgling roots in geography and psychology to embrace a diverse array of interrelated disciplines and cognate areas, including architecture, environmental design, sociology, anthropology, the health sciences (including rehabilitation science, physical and occupational therapy, and behavioral science) as well as counseling, social care, and intergenerational practice. Regardless of disciplinary background and the professional trajectory of its author/s, each chapter in this volume has been firmly grounded in the conceptual and theoretical underpinnings associated with place attachment, environmental meaning, and community living in later life. Each contributor has shared a concern with using and applying research-based knowledge to improve private and public environments and enhance the well-being of older people, wherever they may be residing. In the quotation that opened this chapter, Isamay recognized that, as far as her grandmother was concerned, she needed to "know her place." Our place and that of our contributors is, we hope, to have extended knowledge and understanding of what makes environments age-friendly and thereby to have helped advance the continually developing and exciting field of environmental gerontology.

REFERENCES

Abbott, P. S., Carman, N., Carman, J., & Scarfo, B. (2009). *Recreating neighborhoods for successful aging.* Baltimore, MD: Health Professions Press.

Bernard, M. (2001). Women ageing: Old lives, new challenges. *Education and Ageing, 16*(3), 333–352.

Bernard, M. (2006). Research, practice, policy and theory: Interrelated dimensions of a developing field. *Journal of Intergenerational Relationships: Programs, Policy and Research, 4*(1), 5–21.

Bernard, M. (2008). Critical reflections and personal experiences: Key components of intergenerational research, policy, and practice. *Journal of Intergenerational Relationships: Programs, Policy and Research, 6*(4), 389–393.

Bernard, M., & Phillips, J. (2000). The challenge of ageing in tomorrow's Britain. *Ageing and Society, 20*(1), 33–54.

Bernard, M., & Phillips, J. (Eds.) (1998). *The social policy of old age: Moving into the 21st century.* London, UK: Centre for Policy on Ageing.

Bernard, M., & Scharf, T. (Eds.). (2007). *Critical perspectives on ageing societies.* Bristol, UK: Policy Press.

Bevan, M., & Croucher, K. (2011). *Lifetime neighbourhoods.* London, UK: Department for Communities and Local Government.

City of Peoria. (2012) Zoning Ordinance. Retrieved July 22, 2012, from www.peoria.gov

Estes, C., Biggs, S., & Phillipson, C. (2003). *Social theory, social policy and ageing: A critical introduction.* Buckingham: Open University Press.

Forster, M. (1979). *Mother can you hear me?* London, UK: Martin Secker & Warburg Ltd.

Forster, M. (1989). *Have the men had enough?* London, UK: Penguin Books.

Forster, M. (1995). *Hidden lives.* London, UK: Viking.

Forster, M. (1998). *Precious lives.* London, UK: Chatto and Windus.

Forster, M. (2011). *Isa and May.* London, UK: Vintage Books.

Goltsman, S., & Iacofano, D. (2007). *The inclusive city: Design solutions for buildings, neighborhoods and urban spaces.* Berkeley, CA: MIG Communications.

Grenier, A. (2007). Constructions of frailty in the English language, care practice and the lived experience. *Ageing and Society, 27*(3), 425–445.

Grenier, A. (2012). *Transitions and the lifecourse: Challenging the constructions of 'growing old'.* Bristol, UK: Policy Press.

Holstein, M., & Minkler, M. (2007). Critical gerontology: Reflections for the 21st century. In M. Bernard & T. Scharf (Eds.), *Critical perspectives on ageing societies* (pp. 13–26). Bristol, UK: Policy Press.

Iwarsson, S., Wahl, H-W., Nygren, C., Oswald, F., Sixsmith, A., Sixsmith, J., . . . Tomsone, S. (2007). Importance of the home environment for healthy aging: Conceptual and methodological background of the European ENABLE-AGE Project. *The Gerontologist, 47*(1), 78–84.

Jacoby, S. (2011). *Never say die: The myth and marketing of the new old age.* New York, NY: Pantheon Books.

Kendig, H. (2003). Directions in environmental gerontology: A multidisciplinary field. *The Gerontologist, 43*(5), 611–615.

Kitwood, T. M. (1993). Towards a theory of dementia care: The interpersonal process. *Ageing and Society, 13*(1), 51–67.

Kitwood, T. M. (1997). *Dementia reconsidered: The person comes first.* Buckinghamshire, UK: Open University Press.

Kitwood, T., & Bredin, K. (1992). Towards a theory of dementia care: Personhood and well-being. *Ageing and Society, 12*(3), 269–287.

Lui, C. W., Everingham, J. A., Warburton, J., Cuthill, M., & Bartlett, H. (2009). What makes a community age-friendly: A review of international literature. *Australian Journal on Aging, 28*(3), 116–121.

Pastalan, L. A. (2012). The quest for a new paradigm: A need to rewire the way we think. *Journal of Housing for the Elderly, 26,* 20–25.

Phillipson, C. (2004). Urbanisation and ageing: Towards a new environmental gerontology. *Ageing and Society, 24*(6), 963–971.

Phillipson, C., & Walker, A. (1987). The case for a critical gerontology. In S. De Gregorio (Ed.), *Social gerontology: New directions* (pp. 1–15). London, UK: Croom Helm.

Ray, M. (2007). Redressing the balance? The participation of older people in research. In M. Bernard & T. Scharf (Eds.), *Critical perspectives on ageing societies* (pp. 73–87). Bristol, UK: Policy Press.

Ray, M., Bernard, M., & Phillips, J. (2008). *Critical issues in social work with older people.* Basingstoke, UK: Palgrave-Macmillan.

Relph, E. (1976). *Place and placelessness.* London, UK: Pion.

Rowles, G. D. (1978). *Prisoners of space? Exploring the geographical experience of older people.* Boulder, CO: Westview Press.

Rowles, G. D. (2001). Anguish of the observed but unseen, Guest editor's introduction. *Journal of Applied Gerontology, 20*(2), 139–143.

Rowles, G. D. (2008). Place in occupational science: A life course perspective on the role of environmental context in the quest for meaning, *Journal of Occupational Science, 15*(3), 127–135.

Scheidt, R. J., & Windley, P. G. (2006). Environmental gerontology: Progress in the post-Lawton era. In J. E. Birren & K. W. Schaie (Eds.), *Handbook of the psychology of aging* (6th ed., pp. 105–125). Amsterdam: Elsevier.

Schwarz, B. (2012). Environmental gerontology: What now? *Journal of Housing for the Elderly, 26,* 4–19.

Townsend, P. (2007). Using human rights to defeat ageism: Dealing with policy-induced "structured dependency." In M. Bernard & T. Scharf (Eds.), *Critical perspectives on ageing societies* (pp. 27–44). Bristol, UK: Policy Press.

U.S. Bureau of the Census. (2011). *The Older Population: 2010.* 2010 Census Briefs, November 2011, Washington, DC: U.S. Department of Commerce, Econcomis and Statistics Administration.

Wahl, H.-W., Oswald, F., Schilling, O., & Iwarsson, S. (2009). The home environment and quality of life related outcomes in advanced old age: Findings of the ENABLE-AGE project. *European Journal of Ageing, 6*(6), 101–111.

Wahl, H-W., & Weisman, G. D. (2003). Environmental gerontology at the beginning of the new millennium: Reflections on its historical, empirical and theoretical development. *The Gerontologist, 43*(5), 616–627.

World Health Organization. (2007). *Global Age-friendly Cities: A Guide.* Retrieved from www.who.int/aging/publications/Global_age_friendly

Zanjani, F., & Rowles, G. D. (in press) "We don't want to talk about that": Overcoming barriers to rural aging research and interventions on sensitive topics. *Journal of Rural Studies, 28,* 4.

Index

Accessibility
  defined, 44,177
  ecological theory of aging,
    6, 177,178
  effective signage and, 218–219
  empirical studies on, 179–181
  enabler concept, 177
  environmental barriers to, 187–189
  fear of falling, 178
  and sense of place, 200, 211,
    214–216, 217
  solutions for, 192–195
  usability, 177
Active aging, 256
Activities of daily living (ADLs), 63
Adult care facilities, 235–239
Age-friendly, 301
  age friendly cities, 28,40, 42, 293
  age friendly communities, 25, 26, 35,
    40–43, 45
Age-integrated
  childcare, 235–239
  communities, 29
  environments, 227
  facilities, 230, 236–239
  settings, 239, 243
Ageism, 290
Age-loss continuum, 6
Agency
  housing-related
    belonging and, 61–63, 286,
      291, 296
    processes of, 58–59

indicators of, 66
organizations and, 243
and outcomes of aging
  well, 59–60
Age segregation, 232
  communities, 7, 29, 243, 263,
    264–265, 288
Aging, 289. See also Old age
  diverse options, 18
  ecological theory of, 6, 177, 178
  environmental perspectives on, 55
  environment and, 254–255
  healthy, 179, 256
  individuals, 58
  in place, 110, 202, 204, 205, 217, 219,
    257–258
  planning implications of, 34
  populations, 253–254
  process of, 176
  in residential care
    environment, 143
  spatiality of, 28, 29
    age-friendly communities, 40–43
    Aylesbury, 34–35
    intergenerational interaction,
      35–36
    public areas, safety and security
      in, 37–38
    public space, management and
      maintenance of, 39
    space, shared and contested use
      of, 36–37
Aging-friendly environments, 227

Aging in place, 110, 202, 204, 205, 217,
    219, 257–258
Aging population, 228
Aging well, outcomes of, 59–60
Amphitheater space, 229
Anchor Trust, 259–260, 262
Assistance, provision of, 298
Assisted living residence, 112–113
    becoming at-home in, 113–116
    case examples, 105–108
    developing arena of, 108
    home as place, 108–109
    introduction of, 105
    learning, growth, and future, 121
    place integration, 111–112
    place processes, 110–111
    place transitions and home, 109–110
Attachment, 26, 72–73
    emotional, 10, 11, 83
    forging, 258, 268, 275
    to home, 113, 255
    place/to place, 4, 17, 28, 32, 56–57, 112,
        200, 202–203, 217, 231
    (*see also* Place/s)
Auditory stimulation (EA), 157, 158, 161,
    165, 166, 168
Aylesbury, 34–35

Batch living, 130
BCCs. *See* Behavioral Category Codes
Becoming at-home,
        complex process of
    assisted living and, 107–108, 112–116
    extensions and practical applications,
        116–121
    habits and habitus in, 116–118
    place integration, 111, 112
Behavioral adaptation, 58
Behavioral Category Codes
    (BCCs), 157
Being in place, 5, 12, 14, 15, 18, 19
    concept of "home," 11–13, 17
    importance of, 4
    mode of, 16, 17
Belonging and agency processes, 55
"big family" concept, 238
Binary management, 130
Bio-medical perspectives, dominance
    of, 292

"body awareness," 201
Bonding, cognitive and emotional
    aspects of, 57
British social policy, 34
Building communities, 226
Built environment, 43, 258, 265, 297

Care
    approach, 143
    depersonalization of, 135
    environment, TESS-NH data, 155
    ethos of, 134–135, 146
Care environment, 134–135
Care staff, nurses and, 145
CASI. *See* Cognitive Abilities Screening
        Instrument
Cedarwood Manor, case study, 162–169
Childcare programs, 244
Childcare teachers, 238
Child-friendly environments,
        characteristics of, 227–228
Childlessness in older women, 80
    case examples, 90–98
    in historical context, 83–85
    implications for policy and
        practice, 100
    positioning (*see* Positioning)
    rates for women in United
        States, 84
    and sense of home, 80–81, 83, 85–86
    shaping norms and symbolic
        meanings, 83
Coding schemes, 157
Cognitive Abilities Screening
        Instrument (CASI), 207
Cognitive impairment, 154, 156, 204
Colchester town center, 209, 215
Colocating aging services, 233
Comfort trade-off, cost versus, 255
Communication
    importance of, 45, 140–141, 230, 242,
        244–245, 298–299
    integration handbook, 119–121
Community
    age-friendly, 26, 35, 40–43, 45
    age-integrated, 29
    celebration, 243
    connections/connectedness,
        134, 139–142

identity, 235
importance of, 44
neighbourhoods and, 27
park, 242
planning process, 228
policing, levels of, 33
purpose-built retirement,
    258–259, 260
"Community school" movement, 234
Connectedness, 129, 134, 144,
    147, 287, 296
to community and family, 139–142
Connection pathway, 287
Conscious recognition of
    diversity, 291
Control beliefs, 66, 67
Core category, 181
Cost-sharing for older people, 127
Cost versus comfort trade-off, 255
Counselling, 72, 180, 298, 301
Creating Aging-Friendly Communities
    conference, 225
Creative place-making, 118–119
Critical environmental gerontology,
    294–295
Cues in environment, 247–248
Cultural heritage, importance of, 213
Cultural sensitivity, 245, 300
Culture change movement,
    125, 143–144

Daily activity patterns,
    habituation of, 9
DCM tool. *See* Dementia Care
    Mapping tool
Dementia, 259
    care evaluation tool (*see* Dementia
        Care Mapping tool)
    environmental aspects and
        features of, 157–158
    environmental evaluation
        of, 156
    nature of, 154
    older adults with, 73
    psychosocial and behavioral
        manifestations of, 156
Dementia Care Mapping (DCM)
    tool, 299
    BCCs, 157

description of, 156
design professionals, 169–170
EAT, 155
environmental evaluation tool
    applied implications, 169–170
    case study, 162–169
    pilot testing, 162
evidence-based data, 170
MEAP, 154
NURS, 155
PEAP, 155
physical environment, 153–154
physical environment evaluation
    component
    coding schemes, 157
    ECCs, 157–160
    TGs, 160–161
Press-Competence Model, 154
Progressively Lowered Stress
    Threshold Model, 154
real-time environment-
    behavior, 170
residential environments and public
    spaces, 287
SEAT, 155
TESS-NH, 155
WIB values, 157
Dementia care setting
    built environment evaluation in, 169
    environmental aspects and features
        of, 157
    post-occupancy evaluations, 170
    TGs, physical environment in, 154
Dementia care unit, 155, 162
Dementia-friendly environments,
    203, 204
Denham Garden Village (DGV)
    after redevelopment (2009) of, 260
    contemporary environment
        of, 262
    historical environment of,
        261–262
    meaningful engagement, with
        residents, 276–277
    residents' efforts to home
        re-creation, 266–274
    vision
        clarity of, 275–276
        and home creation, 262–266

Depression, 84
  affect and, 63, 66
  declines, 70
  Geriatric Depression Scale, 64
  symptoms, 64, 67, 72
Design
  age-friendly, 43–44, 227
  community, 140–141, 288
  considerations, 5, 27, 70,
    157–158, 200
  environmental, 20, 170, 207, 227, 229,
    230, 242, 244, 248, 289
  guidance, 43, 45, 216
  inclusive, 216, 230, 254, 293–294
  issues, 144, 229, 288 (*see also* Dementia
    Care Mapping (DCM) tool)
  literacy skills, 245
  principles, 299
  universal, 8, 18, 27, 230, 247, 294, 298
Designers, 8, 45, 70, 169, 218,
    274, 296, 300
DGV. *See* Denham Garden Village
Disability, social model of, 27
Diversification, of environmental
    gerontology, 8
Diversity, 291

EAT. *See* Environmental Audit Tool
ECCs. *See* Environmental Category
    Codes
Ecological theory, 6
Ecological theory of aging (ETA), 58,
    177, 178
Eden Alternative, long-term care
    reform, 80
EDs. *See* Environmental Detractors
Education
  intergenerational spaces and places,
    232–235
  place integration and, 119, 121
Educational material, provision
    of, 119
EEs. *See* Environmental Enhancers
Effective counseling strategies,
    development of, 298
Effective signage, 218
"Elective belonging," importance
    of, 258
Emotional attachment

development of, 11
  layers of, 10
ENABLE-AGE project, 53, 54, 60–61,
    179, 190, 287
  housing and healthy aging, 63–66
  housing-related agency and healthy
    aging over time,
    66–70
  housing-related belonging and
    agency, 61–63
  indicators in, 62
Enabler Concept, 177
  principles of, 178
English Longitudinal Study of Ageing
    (ELSA), 256
Environment
  and aging, 254–255
  human experience of, 8–13
  micro and macro aspects of, 28
Environmental adaptation, visual
    representation of, 6
Environmental assessment tools, 154
  influence of, 181, 187–189
  and usability problems, 184
Environmental Audit Tool (EAT), 155
Environmental barriers, 61, 186, 188
  influence of, 181, 187–189
  and usability problems, 184
Environmental Category Codes (ECCs)
  environmental aspects and features
    of, 157–158
  mapping table for, 159–160
  ME Value, 158–159
Environmental coding scheme, 299
Environmental competence, 255
Environmental congruence theory, 6
Environmental design, 229, 246, 247
  flexibility in, 248
  intergenerational programs, 231
  practices, 230
Environmental Detractors (EDs)
  Awareness and Orientation,
    160, 161
  secondary coding scheme, 170
Environmental docility hypothesis, 6
Environmental Enhancers (EEs)
  Awareness and Orientation,
    160, 161
  secondary coding scheme, 170

Environmental evaluation tools, 155
  applied implications, 169–170
  pilot testing, 162
Environmental experience in
  old age, 13–18
Environmental familiarity, 257–258
Environmental gerontology
  advancement of, 296
  communication and information,
    298–299
  conceptual refinement, 297
  education, training and learning,
    300–301
  importance of theory, 296
  monitoring and evaluation, 299–300
  motivations, individual
    psychological aspects of, 296
  physical alterations and preservation
    of environments, 297–298
  pioneers of, 285
  research, future, 71
  theoretical basis of, 7
Environmental measures
  post-implementation of, 193
  pre-implementation of, 192
Environmental perspectives on
  aging, 55
Environmental positioning, 286
  case examples, 90–98
  concept of, 88–89
  perspective of, 79
  from positioning theory, 81–82
Environments
  interactions between people
    and, 296
  preservation of, 297–298
Environment transactional theory, 8
ER-C. *See* Room configuration
ETA. *See* Ecological theory of aging
Evaluation, 44, 54, 56
  component, 157–161
  dementia care settings, 156
  instruments, limitations of, 155
  monitoring and, 299–300
  tools, 155, 156, 162, 170
  workshops, 276
Experiential walk, 190
External control beliefs, 59,
  67, 70

Facilitative design, 298
Familiarity/unfamiliarity,
  219, 220
  focusing on, 203–204
  for older people, 201–206
  routines and actions in, 201
  places (Unfamiliar places)
  spaces (*see* Unfamiliar spaces)
Family, link between home and, 80
Family photographs, environmental
  positioning, 88–89
Fatherhood, 84
Fellowship and Lifelong Learning at
  Waialae School (FELLOWS),
  232–233
Field theory, 5
Frontline workers, perspectives
  of, 292
Functional decline
  and aging, 176
  compensation for, 176
  complexity of, 176
Functional limitations on mobility,
  184–186
Funding scheme for long-stay
  care, 127
Furniture arrangement (EF-A), 158,
  165, 167
Furniture type (EF-T), 165, 167

Gated senior community, 227
Geographical pragmatism, 111, 116
Geriatric Depression Scale, 64
Gerotechnology, 289
Global Age-Friendly Cities
  Project, 40
Globalization, 205
Global urbanism, 29

Habit, 117, 121
  formation, becoming at-home,
    116–118
  of imagination, 118–119
  reconstruction, becoming at-home,
    116–118
Habituation
  of daily activity patterns, 9
  of environment, 10
  process of, 11

Health, 59, 63, 232
    conditions, 28
    holistic, 96
    problems, 176
    services, 41
Healthy aging, 256
    components of, 179
    housing and, 63–66
    in old age, 60–61
    over time, 66–70
Healthy Cities Project, 40
Help the Aged (HTA), 40
Home
    case examples, 90–98
    for childless older women, 81
    concepts of, 85–86
    defined, 11
    development of, 29
    DGV vision and creation of, 262–266
    dimensions of, 11
    as expression of self, 99
    versus house, 11–13
    idea of, 83
    importance of, 108, 110, 254, 256–257,
        274–275, 301
    issues of, 80
    meaning of, 4, 11, 19, 57, 79–83, 85, 88,
        90, 99–100, 109–110, 112–113
    notion of, 126
    in old age, 88
    physical and mental attributes
        of, 129
    physical aspects of, 89
    as place, 108–109
    place transitions and, 109–110
    Rapoport's definition of, 129
    real and ideal forms, 130
    remaking of, 14–17
    residents' efforts to re-create, 266–274
    and "self," (re)creation of, 256–257
    source of, 128
    transferability of, 132
    understanding the role and function
        of, 274–275
    vision clarity of, 275–276
    women and, 86
Homelike care
    description, 133–134
    physical environment, 135
Homelike environments
    aging, 143
    care approach, 143
    connectedness, 144–145
    negative aspects, 143
    physical environment, 144
    societal attitudes reassess, 145–146
    staff attitudes, 145
Homelike places, creating and
        sustaining, 54
Homeliness, 203
Home-making, process of, 254
Home modifications, 19
Home ownership, 255
House, home versus, 11–13
Housing
    adaptation, 72
    correlations of aspects on, 65
    indicators in ENABLE-AGE survey, 62
    integrative theoretical framework
        for, 54–56
    in old age, 60–61
    for older adults, 226
    variables, 64
Housing enabler concept, 7
Housing enabler instrument, 61
Housing-related agency, 71
    and healthy aging, 63–66
    housing-related belonging and,
        61–63
    over time, 66–70
    processes of, 58–59
Housing-related belonging, 71
    and agency, 61–63
    and healthy aging, 63–66
    interplay, 59–60
    processes of, 56–58
Housing-related control beliefs, 59, 63
"Housing with care," 7
HTA. *See* Help the Aged
Human experience of environment,
        8–13
Hypothesis of changing emphasis, 6

Identity, 138
    construction of, 29
    environment and, 4, 5, 7, 9, 16, 26, 32
    formation, 274
    home and, 11, 17

meaning of, 86–87
personal, 26, 131, 143
and personal history, 12
reinforcement of, 10, 298
social, 28
stripping, 130
and well-being, 7, 17
Imageability, 206
features of, 212
Imagination, habits of, 118–119
Immobility, 182
Implementation process, in municipal
        planning, 180
Inclusive design, 230, 293–294
"Independent living," 28
Indicators
    of agency, 66
    for healthy aging, 63
    housing, 62, 63
Individual's life course, 130
Informal interaction, 238, 247
Institutional care, in Ireland, 126
    connectedness, 144
    financial and tax incentives of, 133
    physical and mental attributes, 129
"Integration handbook," 121, 299
    process of developing, 119
Integrative theoretical framework, for
        housing in later life, 54–56
"Interaction room," 234
Interagency collaboration, 295–296
Interdisciplinary collaboration, 295–296
Intergenerational
    benefits of, 245
    community centers, 240
    converting space to place, 231
    creating a conceptual model for,
        246–248
    defined, 230
    and educational facilities, 229–235
    and environmental design, 229
    environment creation, 227
    facilities, 232
    interaction, 35–36, 230, 235
    at Kotoen, 238–239
    learning, 239
    literature on, 230, 246
    perspective and challenges of,
        243–244

practice, 229
practitioners, 245
programs, 231
propositions of, 231
and recreation, 239–243
relations, 29
school, 232
and sense of belonging, 226
and social services, 235–239
spaces and places for, 232
and staffing development,
        244–246
Intergenerational settings
    challenge of, 246–248
    creating, 230
    development of, 244
    multigenerational and, 229
Intergenerational spaces and
        places, 295
    conceptual model of, 246–248
International Classification of
        Functioning, Disability, and
        Health, focus of, 177
International literature
    long-stay care adaptation, 129
    on quality of life, 143
    theoretical conceptualization of
        home and homelike, 126
Interprofessional collaboration,
        295–296
Ireland, private care in, 126
Isa and May, 284
Iterative process, 255

"Keeping on doing as before," 182
Knowledge
    to ownership to practice, 45–46
    and research about older
        people, 290
Kodaira second elementary
        school, 234
Kotoen age integrated facility, 236–239
Kreativehaus Center, 240

Landmarks, 199, 206, 209, 211–212,
        216–217
LARC. *See* Longitudinal Study
        of Ageing in a Retirement
        Community

Large-scale generational
    segregation, 294
Later life
    housing in, 54–56
    levels of connectivity in, 27–29
    P-E adaptation in, 60
Learning
    intergenerational, 239
    programs, 244
"Let's Go for a Walk" project, 180,
    192–193
Levels of connectivity in later life,
    27–29
Licensed Victuallers' National Homes
    (LVNH), 260–262
Life satisfaction, 63, 67
Lifespan development, psychological
    theories of, 57, 71–72
Lifetime homes, 8, 28, 34, 262, 264
Lifetime neighborhoods, 28
Living room, environmental
    positioning, 89
Local planning strategies, 44
Longitudinal regression analysis, 67, 69
Longitudinal Study of Ageing in a
    Retirement Community (LARC),
    254, 260–261
    surveys, 256
Long-stay care in Ireland
    admissions, 146
    concept of home
        physical environment
            experience, 131
        Rapoport's definition of, 129
        real and ideal forms, 130
        "total institution" concept, 130
    culture change movement, 125
    culture of care, 125
    funding for, 127
    homes, notion of, 126
    institutional control, 130
    national quality standards
        for, 127
    public expenditure, 132–133
    residential care
        care environment and ethos of
            care, 134–135
        community and family
            connections, 139–142

older public residential care
    settings, 133
sense of self maintenance, 136–139
routine, benefits for residents, 135
Long-stay care settings
    homelike environments creation
        aging, 143
        care approach, 143
        connectedness, 144–145
        negative aspects, 143
        physical environment, 144
        societal attitudes reassess, 145–146
        staff attitudes, 145
    homelike places in, 132
    outside world communication, 139
    quality of life, 129
    research on, 130–131
    vulnerability of older people, 127
Long-term care
    communal activity, 146
    and concept of home
        physical environment
            experience, 131
        quality of life, 129
        Rapoport's definition of, 129
        real and ideal forms, 130
        "total institution" concept, 130
    connectedness, 146–147
    facilities of, 19
    setting, family engagement in, 80
Long-term dementia care
    environments, 287
Long-term memory, 162
LVNH. *See* Licensed Victuallers'
    National Homes

Management
    and maintenance of public
        space, 39
    ownership and, 33
Massachusetts, multigenerational
    school, 233
Meaning-making narrative, 258
Meaning of home, 63, 85, 99
    behavioral aspects of, 65
    for childless older women, case
        examples, 90–98
    conceptualizations of, 57
    international literature on, 128

in old age, 79, 88
questionnaire on, 61
renegotiation of, 80
symbolic, 83
for women, 112–113
Meaning of/in place, 4, 5, 10, 20, 79, 83,
109, 119, 284–285, 288
MEAP. *See* Multiphasic Environmental
Assessment Procedure
Memories/memory, 15, 85, 89,
131, 207
Memory cue, 158
Metaphoric position, environmental
positioning, 88
Meta-theoretical perspective, 111
Methodology of OPUS, 206–209
ME Value. *See* Mood and
Engagement Value
Ministry of Health and Welfare, 233
Mixed-method approach, 180–181
Mixed-method longitudinal
study, 260
Mobility
accessibility and ease of, 214–216
case study, 189–192
core category, 181
definition of, 176
devices
for older people, 182
role of, 181, 186–187
types of, 187
use of, 175, 176, 192, 194–195
empirical studies on, 179–181
environmental barriers to,
187–189
functional decline
and aging, 176
compensation for, 176
complexity of, 176
functional limitations and, 184–186
motivation for, 182
in old age, 178, 179
in outdoor environments, old age (*see*
Accessibility)
solutions for, 192–195
transactional perspective, 182–184
usability, 177
Mood and Engagement (ME) Value,
158–159

Motherhood, 81, 84
Motivations
individual psychological aspects
of, 296
for mobility, 182
Multigenerational facilities, 232
Multigenerational school, 233–234
Multigenerational settings,
intergenerational and, 229
Multigenerational site, 242
Multiphasic Environmental
Assessment Procedure
(MEAP), 154
Multivariate regression models, 193
Municipal planning, implementation
process in, 180

Narrative position, environmental
positioning, 88, 89
National Economic and Social Forum,
2005, 133
Neighborhood,42, 216
elder-friendly, 18
home and, 179, 262
lifetime, 28, 34, 42, 45
transformation of, 5
"Neutral ground," 27
Nine micro-observation sites, 35
Nonvisual cues, 219
Nordic countries, 186
mobility devices in, 181, 190
outdoor mobility in, 176
researchers in, 180
NURS. *See* Nursing Unit Rating Scale
Nurse-resident staffing ratios, 126
Nursing care
facility, 128
home care, 126
older people, 132
staff continuity, 140
Nursing Home Support Scheme Act,
2009, 127
Nursing Unit Rating Scale
(NURS), 155

Occupational therapists, 119–121
Occupational therapy, 7, 177
OECD. *See* Organisation for Economic
Co-operation and Development

Old age
acute health conditions, 28
adjustment, patterns of, 13–14
and aging, 289
aspects of mobility in, 179
childlessness in, 80
environmental and structural
barriers, 29
environmental experience in
adjustment within private
space, 13–14
consequences of relocation, 18
patterns of relocation, 14–17
environment and personal
identity in, 4
home in, 88
homeless, 18
housing
adaptation, 72
and healthy aging in, 60–61
housing-related belonging in, 57
human experience of environment,
8–10
being at home, 11–13
meaning of home in, 79, 88
mobility in, 178 , 179
in outdoor environments (*see*
Accessibility)
outdoor mobility in, 176
transactional perspective on,
181–184
quality of life in, 5, 19–20
social exclusion and, 29
social media growth, 19
studying mobility in, 178
Older adults
childlessness for, 80–81
with dementia, 73
housing for, 226
integration of, 227
in wheelchairs, 242
Older participants. *See* Participants
Older people, 179, 181, 182,
185, 189, 217
accommodation for, 254
beds availability, long-stay care settings, 132
community roles, 145
cost-sharing for, 127

familiar environment for, 201–206
in long-stay care settings,
vulnerability of, 127
mobility devices for, 182
nursing care, 132
peer support and one-to-one
mentoring, 301
perceptions of environmental
barriers outdoors and public
facilities, 187
prerequisites for, 176
public spaces and residential
environments, 287–288
public transportation systems for, 176
residential care settings, 133
residential environments and public
spaces
environment relationship, 285
physical-psychological and
emotional components of,
287–288
tourists to new places, 203
understanding diversity of, 291
unfamiliar
places for, 201–206
spaces and familiar places, 201
vulnerability of, 127
Older People's Use of Unfamiliar Space
(OPUS), 199–201
creating meaning in unfamiliar
places, 209–216
design of public spaces, 216–219
methodology, 206–209
unfamiliar spaces—familiar places,
201–206
Older women
childlessness for, 80–81
using environmental positioning, 82
"One size fits all" solution, 291
One-to-one mentoring in older
people, 301
"Open school" program, 234
OPUS. *See* Older People's Use of
Unfamiliar Space
Orderliness, environmental
positioning, 89
Organisation for Economic
Co-operation and Development
(OECD), 133, 258

Outdoor environment-intervention
  project, 180
Outdoor environments, 297
  dementia-friendly, 203, 204
  in old age (*see* Accessibility)
  physical barriers in, 180
  problems in, 176
  urban planning of, 180
Outdoor mobility
  barriers to, 188
  in old age, 176, 181–184
  restraining, 186–187
  traffic dynamics on, 187–189
Outdoor public environments, 200
Outdoor spaces, 30, 43, 169,
    200, 247, 299
  core category, 181
Outdoor walks, 191
Ownership, 30–31, 37
  from knowledge to, 45–46
  and management, 33

Parks, 240–243
Participants, 207, 213
  comment on, 208
  focus groups, 208
  majority of, 210, 211
  in reality cave, 207, 208, 211, 214
Patterns
  of adjustment in old age, 13–14
  of relocation, 14–17
P-E. See Person-environment
P-E-A. See Person-environment-activity
    model
PEAP. *See* Professional Environmental
    Assessment Protocol
Peer
  mentoring, 121
  support in older people, 301
Peoples'
  bench-type seating for, 39
  with dementia, 204, 216
  mental maps of
    environment, 206
Perceived environmental
  barriers, 185
Personal
  autonomy, quality of life, 134
  care options, 14

components, accessibility, 177
  identity, 131
Person-centered
  care, 140, 156
  practice, 292–293
Person-environment (*P-E*), 71
  agency, processes of, 59
  belonging and agency processes,
    59–60, 66
  distinction, 111
  exchange processes, 66
  interaction, 30–31
  interchange processes
    in later life, 54, 55, 70–72
    theoretical view of, 57
Person-environment-activity model
    (P-E-A), 7
Photographs, 19, 88, 89, 95, 107, 160, 162,
    168, 247, 261, 298.
Physical alterations, 297–298
Physical environment, 55, 211–216
  DCM tool, 153–154
  environmental observation
    tools, 155
  evaluation component
    coding schemes, 157
    ECCs, 157–160
    TGs, 160, 161
  evaluation tool (*see* Environmental
    evaluation tools)
  features of, 160
  quality of, 156
  TGs, 154–155
  therapeutic goals, 154–155
Physical environmental barriers, 183
  influence of, 181, 187–189
  and usability problems, 184
Physical position, environmental
    positioning, 88
Placelessness, 201, 204, 220
Place/s, 227, 231
  aging in, 110
  attachment, 17, 28, 32,56–57, 72–73,
    109, 202, 231
  attractiveness of, 211–214
  creation of, 9
  defining, 26–27
  devoted to education, 232–235
  home as, 108–109

Place/s, (cont.)
  identity, 56
    defined, 231
  implement change in, 43–45
  importance of, 18–20
  integration, 7, 105, 111–112, 286, 287
    and becoming at-home in assisted
      living, 113–116
  making spaces into, 8–10
  modification, 116
  and placelessness, 204
  processes, 110–111
  for recreation, 239
    intergenerational community
      centers, 240
    parks and playgrounds, 240–243
  for social services
    Kotoen age integrated facility,
      236–239
    Tampines Three-in-One
      Center, 236
    TTIC, 236
  therapy, 4
  transitions and home, 109–110
  urban, 26
Playgrounds, 240–243
Policy
  British social policy, 34
  initiatives, 43, 219, 235
  intergenerational, 235
  objectives, 204, 259
  outdoor, 202
  policy-makers, 290, 292
  practice, policy and design, 5
  public, 8, 20
  responses, variety of, 254
  rhetoric, 28
  urban regeneration, 39
Positioning
  case examples, 90–98
  environmental positioning, 88–89
  theory
    concept of, 86–87
    environmental positioning from,
      81–82
Post occupancy
  assessment teams, 300
  evaluations, 170
    increased emphasis on, 299

Practical applications
  and ageism, 290
  and critical environmental
    gerontology, 294–295
  and diversity, understanding, 291
  and elderly population, demographic
    visibility of, 290
  inclusive design, 293–294
  interdisciplinary, interagency and
    interprofessional collaboration,
      295–296
  person-centered practice, 292–293
  research-informed practice and
    practice-aware research, 291–292
  translating research into, 119–121
Pregnant women
  and employment, 84–85
  program for, 244
Press-Competence Model, 154
Private care in Ireland, 126
Private nursing homes, 142
  long-stay care in
    design and physical infrastructure
      of, 133
    drawbacks of, 135
    nurse-resident staffing ratios, 126
    sense of self maintenance, 136
Private places, 4
  patterns of adjustment within, 13–14
Private security, 33
Private spaces, design of, 298
Processes of agency, 54, 55, 60. *See also*
    Housing-related agency
Processes of belonging, 55, 61, 71.
    See also Housing-related
    belonging
Professional Environmental
    Assessment Protocol (PEAP), 155
Professional interventions,
    119, 121, 300
Progressively Lowered Stress
    Threshold Model, 154
Provision of educational material, 119
Psychological control theory, 59
Psychological factors in mobility,
    184–186
Psychosocial processes, description
    of, 130
Public environments, mobility in, 176

Public places, 4, 227, 248
Public residential care beds, shortage
    of, 127
Public security, 33
Public spaces, 201, 227, 248
    age-integrated settings in, 243
    conceptualization of, 45–46
    defining, 26–27
    design of, 216–219
    identification of, 244
    implement change in, 43–45
    levels of connectivity in, 27–29
    management and maintenance of, 39
    "public" nature of, 30–34
    residential environments and
        "being at home," 285
        belonging and agency, 286
        "breaking up home," 285
        connectedness, 287
        DCM tool, 287
        "dwelling," 285
        environmental gerontology,
            284–285
        "environmental
            positioning," 286
        "housing with care"
            developments, 288
        institutional care settings in
            Ireland, 287
        older people, 287–288
        older person-environment
            relationship, 285
        older women, 286
        person-environment processes,
            developmental framework, 286
        "place integration," 286, 287
        retirement communities, 289
    safety and security in, 37–38
Public transportation systems for older
    people, 176
Public urban spaces, 201
Purpose-built
    Environments, 253–255, 258–260, 274,
        277, 298
    retirement communities, 258–260
    villages, 254, 258

Qualitative findings, 180–181
Quality of life

conceptualization of, 256
long-stay care settings, 129
in old age, 5, 19–20
personal autonomy, 134
and quality of care, 156
of residents, 126
volunteers, 142

Reality cave, older participants in, 207,
    208, 211, 214
Recognition of achievement,
    138–139
Reconciling process, 16
Religious
    activities, 182
    beliefs, self maintenance
        sense, 137
Relocation
    consequences of, 18
    experience of, 14–15
    patterns of, 14–17
    United States' residents, 15
Research
    circles, 178–179
    practice-aware, 291–292
Research-informed practice, 291–292
Residential care
    community and family connections
        communication and connectivity
            opportunities, 140–141
        "getting out," 139–140
        outward/inward
            perspectives, 139
        private chat rooms, 142
        residents value
            opportunities, 140
        visitors, 141–142
    environment and ethos of care,
        134–135
    older public residential care settings,
        133
    sense of self maintenance
        female residents, 137–138
        photographs, 136–137
        recognition of achievement,
            138–139
        religious belief, 137
        self-identity and esteem, 138
        space restrictions, 136

sense of self maintenance, (cont.)
  settings
    older people, 133
    private and public, 126
    spectrum in United States, 112
  state-operated, 126
Residential environments
  P-E exchange in, 55
  and public spaces
    "being at home," 285
    belonging and agency, 286
    "breaking up home," 285
    connectedness, 287
    DCM tool, 287
    "dwelling," 285
    environmental gerontology,
      284–285
    "environmental positioning," 286
    "housing with care"
      developments, 288
    institutional care settings in
      Ireland, 287
    older people, 287–288
    older person-environment
      relationship, 285
    older women, 286
    person-environment processes,
      developmental framework, 286
    "place integration," 286, 287
    retirement communities, 289
Residential satisfaction, 56
Residential settings, 248
Residents
  home re-creation, efforts to, 266–274
  meaningful engagement with,
    276–277
  mentoring, 119
Retirement communities, 289
Rollator, 186, 190–192
  using in public places, 192
Room configuration (ER-C), 160, 165, 166
Rural population, defining, 40

Safety
  cognitive dimension, 178
  dimensions of, 178
  "fear of crime," security, 178
  "fear of falling," safety, 178
  "fear of moving outdoors," 178

Santa Barbara Sense of Direction Scale
  (SBSOD), 207
SBSOD. See Santa Barbara Sense of
  Direction Scale
SCAMOB. See Screening and
  Counselling for Physical
  Activity and Mobility in
  Older People
School/s
  administrators, teachers and, 234
  age-integrated settings in, 243
  intergenerational, 232
  multigenerational, 233–234
  second elementary, Kodaira, 234
  "sukusuku school," 234–235
Screening and Counselling for Physical
  Activity and Mobility in Older
  People (SCAMOB), 180
SEAT. See Stirling Environmental
  Audit Tool
Security
  cognitive dimension, 178
  dimensions of, 178
  "fear of crime," security, 178
  "fear of falling," safety, 178
  "fear of moving outdoors," 178
Selection, optimization, and
  compensation (SOC)
  mechanisms, 71
Self
  home and (re)creation of, 256–257
  maintenance sense, residential care
    female residents, 137–138
    recognition of achievement,
      138–139
    religious belief, 137
    self-identity and esteem, 138
    space restrictions, 136
Self-acceptance, 182
Self-actualization, element of, 17
Self-identity, stripping of, 130
"Self-narrative," 257
Self-realization process, 256–257
  control and autonomy, 256
Senior care services, administrators
  of, 244
Senior Walking Environment
  Assessment Tool-Revised
  (SWEAT-R), 208, 209

Sense
of coherence, 257
of place, 200, 205
to develop, 201, 211–216
of self, 257
Sense of home, 80–81, 83, 85–86
"dwelling" process, 11
homeliness, 203
home-making, process of, 254
home modifications, 19
house, home versus, 11–13
Shaping norms, 83
Shared sites, 230
facilities, 242
Shared social services sites, 236
Sheltered housing schemes, 7
Single Regeneration Budget, 39
SIZE project, 179–180
Smart homes, 8
Snow, importance of, 189
Social
exclusion, 27, 31
home, 83
interaction, 25, 32
opportunities for, 219
in places (*see* Place/s)
in public spaces (*see* Public spaces)
media growth, 19
problem solving/collaboration, 119
relationships, 255
services
age-integrated settings in, 243
shared sites, 236
Society, mobility and participation
in, 176
Socio-cultural environment, features
of, 131
Socio-emotional selectivity theory, 72
Socio-spatial practices, 27
SOC mechanisms. *See* Selection,
optimization, and compensation
mechanisms
Space/s, 231
age-integrated settings in, 243
devoted to education, 232–235
intergenerational (*see*
Intergenerational
spaces and places)
plan and organized, 248

private and public, 4
public places and, 227
shared and contested use of, 36–37
sharing, 233
Spatiality of aging, 28, 29
age-friendly communities, 40–43
Aylesbury, 34–35
intergenerational interaction, 35–36
public areas, safety and security in,
37–38
public space, management and main-
tenance of, 39
space, shared and contested use of,
36–37
Spatial planning, 201, 207, 209, 218
Special Care Unit, 162
Special transportation services (STS), 190
Spectrum of residential care settings in
United States, 112
Staff training
and development, 244
in workshops, 300
State-operated residential care, 126
Stirling Environmental Audit Tool
(SEAT), 155
Street audit, tools in, 208
STS. *See* Special transportation services
"Sukusuku school," 234–235
Swampscott multigenerational school,
233–234
SWEAT-R. *See* Senior Walking
Environment Assessment
Tool-Revised
Symbolic meanings
explanations of, 100
of home for women, 83
Symbols, associated with home, 80

Tampines Three-in-One Center, 236
Teachers
childcare, 238
and school administrators, 234
TESS-NH. *See* Therapeutic
Environmental Screening
Survey
TGs. *See* Therapeutic goals
Theoretical basis of environmental
gerontology, 7
Theoretical models, 177

Theoretical refinement, 297
Therapeutic Environmental Screening
    Survey (TESS-NH), 155
Therapeutic goals (TGs)
    description of, 161
    EE and ED, 160, 161
    "Maximize Awareness and
        Orientation," 160
    physical environment, 154–155
Tiny Tigers Intergenerational Center
    (TTIC), 236
"Total institution," concept of, 130
Transactional perspective on outdoor
    mobility in old age, 181–184
Transference of belongings, 110, 113
TTIC. *See* Tiny Tigers Intergenerational
    Center

U3A. *See* University of the Third Age
UDQ. *See* Urban Design Quality index
UK national policy, 263
Unattractive spaces, 213
Unfamiliar places, 209–216
    accessibility and ease of mobility,
        214–216
    attractiveness of place, 211–214
    creating meaning in, 209–216
    for older people, 201–206
Unfamiliar spaces, 204, 205
    concept of, 206, 219
    focusing on, 203–204
    older people's use of, 199–220
United States
    assisted living residences in, 112
    childlessness rates for women in, 84
    children role in parents' decisions, 80
    pregnant women and employment,
        84–85
    women in historical context, 83–85

Universal design, 230, 247
Universal public space, 205
University of the Third Age
    (U3A), 207
Urban
    environments
        quality of, 208–209
        walkability of, 208
    planners, issue of, 217–219
    planning of outdoor
        environments, 180
    population, defining, 40
    public place, 26
    regeneration, 203
    residents, 29
Urban Design Quality index (UDQ),
    208, 209
User-friendly manuals, 299

Vicarious engagement, 10
Volunteers, 234, 242

Waialae Elementary School, 232–233
"Walkability," of urban
    environments, 208
"Walking in Old Age," project, 180,
    192–193
Well-being and aging, notions
    of, 256
Well-being-related outcomes, 66–67
Well/Ill Being (WIB) values, 157
Women
    childlessness rates for, 84
    in historical context, 83–85
    and home, 86
    older (*see* Older women)
Workshops, staff training in, 300

Youth-friendly environments, 227